THE FAMILY WELCOME PUB & RESTAURANT GUIDE 1991

CW01584132

JILL FOSTER & MALCOLM HAMER

Macdonald
Queen Anne Press

Jill Foster started out as an actress at the age of 12 and retired at 17. She has been a literary agent for over 20 years and has run her own agency for most of that time. In 1970 she married Malcolm Hamer and they have a daughter, Polly.

Malcolm Hamer had a traditional education at Shrewsbury School and Trinity College, Cambridge. He worked in marketing for 10 years and is now a literary agent and specialises in non-fiction authors and television journalists. His first novel has just been published.

A QUEEN ANNE PRESS BOOK

© Hamer Books Ltd 1991

First published in Great Britain in 1991 by
Queen Anne Press, a division of
Macdonald & Co (Publishers) Ltd
Orbit House
1 New Fetter Lane
London EC4A 1AR

A member of Maxwell Macmillan Pergamon Publishing Corporation

Cover illustration by Andrew Bylo

All rights reserved. No part of this publication may be reproduced, stored in a retrieval system, or transmitted, in any form or by any means, without the prior permission in writing of the publisher, nor be otherwise circulated in any form of binding or cover other than that in which it is published and without a similar condition including this condition being imposed on the subsequent purchaser.

A CIP catalogue record for this book
is available from the British Library

ISBN 0-356-19569-4

Typeset by Tradespools Ltd, Frome, Somerset
Printed and bound in Great Britain by
BPCC Hazell Books,
Aylesbury, Bucks
Member of BPCC Ltd

CONTENTS

Our special thanks to our Northern editor, Tony Halstead, and his wife, Heather; and also to June Bamford, Carol Brunton, Cyril and Rita Carter, Jean Howat, Jackie Mills, Tricia Phoenix, Ann Pollard, Carol Quinn, Jenny Parkhouse, Julia Shuff, Veronica and John Smart and Pam Willmott for all their help.

Our thanks also to our very efficient typist, Adrienne Fell of Lynn Associates.

And our love to Polly.

INTRODUCTION

In its eighth year of publication the Family Welcome Guide has become two books. The Pub & Restaurant Guide offers a selection of nearly 600 places where a family can have a meal or a drink together in the comfortable knowledge that the facilities a family needs will be made available.

The Family Welcome Accommodation Guide provides a wide choice of places for a family to stay: from grand hotels to small pubs and farmhouses.

The Guide was divided in this way for two reasons: first, because the original Family Welcome Guide, at well over 500 pages, was becoming unwieldy in size; second, because it seemed logical to bring the food and drink recommendations together in one guide, and the accommodation recommendations together in another.

We have excluded about sixty pubs and restaurants which were listed in the 1990 edition; in some cases because their standards have fallen and in others because their policies towards families have changed for the worse. Some places have been closed down and it is sad to record that Taylor's, of Market Harborough, an outstanding fish and chipper, has closed its doors with the retirement of its owner, Frank Taylor.

We have made up for these deletions by the introduction of nearly fifty pubs and restaurants which are new to the Guide. Some of them were recommended by readers and we thank you for those recommendations. Don't keep those good family pubs and restaurants to yourselves: tell us about them, please. The forms are at the back of the book.

The additions to and the exclusions from the Guide illustrate how volatile is the pub and restaurant scene; and more so when the economic climate is uncertain. As always, we urge you to use a current edition of the Guide. As you can imagine, a good deal of the 1990 edition is now irrelevant.

Our policy in selecting establishments for inclusion in the Family Pub & Restaurant Guide is unchanging.

We only include those places in which we believe that a family will receive a genuine welcome, where they will feel at home and will be able to relax and enjoy their food and drink together. If we sense a half-hearted or grudging approach to families, that particular pub or restaurant does not get a mention in the Guide.

We should stress that we do not seek any payment or free hospitality from places listed in this Guide. They are only included if they meet our high standards.

Pubs and restaurants must offer some basic essentials and these are as follows:

PUBS must have separate and legal children's or family rooms, i.e. rooms which are separated from the bar areas and which do not have any facility for serving alcohol;
RESTAURANTS must provide at least one high chair and offer reduced portions and/or a special children's menu.

The presence of these bare essentials is by no means enough. We look for appealing and attractive places, with helpful and cheerful staff. Those are the "intangibles"; and we look for the "extras", such as pleasant gardens and play areas, restaurants (and even pubs) which provide a place where a mother can change a baby in comfort, and the presence of no smoking areas.

THE ENTRIES

We have stuck to basic simple information, given in the following order and avoiding confusing codes or symbols:

Name of the town or village and its county or region.

Name of the establishment, and whether we recommend it as a pub (P), a restaurant (R) or both (PR).

Address and phone number.

Directions.

Description: we try to give you an impression of what the place is like and why we have included it and we summarise its facilities.

Food: we give you the serving times, and an idea of the price range and type of food on offer. For restaurant meals (as opposed to bar snacks) we quote the price of a three-course meal and again an extract from a typical menu. Since prices are hard to forecast we have quoted to the nearest £, and have rounded figures upward. We tell you if special menus or smaller portions are available for children.

Credit Cards: we have listed the four major cards: Access, American Express, Diners Club and Visa.

Opening and closing times: except for pubs which, with rare exceptions, are open every day of the year. Pubs can remain open throughout the day, but a relatively small number of the pubs in the Guide have taken advantage of this new-found freedom. When they do, we tell you in our report. But please note that several of them only open all day during the summer season, or on certain days during the week, and these variations are mentioned: so check carefully before you undertake a journey.

• Ale means real ale and we name the variety on offer.

High chairs and cots: if a restaurant has only one high chair we tell you, so that you can check in advance that it will be available.

Parking: very important to know what is available especially with children, luggage, pots and pushchairs in tow.

Some entries are marked "Pot Luck" which usually means that the establishment is useful to know about if you are in the vicinity, but not a place which you should go out of your way to find; or that some aspect of the establishment is not fully known to us.

No smoking: we firmly believe that all family rooms shoud be no smoking areas and have made our views known to the major brewers. It seems to us that some progress is being made, and that more licensees are making their family rooms into smoke free zones. Smokers do, after all, have the rest of the pub in which to puff away.

Music: we tell you which places do not inflict music on their customers. We are amazed at how the music industry has conned hoteliers, publicans and restaurant owners into installing expensive sound systems which hardly anyone wants. It seems to us that the music is often played solely for the benefit of the staff.

We have been encouraged in the past year or two by the growing number of pubs and restaurants which offer real food, freshly cooked. It is noticeable, too, that a choice of vegetarian dishes is no longer unusual on a pub menu.

But we are still dismayed that a children's menu invariably means sausages, fish fingers or burger with chips. It is far better, we think, to offer the children half portions of real food. All parents should resist the parrot cry that chips with everything is "what the children want". It is never too early to start educating children in the joys and benefits of good food.

Amid the many encouraging signs that more and better facilities are being provided for families, we must tell one cautionary tale, which illustrates how the attitudes of some owners are still stuck in the snobberies of the 'fifties or even earlier.

When we questioned a hotel restaurant in Wales about the provision of high chairs, their spokesman replied: "We are not that kind of a place. We are very up-market." Well, that puts every family back in its place, doesn't it – if you have small children, you're down-market.

STORES AND SUPERMARKETS

We continue to list the outlets which provide mother & baby rooms, and most of the major companies in the High Street are adding this essential facility to their outlets. Asda, Boots, Gateway, John Lewis, Mothercare, Sainsbury and Tesco lead the way. Marks & Spencer do not yet provide a single mother & baby room for their family customers; a particularly mean-spirited and highly reprehensible attitude on the part of one of Britain's best known retailers.

We thank all those people who wrote in to us with recommendations and with comments about places already in the Guide. These are invaluable; and we take your comments very seriously. Many establishments have been excluded, and many added as a result. Please keep writing to us.

A–Z Guide

Aberaeron, Dyfed **map 5**

THE HIVE ON THE QUAY, Cadwgan Place – ☎ Aberaeron (0545) 570 445.

R

This white-washed little café, situated on the old wharf between the inner and outer harbour,is in a most attractive spot, ringed by colourful and neat cottages. The recently built conservatory adds to the appeal of the café. It shares the wharf with a Honey Bee Exhibition and occasionally a Punch and Judy show. The emphasis is very much on fresh home-made food and the salads are always interesting and the bread and cakes delicious.

It is good to report that the children's menu is not the usual dreary fish fingers and chips, but a proper offering of soup, salads and hot savoury pancakes. The honey ice creams are an absolute delight, whatever age you are, and there is also a range of honey fruit sorbets, all made from fresh fruit, and yoghurt ices.

It's back to the car if you wish to change or feed a baby – the Ladies is very small.

A new attraction is the "Aeron Express", with its starting point close to the café. It is an aerial ropeway which carries people across the harbour; and is a replica of a device which was built in 1885. The sea aquarium, along the quay, should also appeal to the children.

£1–5: pickled local mackerel, pies, salads, hot savoury pancakes;
DINNER (6–9pm) £10: laverbread roulade, fresh crab, honey ice cream
Children: own menu

Open 10.30am–5pm May, June & Sept; 10am–9pm July & Aug
Closed end Sept-Spring Bank Hol No credit cards
• Ale – Theakston's No music
P – ample street parking

Aberdeen, Grampian — map 12

CAFÉ CONTINENTAL, Beach Esplanade – ☎ Aberdeen (0224) 588 396.

R

On the beach front.

This modern, well-designed restaurant has acres of windows, which give panoramic views of the beach and the sea. The impression as you enter is one of space and even tranquillity; even though the restaurant is a neighbour of the local fun fair – not that you would know it once you are inside.

The bar area is high tech modern with black tables and chairs and marble columns, and the carvery is done out in more conventional style. There is an enclosed terrace and a very agreeable and comfortable conservatory.

There is a table and a chair in the Ladies, if you need to deal with either end of a baby.

There is a good atmosphere here, with a good flow of customers who might drop in for a coffee or a drink, a snack or a full meal.

ALL DAY MENU £2–8: chicken curry mayonnaise, burgers, Texas chilli, oriental chicken, swordfish;
CARVERY £10: tuna & cucumber salad, roast lamb, pudding or cheese
Children: own menu, half portions

Open 10am–10pm, every day
Access/AmEx/Diners/Visa Licensed
P – small car park, or on street

Aberfeldy, Tayside — map 12

COUNTRY FARE COFFEE HOUSE RESTAURANT, Bridgend – ☎ Aberfeldy (0887) 20729.

R

On the main A827 through Aberfeldy between the square and the bridge.

A compact and welcoming self-service restaurant, which comprises two cosy rooms one of which is designated non-smoking, and is therefore better for children (and adults!). Everything here is home-made, including the cakes and bread, and there is an excellent range of salads and toasted sandwiches.

At the back there is an agreeable walled patio with half a dozen tables with parasols.

Although there is not a lot of space to change or feed a baby, the owners will certainly try to find a place for a mother to do this, and by now they may have installed a pull-down shelf in the Ladies.

£1–4: soup, cold buffet, smoked mackerel paté, chilli con carne,
Children: half portions

Open 10am–5pm, Mon to Sat. Closed 3 weeks in Jan/Feb
No credit cards accepted No music
Licensed 4 non-smoking areas
P – street and municipal car park

Abergavenny, Gwent map 2

LLANWENARTH ARMS HOTEL – ☎ Abergavenny (0873) 810 550.

P

On the A40 towards Brecon.
The hotel is more or less halfway between Abergavenny and Crickhowell, and sits in a splendid position above the River Usk. It is a large roadside inn and hotel which has its origins in the 16th century but has been substantially altered and extended in the last two decades.

Past the entrance hall, there is a comfortable bar with a large open fireplace and a very spacious restaurant area alongside. Families can of course eat together there from the extensive menu (and there are four high chairs available), but down some stairs is a good-sized conservatory where they are also welcome to settle. It is appropriately furnished with cane furniture and from here you have a lovely view of the river below – down a steep bank which is crowded with bushes and small trees. On warmer days you can sit on the paved terrace which has the same views of the Usk Valley.

(12–2pm & 6–10pm) £2–12: fresh plaice, vegetable bake, rack of Welsh Lamb, steaks, cannelloni
Children: own menu

• Ale – Bass, Wadworth P – own car park

Also recommended in the Family Welcome Accommodation Guide.

If you wish to recommend an establishment to the Guide please write to us – report forms are at the back of the book. We need your help to extend and improve the guide.

Aberlady, Lothian — map 11

WAGGON INN – ☎ Aberlady (087 57) 204.

P

In the main street, the A198.

The interior of this pub is much larger than the small sandstone exterior indicates and it is all very well laid out with plenty of space for families to park themselves. For example, you can head for the "snug" or an upstairs dining room.

The pub has a friendly atmosphere and the food is all freshly prepared from local produce. In the summer the pub is open all day and food is served throughout opening hours.

There is a gift shop attached to the pub, which is open during pub hours, and a patio at the back, with an aviary.

(12–10pm in summer; 12–2pm & 6.30–10pm in winter) £1–9: smoked salmon, trout, moussaka, fish & chips, fillet steak
Children: smaller portions

• Ale – McEwan's P – own car park

Aboyne, Grampian — map 12

ALFORD HOUSE – ☎ Aboyne (03398) 82249.

R

On the A93.

This is a small and cheerful restaurant cum tea room, with smart white furniture and brightly coloured tablecloths.

There's a nice fresh feeling to the whole place, and the owner and staff are happy to welcome families with small children. Unfortunately there is nowhere to change a baby in comfort, since the lavatory is on the small side.

The food is reasonably priced, and the cost of a high tea includes tea and cakes. It is good to report that the whole restaurant is a no smoking area.

£1–5: soup, haddock, gammon, roast beef & salad, vegetarian salad
Children: small portions

Open 11am–6pm (from 12 on Sunday)
No credit cards accepted No music
Unlicensed One high chair only
No Smoking P – on street

Airmyn, Nr Goole, Humberside — map 7

THE PERCY ARMS, 89 High Street – ☎ Goole (0405) 764 408.

P

Half a mile from the M62. Take exit 36.

This is an excellent pub in a small village just a stone's throw from the motorway and a good spot to know if you want to break a journey. It's built in rustic red brick with a cream frontage and is an attractive sight after the monotony of motorway travel.

Inside there's a smart tap room area with a well restored black range fire and an attractively furnished lounge bar.

Families can use a delightful, centrally heated conservatory with white garden tables and chairs and a profusion of indoor plants and other greenery. The conservatory leads out to a lawned garden with lots of children's play equipment including an excellent playhouse.

This is a well-run pub where families can be sure of a warm welcome; and there is a good selection of food available.

BAR MEALS (12–2.15pm & 6–10pm, not Sun pm) £1–7: burgers, mixed grill, lasagne, fisherman's pie, chicken Kiev
Children: own menu

• Ale – John Smith's P – own car park

Alderminster, Warwicks — map 3

BELL INN AND BISTRO – ☎ Alderminster (078 987) 414.

P

On the A34 near Stratford-upon-Avon.

On the main road to Stratford, you cannot miss this smart, white-painted pub with its bright window boxes. It was converted a few years ago to a large and busy pub/bistro; the cream painted walls, brick pillars and bar, and nice wooden furniture make for a cheerful and relaxing atmosphere.

Families are welcome to use the no smoking area at the far end of the pub, well away from the bar, and French windows lead out to an enclosed and lawned garden with white furniture and parasols.

This is an enterprising family pub with the emphasis very much on food, of which there is an extensive and interesting range on offer. It is all freshly cooked to order and features a good choice of fish. There is a high chair on the premises.

Please note that the pub is shut on Monday evenings in the winter.

(12–2pm and 7–10pm) £2–8: moules marinières, mini rack of lamb, prawn & crab cocotte, London pie, grilled sea trout
Children – half portions

• Ale – Flowers **P** – own car park

Aldworth, Berks map 3

THE BELL – ☎ Compton (063 522) 272.

P *Just off the B4009 south-west of Streatley.*

This is a real village pub, with dark red brick walls crowned with a deep roof, and it looks out to its tiny hamlet on one side and open countryside on the other. A few yards from the front door is the village well 'sunk in 1868 with monies raised in this parish'.

Inside there is one bar, L-shaped with a low-beamed ceiling and with an alcove where a bread oven used to be. Photographs of past village cricket teams decorate the walls. The children's room is off to one side, and is also a low-beamed, wood-panelled room with a few tables and benches and a huge and splendid open fireplace. The room houses the dart board too. On warmer days you can sit at ease in a large and beautifully kept lawned garden, which is enclosed by hedges and dotted with trees and bright flowers.

Very little, if anything, seems to have been done to change this unpretentious and delightful pub during the last few decades. The landlord likes it that way, and so do we – long may it remain so.

(12–2pm and 6–10pm): hot crusty rolls (stilton, ham, turkey etc) under £1.

• Ale – Arkell's, Hall & Woodhouse, Morland
P – own car park No music

Alfriston, East Sussex map 4

DRUSILLAS PARK – TOUCANS FAMILY RESTAURANT – ☎ Alfriston (0323)870 235.

PR *Just off the A27, near the village – it's well signposted.*

This restaurant is an integral part of Drusillas, but you can call in here for a meal or a drink without having to pay the entrance fee to get into the park. Not that any parent would be able to resist taking the children into the splendid zoo, a compact and very well-organised one, which is laid out very much with the enjoyment of children in mind, and adults will find it just as interesting, too.

The restaurant is very spacious, has masses of high chairs, and offers a pretty good range of food. It is particularly popular at weekends, and entertainment of various kinds is provided for children on Sundays. Children's parties are quite a speciality, too. Attached to the restaurant there is a pub, the Inn at the Zoo, and this has a family room, so that the adults can enjoy a drink with the whole family.

There are excellent facilities for parents with babies: in the toilet area opposite Toucans there is a large changing table, chairs, paper towels, etc.

There is plenty of space for picnics within the park and a huge and splendid play area. The whole family can certainly enjoy a visit to Drusillas.

£1–6: spaghetti Bolognese, seafood pie, Sussex pie, tuna fish mayonnaise, cheeseburger
Children: own menu

Open 10am–6pm every day (except Xmas Day)
Access/AmEx/Visa • Ale – Harveys
No smoking area P – own car park

Also recommended in the Family Welcome Leisure Guide.

Alnwick, Northumberland — map 10

COTTAGE RESTAURANT – ☎ Alnwick (0665) 602 011.

R

In the town centre.

This is very much the traditional English restaurant, housed in an 18th century town house in a busy and narrow street in the centre of the town. It is very convenient if you plan to visit the remarkable Alnwick Castle, home of the Percy family since the 14th century.

The restaurant has pleasant, light and airy rooms and friendly and capable service. The lavatories are small, but they are carpeted and you could probably change a baby on the floor.

£1–6: seafood platter, chicken Cordon Bleu, mixed grill, vegetarian lasagne, sirloin steak
Children – own menu

Open 9am–9pm (from noon on Sun), June to October; 9am–5pm winter
P – public nearby Licensed

Alstonfield, Nr Ashbourne, Staffs map 6

GEORGE – ☎ Alstonfield (033 527) 205.

P

Off the A515 from Ashbourne to Buxton.

This old stone building overlooks the village green and its spreading chestnut trees. The grey stone can look drab but even on a wet evening Alstonfield has an ageless charm. It is high above Ashbourne and Dovedale and is a gathering place for walkers and climbers.

The main bar is a charming room with oak beams and an open fire. The long, low-ceilinged family room has six stout tables, and the walls are decorated with copper bric-a-brac.

There is a large field enclosed by stone walls at the rear, where children can play; it is also used by campers.

If you are keen on walking and the outdoor life you can recover from your exertions here with a few draughts of Burton, and a substantial plate of food.

(12–2pm & 7–10pm) £1–5: meat & potato pie, fillet steak, plaice & chips, lasagne, smoked trout
Children: small portions

• Ale – Ansell's, Ind Coope Burton P – own car park

Alvediston, Wiltshire map 2

THE CROWN – ☎ Salisbury (0722) 780 335.

P

Off the A30 between Shaftesbury and Salisbury.

A couple of years ago this 15th century thatched inn burnt down, but within a few months it was open for business again, and looks as welcoming as it ever did. The only difference is that the name has reverted to what it used to be – the Crown. It is situated in a lovely small village in the Chalke Valley and on the edge of Cranborne Chase.

The large bar is fully equipped with wooden doors, low beams and pillars, and has a large open fireplace with a stove: an appealing and comfortable room with its cushioned benches. Off the bar is another lounge, and fami-

lies are welcome to park themselves here. It's a delightful room with low beams, a large open fireplace and nice wooden tables. Towards the back of the pub there is a spacious restaurant.

The garden will delight any family: a large rambling grassy place with a goldfish pond and patches of flowers and shrubs, and occasional bench tables under the trees. There is a play area with a slide, a wooden fort and a toy tractor to ride on, and the whole area is safely enclosed.

You can have a Sunday roast here for around a fiver, and a further modest sum will bring jam roly poly or treacle sponge to your table, thus ensuring a sound afternoon sleep.

(12–2pm & 7–9.30pm) £2–9: Dorset paté, chilli with garlic bread, plaice & chips, cottage pie, steaks
Children: own menu

• Ale – Palmer's, Wadworth's & guests
P – own car park

Amberley, Nr Stroud, Glos — map 2

BLACK HORSE INN – ☎ Amberley (045 387) 2556.

P

In the centre of the village.

This attractive old inn, situated in an equally appealing village, had a beer licence only for about 150 years and still offers a good range of real ales.

Families are now very well provided for in the new conservatory at the back of the pub, but children must not linger beyond 8 o'clock at night. The conservatory leads out to a garden from where there are spectacular views of a valley below and a range of hills beyond. There is another very pleasant garden, safely enclosed, at the front of the pub.

(11.45am–2pm and 6.30–9.30pm) £1–5: whitebait, ploughman's, steak & kidney pie, salads, steaks
Children – own menu

• Ale – Archer's, Tetley, Timothy Taylor's, Wadworth's and guests
P – on the common

Please let us have reports – good or bad – on any establishments listed in the Guide as soon as possible after your visit.

Amersham, Bucks **map 3**

ETON WINE BAR, 1 Market Square – ☎ Amersham (0494) 727 242.

R

On the A413 in the Old Town.

This appealing restaurant, housed in a 17th century listed building, was in the Guide for many years as the Willow Tree and has become a wine bar and brasserie.

The restaurant forms an L shape around a small bar and is nicely furnished with pine tables. The old ceiling beams are still in place, as is the central brick fireplace and the place has bright posters on the walls.

You can still enjoy a little patio by the front entrance, and the willow trees provide some shade on sunny days.

The new owners have retained the pleasant ambience of the place and welcome families. Some space can always be found for a mother who needs to change a baby.

Last summer we had a really excellent lunch here from a small but enterprising menu.

£2–9: smoked salmon & mushroom mousse, seafood & mushroom roulade, lamb & fennel & cucumber pie, smoked fish platter
Children: smaller portions

Open 12–2.30pm and 7–10.30pm
Licensed P – ample nearby

Ansty, Dorset **map 2**

THE FOX – ☎ Milton Abbas (0258) 880 328.

P

Signposted in the minor roads near Milton Abbas and south-west of Blandford.

A major reconstruction was completed a couple of years ago at this well-known pub. The facilities for families were expanded with the provision of a play room for smaller children with a Wendy house, TV cartoons, etc; a large games room for adults and children; and an eating (and drinking) area in which smoking is forbidden. Despite the refurbishments and additions to the inn, the wonderful collection of Toby jugs and of coloured plates have been retained.

The owners were very conscious of the need to preserve the character of this handsome old pub, and the new wing, with more bedrooms on the upper floor, is an excellent match in flint and brick to the original building.

The front garden has a Wendy house and a slide, as well as bench tables where the adults can sit; and the rear garden has a swimming pool and more bench tables on the patio.

(12–2pm & 7–10pm) £1–7: Dorset paté, sirloin steak, spare ribs, swordfish, vegeburgers
Children: small portions

• Ale – Hall & Woodhouse, Wadworth's, Tetley & guests
P – own car park

Also recommended in the Family Welcome Accommodation Guide.

Appleby, Cumbria **map 9**

ROYAL OAK INN, Bongate – ☎ Appleby (07683) 51463.

P

Half a mile off the A66.

This delightful old coaching inn, long and low, is an attractive sight with its colourful hanging baskets and window boxes. It enhances an already

appealing town, which used to be the county town of Westmoreland. Parts of the building may date back to the 12th century, and the River Eden is nearby.

You will not be disappointed with the inside, with its wealth of brasses, old furniture, and low dark beams. Families can use a spacious room just inside the front door and it is comfortably furnished. There is an equally agreeable dining room alongside.

The long and varied menu doubles up for both bar meals and dinner, and also includes vegetarian dishes and daily specials. A high chair is provided.

(12–2pm & 6.30–9pm) £1–8: langoustines, savoury crumble, seafood Mornay, Cheddar chicken, steaks
Children: half portions

• Ale – Yates, McEwan's, Younger's No music
P – on forecourt

Ardentinny, Strathclyde **map 11**

ARDENTINNY HOTEL – ☎ Ardentinny (036 981) 209.

P *In the village at the end of the A880.*

You will find this cheerful, white-washed inn on the shores of the busy restaurant.

Unfortunately there is nowhere to feed or change a baby, though there is a special small lavatory for infants out of nappies.

£1–10: hot garlic bread, boiled salt beef dumplings, steak au poivre, plaice & chips, Wiener schnitzel
Children: own menu

Open 10am–11pm, every day   Access/AmEx/Visa
Licensed   One high chair only
P – public car park

Nr Arundel, West Sussex — map 3

BLACK RABBIT – ☎ Arundel (0903) 882 828

P

From Arundel follow the signs to the Wildfowl Trust and keep going.

The pub has the great bonus of a superb position on the River Arun, and next door to the Wildfowl Trust. You have a lovely view of Arundel Castle, too.

The Black Rabbit underwent a major face-lift last year and offers excellent facilities for families, including several high chairs. A family room, nicely furnished with wicker chairs, adjoins a pleasant restaurant and both look on to the river. The main bar has the same lovely views of the river and a verandah runs the length of the building.

On summer days you can settle in the garden and enjoy the view. There are bench tables on the lawns, and cheerful baskets of flowers are hung here and there.

During the summer months you can take a trip by boat from Arundel Quay to the Black Rabbit (at lunchtimes). The pub is open all day from Monday to Saturday, and food is available at all times.

(12–10.30pm) £2–9: crudités, lamb kebab, seafood enchilada, Hawaiian chicken
Children: small portions

• Ale – Hall & Woodhouse   P – own car park

Never use an out-of-date Guide. Many places are excluded because their standards have dropped or their policies towards families have changed. Many new establishments are added each year.

fireplace at one end where there is a collection of very lifelike stuffed birds and animals; a stag's head looks approvingly over the smart bar, with its comfortable seats and polished tables.

The family room doubles as an eating area and its windows look out on to the quiet grassy garden, with several tables and chairs, shady trees and a distant view of Ashwell's church tower – 176 feet high with a distinctive spike on top.

This pub has opted to stay open throughout the day (11am to 11pm) from Monday to Saturday.

(12–2pm & 6.30–10.30pm) £2–9: savoury Stilton pancake, Scotch salmon, beef in Guinness, entrecote Bordelaise
Children: own menu

• Ale – Greene King P – own car park

Askham, Cumbria **map 9**

PUNCH BOWL INN – ☎ Hackthorpe (09312) 43.

P

Two miles off the B5320 and the A6. At the bottom of the village.

This delightful pub is situated in the pretty village of Askham, alongside Lowther Park and its impressive castle.

You enter a spacious and low beamed bar, comfortably furnished and welcoming, and families are able to use a room at the far end. It's two rooms really, on different levels, with several tables and chairs. It's pleasantly cosy in there, and an alternative is a tiny little room, off the bar, with a padded bench running along the walls. A real snug.

On warmer days you can sit on the terrace at the side of the pub and watch the world go quietly by.

An enterprising range of bar meals is served lunchtime and evening, seven days a week, and on Sunday lunchtimes you can have roast beef and Yorkshire pud for around £4.

(12–2pm & 6.30–9.30pm) £1–9: shrimp bake, slamon en croute, fisherman's pot, cashew & pepper loaf, steaks
Children: own menu

• Ale – Castle Eden & guest beers P – own car park

Aston Crews, Nr Ross-on-Wye, Hereford & Worcs map 2

WHITE HART INN – ☎ Lea (098 981) 203

P

East of Ross-on-Wye on the B4222.

You will enjoy the fine views of the countryside from the well-tended, lawned garden of this appealing pub. On one side is the Forest of Dean and to the other the Welsh mountains. It sits in a tiny and quiet village, and part of the pub is reputed to be four hundred years old, as the main bar with its exposed beams and big open fireplace would indicate. A family room cum dining room, comfortable and well carpeted, is available, and a conservatory has been added.

The owners are happy to serve smaller portions to children and charge accordingly, and an excellent range of food is on offer every day, and includes a good choice of vegetarian dishes.

(12–2pm & 7–10pm, not Mon) £1–7: tuna & prawn mayonnaise, beef 'n beer, plaice & chips, turkey & cider pie, steaks

Children: own menu, half portions

• Ale – Wadworth's P – own car park

Aust, Avon map 2

BOAR'S HEAD – ☎ Pilning (045 45) 2278.

P

Follow the A403 to Avonmouth (at Junction 21 of the M4 by the Severn Bridge) and turn left to Aust village.

Only a few seconds from the M4, this attractive 17th century pub has an excellent children's room (extended last year) with low ceilings and a large, stone fireplace complete with iron stove. The main bar is also very appealing, with its stone walls, large open fireplace and various wooden tables and settles. On warmer days the children will perhaps be interested in the collection of rabbits and guinea pigs in the charming garden, which also has a swing and a climbing frame on the lawn.

There's a wide range of food and, with a couple of exceptions, it is all home-made. Snacks are available every day except Sunday and the buffet lunch from Monday to Friday offers around thirty different salads and pickles to accompany quiches, cold meats, salmon, game pie, turkey, etc. There are two high chairs on the premises.

This pub has excellent facilities for all the family in a very accessible place for travellers. The staff are not, however, at all flexible over meal times. If

you arrive even one minute after 2 p.m. and ask for food you will be denied it – as we were one afternoon last summer.

✕ (12–2pm & 7.30–9.45pm) £1–8: buffet lunch, ploughman's, potato and cheese and onion hot pot, omelettes
Children: half portions

• Ale – Courage   No music
P – own car park

Avebury, Wilts **map 3**

STONES RESTAURANT – ☎ Avebury (067 23) 514.

R

Off the main street of the village.

The village is encircled by the famous Neolithic stones which brood across the landscape in all directions, and were thought by John Aubrey in the 17th century to be of more historical importance than Stonehenge.

The restaurant is housed in a fine old stone barn next to the National Trust Shop and the Tourist Information Centre. There's a cobbled patio outside, a farmyard pond, a dovecote, a backdrop of lime trees, and across the way is the manor house. Inside the restaurant is long and spacious, plainly and attractively furnished with pine tables, chairs and settles.

All the food is home-made including the bread and the cakes (from organic flours), the jams and the chutneys. The herbs are home-grown, and the food will not contain any artificial additives. There are plenty of morning snacks available, including rolls, quiches, salads, cakes and various savouries; afternoon teas are served from 2.30pm, and there is an excellent choice of teas. The lunch we had here last Autumn was first rate, and very good value.

£1–3: soup, salads, hot savoury dishes, cream tea
Children: smaller portions

Open 10am–6pm every day during summer; weekends only in winter
Closed mid-Dec to Jan No credit cards accepted
• Ale – Bunce's No smoking area
P – in the village No music

Axminster, Devon **map 2**

NEW COMMERCIAL INN, Trinity Square – ☎ *Axminster (0297) 33225*
Pot Luck

R

In the town centre, opposite Boots and the Midland Bank.

This is a useful place for families to know about since it is open all day from Monday to Saturday, has several high chairs on the premises and offers special children's meals. You can also get breakfast at any time of the day and the meals are reasonably priced.

It is an unusual combination of a baker's shop, function room, pub and restaurant; and the food will mostly be fresh because the owners grow a lot of their own fruit and vegetables.

£1–6: beef curry, chilli con carne, burgers, sirloin steak, plaice
Children: own menu

Open 7.30am–11pm Mon-Sat; 12–2pm & 7–10pm Sunday
• Ale – Palmer's P – public car park nearby
Access/Visa No music

Aysgarth, Nr Leyburn, North Yorks — map 9

PALMER FLATT HOTEL – ☎ Wensleydale (0969) 663 228

P

On the A684 between Hawes and Leyburn.

This ivy clad roadside inn is an excellent base for exploring the nearby beauty spots which include the spectacular Aysgarth Falls.

The cosy public bar serves snacks and grills. The family room is a small functional place located at the end of the main bar area down some steps.

There is a well-kept garden at the back of the pub, laid out in lawns and terraces, and with a rockery and pond.

(12–2.30pm & 7–9.30pm) £1–4: plaice & chips, ham & egg & chips, chicken & chips, quiche, toasties.
Children – own menu

• Ale – Webster's, Ruddles, Theakston's
P – own car park

Please let us have reports – good or bad – on any establishments listed in the Guide as soon as possible after your visit.

Bamford, Derbyshire **map 7**

DERWENT HOTEL– ☎ Hope Valley (0433) 51395.

P

In the centre of the village, just off the A57.

Don't be put off by the imposing half-timbered exterior, this is an establishment which is clearly used to the demands of families and accommodating them with a smile.

The large family room is adorned with bric-a-brac and it feels as though you can relax without looking over your shoulder all the time.

There is a large garden with tables and umbrellas and it is walled off from the road so the children can play in safety.

The pub is open throughout the day from Monday to Saturday.

(12–2pm & 7–10pm) £1–7: Fisherman's platter, cauliflower cheese, country bumpkin, lasagne verdi, fillet steak
Children: own menu

• Ale – Ward's, Stone's, Tetley's **P** – own car park

Bampton, Devon **map 1**

THE ROSE GARDEN – ☎ Bampton (0398) 31788.

R

On the Dulverton r… Bampton.

An inform… ng atmosphere is the aim of the friendly owners of this r… u can have anything from baked beans to venison, and are… go into the kitchen to choose your meal, if you wish.

A grea… for parents is the availability of a baby-sitter, who, if you book in … ance, will take the children off your hands if you want to enjoy a meal on your own. If you need to change a baby, room will be found for you upstairs.

The restaurant is aptly called the Rose Garden, because the blooms are everywhere – on the china, the tablecloths, the chairs, and in their natural form on the tables. They are in the large garden too, with its wide lawn. There are plenty of tables, a fish pond, a waterfall and a wooden parrot in a cage spins away in the breeze.

You can get a good range of snacks throughout the day, with a more ambitious menu available in the evening.

£1–3: lasagne, scampi, poached egg on toast, pizza, salads
Children: own menu, half portions

Open 10am–10pm. Closed Mon to Wed during winter
No smoking in restaurant Access/Visa
P – own car park One high chair only

Bantham, Devon map 1

THE SLOOP INN – ☎ Kingsbridge (0548) 560 489.

P

West of Kingsbridge off the A379/B3197.

In a marvellous stretch of holiday country between Bigbury and Thurlestone, you will find this white-painted stone pub, a 16th century building, once owned by a notorious local smuggler called John Widdon.

Inside, it resembles a ship with wood-panelled walls and windows like port-holes. It is very spacious, and so is the family room, again with wood panelling, lots of tables and chairs: a bright, well-furnished room.

Food is on the go every day and there is always an excellent choice of locally caught fish. There is a fine sandy beach a few hundred yards from the pub.

(12–2pm & 7–10pm) £1–8: turkey broth, local smoked mackerel, plaice & chips, lamb chops, steaks

• Ale – Bass, Flowers, Usher's P – own car park

Also recommended in the Family Welcome Accommodation Guide.

Barcaldine, Nr Oban, Strathclyde map 11

SHORELINE RESTAURANT, Sea Life Centre – ☎ Ledaig (063 172) 386.

R

Off the A828 ten miles north of Oban.

The restaurant is part of the Sea Life Centre, with its huge display of marine life; the children will love the seals. It has a delectable situation on the shores of Loch Creran. You can sit at peace at the outside tables, surrounded by tall and shady trees.

The restaurant is a large and airy place with lovely views of the rocky shore. There are pine tables and chairs, and a tiled floor, under a high vaulted wooden ceiling.

If you need to change a baby there is a table and chair in the disabled toilet area; and there are several high chairs on the premises.

✕ £1–4: salmon, fisherman's pie, pizzas, baked potatoes
Children – half portions

Open 10am–6pm, mid-February to end-November
No credit cards Licensed
No smoking in part of restaurant No music
P – own car park

Also recommended in the Family Welcome Leisure Guide

Barngates, Nr Ambleside, Cumbria **map 9**

THE DRUNKEN DUCK – ☎ Hawkshead (096 66) 347.

P

Off the B5286.

Standing alone at a crossroads in a lovely part of the Lakes, and not far from Tarn Hows, you will find this welcoming 16th century pub. The name derives from some ducks which, in Victorian times, were inadvertently given ale with their usual feed. Modern visitors will not be disappointed by the range of beers available.

It's not ducks but a row of foxes' heads on one of the low beams which greets you as you enter. Various hunting trophies, brasses, pewter mugs and stuffed birds are a feature of the inn.

Families are welcome to use a small room with pine settles or the dining room, which is divided by beamed stalls.

A little verandah at the front of the pub gives you a wonderful sight of rolling countryside and at the back is a patio.

✕ (12–2pm & 6.30–9pm) £1–5: lamb & apricot casserole, gammon steak, lasagne, beef Stroganoff
Children: half portions

• Ale – Marston's, Tetley's, Theakston's, Jennings
P – own car park No music

Places included in the Guide must offer the following basic facilities: Pubs – a separate area or room for families where alcohol is not served; Restaurants – high chairs and special menus/reduced portions.

Loch Long. It was built in 1720, and was on the drovers' route to Glasgow from the Highlands. The surroundings are delightful as you look across the water to the mountains beyond. You can sit on the terrace and admire the views; and a lawn, sheltered with trees and hedges, goes down to the edge of the loch. There are moorings if you should arrive by boat.

A room next to the bar serves as a family room or you can head for the spacious buttery.

There are bar lunches and suppers, and the restaurant, which has two high chairs, is open for dinner. The menus concentrate on 'Taste of Scotland' dishes.

The Ardentinny is open all day every day, and on Sundays food is available throughout opening hours.

(12–2.30pm & 6–9.30pm) £1–9: haddock & chips, venison & mushroom pie, grilled salmon steak, fillet steak
Children: half portions

P – own car park

Ardkinglas, Argyll, Strathclyde **map 11**

LOCH FYNE OYSTER BAR – ☎ Cairndow (04996) 264.

R

On the A83 at the head of Loch Fyne.

The oyster bar is housed in an old farm building and its character is retained. The timbered roof is draped with nets, the walls are whitewashed and the furniture is natural wood, with some padded benches in booths. There are lovely views over the loch.

The accent is on informality. The customer can have a quick snack or tuck into a series of courses in any order he pleases. All the food is produced by the owners, who have their own oyster beds and their own smokehouse.

There are some non-fish items, such as smoked venison; and there is a shop alongside the oyster bar.

There are no facilities for changing a baby – it's the floor of the Ladies only.

£1–8: oysters, smoked mussels, dressed crab, smoked chicken, fresh salmon
Children: small portions

Open:mid-March to mid-April, 9am to 6pm
mid-April to end-October, 9am to 9pm
Otherwise, 9am to 6pm weekdays and 9am to 9pm weekends.
Closed at Christmas

Access/AmEx/Visa
P – own car park

Arreton, Isle of Wight — map 3

ARRETON MANOR – ☎ Isle of Wight (0983) 528 134.

R

Just off the A3056 in the centre of the island.

Arreton Manor, built in the late 16th century, is a real treasure house and well worth a visit for its various exhibitions.

When you need a rest and a sustaining cup of tea and a bite to eat you can head for the tea shop, which is housed in a garden room with sliding walls of leaded glass. It is a large and functional place, but is in a most attractive setting with more tables in a courtyard, and with a beautiful garden alongside which is loaded with bright flowers and mature trees.

There is pretty standard tea shop food available, but served in generous portions. There is nowhere to change a baby in comfort.

£1–4: baked potatoes, salads, paté, cottage pie, lasagne
Children: smaller portions

Open 10 am–6pm Mon to Fri; 12–6pm Sun; Closed every Saturday and from November to Easter
P – ample   No music
Licensed   One high chair only

Arundel, West Sussex — map 3

CAFE VIOLETTE – ☎ Arundel (0903) 883 702.

R

You will find this smart and cheerful restaurant in the main street of lovely Arundel with its superb castle.

The café has quite a history. It sits on Roman foundations, and the existing building has 17th century origins. It is worth a visit just to look at the famous ceiling, originally installed in the Medici Palace in Florence and removed to Penn Place in 1918. The frescoed walls were painted by Allan Dodds in 1954.

Throughout the day there is a comprehensive and eclectic menu and this includes a few vegetarian dishes, as well as fresh fruit and vegetable juices.

There is a good atmosphere here: it's bright and friendly, and to aid the 'Continental' atmosphere there's a very small terrace at one side of the

Barnstaple, Devon — map 1

HEAVENS ABOVE, 4 Bear Street – ☎ Barnstaple (0271) 77960.

R

In town centre (Queen Street car parks).

Everything is cooked on the premises at this vegetarian wholefood restaurant, and organic produce is used whenever possible. Vegan food is also available, and most dishes are salt free, while the sugar levels in the puddings are kept well below the norm.

The restaurant is up some stairs above a shop, and is a functional sort of place with pine furniture.

The sensible owners provide baby mugs and plastic bibs and will warm up baby food. Babies can be changed in the lavatories.

£1–2: pizza, rice loaf, cashew nut rissole, baked potato, salads
Children: half portions

Open 10am–6pm, Mon-Sat No credit cards accepted
Closed Sunday & Xmas through New Year Licensed
No smoking in half the restaurant P – public car parks

Bath, Avon — map 2

CRYSTAL PALACE, 11 Abbey Green – ☎ Bath (0225) 423 944.

P

In a central position very close to the Roman Baths and the Abbey.

The Georgian square where this pub is situated is a very busy spot during the tourist season, and it's useful to know of a pub with a pleasant atmosphere which is so central. The pub was originally called the "Three Tuns", and owed the change in its name to the popularity of the Great Exhibition of 1851, which was housed in the specially built Crystal Palace in Hyde Park.

Children are welcome in a conservatory room, with a paved floor, lots of pine tables and chairs, and a wall of glass doors which lead on to the courtyard attractively laid out with a vine, hanging flower baskets and bench tables.

Food is available every day at quite reasonable prices, and the staff will heat baby food for you, if asked. There is also a high chair on the premises.

(12–2pm) £1–3: range of ploughman's, plaice & chips, lasagne, shepherd's pie, baked potatoes
Children: own menu

• Ale – Eldridge Pope P – street parking

NO.5, Argyle Street – ☎ Bath (0225) 444 499.

R

Near Pulteney Bridge.

This is another restaurant run by Milburns, and a number of them are recommended by us: the Pump Room in Bath and the New Restaurant at the V & A Museum, for example.

This restaurant is close to Pulteney Bridge and offers a wide and interesting range of dishes. The surroundings are simple and uncomplicated, with wooden floors, mirrors and prints on the walls, and some potted palm trees. For those who like to watch the chef at work, the kitchen is in full view.

There are no facilities for changing a baby.

£2–6: rabbit casserole, mushroom & caraway roulade, trawlerman's pie, beef & Guinness stew, crisp pancakes with ratatouille
Children – small portions

Open 10am–10pm Mon to Sat; 12–5pm Sunday
No smoking at three tables Licensed
P – public car parks Access/AmEx/Diners/Visa
One high chair only

JOLLY'S, Milsom Street – ☎ Bath (0225) 62811.

R

In the centre.

On the first floor of this House of Fraser store you will find the self-service restaurant called Circles; and there is a lift service, if you are encumbered with shopping, push chairs, infants and all the usual paraphernalia of parenthood.

There are tables and seats, arranged in booths, on one side and a long counter on the other side, which displays some very tempting food. The emphasis is very much on healthy, fresh foods, with a good choice of vegetarian meals and salads.

Facilities for dealing with babies are provided on request: the mother and baby room has a chair, a table, wash basin and paper towels.

£1–4: vegetarian pizza, savoury pie, vegetable curry, roast beef.

Children: own menu, smaller portions

Open 9am–5pm Mon-Sat (till 7.30pm Thurs)
Open all year Licensed
Access/AmEx/Diners/Visa No music
No smoking in most of the restaurant P – public car parks

MILBURNS RESTAURANT, The Pump Room – ☎ Bath (0225) 444 477.

R

The famous Pump Room was built in the late 18th century, and an extension was built at the end of the next century by John Brydon. This was a haunt of fashionable society when they were in Bath to "take the waters" and it faces on to the Abbey churchyard.

Milburn's are expert at running restaurants in museums and other historical surroundings, and there is an elegant atmosphere to this one. The room is spacious, with starched white cloths on the tables, and you can still buy a glass of health-giving water from the original drinking fountain. Two 18th century sedan chairs occupy a corner, and some fine portraits adorn the walls, including one of Sir Robert Walpole.

Back to more mundane matters: mothers will find reasonable facilities for baby-changing; there is a table and a pull-down shelf in the Ladies.

The food ranges from breakfasts to hot meals, afternoon teas and snacks and there is an excellent choice of dishes. You can eat al fresco at the tables in the Abbey churchyard.

£1–6: club sandwich, avocado & celery salad, fish pie, steak & kidney pie, cold meat board.
Children: half portions

Open 10am–6pm, every day No credit cards
Licensed No smoking area
P – public car parks nearby

ROSSITER'S, 38-41 Broad Street – ☎ (0225) 62227.

R

In the town centre.

The restaurant is part of a small and up-market department store, which is housed in several old and interesting buildings. If you are encumbered with shopping, children, push chairs, etc you are warned that the restaurant is up two flights of stairs, and there is no lift.

But the two rooms are bright and pretty with wicker chairs, flowery oilcloths on the tables, a couple of sofas in one room, and prints for sale on the walls.

The limited menu offers some interesting dishes and some tempting cakes. There is a large shelf in the Ladies where a baby could be changed.

£1–4: parsnip soup, vegetable cobbler, smoked trout profiteroles, salads
Children: small portions

Open 10am–5pm, Mon to Sat   Access/AmEx/Diners/Visa
One high chair only   Licensed
P – public car parks   No smoking

SALLY LUNN'S, 4 North Parade Passage – ☎ Bath (0225) 61634

R

In the town centre, not far from Abbey Green.
This is one of the oldest houses in Bath and dates from 1482. Excavations in the cellar revealed items such as pottery and bits of mosaic from Roman times, and these are on display in the little museum, along with an ancient oven. Sally Lunn started baking her famous buns in the latter part of the 17th century and buns made from the same recipe are still sold here – both the savoury and the sweet variety.
The café is on two floors: there is a pretty, chintzy room on the first floor with a large fireplace; and the larger ground floor room is an attractive beamed area with an archway in the middle.
Space is at a premium here, and there is nowhere to change a baby.

£1–5: Sally Lunn buns – Welsh rarebit, chicken curry, turkey & salad, baked beans, salads

Open 10am–6pm (from midday on Sun)   No credit cards
Licensed   No smoking

SWEENEY TODD'S, 15 Milsom Street – ☎ Bath (0225) 462 368.

R

In the centre.
Part of a large chain of fast-food restaurants, this is a most attractive spot. It is housed in a long and spacious room with a high roof, and is simply and effectively furnished with rows of wooden tables and chairs. The place is a mass of green plants and the garden effect is enhanced by the pale green decor, the latticed walls and trompe l'oeil windows.
The restaurant is in action almost twelve hours a day, seven days a week; and families are well cared for with an array of high chairs, mini-pizzas, and burgers for children. The Ladies is roomy and has a pull-down shelf on which to change a baby.

£1–7: pizzas, burgers, chef's salad, barbecued chicken and ribs
Children: own menu

Open 12–11pm every day Open all year
Licensed Access/Diners/Visa
P – public car parks

Bathampton, Nr Bath, Avon — map 2

THE GEORGE – ☎ Bath (0225) 425 079.

P

Off the A4, east of Bath. Look for sign to Toll Bridge and Bathampton.

This large and rambling stone inn, its facade festooned with climbing plants and flowers, sits alongside the canal. From the family room, which is on the upper floor of the pub, you can gaze at the water. This room is divided into two areas within its stone walls and is comfortable enough with plenty of tables and chairs.

The pub itself is busy and cheerful, with several rooms to choose from, all with beamed ceilings, a profusion of copper and brass on the walls, mirrors, prints, and sporting artefacts such as old guns, stuffed fish, etc.

At weekends when it gets really busy the Garden Bar is opened up for families, and this is (funnily enough) alongside an enclosed lawned garden with bench tables and a climbing frame for the children.

(12–2pm & 6.30–9.45pm) £2–6: vegetable chilli with rice, salads, steaks, beef curry, baked ham with cauliflower cheese

• Ale – Courage P – own car park

Bathford, nr Bath, Avon — map 2

THE CROWN, 2 Bathford Hill – ☎ Bath (0225) 852 297.

P

At the junction of the A4 and A363 east of Bath.

This stately stone pub dates back to the 18th century but was substantially altered in the early years of this century.

There is plenty of space inside, with a large bar area, but the interior is well designed to give the effect of a number of small rooms. One of these is for families: the Garden Room is (quite rightly) a no smoking area and a door leads out to a terrace, and then to a large lawned garden, which is safely enclosed. In summer a sand pit, paddling pool and some toys are put out.

An alternative to the Garden Room for families is the Burgundy Room on the other side of the pub. This is a spacious and well-proportioned room with plenty of tables and chairs and particularly comes into play at weekends. There are several high chairs available and a changing table in the Ladies.

It is good to report that the enterprising range of food is freshly prepared, and you must be prepared to wait at busy times (weekends for example); even better to report that chips do not sully the premises, and that children are offered smaller portions of the adult dishes – not the inevitable things and chips.

(12–2pm & 7–10pm, not Mon lunch) £1–9: sirloin steak, Thai chicken & rice, steak & mushroom & ale pie, veal cordon bleu, lentil nut casserole
Children: small portions

• Ale – Ruddles, Usher's P – own car park

Beauworth, Nr Alresford, Hants **map 3**

THE MILBURY'S – ☎ Bramdean (096 279) 248.

P

About two miles south of the A272, and one mile beyond the hamlet of Beauworth.

Standing alone on top of the hill, the 17th century pub is built in soft warm Hampshire brick with hung tiles, flint walls and dormer windows set in a many angled roof line. Much renovation has been done, and families are welcome in various areas. A new family room has been built in a converted barn, where dark wooden settles and chairs are set around half a dozen tables. The dark beams of the ceiling contrast with the whitewashed walls. A door leads out to the garden. Families can also frequent the Gallery, a splendid room under the rafters.

The garden contains a pergola, a barbecue, and two swings and a see saw in the corner, near some neatly fenced off farm buildings. There are ten picnic tables and wonderful views across the fields to the wide open countryside beyond. Barbecues are held at weekends in summer and a Sunday brunch is served from 9.30 to 11.30 am.

This is a marvellous pub, with interesting food and an excellent range of real ales – seek it out!

(12–2.30& 7–10pm) £1–9: smoked salmon, cod fillet Mornay, steaks, plaice, chilli con carne.

Children: own dishes, half portions

• Ale – Courage, Gale's No music
P – own car park

Also recommended in the Family Welcome Accommodation Guide.

Beckhampton, Wilts — map 3

WAGGON AND HORSES – ☎ Avebury (067 23) 418.

P *On the A4 just east of its junction with the A361.*

This stone inn, thatched and substantial, has been a familiar landmark to travellers since the 16th century and an especially welcome sight in the days of horse-drawn coaches.

You enter a pleasant bar with an old curved settle, wooden tables and padded benches; and off this bar there is a room where families can settle. It is an agreeable room with a few wooden tables and a nice wooden settle.

There is another bar in the middle of the pub – again with good wooden furniture – and another room at the far end where families can sit together, particularly if they are having some food.

Behind the pub there is an enclosed grassy garden with lots of picnic tables; and by now an adventure playground will have been installed on an upper level.

(12–2pm & 7–9.30pm) £1–13: crudités, mixed grill, steaks, plaice, broccoli & cauliflower bake
Children: own menu, half portions

• Ale – Wadworth's
P – own car park

Beeley, Derbyshire — map 7

DEVONSHIRE ARMS – ☎ Matlock (0629) 733 259.

P *On the B6012, north of Matlock.*

An absolute beauty of a pub which nestles in a charming village only a couple of miles from Chatsworth House. The thick stone walls and mullioned windows ooze history and with the river meandering by it is a perfect spot.

Inside you will not be disappointed since the low ceilings and blackened beams are genuine as befits a hostelry dating back to the 18th century.

The flag floored family room is simple but has the added attraction of a stone wishing well – with all the money going to charity.

There are both restaurant and bar snack meals available and Sunday lunch at £8 is very popular. Indeed the only problem is that the pub's reputation has spread so much that it can get busy, but it is worth seeking out.

BAR MEALS (12–2.30pm & 7–10pm) £1–7: country casserole, haddock & chips, steak pie, crispy fried chicken, lasagne
Children: half portions

• Ale – Theakston's, Marston's   P – own car park

Berrynarbor, Nr Ilfracombe, Devon — map 1

YE OLDE GLOBE – ☎ Combe Martin (027 188) 2465.

P

Off the A399 east of Ilfracombe.

This is a picturesque village of stone cottages, brightly decorated with flowers, and with a handsome church, St Peter's. The pub was here as long ago as 1675, and was probably converted from a row of cottages of an even earlier vintage. It now has pink washed walls, and the various rooms, which run off the bar, are packed with antiques and curios – horse brasses and tackle, copper flasks, cases of miniatures, etc. The beamed ceilings and timbered walls testify to the age of the building, and there is a surprising amount of room inside.

The family room is very large, with French windows at one end which open on to the garden. There are plenty of wooden tables and wheel back chairs, a Wendy House, and toys for younger children, and books and puzzles for older ones. An alternative for families is a small room as you enter the pub. There is a nice open fireplace and a couple of wooden tables. One of our readers complained that the large room was sometimes closed and that the welcome given to her and her family was far from friendly, but we visited the pub last summer and found nothing amiss.

There is a small terrace at the front of the pub, and to the rear quite a large, enclosed garden with many bench tables on the lawn. A marvellous array of flowers greets your eyes: dahlias, fuchsias, sweet peas, petunias and many others.

(12–2pm & 7–10pm) £1–6: spaghetti Bolognese, Cornish pasty, plaice & chips, rump steak, lasagne, pizzas
Children: own menu

• Ale: Usher's
P – limited, but large public car park nearby

Berwick Station, East Sussex — map 4

BERWICK INN – ☎ Alfriston (0323) 870 002.

P

Off the A27 east of Lewes – signposted to Berwick Station.

A big, rambling white-washed pub, next door to the station. Youngsters will love the large playground and garden with paddling pool, Wendy house, slide, swing and climbing frame. The pub gets very crowded at weekends and on sunny days, but there is plenty of space in the children's room, a conservatory off the main bar.

Food is available seven days a week and includes vegetarian dishes; and Sunday lunches are also served at around £4. There are two high chairs on the premises.

(12–2pm & 7–10pm) £1–7: salmon salad, fresh trout, plaice & chips, vegetarian lasagne, steaks

Children: own menu

• Ale – Harvey's, Hall & Woodhouse   P – own car park

Berwick Upon Tweed, Northumberland — map 11

CANTY'S BRIG – ☎ Berwick (0289) 86255.

P

On the B6461 (signposted Paxton) about a mile west of the A1 (Berwick by-pass).

The aim of the splendid landlady who owns this pub is to make it into a true family pub, and she has already achieved a great deal. The main floor appears to be a traditional pub, but underneath is a family room which can be reached either down a spiral staircase or from its own door outside the pub. It is a comfortable and well-carpeted room, and has several chairs and tables and a box of toys. A high chair is also available.

Alongside is a sun lounge with patio doors to a lawned garden with swings, a slide and a pets' corner with rabbits, hens and ducks. It overlooks the river, as do many of the rooms.

(12–2pm & 7–9pm) £1–4: leek & potato soup, roll mop herring, cottage pie, chicken curry, haddock & chips

Children: own menu, half portions

• Ale – Greenmantle P – own car park

Betws-y-Coed, Gwynedd map 5

THE BUBBLING KETTLE – ☎ Betwys-y-Coed (069 02) 667.

R

On the A5 west of the centre of the town.

The cafe is housed in what was once a Victorian semi-detached house. It has the look of a traditional tea shop with a mixture of furniture, an oak dresser and a Victorian fireplace.

The owners do all the cooking on the spot from fresh ingredients, and the food looks good and is reasonably priced. It ranges from snacks and sandwiches to dishes of the day and cream teas.

There are two tables outside, one on each of the small lawns which are linked by an arch of honeysuckle; and there are also a couple of tables in a small conservatory.

If a baby needs to be changed there is a table, a chair and paper towels available in the Ladies.

£1–4: plaice & chips, prawn salad, cottage pie, filled jacket potatoes
Children: half portions

Open 11.30am–5.30pm Mon-Fri, & Sun. Closed Saturday and from end Oct to Easter
Unlicensed No music
No smoking P – on street

Bewdley, Hereford & Worcs map 6

LITTLE PACK HORSE, High Street – ☎ Bewdley (0299) 403 762.

P

This pub is tucked away off the High Street of this interesting town, and does not have a car park and you are advised to park in the main public car park and go on foot. It is a fascinating little pub, which is determinedly traditional. You enter down a corridor with an interesting mosaic on the walls, and then find a number of small rooms with flagstone floors, ancient black beams, and old photographs and advertisements on the walls.

The old stable room at one end of the pub is designed for families, a pleasant and cosy room with wooden tables and chairs, an old wooden desk complete with ink well, and a wood burning stove. There are more photographs, wood working tools and horses' tack on the walls.

You will find an interesting choice of food, including Desperate Dan pie and jam suet roly poly – but, we are delighted to report, no chips.

(12–2pm & 6–10pm) £1–5: grilled fresh sardines, filled jacket potatoes, vegetable samosa, chicken & ham pie, cauliflower cheese
Children: half portions

• Ale – Ind Coope Burton, Lumphammer (own brew)
P – public car park

Bibury, Glos **map 2**

CATHERINE WHEEL – ☎ Bibury (028 574) 250.

P

On the A417.

The pub was built of stone in the 15th century and is a delightful and unspoiled pub, with two bars furnished in traditional style and with low, black-beamed ceilings. Log fires add to the air of comfort.

Children are welcome in a neatly furnished, wedge-shaped room with some good wooden tables, smart padded benches and an iron stove. If the sun shines you should head for the spacious, enclosed grassy garden, with its several apple trees and bench tables. To one side is open farming country.

A good range of food is available here every day; all in all it is a very appealing pub which welcomes families, who will enjoy a stroll round this super village – "the most beautiful village in England", according to William Morris.

(12–2pm & 7–10pm) £1–8: lasagne, fresh haddock, vegetable chow mein, steak au poivre

• Ale – Courage P – own car park

Bickerton, Cheshire **map 6**

DURHAM HEIFER – ☎ Broxton (082 925) 253.

P

On the A534 West of Nantwich.

This is an odd-looking place: rather like a miniature fort at the front, but it was apparently once a farmhouse. However, it has a large family room, well-furnished with plenty of tables and upholstered wall seating. In addition there is a very pleasant dining room at the back, and this looks out to open countryside.

The large garden has swings and seesaws with a mixture of garden furniture.

Beware of their opening hours: 12 o'clock and 7 pm.

(12–2pm & 7–10pm) £1–6: whitebait, coq au vin, steak Chasseur, plaice, lasagne, salads
Children: own menu, half portions

• Ale – Banks P – own car park

Biddenden, Kent — map 4

THREE CHIMNEYS – ☎ Biddenden (0580) 291 472.

P *On the A262 about one mile from the village of Biddenden.*

A couple of miles down the road from the famous Sissinghurst Gardens you will find this splendid old pub; very busy and very well-organised. Families are welcome to use the Garden Room, and the landlord warned us that it is wise to book a table there at weekends. This room looks out to a lovely garden, with its lawns winding amongst the shrubberies and flowers.

The rest of the pub is made up of a series of rooms with wooden beams and brass ornaments and good wooden furniture which is easy on the eye. That same eye will be drawn to the serried ranks of the beer barrels behind the bar, business-like but inviting on their stillages.

A very wide range of dishes is rotated on a daily basis; a selection goes on to the blackboard each day, but the smoked salmon and potted shrimp starter, and a sirloin steak is always available in the Garden Room. More vegetarian dishes have been introduced and it is good to report that there is a good selection of half bottles of wine.

(12–2pm & 6–10pm) £1–8: chilled avocado & mint, Kentish smokies, seafood casserole, ragout of lamb, aubergine & tomato pie.

• Ale – Adnams, Fremlin's, Harvey's, Marston's, Goacher's etc
P – own ample car park No music

Billingford, Nr Dereham, Norfolk — map 8

FORGE – ☎ Elmham (036 281) 8980.

P

Just off the B1145 north of East Dereham.

It was indeed once a forge, and is a long and low building of attractive dark brick, which was converted and extended with style.

There is a separate family room at the back of the pub, a spacious area with plenty of tables and chairs, and a pool table. There are even baby-changing facilities in the Ladies: a rare and very welcome facility in a pub.

Outside the family room there is a sizeable garden, safely enclosed and lawned, and with several bench tables. For children there are a wooden climbing frame, swings and a see-saw.

An alternative room for families is the dining area at one end of the bar, but separated from it. This is an attractive room with a high vaulted and timbered ceiling. There is a high chair here, as there is in the family room.

(12–2pm & 7–9pm) £1–4: plaice & chips, lasagne, filled jacket potatoes, salads, chicken Kiev
Children: own menu

• Ale – Greene King, Adnams P – own car park

Nr Billingshurst, West Sussex — map 3

BLUE SHIP, The Haven – ☎ Rudgwick (040 372) 2709.

P

Off the A29 just north of the junction with the A264. There is a sign to The Haven and you should then take the turning to Garlands and Okehurst.

This 15th century pub is a lovely sight with its half-tiled brick walls, and dormer windows above, all festooned with Virginia creeper.

There is a timeless look to the place, especially as you see the superb low-ceilinged bar, with a collection of wooden tables, scrubbed white, the old brick floor, and the large inglenook fireplace. There is just a serving hatch, and the beer is served direct from the barrels.

There are a couple of rooms away from the bar where families can sit; one has a pool table and the other is comfortable enough with its various wooden tables.

There is a very large grassy garden at the back of the pub and it includes some swings and a climbing frame for the children. From here you will see some of the landlord's Newfoundland dogs. There is more garden alongside the pub, with bench tables and a pretty display of roses, snapdragons and other flowers, plus a small patio at the front.

(12–2pm & 7–9.30pm, not Sun or Mon pm) £1–7: paté, ham & eggs & chips, plaice & chips, cheesy cottage pie, ratatouille
Children: own menu

• Ale – King & Barnes   No music
P – own car park

Bishop's Caundle, Dorset   map 2

WHITE HART – ☎ Bishops Caundle (096 323) 301.

P

On the A3030 south west of Sherborne.
Once a courthouse for the infamous Judge Jeffries, this 18th century pub stands close to the roadside, and still retains its old mounting block. Pebble dash now covers the original stone, but don't be put off by its rather ordinary appearance because the interior is attractive: lots of wooden tables under the low beamed ceilings, open fires and old agricultural implements on the walls.
The square family room has been added at the back of the original building but is completely in keeping with the rest of the attractive bar. It has easy access to the garden.
The wooden skittle alley (a feature of any Dorset pub worth its salt) is available for families too. It is quite light and airy with plenty of chairs and tables, and is often used as an overflow family room.
The attractive lawned garden has views of Blackmore Vale. A wooden playhouse with a slide has been built for the children, and there are a couple of trampolines for them to play on – but make sure that they are properly supervised.

(12–2pm & 6.30–10pm) £1–10: Somerset pie, steaks, Dorset trout, vegetable curry, fisherman's pie
Children: own menu, half portions

• Ale – Hall & Woodhouse   P – own car park

If you wish to recommend an establishment to the Guide please write to us – report forms are at the back of the book. We need your help to extend and improve the guide.

Bishop's Frome, Hereford & Worcs — map 2

GREEN DRAGON – ☎ Munderfield (0885) 490 607.

P

Just off the B4214 north of Ledbury.

This is an excellent pub with the right basic ingredients – a good choice of food and of real ales, which are augmented by guest beers. You enter a marvellous old bar, with a beamed ceiling, ancient stone floors, good wooden furniture and a huge open fire. Through a doorway there is an equally charming family room, with half a dozen tables, a thickly beamed ceiling and an open fire.

On summer days it would be a treat to sit in the large lawned garden, which is safely enclosed and has several bench tables. At one end there is a swing and a climbing frame to amuse the children.

The owners have now implemented their plans to extend the pub with a games and function room on the side of the pub. It's a delightful family pub in a lovely part of the country.

(12–2pm & 7–9.45pm) £1–7: whitebait, plaice & chips, vegetable curry, cidered chicken, venison pie
Children: own menu

• Ale – Wadworth's, Hook Norton, Timothy Taylor's, Robinson's & others
P – street parking

Bishop's Lydeard, Somerset — map 2

BELL INN – ☎ Bishop's Lydeard (0823) 432 968.

P

In the village off the A358 north west of Taunton. Head for the church.

The lovely garden gives visitors a good introduction to this old pub. It has a terrace with some bench tables and is ringed with bright flowers and greenery. The pub, built in the 15th century, is alongside the ancient village church.

Inside, the stone walls and beamed ceilings give an appealing atmosphere to the place and families are welcome either in the Cellar Bar, which has a pool table and various amusement machines, or in the restaurant area, a lovely bright room on the far side of the lounge bar.

Food is served every day and a Sunday lunch is also available at under £3. There is an excellent range of real ales to be tried.

(12–2pm & 6–10pm) £2–8: cheesy chilli, chicken curry, steaks, ratatouille

Children: own menu, half portions

• Ale – Marston's, Golden Hill, Wadworth's, Websters,
P – own car park

KINGFISHER'S CATCH, Taunton Road – ☎ Bishop's Lydeard (0823) 432 394.

R

On the A358 north west of Taunton (not actually in the village of Bishop's Lydeard).

This roadside restaurant was originally a sheep drovers' inn, and looks bright and welcoming by dint of the tubs of sweet peas and begonias which decorate the walls.

The owners offer a wide range of freshly cooked dishes, and the choice is augmented by daily specials. There is also a three course Sunday lunch at under £7. It's a relaxing place and nicely decorated: the dark wood of the tables and chairs contrasts with the paler paint of the walls.

If you need to change or feed a baby there is a chair in the Ladies, and a shelf.

£1–9: haddock smokies, lasagne, seafood pancake, fresh plaice, steaks
Children: half portions

Open 11am–2.30pm & 6–11pm, Mon to Sat. Closed on Monday from October to May
• Ale – Cotleigh Access/Visa
P – own car park

Blackawton, Devon — map 1

NORMANDY ARMS – ☎ Blackawton (080 421) 316.

P

Take a minor road from the B3207 – it's not far, though some of the lanes are single track. Use the church tower as a guide – the pub is only a little way from there.

This pub was renamed the "Normandy Arms" in honour of the Normandy landings of the Second World War since many of the troops were trained on nearby beaches. Helmets and berets on the walls of the charming bar, and some caricatures of WW2 leaders, commemorate this.

There's a good atmosphere in this pub and a pleasant children's room upstairs, where there are tables and chairs and lots of toys and games. It

is nice to report that there are no gaming machines nor pool tables.

There's one high chair in the restaurant, but book if you want to eat there at the weekend. There is a very good choice of food all of which is freshly prepared on the premises; and small portions of most dishes can be served up for children.

(12–2pm & 7–10pm, not Sun pm in winter) £1–4: plaice & chips, chicken & ham pie, vegetable pancake, steak sandwich
Children: own menu, half portions

• Ale – Blackawton, Bass, Ruddles   P – own car park

Also recommended in the Family Welcome Accommodation Guide.

Blairgowrie, Tayside — map 11

THE PENNY BLACK – ☎ Blairgowrie (0250) 5294.

R

In the centre of Blairgowrie on the High Street.

This bright and cheerful place is a real find in Perthshire. The pine panelled walls and pine tables give it a welcoming air, and you can be assured that the food is all made on the spot from fresh ingredients.

A great bonus for parents is the presence of a separate play area within the restaurant and within full view of the customers. It is well stocked with toys and is a welcome addition to a family restaurant.

There are excellent facilities for dealing with babies: a pull-down shelf, a changing mat, a chair and paper towels.

£2–6: steak & vegetable pie, chicken Kiev, scampi, vegetable curry, haddock & chips
Children: own menu, half portions

Open 9am–7pm (from 11am on Sundays)
Access/Visa No smoking at 4 tables

Bledington, Oxon — map 3

KINGS HEAD INN – ☎ Kingham (0608) 658 365.

P *Off the B4450 East of Stow-on-the-Wold.*

Situated in a charming Cotswold village, the pub is in a marvellous position by the immaculate village green, with its stream and attendant ducks. There are even some swings and a slide on the green quite close to the pub and within easy shouting distance of a small garden at the front.

It's a superb 15th century stone inn, with steep slate roofs; you enter directly into a delightful bar, with black beams and pillars, wooden settles and a big open fireplace at one end. A really excellent cold buffet, with everything home-made, is laid out here, and it is worth a trip just for the imaginative food alone.

Families are welcome in the garden room, which is furnished in the same style as the rest of the pub, with wooden tables and chairs, stone flagged floors and wooden beams. It's a pleasant atmosphere here, and smoking is forbidden.

(12–2pm & 7–9.45pm) £1–10: kipper & horseradish paté, rack of lamb, local trout, Oriental veal, steaks
Children: smaller portions

• Ale – Wadworth's, Hook Norton, Tetley
P – own car park

Bledlow, Bucks — map 3

LIONS OF BLEDLOW – ☎ Princes Risborough (084 44) 3345.

P *Off the B4009 near Chinnor. Look out for West Lane – the pub's at the top of the hill.*

The pub is housed in a long and low-slung white painted 16th century building, with dormer windows set in a steep roof, and is situated in lovely countryside at the foot of the Chilterns. When the sun shines you might sit on the patch of green which fronts the pub and be quite at peace with the world; and the pub also has a large garden at the rear.

The interior has all the delightful attributes of a classic English pub: low beamed ceilings, huge open fires, alcoves here and there with padded wooden settles and wooden tables. It's a busy and cheerful place, with a really pubby atmosphere. At one end of the pub there is a sizeable family room; it used to be the games room and is functional and comfortable enough.

(12–2pm & 7–9.30pm, not Sun pm) £1–4: steak & kidney & mushroom, moussaka, spicy chicken, spare ribs, salads

• Ale – Young's, Wadworth's, Courage, Wethered, & guests
P – own car park No music

Bodfari, Clwyd **map 6**

DINORBEN ARMS – ☎ *Bodfari (074 575) 309.*

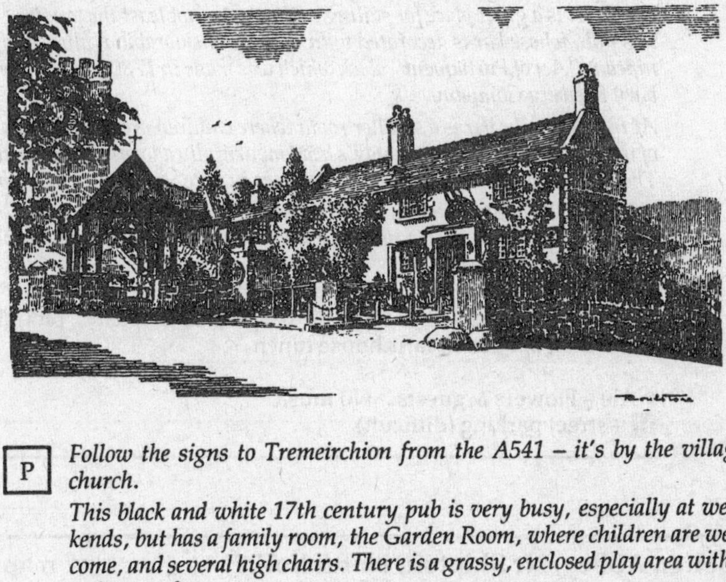

P *Follow the signs to Tremeirchion from the A541 – it's by the village church.*

This black and white 17th century pub is very busy, especially at weekends, but has a family room, the Garden Room, where children are welcome, and several high chairs. There is a grassy, enclosed play area with a swing nearby.

The gardens are terraced, with ponds and alcoves and plenty of seating, and indeed won a pub garden award a couple of years ago.

The smorgasbord is only served at lunchtimes and is so popular on Sundays that it is impossible to provide ordinary bar meals as well. It is advisable to book, or you might go hungry. We think that it is excellent value at £6.50 for adults and £3.95 for children. At other times, there is a wide-ranging selection of bar meals.

(12–3.30pm & 6–10.30pm) £1–8: smorgasbord, grilled halibut, steaks, poached salmon, roast poussin
Children: own menu, half portions

• Ale – Thwaites   P – own car park

Bodinnick-by-Fowey, Cornwall — map 1

OLD FERRY INN – ☎ Polruan (072 687) 237.

P

In the minor roads West of Looe and Polperro.

This fine old inn, of 16th century vintage, has a splendid view across the estuary and is right by the ferry which runs from the village across to Fowey. It is a great place for sailing enthusiasts, not least the landlord of this pub, whose bar is decorated with nautical memorabilia; plus a magnificent "Act of Parliament" clock which was made in 1780 for the Aylesbury Brewery Company.

At the side of the bar is a smaller room where children are welcome. Part of the wall is solid rock and a stag's head mournfully adorns another wall. There are a couple of amusement machines in here, too, and a pool table makes its appearance during the winter months.

Basic bar food is available morning and evening, while the restaurant opens only in the evenings.

BAR SNACKS (12–2.15pm & 6–9pm) £1–4: pasty, ploughman's, quiche, farmhouse lunch

• Ale – Flowers & guests   No music
P – street parking (difficult)

Bolton Abbey, Nr Skipton, North Yorks — map 9

CAVENDISH PAVILION AND TEA ROOMS – ☎ Bolton Abbey (075 671) 245.

R

Look for the stone archway in the village and then for the tea rooms sign. You will find the Cavendish Pavilion at the centre of the Bolton Abbey estate picnic area.

It's a gloriously old-fashioned establishment set in an environment of great natural beauty. Here you can sit in front of the tea rooms, beneath attractive hanging baskets and colourful umbrellas and enjoy the wonderful scenery with the river rumbling past only a few yards away. To one side the children will be amused by the bumper cars, mini-roundabout and other rides.

The interior is still somewhat Spartan with its strip lighting and concrete floor, but offers a good range of food. There's a gift shop, but, as yet, nowhere to change or feed a baby in comfort.

On a warm summer's day it is an idyllic place to have a meal or a drink.

£1–8: soup, salads, burger with salad & chips, local trout, steaks
Children: own menu, half portions

Open 10am–6.30pm March-Oct, weekends only in winter to 5pm
Closed Mon-Fri Nov-Mar Access/Visa
Licensed No music
P – £1 at nearby car park refunded if taking full meal

Bolventor, Cornwall **map 1**

JAMAICA INN – ☎ Pipers Pool (056 686) 250.

P

On the A30 north of Bodmin.

Pop in to see this famous inn on rolling Bodmin Moor because it was the setting for Daphne du Maurier's tale of villainy and derring-do. She is commemorated with a special room here. The inn was once owned by the thriller writer, Alistair Maclean.

If you are travelling down this busy main road in the summer you will find food available most of the day from just after 9 in the morning till about 10.30 at night, and there's a high chair in the restaurant area. Children are welcome there anyway – and probably the adults will prefer it to the children's room which will attract youngsters with its rows of games machines.

There is a large garden and the children's play area, at the back of the pub, has swings, a slide, climbing frame, etc. There are also plenty of bench seats here. The Potter's Museum of Curiosity is an added attraction.

(11am–11pm; until 10.30pm in winter) £1–4: scampi, chicken & chips, Cornish pasty, salads
Children: own menu

• Ale – Flowers and guests P – own car park

Bowness-on-Windermere, Cumbria — map 9

HEDGEROW VEGETARIAN RESTAURANT, Lake Road – ☎ *Windermere (09662) 5002.*

R

Near the centre of town.

New owners have changed the menus at this restaurant, and despite its name it is no longer a vegetarian one. There is a range of sandwiches, light meals and tea available, and the restaurant opens throughout the day, but not in the evening.

A mother wishing to change a baby can just about cope in the Ladies.

£1–4: vegetable curry with rice, houmous with pitta bread, trout mousse, jacket potatoes, cream teas
Children: small portions

Open 9.30am–5pm
Licensed Access/Visa
P – public car park opposite One high chair only

Boyden Gate, Nr Canterbury, Kent — map 4

THE GATE INN, Marshside – ☎ Chislet (022 786) 498.

P *North east of Canterbury on the minor roads between the A28 and the A299.*

This attractive building houses a friendly pub with a charming bar with a large open fire. The pub manages to be one of the hubs of local life while still welcoming tourists and families, who are usually very much in evidence in the garden and the family room. All sorts of events are arranged at the pub: from a Burns Night supper to quiz nights, folk evenings, bell ringing, and all manner of traditional pub games.

It is a relaxing and "pubby" place and the family room echoes the character of the inn. It has an eccentric collection of odds and ends on the walls, and several easy chairs, books and board games. There is a small and pleasant garden with a river alongside which is home to great numbers of loquacious ducks, geese and chickens.

It is good to report that food is available throughout opening hours; and that this pub is one of the first to receive a "Heartbeat" award for its menu.

The pub also has a place in sporting history since it was once the home of William Webb Ellis, the founder of rugby union.

(11am–2.30pm & 6–11pm) £1–3: hot pot, burgers, ploughman's, vegetarian pie, black pudding

Children: portions of any size

• Ale – Shepherd Neame   No music
P – own car park

Bradley Green, Nr Cannington, Somerset   map 2

MALT SHOVEL – ☎ Combwich (0278) 653 432.

P

Just off the A39 west of Bridgwater. Look for the sign (to Bradley Green).

This is not the most appealing exterior we have seen; but no matter since the inside of the pub is pleasant and comfortable enough with its cream painted stone walls and wooden tables and settles under the low beams.

There are three bars to give plenty of space, and families are welcome to use a room separated from the main bar. It has several tables and is furnished and decorated in the same agreeable style as the rest of the pub.

The family room opens on to a large lawned garden with a few tables and chairs.

(12–2pm & 7–9.30pm) £1–8: fisherman's pie, curried vegetable bake, steaks, smoked haddock cheesy bake
Children: small portions

• Ale – Butcombe, Marston's, Wadworth's
P – own car park

Bramber, West Sussex   map 3

OLD TOLLGATE RESTAURANT, The Street – ☎ Steyning (0903) 813 362.

R

Just off the A283 as you enter the village.

Situated in a pretty village, this is a bright and busy restaurant with paved floors, wood panelling and beams and wallpaper with a red brick pattern. It sounds eccentric, but is very effective.

There are two long rooms, which both look out to the garden and a charming conservatory was last year added to the one end of the bar. The garden itself has a pleasant lawned area, with flower beds around the edges and a fish pond, which is safely netted over. There are benches and tables here.

The menu is uncomplicated – either two or three courses – with a good choice of hors d'oeuvres, fish, roasts and casseroles and a wide variety of salads.

The Ladies has adequate room to deal with a baby's needs, or the staff can provide facilities elsewhere.

LUNCH (12–3pm) £9–12
DINNER (7pm onwards) £14
Children: any size meal and charged accordingly

Closed Sun evenings Access/AmEx/Diners/Visa
P – own car park One high chair only

Branscombe, Nr Seaton, Devon — map 2

THREE HORSESHOES – ☎ Branscombe (029 780) 251.

P

On the A3052 above Branscombe.

This is a huge and very busy roadside pub, whose owners have gone for the family market in a most determined and commercial way. There are two large rooms where families are welcome to eat or drink together (with several high chairs available) and an even larger function room alongside is pressed into service if necessary.

The large garden, safely enclosed, has a great array of things to swing on, climb on, sit on, etc.;there are swings, slides, a wooden fort, a carriage with wooden horses, a rocking horse, etc.

The pub is open all day during the season, and food is always available.

(12–10pm) £1–6: plaice & chips, chicken & chips, salads
Children: own menu, half portions

• Ale – Wadworth's, Bass & guests
P – own car park

Brent Knoll, Somerset — map 2

THE GOAT HOUSE, Bristol Road – ☎ Burnham-on-Sea (0278) 760 650.

R

On the A38 just north of Junction 22 of the M5.

This self-service restaurant, with a bias to the vegetarian, looks a bit like a glorified transport caff, with a simple decor, but of course the food is the important thing.

The owners set the place up to develop and sell a range of products derived from goats, of which they have over a hundred of various breeds. The children will certainly love the goats, some of which are in stables around the

courtyard at the back. There are plenty of tables here.
There are no facilities to change babies.

£1–3: lasagne, flans and quiches, baked potatoes, ploughman's
Children: own menu, half portions

Open 9am–5.30pm Mon to Sat (from 10am Sunday & from noon on Tuesday)
No smoking area Unlicensed
P – own car park

Bretforton, Hereford & Worcs — map 2

THE FLEECE – ☎ Evesham (0386) 831 173.

P

In the centre of the village off the B4035 east of Evesham.
This is one of our favourite pubs, a gem of a medieval building, which started life as a farmhouse, became an inn in 1848, and was left to the National Trust by Lola Taplin, who ran the pub for over thirty years. Her bequest stipulated that there should be no crisps, music, fruit machines, pool tables, or advertisements. A lady of great taste and perception. It is beautifully furnished throughout with old oak tables, high-backed settles, dressers, brass and copper pub measures and so on.

Families are welcome in a room next to the servery; this houses a superb collection of pewter, which dates from the Cromwellian period and may indeed have been left there by the infamous Oliver.

There is a very large garden with a swing, a climbing frame, and a log Wendy House. There are tables and benches to seat up to sixty people.

At weekends, if the weather is kind, a barbecue is set up in the garden; and this is supplemented by a salad bar in the restored barn. Prices range from £1 to £4.

(12–2.15pm & 7–9.30pm, not Mon pm) £1–5: ploughman's, gammon steak, chicken & mushroom pie, plaice & chips, Gloucester sausages & chips
Children: smaller portions

• Ale – Hook Norton, Marston's and guest beers
P – in village square No music

Bridport, Dorset — map 2

GEORGE HOTEL, 4 South Street – ☎ Bridport (0308) 23187.

P

In the centre of Bridport, near the town hall.

The George Hotel is a stone Georgian building standing almost on the crossroads in the centre of town. It is unpretentious with its dark low-ceilinged rooms, but the warmth of the long dark mahogany bar is matched by the friendly atmosphere and it is obviously well used by regulars. On market days and weekends the bar gets very busy.

The food is served at the end of the room. It is all home-made and has a good local reputation.

The dining room doubles as a family room and orders are taken through a hatchway at the back of the bar which runs parallel to the corridor that separates the two rooms.

The pub is open throughout the day, from Monday to Saturday.

✕ (12–3pm & 6.30–9.30pm, not Sun lunch) £1–6: crudités, smoked fish paté, entrecote steak, home-made pies, stuffed aubergines
Children: small portions

• Ale – Palmer's P – public car park nearby

Brighton **map 3**

BROWNS RESTAURANT, 3/4 Duke Street – ☎ Brighton (0273) 23501.

R

On the western side of The Lanes, not far from the Old Ship Hotel.

This is very much in the same style as their Cambridge and Oxford restaurants (qv) and is a busy, gregarious place in the centre of a seaside town which continues to retain its charm and style.

The restaurant serves an excellent range of food, with the emphasis on pastas, salads, and grills. We have invariably enjoyed our meals here, and the lively atmosphere. Families are well cared for here: for example there were seven high chairs at the last count; and the toilet area is being enlarged and it is hoped that a pull-down shelf will be installed in the Ladies.

£1–8: spaghetti with various sauces, fisherman's pie, chicken pie, burgers, poached salmon
Children: own menu, half portions

Open 11am–11.30pm (from noon on Sundays)
Closed at Xmas Access/AmEx/Visa
P – multi-storey nearby

FOOD FOR FRIENDS, 17/18 Prince Albert Street – ☎ Brighton(0273) 202 310.

R

Quite close to the back of the Ship Hotel.

A small and very busy self-service wholefood restaurant, which has been revamped and the interior seems less cramped, while the flow of customers has been improved. It is open all day and every day and always has very interesting vegetarian food. You can eat well here at a reasonable price, and the menu changes daily. The restaurant has a relaxed and informal atmosphere, and a relatively youthful clientele.

It is good to report that a pull-down shelf, on which a baby could be changed, has now been installed in the Ladies.

£1–3: cauliflower & paprika quiche, stir-fried vegetables & tofu, Hungarian goulash soup, Virginia spoonbread bake
Children: half portions

Open 9am–10pm. Closed at Xmas. Visa only
P – public car parks nearby Licensed

Bristol, Avon map 2

51 PARK STREET – ☎ Bristol (0272) 214 616.

R

In the shadow of the impressive University tower this restaurant, built in the Georgian era and edged with large flower boxes, is situated half-way down a steep hill. The decor is simple yet tasteful, echoing the days when it was an antiques shop, and even the babies' high chairs reflect a bygone age.

Downstairs there is a large room and a smaller one above, each with a licensed bar. With wooden floors, white walls and large mirrors surrounding the walls, the establishment is light and spacious. A window the length and breadth of the building fronts the premises and gives a clear view of bustling Park Street. A very small whitewashed courtyard is open on warm days.

The menu caters for a very wide range of tastes and is served by friendly staff. There is a relaxed atmosphere about the place, a bit like a French brasserie, into which you might pop for a cup of coffee and a read of your newspaper. Background music, usually jazz or classical, is unobtrusive.

No special areas are set aside to feed and change a baby, but the staff will be happy to provide a room if requested.

£2–8: corned beef hash, crudités, burgers, tagliatelle and spaghetti, entrecote steak
Children: half portions

Open 12–11pm, every day
Access/AmEx/Diners/Visa Licensed
P – meters or public car parks

GUILD RESTAURANT, 68-70 Park Street – ☎ Bristol (0272) 291 874.

R

Close to the centre of the city and near the Cathedral.

At the back of this smart store the restaurant, with windows looking out on to gardens and greenery, is light and bright and airy. There are two rooms, and the Garden Room, as the name suggests, is decorated with lots of plants, has white tables and chairs, and is really a conservatory and very cheerful too.

A good array of home-made cakes and biscuits will greet you in the morning, and lunchtime brings a similarly wide choice of salads, as well as hot dishes of the day, at reasonable prices.

You would change a baby with difficulty – the lavatories are cramped.

LUNCH (12–2pm) £2–5: soup, salads, quiche, spinach & cheese lasagne, tarragon chicken
Children: half portions

Open 9.30am–4.45pm, 4.30pm Sat Closed Sun & Xmas
No credit cards accepted Licensed
No music No smoking
P – street or nearby NCP

Brodie, By Forres, Grampian map 12

BRODIE COUNTRY FARE – ☎ (0309) 4555.

R

On the A96 east of Nairn.

This excellent roadside café has been completely refurbished and now boasts a smart glass frontage. The interior is spick and span and functional and you can choose from a really good range of hot dishes and salads, puddings, cakes and scones.

If you need to attend to a baby there is a table and a chair in the Ladies, and a supply of paper towels.

The outdoor eating area has plenty of bench tables on the well-kept lawn, which is fringed with flowers, shrubs and trees. Next door you will find craft and farm produce and gift shops.

£1–8: burgers, pizzas, haddock & chips, gammon steak, sirloin steak
Children: half portions

Open 9.30am–5.30pm every day (9am–7pm in July and August)
Closed Xmas & New Year Access/Visa
Licensed No smoking at most tables
P – own car park No music

Buckfastleigh, Devon map 1

DARTBRIDGE INN, Totnes Road – ☎ Buckfastleigh (0364) 42214.

P

On the A384 close to the A38 – not in Buckfastleigh.

This is a popular pub and especially so in summer, when cream teas are available through the afternoon. The family room is very large, but not barracky, and is comfortably furnished with plenty of tables and chairs – and two high chairs. Children are welcome here in their parents' company. At the back of the family room there is also a covered verandah with lots of white picnic furniture. Some mechanical rocking horses and a slide will entertain the children.

The Dartbridge is an appealing pub and very conveniently situated close to the main road and to many of Devon's tourist attractions. It offers a good selection of special dishes, a cold buffet and a restaurant menu, and is now open throughout the day.

(12–2pm & 7–10pm) £2–7: fresh Dart salmon, lamb & vegetable casserole, cold buffet, plaice, sirloin steak
Children: own menu

• Ale – Bass, Flowers P – own car park

Buckland Brewer, Nr Bideford, Devon map 1

COACH & HORSES – ☎ Horns Cross (02375) 395.

P

Off the A388 south of Bideford.

It is well worth a short detour to visdit this charming village pub, which offers a cheerful face to the world. It is housed in a long white painted thatched building, brightened with many tiles and hanging baskets of flowers. The educated guesses of the licensees and the customers put the pub as anything from the 13th to 16th century in origin.

Of course it evolved, as all buildings do, over the years; but suffice to say that the main bar is a delightful spot, with its thick stone walls, low beams, old wooden settles and large open fireplace with a stove.

There is a smaller bar on the other side and a very attractive little dining room. Familiies should head for a pleasant room at the back of the pub, and there are a few tables and chairs and a padded settle.

On warmer days you can enjoy the lovely garden: peaceful and enclosed by shady trees. There are bench tables and some slides and swings for the children. Alternatively you might sit on the terrace at the front of the pub.

(12–2pm & 7–9.30pm) £1–8: chilli con carne, vegetable curry, steaks, trout, burgers
Children: small portions

• Ale – Flowers P – on street

Buckland in the Moor, Nr Widecombe, Devon — map 1

ROUND HOUSE CRAFT CENTRE – ☎ Ashburton (0364) 53234.

R

In the centre of the village.

Buckland is one of the prettiest villages on the moor and lies a few miles north west of the A38 at Ashburton. The more famous Widecombe is a little further north. The church at Buckland is well-known because of its clock face, on which the letters "My Dear Mother" replace the numerals.

The craft centre has a delightful restaurant where families are very welcome. Attractive gardens surround the centre, and there is also a field where you can have a picnic and the children can also play there.

The toilet area is well-equipped, and now has a table in it to assist the changing of babies.

A delightful village with a craft centre which is well worth a visit.

£1–3: salads, snacks, cream teas
Children: small portions

Open all year 9.30am–6pm No smoking
One high chair only No music
P – own car park

Burford, Oxon — map 3

BULL HOTEL, High Street – ☎ Burford (099 382) 2220.

P

In the main street.

This delightful town boasts many handsome hostelries and this is certainly one of them: an old coaching inn which extends well back from the street and shows its 15th century origins with a heavy stone roof above rough stone walls. The brick and stone front was added later.

Families are welcome to use the back part of the main bar, which is cut in two by a huge fireplace. It is a splendid old room and the family part is all ancient carved oak panelling and black beams. There are tables in the courtyard at the side of the inn.

A wide range of bar snacks are freshly cooked to order, are served every day and include a vegetarian selection.

(11.30am–3pm & 6–10pm) £2–7: moules Marseilles, vegetable pie, spicy sausages, salmon steak, chicken tikka
Children: own menu, half portions

P – small car park and on street

LAMB INN – ☎ *Burford (099 382) 3155.*

P

Off the main street (A361).

This is as near-perfect an example of the English inn as it is possible to find: the mellow stone facade is covered in greenery and climbing roses; and the large walled garden at the back, with a velvety lawn and a fine display of flowers, is a real haven on summery days.

The comfortable lounge bar, with its worn stone floors, large open fire, pewter tankards displayed on the ceiling beams and willow pattern plates above the bar epitomises the charms of this 14th century inn. To one side, and curtained off from the bar area, is a room where families are welcome – a comfortable area with padded benches and settles and a nice cased clock on the wall; or they can use a most attractive lounge adjoining the bar.

(12–2pm, not Sun) £1–5: beef goulash, duck casserole, jacket potatoes, courgette & prawns au gratin, smoked salmon salad
Children: half portions

• Ale – Wadworth's **P** – street parking

Burley, Hants **map 3**

MANOR FARM TEA ROOMS, Ringwood Road – ☎ *Burley (042 53) 2218.*

R

In the main street.

A traditional 16th Century tea shop which is smartly painted in white under its trim, thatched roof. Inside are three rooms which will seat nearly a hundred people. The rooms have low, beamed ceilings and an original inglenook fireplace, and one room is designated for non-smokers.

The food centres around coffee and home-made scones and cakes, cream teas and light meals for lunch, but smaller portions can be ordered of some items for children. Unfortunately there is nowhere you can change a baby in any comfort.

Gifts, confectionary and home-made preserves and chutneys are sold at the front of the shop. All the baking is done on the premises.

£1–4: Cornish pastie, high tea, ploughman's, haddock & chips, omelettes
Children: half portions

Open 10am–5.30pm (shorter hours in winter)
Closed Mon in winter   No credit cards accepted   Licensed
One no-smoking room
One high chair only   No music
P – own car park

Burnsall, North Yorks   map 9

RED LION HOTEL – ☎ Burnsall (075 672) 204.

P

On the B6160, in the centre of the village.

A wonderfully traditional old inn set in one of the classic Yorkshire Dales villages. Dating from the mid 17th century, this old building enjoys a perfect setting only a stone's throw from the attractive village green which goes down to the River Wharfe. With the magnificent Burnsall Fell and the rolling Dales countryside as a backdrop, it's a perfect spot in which to spend a few hours.

The pub is geared up to cater for its many tourists and you will find a comprehensive bar snack menu plus lunch and dinner menus.

There are two rooms where families may sit; a small room just across from the main bar or up some stairs a larger room which is furnished in attractive style. It was originally an old barn and some of the stonework has been retained. It has plenty of tables with comfortable chairs to match, and overlooks the garden, which comprises a terrace, a rockery and a patch of lawn. There are other stretches of lawn alongside the peaceful river, and you can also sit on the cobbled forecourt at the front of the pub.

(12.30–2pm & 7.30–9pm onwards) £2–6: scampi & chips, steak & potato pie, gamekeeper's lunch, trout with salad
Children: half portions

- Ale – Theakston's, Tetley's   No music

P – own car park

If you wish to recommend an establishment to the Guide please write to us – report forms are at the back of the book. We need your help to extend and improve the guide.

Butterton, Nr Leek, Staffs — map 6

BLACK LION INN – ☎ Onecote (053 88) 232.

P

Off the B5053 east of Leek.

An 18th century stone inn, with white doors and windows, which sits by the church on the edge of the village, and has lovely views over the Peak National Park, and is about a mile from the Manifold Valley.

The interior is notable for its exposed oak beams, low ceilings and stone walls, and the walls are crowded with brass, china and pictures. There is a splendid collection of beer mugs and jugs on the beams. There are several rooms off the main bar where families are welcome: a dining room at the back of the pub, with a beamed ceiling and an open fire; a games room away from the bar through an archway; and the high-ceilinged pool room.

It is a warm and friendly place in lovely surroundings, and on summer days you can also enjoy the grassy, sloping garden, with its bench tables, and the paved terrace.

(12–2pm & 7–9.30pm, not Wed lunchtime) £1–5: roast chicken, salads, gammon steak, lasagne, haddock & chips, chicken curry
Children: own menu

• Ale – McEwan's, Younger's, Theakston's
P – own car park

Buxton, Derbyshire — map 6

NATHANIEL'S, High Street – ☎ Buxton (0298) 78388.

R

In the town centre (on the A55).

A cheery welcome awaits families at this smartly furnished town centre restaurant which has a definite French atmosphere – perhaps it's the superb marble tiled floor, or the tiny indoor garden complete with miniature pond. You can choose from a simple lunchtime set menu, the midweek bistro fare or the more adventurous à la carte dishes.

Children can choose half portions but youngsters should not arrive here expecting the usual junk offerings of burgers or chips – they don't feature on the menu! They can also enjoy a half price Sunday lunch. Vegetarian dishes are also available.

There is just about room to change a baby in the Ladies, or the owners will offer a room upstairs.

LUNCH £6: soup, hot seafood cocktail, liver & onions, apple pie;
BISTRO MENU £10: avocado Stilton, whole plaice, pudding
Children: half portions

Open 12–2.30pm & 7–10.30pm Closed Monday, & Sunday pm
Access/AmEx/Diners/Visa Licensed
One high chair only P – public car park nearby

Byland Abbey, Nr Coxwold, North Yorks — map 10

ABBEY INN – ☎ Coxwold (034 76) 204.

P

Off the A170 east of Thirsk.

The ruins of the abbey, founded by the Benedictine order in 1134, are opposite the inn, which is situated in a lovely stretch of country-side.

The inn itself was derelict until it was restored about three years ago by the current owner. The interior is delightful; a series of rooms have flagged floors, oak tables and carved oak seats, sofas and large open fireplaces.

Families are welcome to use the rooms which are well away from the bar and there is a large and attractive garden.

You should note that the pub is closed on Mondays.

(12–1.45pm & 6.30–9.30pm) £2–9: venison pie, calves' liver, smoked pheasant, lamb curry, chicken with lemon
Children: half portions

• Ale – Tetley, Theakston's P – own car park

Byworth, West Sussex — map 3

BLACK HORSE – ☎ Petworth (0798) 42424.

P

Close to Petworth – look for the sign off the A283.

This fine medieval pub has a small terrace at the back with lovely views of the countryside below. The garden rambles in steps down to the open fields, and adults should therefore keep a wary eye on their young. The interior has not been messed about and indeed deliberately projects a 'spit and sawdust' image, which works well. Children may be taken into two rooms at the rear of the pub which are primarily intended for eating and where an enterprising array of food is available seven days a week.

The pub is only a mile or so from Petworth House with its magnificent collection of paintings by Turner, Van Dyck, Holbein, Rembrandt, Gainsborough, et alia, and is a good place to repair to after the rigours of sightseeing.

(11.30am–1.45pm & 6.30–9.45pm) £2–10: courgettes & prawn au gratin, chicken Kiev, whole plaice, escalope of lamb, steaks

• Ale – Young's, Ballard's No music
P – own car park

Cadeby, South Yorks **map 7**

CADEBY INN – ☎ *Rotherham (0709) 864 009.*

P

Off the A630 between Rotherham and Doncaster.

Be careful you don't drive past this former farmhouse because at first glance, surrounded by outbuildings, it looks as though matters agricultural are still its prime concern. However on closer inspection the long lawn with tables and chairs leading up to the front door and the swing in the garden give a clue that this is a pub geared to families.

Inside you could spend so long looking at the walls, you might run out of time to order. All sorts of things, from mounted fish to cricket caps, are on display.

The family room is simple but cheerful and an added bonus is that there is ample space in the Ladies to change a baby.

The carvery offers excellent value and the Sunday lunch for around £4 is extremely popular.

When we called plans were afoot to extend the pub and create several smaller rooms and alcoves.

(12–2pm & 5–10pm) £1–7: gammon steak, half chicken, Cumberland sausage, seafood platter
Children: own menu and half portions

• Ale – Ind Coope Burton, Sam Smith's, Tetley's plus guest beers
P – own car park

Places included in the Guide must offer the following basic facilities:
Pubs – a separate area or room for families where alcohol is not served;
Restaurants – high chairs and special menus/reduced portions.

Calver, Derbyshire — map 7

DERBYSHIRE CRAFT CENTRE – ☎ *Hope Valley (0433) 31231.*

R

On the A623, north of Baslow.

A good place to know if you want to eat quickly with the minimum of fuss – an excellent stopping off place for families in a hurry.

You pick your food from a self service area and eat it in a pleasant – if fairly small – dining room, which has some attractive exposed stone walls, wooden settles and pictures of local scenes on the walls. All the food is home-made and is displayed in an enticing way.

The restaurant is attached to a craft centre and there is a small childrens' playroom where a mother could feed a baby, but the Ladies is tiny.

This informal restaurant is handy for walkers and for other tourists: Chatsworth House and Gristone Edges are close at hand.

£2–4: ploughman's, salads, quiches & salad, pizza, fidget pie
Children: half portions

Open 10am–5.30pm Closed weekdays in Jan and Feb
No credit cards Unlicensed
P – own car park No smoking

Cambridge, Cambs — map 8

BROWNS, 23 Trumpington Street – ☎ *Cambridge (0223) 461 655.*

R

Part of a small chain of restaurants (see the entries for Oxford and Brighton), this is a huge barn of a place, opposite the Fitzwilliam Museum. We were told that it was once the casualty department of the old Addenbrookes Hospital. It has the familiar and effective decor of cream walls, bentwood chairs, and overhead fans, Edwardian mirrors and converted gas lights.

It is a cheerful place which offers an excellent range of food to suit most palates, including young ones. If you need to change a baby there is a changing table in the Ladies.

We should warn you that parking is a nightmare in Cambridge, as it is, strangely, in Oxford. So it is best to get rid of your car into a public car park and enjoy the sights on foot.

£2–9: spaghetti, Caesar salad, fisherman's pie, venison steak, peasants pot
Children: own menu, half portions

Open 11am–11.30pm (from 12 on Sunday) Licensed
No smoking in part of restaurant • Ale – Theakston's
P – Meters

HOBBS PAVILION RESTAURANT, Park Terrace – ☎ Cambridge (0223) 67480.

R

Right on Parker's Piece, and alongside the University Arms Hotel.

The restaurant is plainly and attractively furnished under its high ceiling, with pine tables, a dresser, old advertising plates and the owner's own drawings. It really is the old brick-built pavilion on Parker's Piece where the maestro learned his cricket, and sporting romantics can let their imaginations flow.

You can eat salads and soup but the restaurant concentrates now on a very full range of pancakes, savoury and sweet. The fixed price menu at just over £6 for three courses is excellent value, or you can have two courses at lunchtime for just over £5. All the food is made, on site, by the owners.

There is a small terrace outside with a few tables and children have the whole of Parker's Piece on which to romp – and the perimeter measures nearly a mile. The restaurant has some lavatories and a baby might be attended to there.

£2–7: pancakes – Florentine, black-eye bean Stroganoff, Arnold Bennett, curried chicken, cyclists (steak, mash, spinach and egg), date syrup, etc
Children: half portions

Open Tue-Sat 12–2.30pm & 7–10pm (Thur dinner starts 8.30pm)
Closed mid Aug to mid Sept, Xmas and Easter, Sun and Mon
No credit cards accepted   Licensed
No smoking in half the restaurant
P – not easy, street parking only

SWEENEY TODD'S, The Watermill, Newnham – ☎ Cambridge (0223) 67507.

R

By the Granta Inn on the ring road at Newnham.

The restaurant is in a lovely spot by the studious calm of the mill pond, which is surrounded by willow trees. An occasional fisherman on the bank, and a quiet punt on the water add to the scene.

The restaurant is housed in the old mill, an attractive, flat-fronted brick building, and the huge wheel is still in place inside. It is a lively, well-designed place, with tiled floors, bentwood chairs, and exposed brick walls, and there is loads of space available. The restaurant will have been expanded by now, with two extra floors brought into use.

Families are well catered for, with several high chairs, and a pull-down shelf for baby-changing, in the Ladies.

£1–7: crudités, pizzas, chef's salad, burgers, barbecued meats
Children: own menu

Open 12–11pm every day   Access/Visa
Open all year   Licensed
P – car park at rear

Canterbury, Kent — map 4

SWEENEY TODD'S, 8 Butchery Lane – ☎ Canterbury (0227) 453 148.

R

Part of a well-known chain of restaurants, where families will be made welcome by the cheerful staff. There are a couple of high chairs, and mini-pizzas and small burgers for children at £1.99. Alas, there is no room at

present to provide baby-changing facilities.
The restaurant is in a basement with dark wooden pillars and beams, exposed stonework, a tile floor, and the various nooks and crannies create a relaxed atmosphere.

£2–8: crudités, pizzas, burgers, barbecued meats
Children: own menu

Open noon–11pm Sun to Thurs; till midnight Fri & Sat
Access/Visa Licensed
P – multi storey nearby

Capel Curig, Gwynedd **map 5**

TY'N Y COED – ☎ Capel Curig (069 04) 331.

P

On the A5 – look out for the black and yellow stage coach.
A long white roadside inn, in the heart of Snowdonia and well situated for tourists wanting food and drink. There is plenty of seating space for children in and off the entrance to the bars, and also a small grassy garden where you can sit and gaze at the mountains.
You will find a varied choice of food here either among the bar snacks or in the restaurant, and there is always an excellent selection of vegetarian dishes. Cream teas are served in the afternoon.

(12–2.30pm & 6–9.30pm) £1–11: vegetable chilli, baked potatoes, trout, steaks, hazelnut & rice burger
Children: own menu, half portions

• Ale – Castle Eden P – own car park

Cardross, Strathclyde **map 11**

MUIRHOLM HOTEL – ☎ Cardross (0389) 841 286.

R

On the A814 in Cardross.
This pleasant hotel welcomes families and you have a choice of a small family room off the bar, a comfortable place with its upholstered bench seats, or the restaurant which is now housed in an attractive conservatory, with its array of plants.
On a warm day you might opt to sit at a table on the patch of lawn at the front of the hotel.

There is quite a wide ranging menu here, and children are welcome to have half portions of most of the available dishes.

The facilities for changing a baby are limited, but there is a space between the basins in the Ladies.

£2–10: garlic mushrooms, vegetable Stroganoff, tiger prawns, trout, steak au poivre
Children: own menu, half portions

Open 11 am to 9.30pm Access/AmEx/Diners/Visa
P – own car park

Carlisle, Cumbria — map 9

HUDSON'S COFFEE SHOP, Treasury Court, Fisher Street – ☎ Carlisle (0228) 47733.

R

In the town centre to the right of the town hall. Well signposted.

This popular coffee shop is found in Treasury Court off Fisher Street, part of the pedestrianised area of the city. The flagged Victorian courtyard is a haven within the modern shopping precinct.

Parents of babies will be relieved to know that high chairs, trainer mugs, bibs are available on request and bottles or jars of baby food will be warmed by the friendly staff. Even emergency toys will be produced for any tearful toddler.

There is a table and bench in the Ladies for baby changing (ask for key at food counter).

£1–6: beanburger, Cumberland mixed grill, pizzas, plaice, lasagne
Children: own menu

Open 9am–5pm daily (closed Sundays)
No credit cards All non smoking
Licensed P – municipal car parks

Carnwath, Strathclyde — map 11

WEE BUSH INN, 99 Main Street – ☎ Carnwath (0555) 840 587.

P

On the A721 near to the junction with the A70.

This is an unusual pub to find in Scotland, by dint of its thatched roof. It was built in 1750 in readiness for the new turnpike road from Edinburgh to Ayr.

It's a small and cosy pub, although plans are afoot to build an extension before the end of the year. At present, like all the rooms here, the family room is quite small and is just off the bar, and can get rather crowded at busy times.

There is a good range of food, generously served, and it includes daily specials and a children's menu. During the summer the pub is open throughout the day (11am to 11pm) on Friday and Saturday.

(12–2.30pm & 6–10.30pm) £1–7: haddock & chips, beef-steak pie, sirloin steak, liver casserole, Hungarian goulash
Children: own menu

• Ale – McEwan's P – on street

Cartmel Fell, Nr Windermere, Cumbria map 9

MASONS ARMS – ☎ Crosthwaite (04488) 486.

P

Two and a half miles off the A5074. Follow the signs to Bowland Bridge.

This superb country pub is wonderfully situated on Strawberry Bank overlooking the Winster Valley. Although the Masons is a typically quaint English inn, the cuisine and the remarkable range of beers offered has a distinctly international flavour.

The menu, which is always varied and interesting, includes several vegetarian dishes and also offers unusual delights such as Russian vegetable pie. Real ale lovers will enjoy it here – the owners of the Masons offered nearly 200 guest beers last year. They also have their own mini-brewery in operation.

The pub provides a family room just off the main bar with low beams and oak furniture. There is a terrace and patio outside the main door of the pub which is always a popular spot when the weather is fine.

At weekends the Masons is understandably busy and in summer it is worth turning up early to get one of the tables overlooking the valley. Last orders at 1.45pm and 8.45pm mean exactly that – be warned!

(12–1.45pm & 6–8.45pm) £1–6: lasagne, chicken tikka, French-style fish soup, beef in red wine, taramasalata
Children: half portions

• Ale – Amazon, Yates and guest beers
P – on road and rear No music

Casterton, Cumbria — map 9

PHEASANT INN – ☎ Kirkby Lonsdale (05242) 71230.

PR

On the A683.

This well-organised country inn is just a couple of miles from the market town of Kirkby Lonsdale. It is deceptively spacious inside with two roomy bar lounges and a couple of other snug rooms, one of which can be used by families. The attractive garden lounge is for adults only, and is a no smoking room. The garden itself is large and safely enclosed.

The Pheasant has long had a fine reputation for its food but it also sets out to cater for its customers in a friendly and unfussy way, and to look after families.

It is a good base from which to explore the attractive countryside of the nearby Lake District; and Lancaster and Morecambe are not too far away.

(12–1.45pm & 6.40–9.30pm) £1–8: steak & kidney pie, black pudding, seafood crepe, roast duckling
Children: own menu, half portions

• Ale – Jennings, Tetley Access/Visa
No smoking in Garden Lounge and dining room
P – own car park

Castle Acre, Nr Kings Lynn, Norfolk — map 8

OSTRICH INN – ☎ Swaffham (0760) 755 398.

P

Off the A1065 three miles north of Swaffham.

In a small and quiet village, you will find this splendid pub, built of brick and flint with a flat front, and its origins lie back in the 16th century. There's a lovely feel to the pub, with its large and unfussy bar, and a notable feature is the large brick-built open fireplace.

It is dwarfed, however, by the fireplace in the family room; it is in the same style and soars high into the vaulted roof. This is a most attractive and spacious room, with a wall at one end which is made of various types of stone and brick. It was once the kitchen, and opens on to the garden.

The garden is quite a large, grassy area, mostly enclosed with flint walls, and has a vegetable patch at the far end. There are bench tables on the lawn, and some caged birds and a few rabbits at the side.

There is an interesting selection of meals available every day – mostly cold food at lunchtimes, and hot in the evenings.

The village is well worth a visit to see the Norman castle and the medieval Priory.

(12–2pm & 7.30–10.30pm) £1–8: omelettes, burgers, salads, trout, seafood platter, steaks

Children: own menu, half portions

• Ale – Greene King P – own car park

Castle Combe, Wilts **map 2**

WHITE HART – ☎ *Castle Coombe (0249) 782 295.*

P

Directly opposite the cross in the centre of the village.

The lovely old pub, sprucely painted white, sits opposite the church in this famous village. The pub has small wooden mullioned windows under its steep roof of Cotswold stone tiles.

As you enter, the bar is on one side and quite a sizeable family room on the other. It has a low ceiling, with wooden beams, plenty of tables and chairs and wooden settles, and the walls are decorated with prints of hunting scenes.

If the weather is warm, you can head for the secluded garden terrace, enclosed by stone walls, and with a paved floor. There are picnic seats, and shrubs and trees around the walls. You have a good view from here of the eccentrically shaped roofs of the surrounding cottages.

(12–2pm & 6.30–9.30pm) £2–7: filled jacket potatoes, lasagne, garlic mushrooms, steaks, chicken Kiev

Children: own menu

• Ale: Ruddles, Tetley, Usher's, Wadworth's

P – public car park

Castle Douglas, Dumfries & Galloway **map 11**

THE SCOTTISH PANTRY, 184 King Street – ☎ *Castle Douglas (0556) 3878.*

R

On the main street.

This is a cheerful restaurant, bright and appealing with its colourfully decorated walls with paintings by local artists thereon, and pine furniture. The emphasis is on fresh local produce whenever possible, served by efficient and friendly staff. It is mostly very busy, and you will usually find a few families with small children tucking into their food. A testimony, no doubt, to the excellent value which is offered here.

If you need to change or feed a baby there is a table, a chair and paper towels provided in the Ladies.

£1–9: haddock & chips, grilled salmon steak, steaks, roast pheasant, smoked duck
Children: own menu

Open 9am–9pm Open all year
Access/Diners/Visa No music
No smoking in half the restaurant One high chair only
P – in main street and car parks

Castle Hedingham, Essex **map 4**

BELL, 10 St. James Street – ☎ Hedingham (0787) 60350.

P

On the B1058.

This splendid pub is in the main street of an attractive village with a notably well-preserved Norman castle. The large bar has exposed brick walls, black wooden beams and pillars, and good collections of coins and matches decorating the walls. It is well furnished with easy chairs and wooden tables.Families are welcome to use a room between the two bars. It is quite small, with a few tables and a sofa, and it looks on to a little terrace.

The large walled garden is more like an orchard with shady trees, bench tables, and a couple of swings. A good place to relax on a summer day.

(12–2pm & 7.30–10pm, not Mon evenings) £1–6: prawns or mussels in garlic, ratatouille, fisherman's pie, sirloin steak, savoury pancakes
Children: half portions

• Ale – Greene King P – own car park

Please let us have reports – good or bad – on any establishments listed in the Guide as soon as possible after your visit.

Castleton, Derbyshire — map 7

CASTLE HOTEL – ☎ Hope Valley (0433) 20578.

P

In the main street of the village near the parish church.

A solid looking inn built of stone in the 17th century which is the focal point of life in this Peak District village, and is a popular venue for hikers and tourists.

The comfortable bar has stone walls, dark wooden beams and a welcoming fire in the stone fireplace. The family room is located at the back of the pub and leads out to the lawned garden via the car park. It is carpeted and has similar dark beams and stone walls and boasts plenty of tables and cushioned stools. The management will provide an extra plate to divide portions for children

The pub is open throughout the day during the summer months (except on Sunday) and the bar meals at lunchtime and during the evening are augmented by sandwiches during the afternoon. There is an excellent range of food on offer at reasonable prices; the roast of the day with all the trimmings is a bargain at under £4.

Apart from the sizeable garden at the back of the pub, you might like to sit out at the front of the pub on the bench tables and watch the world go by.

BAR MEALS (12–2.30pm & 7–9.30pm) £1–6: Castle club sandwich, cauliflower cheese, vegetable lasagne, joint of the day, chilli bake
Children: half portions

P – own car park

Also recommended in the Family Welcome Accommodation Guide.

Cauldon Low, Nr Waterhouses, Staffs map 6

OLD SCHOOL RESTAURANT, Old School – ☎ Waterhouses (053 86) 431.

R

On the A52 seven miles west of Ashbourne.

Housed in the old village school, this wholefood restaurant is a part of an interesting arts and craft centre with lots of products on display, including paintings, prints and woodcuts on the walls of the restaurant itself. It's a large lofty room with big windows and old school chairs. On summer days you can sit in the lawned garden which overlooks farmland.

The big stove will comfort you on winter days, but the lavatories will not – they're in an outhouse – so feeding or changing a baby is not really practicable here.

The new owners no longer offer exclusively vegetarian meals, but there is an excellent selection of interesting food at reasonable prices. This includes a good choice for children; homity pie, mushroom burger etc, all served with jacket or new potatoes and vegetables. Adults should note that there is an excellent selection of English country wines.

£1–3: filled jacket potatoes, salads, Somerset chicken, spicy beef & herb dumplings, vegetable curry & brown rice
Children: own menu, small portions

Open 10.30am–5.30pm (till 8.30pm at weekends) Easter to October, 12–4pm November to Easter
Closed weekdays Nov-Mar Access/Visa
Licensed No smoking
P – own car park No music

Never use an out-of-date Guide. Many places are excluded because their standards have dropped or their policies towards families have changed. Many new establishments are added each year.

Chacombe, Nr Banbury, Northants — map 3

GEORGE AND DRAGON – ☎ *Banbury (0295) 710 602.*

As we went to press, the management of this pub changed and we will re-assess it for the next edition.

Chailey, East Sussex — map 4

FIVE BELLS – ☎ *Newick (082 572) 2259.*

P

On the A275.

This lovely roadside inn, built in the 17th century and with a weather boarded facade, is a handsome building. There are three very attractive inter-connected rooms, well away from the bar, where families are welcome. With their low beams, tiled floors, brick walls and smart wooden furniture they are very pleasant places to sit, and there is a huge inglenook fireplace in the middle room. The main bar is splendidly in character with its oak beams.

The pub is surrounded by open countryside, and has a large, lawned garden with lots of flowers – a good place to be on a warm summer day. There are swings and a climbing frame for the children. But keep a wary eye on the children: the garden is enclosed with a low fence, but it might not deter a determined child. Barbecues are held here on summer weekends.

The Five Bells is open from 11 o'clock in the morning to 11 at night from Monday to Saturday.

(12–2pm & 7–9.30pm) £1–6: plaice & chips, Cumberland sausage & egg, salads, steak & kidney pie.
Children: own menu

• Ale – Flowers, Marston's, Wadworth's
P – own car park No music

Chale, Isle of Wight — map 3

WIGHT MOUSE INN – ☎ Isle of Wight (0983) 730 431.

P

Just off the A3055 in the south of the island.

The inn is attached to the Clarendon Hotel, a 17th century coaching inn of some character, which has won numerous awards.

It is a large, convivial and cheerful pub, open all day and usual busy in the three bar areas. Families are made welcome and there is plenty of room for them; they can use their own separate room, a warm and cosy one with several large old tables, pictures of the pub on the white-painted stone walls, and oil lamps hanging from the low ceiling.

On summer days you can enjoy the large grassy garden which looks out to the sea. There are plenty of tables and chairs, and a separate play area for the children with swings, climbing frames and a petanque pitch.

Entertainment is laid on every night – jazz, pop and country and western. The pub is open throughout the day, and there is an extensive menu. There are several high chairs and you could change a baby in the Ladies.

£1–9: gravad lax, steaks, crab & prawn Mornay, burgers, pizzas
Children: own menu, half portions

• Ale – Boddington, Burt's, Marston's, Strong's
P – own car park

Champany, Nr Linlithgow, Lothian — map 11

THE CHOP AND ALE HOUSE – ☎ Philpstown (0506) 834 532.

R

On the A904 just off junction 3 of the M9.

The Chop and Ale house is a comfortable restaurant within the Champany Inn which was created from a 16th century building. Mary, Queen of Scots, was born down the road at Linlithgow Palace.

The low beams of the ceiling, and the dark oak tables and chairs contrast well with the bright tablecloths, and there is a fine central fireplace.

There is another restaurant (older children only in here), a wine loft, and a main bar. There is plenty of room in the Ladies to feed or change a baby.

On warmer days, families might head for the courtyard, which is enclosed on three sides, has white tables and chairs, and pretty flowering plants here and there.

Lovers of good wine should know that there is a notable cellar here, and it is particularly strong on clarets. There is also a notable selection of malt whiskies and of brandies.

£1–10: cold buffet (lunchtimes), lamb chops, veal chops, scampi, salads, grilled chicken.
Children: small portions.

Open 12–2pm & 6.30–10pm, every day
Access/AmEx/Diners/Visa
Closed two weeks at Xmas • Ale – McEwan's
No music P – own car park

Chedington, Dorset map 2

WINYARDS GAP INN – ☎ Corscombe (093 589) 244.

P

On the A356 on the way to Dorchester, four miles from Crewkerne.

A smart white-painted pub, which is situated on National Trust land, and has wonderful views of the Axe Valley and the Quantock and Blackdown hills. The pub is mentioned several times by Thomas Hardy in his books and poems.

Below the main bar is a very large room which fulfills several purposes – it is a function room and it has a skittle alley and a pool table. But there is plenty of space left for families and it is well furnished with plenty of tables and chairs. When we visited the owners were refurbishing it.

There's a large grassy garden from which to view the fine countryside below; and a patio with wrought iron furniture and tubs of bright flowers.

Two self-contained flats, converted from an old barn, are available for letting.

(12–2.30pm and 7–9.30pm) £1–8: smoked trout, braised beef & vegetable pie, fisherman's pie, chicken curry, tenderloin of pork
Children: own menu, smaller portions.

• Ale – Bass, Hook Norton, Golden Hill
P – own car park

Nr Cheltenham, Glos **map 2**

FROGMILL INN – ☎ Shipton (0242) 820 547.

P

200 yards south of the junction of the A40 and the A436.

The Domesday Book recorded a mill on this site and it later became a noted coaching inn on the Oxford to Gloucester route. There have been many additions to make a rambling stone hotel and restaurant and children are welcome with their adults in a room off one of the bars. It is set up mainly for eating with plenty of tables and there is another alongside – part lobby and part lounge – where you might also settle. Several high chairs are available for the restaurants.

Although there is nowhere specific to change or feed a baby the staff are instructed to find a spot – there might be a bedroom spare, for instance.

Outside is a lawned garden with an extensive patio and an adventure playground.

BAR MEALS (12–2pm & 6–10pm) £1–10: Cotswold smokies, braised venison, chicken Marengo, cottage pie, steaks
Children: own menu

Open all year Access/AmEx/Diners/Visa
P – own car park • Ale – Flowers

Chester, Cheshire **map 6**

ABBEY GREEN RESTAURANT, 2 Abbey Green, Northgate Street – ☎ Chester (0244) 313 251. *Pot Luck*

R

Off Northgate Street, in the city centre.

The restaurant is housed in a tall brick building of 18th century vintage, although the arches below are probably Roman. It is a pleasantly decorated place with an appealing atmosphere and also has a garden.

The owners describe the cooking as gourmet vegetarian and certainly there are some interesting dishes on the menu, and the day menu offers good value for money.

Only one high chair is provided, and there are no facilities for baby changing.

DAY MENU £1–5: houmous & pitta bread, carrot & apricot paté, tostados, mushroom & carrot & aduki burgers
Children: small portions

Open 12–2.30pm and 6.30–10pm. Closed Sunday
Access only   No smoking
One high chair only   Licensed
P – own car park

FARMHOUSE RESTAURANT, 9–13 Northgate Street – ☎ Chester (0244) 311 332.

R

In the city centre.

This modern self-service open-plan restaurant (part of a Millet's store) has pine tables and padded pine settles, and is set up in three sections surrounded by plants. This gives the place a cool and fresh aspect; and one of the sections is a no-smoking area. It is a useful place to know about if you are out shopping and fancy a snack, but unfortunately there isn't a mother and baby room here.

(9am–5.15pm) £1–3: salads, haddock & chips, moussaka, liver & onion casserole
Children: own menu

Closed Sun   No credit cards accepted
Licensed   No smoking area
P – public car park

FOURGATES, 126 Foregate Street – ☎ Chester (0244) 315 046.

R

The restaurant is close to the centre of the city and offers an enterprising choice of food at reasonable prices. It is housed in a 17th century building and has a very attractive dining room, furnished with oak tables and wheel back chairs. The pale pink walls are hung with paintings and prints of old Chester and most of them are for sale.

You could change a baby in the Ladies, which has a tiled shelf, a chair and a good supply of paper towels.

LUNCH (12–3pm) £1–3: devilled herring, cauliflower cheese, venison & port paté, spaghetti carbonara, steak pie;
DINNER (6–10.30pm) £9: tuna cannelloni, chicken Hungarian, pudding
Children: own menu, half portions

Open 11.30am–3pm & 6–10pm Access/AmEx/Diners/Visa
P – public car parks Licensed

SPRINGLES RESTAURANT, 34 Eastgate Road – ☎ Chester (0244) 350 001.

R

In the city centre.

This self-service restaurant is on the third floor of the well-known Brown's of Chester store, which is part of the Debenham group. It is a useful place to know about if you are out shopping with children because it has six high chairs, and a wide selection of food throughout the day. There is also a no smoking section, and mothers can use the nursing sister's room if they need to change or feed a baby; the Ladies is also spacious.

£2–4: steak & kidney pie, fish & chips, salads, lasagne
Children: own menu

Open 9am–5.30pm Mon to Sat Access/AmEx/Diners/Visa
No smoking in part of restaurant Unlicensed
P – public car parks

Chichester, West Sussex map 3

SHEPHERDS TEA ROOMS, 35 Little London – ☎ Chichester (0243) 774 761.

R

Near the back of Marks and Spencers in the centre of the town.

This listed building looks like a private house from outside, but inside you will find a bright and attractive tea room, with lace tablecloths and bowls of fresh flowers on the tables. There's plenty of space between the tables, if you are encumbered with children and shopping and the other accoutrements of parenthood.

The food is freshly cooked and generously served, and there is a wide range of meals and snacks, and the various rarebits are specialities. It's obvious that there are many regular customers, a testimony to the friendly and efficient staff.

There are no special facilities for baby-changing, but the lavatory is reasonably spacious.

£1–4: filled jacket potatoes, rarebits, home-made pies, salads, cream teas
Children: half portions

Open 9.30am–5pm, Mon to Sat No credit cards
One high chair only P – public car parks nearby

Chidham, West Sussex map 3

THE OLD HOUSE AT HOME, Cot Lane – ☎ *Chichester (0243) 572 477.*

P

Off the A259 west of Chichester. Don't try to reach it from the new A27, there is no exit – another triumph for Britain's road planners.

The pub is situated on one of several flat but interesting pieces of land which jut into Chichester Harbour; and it is a handsome flat fronted building which looks Georgian. The interior looks much older with its ancient beams, collection of old farm implements, and open fireplaces.

Families are welcome to use a room at one end of the pub: a pleasant spot with low beams, wooden settles and sloping ceilings. At the back of the pub there is an enclosed, grassy garden with a few bench tables, a shady tree and an aviary.

The menu is extensive and includes a children's menu and a Sunday roast for under £5.

(12–2pm & 7–10pm) £1–10: Dover sole, fresh plaice, fisherman's pie, steaks, liver & bacon
Children: own menu, half portions

• Ale – Ballard's, Ringwood and guests
P – own car park No music

Chisworth, Cheshire map 6

WOODHEYS FARM RESTAURANT, Glossop Road – ☎ *Glossop (0457) 852 704.*

R

On the A626 between Murple and Glossop.

The large and busy restaurant has expanded over the years, and the owners have a continuous programme of development. A couple of years ago a spacious lawned garden was added and it is planned to build a children's play area.

From the garden and the terrace you have fine views of Etherow Country Park and Werneth Low; and similar commanding views of the countryside from the generous windows of the restaurant. The Peak National

Park is only minutes away.

The food is based on a cold buffet and hot carvery and children under 12 are charged half price. The weekend family buffet lunch is very good value and deservedly popular. The Ladies has plenty of room and contains a chair, and a large vanitory unit on which a baby can be changed.

LUNCH (12–2pm) £10: hors d'oeuvres, roast of the day, pudding or cheese
DINNER (7–10pm) £11: Cumberland chestnut pie, chicken & pork Victoria, pudding or cheese
Children: half portions

Open 12–2pm & 7–9.30pm Access/Visa
P – own car park Licensed

Cholmondeley, Nr Malpas, Cheshire map 6

CHOLMONDELEY ARMS – ☎ Cholmondeley (0829) 720 300.

P

On the A49 5 miles north of Whitchurch.

The Harrison family used to own the excellent Crown at Hopton Wafers, which has been listed by us for many years. They have now converted this Victorian school (it was the local school until 1982) and have made a really splendid job of it.

The original building has not been altered, but the interior has been opened into three sections; in the centre is a bar and there are two areas, away from the bar,which are intended mainly for food and where families can settle.

The high schoolhouse windows are curtained from top to bottom, and there is a mixture of oak and pine furniture: oblong and round tables, settles, bucket and cane chairs, standard lamps in the corners, and china plates and prints scattered on the walls. It all hangs together very well.

There is a huge lawned garden with plenty of bench tables, and a children's play area with swings and a large wooden climbing frame.

(12–2.15pm & 6.30–10pm) £1–10: hot crab paté, king prawn & chicken brochette, chicken piri piri, fillet steak
Children: own menu

• Ale – Ind Coope Burton, Marston's and guests
P – Own car park

Also recommended in the Family Welcome Accommodation Guide.

Church Stretton, Shropshire — map 6

ACORN WHOLEFOOD RESTAURANT – ☎ Church Stretton (0694) 722 495.

R

In the town centre.

The owners of this wholefood restaurant, which is situated over a gift shop in the centre of this attractive little town, clearly set out to welcome families. Their motto is "small is beautiful" and all the food (except the bread) is made on the spot.

There are two pleasant and functional rooms, one of which is a no smoking area, and a small and sheltered tea garden with a few tables for warmer days. It is safely enclosed.

If you need to change a baby the owners will find some space for you in their office.

£1–4: lamb kebabs, meat & potato pie, Provencale bean stew, kidney bean & chicken paella
Children: half portions

Open 10am–6pm (9.30am–5.30pm winter)
Closed on Tuesdays, 2 weeks in November and 1 week in March
No credit cards No smoking in one room
P – on street or main car park Unlicensed

Churchstow, Devon — map 1

CHURCH HOUSE – ☎ Kingsbridge (0548) 2237.

P

On the A379 West of Kingsbridge.

In the 13th century the building was a rest home for Benedictine monks and it was renovated in the 16th century, and that basic structure remains to this day.

The delightful bar is long and narrow, with a large inglenook fireplace, old black wooden beams holding the ceiling up and a number of wooden settles. There are two alcove rooms at one end of the bar.

The new family room is a stylish conservatory, a very pleasant place to sit. There is loads of space, a tiled floor and marble topped tables. The landlord asks that children be properly supervised – and so say all of us.

The large terrace at the side of the pub is well provided with bench tables, with sun umbrellas, and is bright with trailing flowers and greenery.

When we called in last summer it was packed with families enjoying their food and drink together.

You will always find some food on the go including a carvery at Sunday lunchtimes at around £6 for two courses, and this is also in operation from Wednesday to Saturday in the evening.

(12–1.30pm & 6.30–9pm) £1–7: whitebait, fish pie, devilled chicken, mixed grill, rump steak
Children: smaller portions

• Ale – Bass, Ruddles, Usher's No music
P – own car park

Clachan Seil, by Oban, Strathclyde **map 11**

TIGH-AN TRUISH – ☎ Balvicar (085 23) 242.

P

Twelve miles south of Oban on the B844.

This long and low, 18th century white-washed pub is situated in an idyllic setting next to the famous 'Bridge over the Atlantic Ocean' built in 1791 which connects Seil Island to the mainland of Scotland. There are two small but comfortable family rooms where children are welcome, and a pleasant garden with tables and chairs where you can sit and admire the bridge and Seil Sound (weather permitting).

The summer menu varies slightly each day, but there's always something fishy; and in the winter it's more limited with things like 'toasties' available. Special children's meals will be prepared by request and charged accordingly, and there is a high chair in the pub.

The pub is open throughout the day during the summer months.

(12–2pm & 6–8pm) £1–5: hot pie and beans, hot dish of the day, local salmon & salad, dressed crab
Children: special meals on request

• Ale – McEwan's P – own car park

Clanfield, Oxon **map 3**

CLANFIELD TAVERN – ☎ Clanfield (036 781) 223.

P

On the A4095.

A Cotswold pub in all its glory, with mellow stone walls, and an interior of black beams and polished stone floors, it's a delightful watering-hole in a very pleasant Oxfordshire village. Children are welcome in two rooms: there is a small, very attractive room just by the entrance, its walls ringed with padded bench seats, and a larger room at the side with a heavily beamed ceiling and a number of wooden settles. This latter room has recently been enlarged.

A very pleasant lawned garden, with plenty of bench tables, runs round two sides of the pub.

The inn has a restaurant which serves traditional Sunday lunches at around £9. There is a high chair on the premises. Such a splendid pub is of course very busy at weekends, so you should plan to arrive early if you have a family meal in mind. There is a welcome emphasis on healthy food at the pub, which secured the Heartbeat Award last year.

(11.30am–2pm & 6–10pm) £1–6: ploughman's, whitebait, local trout, steaks, stuffed aubergine & salad
Children: own menu, half portions

• Ale – Morrell's, Hook Norton, Morland's
P – own car park No music

Also recommended in the Family Welcome Accommodation Guide.

Clavering, Essex **map 4**

CRICKETERS – ☎ Saffron Walden (0799) 550 442.

P

On the B1038 on the outskirts of the village.

This is a good-looking pub, parts of which date from the 16th century. The spacious gravelled patio in front of the pub has lots of bench tables for summer days and there is also a small garden at the back.

Inside the pub is just as appealing. There is a long L-shaped bar, with brick walls, heavy wooden beams and pillars, a low ceiling and an open fire at one end. It is very smartly and comfortably furnished. So is the family room, which is a few steps away from the food bar and has attractive padded benches and seats. There is an excellent range of food and the roast beef and Yorkshire pudding with all the trimmings seems good value at under £6.

(12–2pm & 7–10pm) £2–10: crab cocktail, chicken Tandoori, escalope of veal, grilled trout, steaks
Children: own menu

• Ale – Wethered, Flowers, Boddington's
P – own car park

Cleveleys, Lancs — map 9

CLEVELEYS WHOLEFOOD AND VEGETARIAN RESTAURANT, 44 Victoria Road West – ☎ *Cleveleys (0253) 865 604.*

R

Enter Cleveleys on the B5412. The restaurant is in the town centre on Victoria Road West.

This pretty restaurant, over a health food store, offers a most unusual and interesting menu which has gained the establishment a deserved reputation. Ideally situated close to the beach, the restaurant serves morning coffee and afternoon teas with a delicious assortment of wholemeal muffins, scones, flapjacks and the like. Speciality coffees including dandelion and decaffeinated are also available. The lunch and evening menu, which offers a wide selection of both savoury and sweet dishes, changes daily and everything is freshly made on the premises.

If you need to change a baby there is enough space in the Ladies.

£1–4: parsnip and apple soup, cashew paella, oaty broccoli & cauliflower, vegetable crumble, rice & vegetable bake
Children: half portions

Open Tues to Fri 11am–3pm, Sat 10am–5.30pm, Sun midday–5.30pm, Fri evening 6.30pm–9pm Closed Mondays
No credit cards Licensed
One high chair only No smoking
P – Public car park opposite

Clifton Campville, Staffs — map 6

GREEN MAN – ☎ *Clifton Campville (082 786) 262.*

P

Off the A5134 or A453 north of Tamworth.

This is an old coaching inn which presents a traditional face to the world, black woodwork against white walls. It is a smart and well maintained place, with low, oak beamed ceilings and good wooden tables and chairs. There is a cosy family room – it's a snug, really – and this is furnished with oak tables and wheelback chairs. It's a pleasant room, and an alternative on warm days is the large lawned garden, which is safely enclosed.

There is an excellent play area with swings, a slide and a rocking horse; and there are two docile donkeys for the children to pet, and an aviary. A small pavilion houses pool tables and slot machines, and there is a barbecue on the patio.

It's an excellent family pub.

(12–2pm & 6–9.30pm) £1–7: steak & kidney pie, place & chips, lasagne, ploughman's, steaks
Children: own menu

• Ale – Ansell's   P – own car park

Clifton Dykes, Nr Penrith, Cumbria — map 9

WETHERIGGS POTTERY – ☎ *Penrith (0768) 62946.*

R

Off the A6, four miles south of Penrith. There is a sign to the Pottery.

This is a splendid little complex based around a working pottery which has been going since 1855. Today it comprises an excellent and well stocked pottery shop, gallery, museum, restaurant and tearoom. The tables set up in the gallery look over the pottery workshops and this is an interesting place to sit.

All the food is home-made with a strong vegetarian theme although one of the specialities is an American Sunday brunch – ham and eggs etc for around £5. All the food is cooked with fresh ingredients.

You can get light snacks all day and there are daily specials at lunchtimes, all made from fresh ingredients.

Children are very well looked after. Outside in the garden there are picnic tables and a playground but the owners also encourage their young visitors to try their hand on the potters wheel. It is refreshing to find a place which is a little bit different and where the owners give families such a good welcome.

If you need to change or breast-feed a baby there is plenty of room in the Ladies, which has a specific section for mothers and babies.

£1–5: pizzas, moussaka, mushroom and yoghurt quiche, homemade soup and bread, American Sunday Brunch
Children: own menu, half portions

Open 10am–9pm daily   Access/Visa
Licensed   No smoking
P – own car park   One high chair only

Also recommended in the Family Welcome Accommodation Guide.

Clifton Hampden, Nr Abingdon, Oxon — map 3

BARLEY MOW – ☎ Clifton Hampden (086 730) 7847.

P

Off the A415.

This very smart pub, thatched and white-painted, with its origins in the 13th century, is best described in Three Men in a Boat – 'It is, without exception, I should say, the quaintest, most old-world inn up the river. It stands on the right of the bridge, quite away from the village. Its low-pitched gables and thatched roof and latticed windows give it quite a story-book appearance, while inside it is even still more once-upon-a-timeyfied.'

The family room, like the lounge bar, is delightful with its oak beams and panelling and wooden settles, and leads on to a large, enclosed, lawned garden.

A good choice of bar food is always available and there is a traditional Sunday lunch at around £5, and there are a couple of high chairs.

(12–2pm & 7–10pm) £2–5: roast and vegetables, beef in beer pie, beef pepperoni, salads
Children: small portions

• Ale – Usher's, Ruddles, Webster's P – opposite

Clyst St Mary, Exeter, Devon — map 1

CAT AND FIDDLE – ☎ Topsham (0392) 873 317.

P

On the A3052 just East of Exeter.

This 16th century roadside pub is about half a mile from Clyst St. Mary and has a large car park on either side. Originally a Tithe barn, some of the old features remain – there are the most extraordinary Jacobean fire-places, huge and dark and carved from oak, and the main restaurant seating is in the old part of the building. The extensions are in keeping with the original with low ceilings and black beams.

There are three rooms where families are welcome, two of which have amusement machines and a pool table. There is the usual pub furniture and red carpeting throughout gives a feeling of continuity.

Outside there is a large terrace at the back and a patio at the side contain-

ing the play area for younger children. There are swings, a roundabout, a seesaw, a rocking horse, two rabbits in a hutch and picnic tables. The other children's play area, an adventure playground, is across the car park.

(12–2pm & 6.30–10pm) £1–11: smoked mackerel, fish & chips, steaks, cold buffet, lentil crumble
Children: own menu, half portions

• Ale – Courage P – own car park

Cobham, Surrey **map 3**

VERMONT EXCHANGE – ☎ *Cobham (0932) 62015.*

R

On the A245 when you approach the town from the A3.
This restaurant is part of a small chain and the very spacious premises are modelled on an American diner.

There is a huge bar and the dining area is a large and well-proportioned room with wooden pillars and beams, huge open fireplaces at each end, cheerful check tablecloths, and an eclectic decor – old film posters, photos of racehorses, metal advertising signs, golf bags, musical instruments and so on. You've seen it all before, but it is agreeable enough.

There are several high chairs – in a rather stylish basket-weave design – and shelf space in the Ladies where a baby can be changed.

£1–9: sesame prawns, Vermont salad, steaks, burgers, Cajun chicken
Children: own menu

Open 12–11pm every day Licensed
Access/AmEx/Diners/Visa P – own car park

Cockfield, Suffolk **map 4**

THATCHERS RESTAURANT, Cross Green – ☎ *Bury St Edmunds (0284) 828 246.*

R

On the A1141 north of Lavenham.
You will easily spot this restaurant by the road side. It is a lovely sight; as the name tells you it has a fine thatched roof over pink-washed walls, with windows and shutters smartly painted white. The front of the

16th century building is a blaze of colour, with tubs of flowers and climbing plants on show.

There are a few tables and chairs by the entrance and a delightful garden at the back. A long lawn is fringed with trees, a very inviting spot on a warm summer's day; and you will perhaps be greeted by some of the owners' ducks.

The inside is just as appealing. A low-ceilinged lounge with a bar has a comfortable sofa and plush chairs, and this leads into the restaurant. This is on two levels, with oak pillars and beams, and brick fireplaces at either end. It all looks very smart.

The set lunches are excellent value, and this includes a traditional Sunday lunch at around £7. There is a good range of bar snacks, too. Morning coffee and afternoon teas are also served.

At present there are no special facilities to change a baby, but the lavatories are spacious, and the new owners may do some re-organising of these. There is one high chair plus a booster seat for older children.

BAR SNACKS £1–4: prawn salad, shepherd's pie, plaice & chips, roast chicken & chips;
LUNCH £6: leek soup, Barnsley chop, pudding;
DINNER £15: Mediterranean prawns, supreme of chicken, pudding or cheese
Children: half portions

Open 10am–9.30pm Closed all Mon & Sat pm
Access/Visa Licensed
No smoking at some tables P – own car park

Coldharbour, Nr Dorking, Surrey — map 3

PLOUGH – ☎ Dorking (0306) 711 793. — *Pot Luck*

P

Off the A24 south of Dorking.

The Plough is situated at the highest point in south east England, on Leith Hill, which is owned by the National Trust. Leith Hill Tower was built in 1766 and on a clear day it is claimed that you can see across a dozen counties.

The pub is 15th century in part, a black and white building with bench seats outside from which you can contemplate the glorious countryside. The grassy garden has several tables and chairs and a paved area with a barbecue.

The family room is small but adequate and the cosy oak-beamed restaurant is an alternative if you have children in tow.

✕ (12–2.15pm & 7.30–9.30pm) £1–5: cottage pie, lamb stew, chicken curry, lasagne
Children: own menu, half portions

• Ale – Bateman's, Ringwood, Theakston's
P – own car park

Colehill, Nr Wimborne, Dorset **map 2**

BARLEY MOW – ☎ Wimborne (0202) 882 140.

P *Off the A31 east of Wimborne. In the village turn into Colehill Lane (opposite a church), and keep going until you see the pub's sign.*

Surrounded by fields, this 16th century country pub with its steeply pitched thatch and tiled roof sits comfortably at an open crossroads, a mile from the extended suburbs of Wimborne. It is bright with tubs of flowers, hanging baskets and complete with neat white picket fence in front.

The bar has a working inglenook fireplace, oak panelling and beams and is comfortably furnished with red carpets and traditional pub furniture.

The family room is housed in a new extension, with a couple of steps down from the bar. It is furnished in much the same style as the main bar, with several tables, and has its own lavatories. There is also a pool table and a dart board in here.

French windows open on to a large and attractive, lawned garden which is protected by a high hedge and fir trees. A big yew tree stands in the middle of the lawn with a tyre swing, and there is another set of swings at one side. There are plenty of picnic tables and a barbecue area.

✕ (12–2pm & 6–10pm) £1–9: Dorset paté, fisherman's pie, moussaka, steaks
Children: half portions

• Ale – Hall & Woodhouse & guests P – own car park

Nr Colne, Lancs **map 9**

THE HERDERS INN, Lancashire Moor Road – ☎ Colne (0282) 863 443.

P *Turn off the A6068 at Laneshaw Bridge. Go down School Lane, a turning opposite the Emmott Arms, for two miles.*

You're on the fringe of Bronte country here. This isolated stone-built pub, with commanding views over the moors, is situated on the only direct route from Lancashire to Haworth where the famous literary sisters lived and which is now overrun by tourists.

A short walk from the pub, down an excellently-marked path, is the preserved hamlet of Wycollar which includes the ruins of the old village hall. This was almost certainly the setting which Charlotte Bronte used for Ferndean Manor when she wrote "Jane Eyre". Elsewhere in this charming spot, which is now a country park, you'll find an information centre, refreshments and some glorious walks.

Back at the pub you can relax in the comfortable interior which includes two areas away from the bar where families can settle. They are nicely furnished with bench seats and tables. All the rooms here are liberally dotted with brass jam pans, copper kettles and the like.

There's an enclosed lawn outside with bench tables and a marvellous view of the haunting Bronte countryside.

(11.30am–2.30pm & 7–10.30pm) £1–5: beef curry, haddock & chips, steak & kidney pie, scampi
Children: half portions

● Ale – Tetley, Younger's No music
P – own car park

Combeinteignhead, Devon — map 2

COOMBE CELLARS – ☎ Newton Abbot (0626) 872 423.

P

Just off the B3195 east of Newton Abbot.

This pub has a magnificent position on the Teign Estuary and takes full advantage of it with a number of terraces from where you can view the water and the abundance of bird life.

The pub is housed in a very large and smartly maintained building and the interior is well organised, with light wood panelling lending an attractive air to the decor. An appealing dining room has wonderful views over the water and the family room is on the other side of the pub.

This is another spacious and attractive room, down some stairs and separated from the bar; it has wood panelled walls, some good wooden tables and an open fire at one end. What a pity that there is one of the obtrusive amusement machines in here. There is an excellent choice of food here, and the menu is understandably strong on fish.

On warm days you can sit on the terraces and when we visited a huge wooden play boat was being built, so the children are well cared for, too.

(11.45am–2.15pm & 6.30–10.15pm) £1–9: seafood chowder, monkfish Provencal, poached salmon, rack of lamb, supreme of chicken
Children: own menu

• Ale – Bass, Tetley P – loads

Compton Martin, Avon map 2

RING O'BELLS – ☎ West Harptree (0761) 221 284.

P

On the A368.

This excellent family pub – long low and white-painted – sprawls welcomingly against a backdrop of wooded hills, and has a large and splendid garden. It's well-grassed with plenty of log tables and benches and has a slide and some swings and a scattering of apple trees. It is a delightful spot, which we singled out for special praise in the very first edition of the Guide.

The family room is extremely well organised: spacious and attractive with stone walls topped by a high vaulted ceiling and with a good array of wooden tables, chairs and settles and a rocking horse.

It is a rare pub which boasts more than one token high chair – but this one has six.

There's a very extensive menu for the adults, and a particularly good choice of salads, and a Sunday lunch at under £5 for a main course. There is always a good range of real ales, too.

(11.30am–2pm & 7.30–10pm) £1–11: smoked salmon, ham & eggs, cottage pie, steaks, ocean pie
Children: own menu, half portions

• Ale – Butcombe, Wadworth's and guests
P – own car park

Comrie, Tayside map 11

TULLYBANNOCHER FARM FOOD BAR – ☎ Comrie (0764) 70827.

R

Just west of Comrie on the A85.

There is plenty of room for children, both inside and out, at this large café and craft centre, which is surrounded by woodland and hills. The café itself has a simple lay-out, high-ceilinged like a barn, and with an array of long wooden tables and benches. There is an excellent choice of salads, and of home-made cakes and pastries.

A table and a chair are stationed in the Ladies for the benefit of mothers with small children, and paper towels are also provided.

A large, grassy garden at the front, with several picnic tables, will attract you on summer days, and there is loads of room for the children to play.

It is a lovely spot to stop for a meal or a snack, and has the added attraction of having a craft and gift shop and a garden centre on the site. Exhibitions of local paintings are also held throughout the summer.

✕ £1–4: baked potatoes, burgers, salads, trout, quiches
Children: own menu, half portions

Open 9.30am–6pm every day Closed Oct-Easter
No credit cards Licensed
No music
P – own car park

Congresbury, Avon **map 2**

WHITE HART, Wrington Road – ☎ Yatton (0934) 833 303.

P

Off the A370. Take the signs to Wrington/Redhill.

In the Avon countryside you will find two pubs facing each other across a wide car park. Head for the White Hart because it has an excellent family room – spacious and well-furnished under a vaulted glass roof, and it even has a selection of toys to keep the children occupied.

It is a popular pub with families and especially so when the sun shines because there is a big grassy garden with plenty of bench tables, a slide, swings and a climbing frame. The children will also be interested in the aviary, and there is a rocking horse on the patio.

There is a large and varied menu, and it includes a vegetarian dish of the day.

✕ (12–2pm & 6.30–10pm) £1–5: filled jacket potatoes, salads, curry of the day, steak sandwich.
Children: own menu

• Ale – Butcombe, Hall & Woodhouse, Wadworth's
P – own car park

Corfe Castle, Dorset **map 2**

GREYHOUND INN, The Square – ☎ Wareham (0929) 480 205.

P

This pleasant cream-painted pub, with a steeply pitched, heavy stone roof, sits in the middle of the touristy village. Behind the pub, and dominating the area from its high knoll, is the gaunt outline of Corfe Castle, which, after a singularly bloody history, was mostly destroyed during the Civil War.

The pub is a cheerful and busy place with a big main bar on two levels, and an alcove room to one side. Tucked away down the corridor is an attractive and smart family room with several tables and a juke box. Reports tell us that the juke box is, thank goodness, a quiet one; and we are also happy to tell you that the room is a no smoking area. There is also a comfortable Ladies with a shelf on which a baby could be changed. If the sun shines you can take advantage of it by sitting at one of the bench tables which are set out in front of the pub.

(11.30am–2pm & 6.30–9pm) £1–7: prawns in garlic butter, cockles, fisherman's pie, lasagne, salads
Children: small portions of some dishes

• Ale – Flowers and guest beers P – street parking only

Cotebrook, Nr Tarporley, Cheshire **map 6**

ALVANLEY ARMS – ☎ Little Budworth (0829) 760 200.

P

On the A49 just north of Tarporley.

This is an attractive, busy and efficiently run pub, well established on this busy main road. It is built of brick and sandstone, overlaid with ivy. Carved in the stone of the back door is the date 1666.

There is a cheerful and well decorated room where families can park themselves while they browse through the extensive menu. The walls under the low beams are hung with prints and pictures and flower baskets hang in the windows.

There is plenty of space outside. The lawned area has pine and apple trees, swings for the children, and a pond with resident geese. A five-a-side football pitch can also be used.

(12–2pm and 6–9pm) £1–7: rollmop herring, steak pie, cod & chips, grilled lamb chops
Children: half portions

• Ale – Robinson's **P** – own car park

Cottesmore, Nr Oakham, Leics — map 7

SUN INN – ☎ Oakham (0572) 812 321.

P

On the B668 about three miles north-east of Oakham.

In the middle of this pretty village and set back from the main street, you will find this attractive white-washed stone pub with its steep partly-thatched roof. The main bar is much in keeping, with oak beams and a large open fireplace. On summer days you can take advantage of the patio and small, grassy garden at the back, or the tables and benches set out at the front of the pub, which is enlivened by patches of garden, and hanging baskets of flowers.

Families are welcome to use a small garden room at the back of the pub or a comfortable lounge area on one side, and separated from the bar.

There is a good selection of food, but note that it is available at lunchtimes only.

(12–2pm, Mon-Sat) £2–7: chicken & ham & leek pie, haddock, chicken Kiev, sirloin steak, lasagne
Children: half portions

• Ale – Adnams, Everard's **P** – own car park

Cowley, Glos — map 2

GREEN DRAGON INN – ☎ Coberley (024 287) 271.

P

Off the A435 south of Cheltenham. Take a road signposted to Elkstone.

The building has its origins in the 17th century, and was a cider house. It is built of mellow stone, and the rooms have their full complement of heavy wooden beams. In winter the open fires add to the charm of the place.

It is of course an extremely busy pub, but families are welcome to use a small room off the bar, with wooden furniture and stone walls. At weekends and Bank holidays the Long Room is opened for lunches. It was a farrier's building and was recently converted to a function room. You can get a carvery lunch here for around £5.

There is a patio area at the front of the pub with bench tables.

(12–2pm & 7–10pm) £2–10: grilled sardines, Mexican spiced beef, halibut, vegetable lasagne, steaks
Children: half portions

• Ale – Bass, Hook Norton, Butcombe, Boddington, Marston's, Wadworth's
No music

Coxwold, North Yorks — map 10

FAUCONBERG ARMS – ☎ Coxwold (03476) 214.

P

Four miles off the A19. In the middle of the village.

This fine village of stone houses with verges of grass and cobbled stones was given to the Fauconberg family by Henry VIII. One of its famous inhabitants was Laurence Sterne, vicar at St. Michael's, and he named his house Shandy Hall after his most famous novel. It is now a museum.

The long and low stone inn was built in the 17th century and is an attractive sight with its hanging baskets of flowers. The interior has some fine furniture in the attractive bar with its paved floor: a canopied chair and a splendidly carved settle are particularly striking. Families are welcome to use the comfortable entrance hall which, like the bar, has a huge stone fireplace, or the spacious dining room. There is an unusual Yorkshire loving seat in the entrance hall.

There is a large, grassy garden at the back of the pub.

BAR SNACKS (12–2pm) £1–3: steak & kidney pie, halibut cobbler, Cumberland sausage

• Ale – Theakston's, Younger's, Tetley's
P – on forecourt

Nr Craven Arms, Shropshire — map 6

SUN INN – ☎ Seifton (058 473) 239.

P

On the B4368 north of Ludlow.

The pub has been in business as a roadside tavern since the 17th century and is situated in the lovely Corve Dale area of South Shropshire. It fell on hard times and the new owners, Mr and Mrs Pearce, devoted a lot of hard work to restoring the nearly derelict building.

It now looks very smart again and has a welcoming and comfortable family room, furnished with pine tables and padded chairs and settles. On summer days families can head for the large enclosed garden which has plenty of wooden bench tables, and for the children some swings and a slide, and an old tractor to climb on.

There is a good choice of food on offer including a two-course Sunday lunch at under £4. There is also a high chair on the premises.

All the family will receive a warm welcome from the Pearces, who have several children of their own.

✕ (11am–3pm & 6–9.30pm) £1–9: vegetarian pie, chicken Kiev, grilled trout, chicken & ham pie, mixed grill
Children: own menu

• Ale – Marston's, Wood's and guests   P – own car park

Criccieth, Gwynedd map 5

MOELWYN RESTAURANT, Mona Terrace – ☎ *Criccieth (0766) 522 2500.*

R

By the sea front off the A497.

This restaurant, as always, is bright, well-kept and welcoming, added to which it's in a splendid position with a view of Cardigan Bay, the hills and the distant Harlech Castle.

The building is Victorian (Criccieth was a well-known bathing resort in the 19th century) and framed with creeper, and the interior is smartly turned out with patterned wallpaper and pink tablecloths. A small garden, with four tables, gives lovely views of the sea and the mountains, and there are children's toys here.

There is always an interesting choice of food here, from the reasonably priced lunchtime snacks to the à la carte evening menu; and the three course Sunday lunch is great value at around £8. The children's menu offers a much better than usual choice, also.

Room can always be found for a mother who needs to tend her baby.

✕ LUNCH (12–2pm) £1–6: crab paté, herb pancake with chilli con carne, fried sea clams, grilled Welsh lamb chops;
DINNER (7–9pm) £16: smoked trout, escaloppe of Dwyfor salmon, pudding or cheese
Children: own dishes, half portions

Closed Xmas-March   Access/Visa
Licensed   P – roadside parking

Also recommended in the Family Welcome Accommodation Guide.

Cropton, Nr Pickering, N Yorks   map 10

NEW INN – ☎ Lastingham (07515) 330.

P

Off the A170 north west of Pickering.

This pub sits in the heart of the North York Moors and is especially popular not least because it has its own little brewery. The food is reasonably priced, and particularly so for the Sunday lunch carvery which costs less than a fiver.

Families are particularly welcome here and there is a family room, which was extended last summer as well as a garden and another large grassy area at the side of the pub where the children can play.

There are three self-catering cottages in the grounds of the pub – a pretty good place to use as a base in this delightful part of Yorkshire.

(12–2pm & 6–9.15pm) £1–4: steak & kidney pie, lasagne, chilli con carne, scampi, fish & chips
Children: own menu, half portions

• Ale – Cropton, Tetley's No music
P – own car park

Croscombe, Nr Wells, Somerset map 2

THE BULL TERRIER – ☎ Shepton Mallet (0749) 3658.

P

On the A371 East of Wells.

A traditional stone village inn, which has a long history, since it was probably built towards the end of the 15th century and was first licensed to sell beer in 1612. It is close to the very fine village church.

Inside you will find three rooms grouped around a central bar area; and the stone-flagged floors are complemented by the beamed ceilings and a large inglenook fireplace in one of the rooms. Families are welcome in another separate room which has three tables and an old dresser against one wall. As the landlord emphasised it can get very busy, especially at weekends, so don't come in a coach party.

Between the pub and the church is a compact walled garden with seating for around thirty people. It is partly paved and partly lawned.

There is an extensive bar menu, and it is notable for a daily choice of several vegetarian meals.

(12–2pm & 7–9.30pm, not Sun pm or Mon in winter) £1–10: tuna & egg mayonnaise, Barnsley chop, Indian spiced beans, fillet steak
Children: small portions

• Ale – Butcombe, Greene King, Palmer's, Bull Terrier
P – own small car park

Croyde, Devon map 1

THATCHED BARN INN, Knob Hill – ☎ Croyde (0271) 890 349.

P

On the road through Croyde, the B3231.

This building, with its origins in the 15th century, has had an interesting history. Originally it was used by monks for keeping farm animals, was then made into two dwellings and became a teashop in the thirties. It was converted to a pub in the late seventies. Long and low, it sits on the main road through this very popular village. Tubs of flowers decorate the front of the building, and there is a sizeable terrace here with lots of bench tables.

A lounge bar and dining area are combined and overlook the patio. The room is spacious with several oak tables and a large dresser at one end with a collection of china. Away from the bar there is an alcove, and beyond that a family room with cane furniture and marble topped tables. It is a pleasant room with a beamed ceiling, wooden pillars and a large open fireplace. At the far end of the pub there is another area where families are welcome: a delightful room, its ceiling cross-hatched with wooden beams. It looks out to a small lawned garden.

(12–2pm & 6–10pm) £1–10: poached salmon, steak & kidney pie, lemon sole, roast duck, steaks
Children: own menu, half portions

• Ale – Courage P – own car park

Damerham, Fordingbridge, Hants — map 3

THE COMPASSES INN – ☎ *Rockbourne (072 53) 231.*

P

On the B3078 west of Fordingbridge.

It's good fishing country around here, and you will usually find a plump local trout on offer at this village pub. There are five different buildings incorporated in the structure, including an old brewery and a Victorian wing, which houses the dining room, where families are welcome to park themselves. It's a long room with plenty of space, with sofas at one end by the fire. The bar is a cosy room with a couple of nice wooden tables, a large bow window and an open fire with a Victorian surround.

There's a stretch of garden at the front of the pub and a very large and grassy garden at the back with several swings and a see-saw. It's enclosed and has an uninterrupted view of a playing field and open countryside.

Food is on offer every day, including a traditional Sunday lunch at around £5.

(12–2pm & 7–9.30pm) £1–5: ploughman's, salads, cottage pie, Damerham trout & salad, haddock or plaice, steak
Children: own menu, half portions

• Ale – Wadworth's, Ind Coope Burton
P – own car park

Dartington, Devon map 1

CRANKS HEALTH FOOD RESTAURANT, Shinners Bridge – ☎ Totnes (0803) 862 388.

R

Look out for the Cider Press sign on the A384.

Within this very interesting crafts centre you will find a Cranks self-service restaurant, one of the first of the chain of vegetarian restaurants, and it offers a good array of fresh and healthy vegetarian dishes, salads, quiches, fresh orange juice, home-made lemonade, and many other good things. There are many shops in which to browse – Dartington glass, farm food, pottery, clothes, toys, etc., and there is, of course, an old cider press.

There are plenty of grassy areas, with bench tables and shady trees – a pleasant spot to have a picnic.

There is a pull-down shelf in the Ladies in the Cider Press Room.

£1–3: baked potato, mixed salads, pizzas and quiches, cauliflower croustade
Children: small portions

Open 10am–5pm Mon-Sat (and on Sundays during summer)
No credit cards accepted Open all year
P – in the complex Licensed

Dartmeet, Devon map 1

BADGER'S HOLT – ☎ Poundsgate (036 43) 213.

R

On the B3357 east of Princetown.

The 'meet' is between East and West Dart and it is worth a visit to Badger's Holt for the pleasure of the walk by the rushing river or even, for the adventurous, on the river on the giant stepping stones. The walk from the huge car park to the spacious wooden-walled café can also take you through the rockery gardens where some rare birds can be seen and heard.

There are plenty of high chairs available here plus a good choice of hot and cold food all day including a hot special at lunchtime; and they make all their own bread, cakes, pies, etc. The three course menu at under £5 is pretty good value.

The Ladies is sizeable and space can be found for a mother wishing to change or feed a baby.

Souvenirs, toys, Devon cream and so on are on sale here.

£1–4: Welsh rarebit, plaice & chips, vegetable lasagne, Cornish pasty, salads
Children: own menu, half portions

Open 10am–6pm Closed end Oct-Easter Access/Visa
Licensed No music
P – own car park

Dartmouth, Devon — map 1

SPINNING WHEEL CAFE, Hauley Road – ☎ Dartmouth (0803) 832 645.

R

Close to the harbour.

First of all you will see this restaurant's lovely patio garden, which is ablaze with colourful flowers, and not so long ago won an award.

Second, the restaurant is famous for its cream teas, and these are so substantial that tea for two would probably feed four. And you will be served real tea; no tea bags gain admittance here.

Everything is home-made on the premises, and the children's meals are all below £1, including that great favourite, boiled eggs and soldiers. The friendly owner will do her best to supply any food a child likes (within reason).

If you need to change a baby you can just about manage it in the toilet area.

£1–3: cream teas, omelettes, smoked mackerel, salads, fresh Dart salmon
Children: small portions

Open 10.30am–5pm, every day (excluding Mon in winter)
Unlicensed No smoking in one room
One high chair only P – public car parks

Dedham, Essex — map 4

MARLBOROUGH HEAD – ☎ Colchester (0206) 323 250.

P

The painter, John Constable, went to school in this lovely village, and it is good to include this excellent pub in a part of the country where we are very short of places to recommend. It is an ancient and delightful inn, with a wooden framed upper storey, and inside is plenty of space in the various bars and eating areas.

The main bar is very comfortable and the timbered beams and pillars are easy on the eye. At one end is a room where families are welcome – it has a bar, but it is not used to serve alcohol, and a notice confirms this. At the other end, past a well-furnished lounge with a huge fireplace with a carved wooden mantle, is another large room with plenty of tables and chairs, and families can also park themselves there – but it is sometimes used as a function room.

There is a pleasant lawned garden at the side of the pub, enclosed by walls, and with some nice shrubs and trees.

A good choice of food is served every day, and includes a Sunday roast at around £5.

(12–2pm & 7–9.30pm) £1–8: fried skate, fricassé of veal, minty English lamb, braised wild rabbit, baked mushrooms
Children: small portions

• Ale – Adnams, Benskin's No music
P – on street

Dent, Cumbria **map 9**

DENT CRAFTS CENTRE – ☎ Dent (058 75) 400.

R

Two miles out of Dent on the road to Sedbergh.

This converted roadside hay barn is an ideal spot to break your journey. As the name suggests there are many traditional crafts on display including wooden toys, local pottery, wrought ironwork and even a large picture gallery. There is also the chance to see a Victorian printing workshop operating as it did over a hundred years ago.

The stone-flagged restaurant only has a handful of tables, but they look out on to the surrounding hills through a huge picture window. Snacks are on offer during the week, and more substantial meals available at weekends. A good selection of teas is served.

There are bench tables on the patio and a small play area for children. There is a changing table and a chair in the toilet area.

There are regular craft demonstrations here, and the owners are planning some musical events, such as jazz brunches and suppers.

£1–2: pizza, quiche, carrot cake, filled baps, salads
Children: small portions

Open 9.30am–6pm daily Easter-November
Access/Visa Licensed
No smoking One high chair only
P – own car park

STONE CLOSE – ☎ Dent (05875) 231.

R

In the centre of the village.

This is an archetypal 17th century cottage teashop with flagged floors, exposed beams and open fires in its two cast iron ranges. It is situated in the beautifully preserved village of Dent, about fifteen miles south east of Kendal. It's a haven for walkers who come to enjoy the magnificent countryside but the village with its pretty cobbled main street and fine stone cottages is well worth a wander.

The food is all cooked on the premises including the cakes and the pastries. Meals are available all day and there's a daily changing choice of blackboard specials; there are a number of speciality teas which you are encouraged to try. Evening meals are available from 7.30 onwards.

A bathroom is available for mothers who need to change or feed a baby.

£1–5: paté, cheese & onion pie, crispy mushroom layer, gammon & eggs
Children: half portions

Open 10.30am–6pm
Closed January/February and weekdays in winter
No credit cards accepted Licensed
P – public, nearby

Dirleton, Lothian map 11

THE OPEN ARMS HOTEL – ☎ Dirleton (062 085) 241.

R

On the A198 west of North Berwick.

The hotel is included because of its position opposite Dirleton Castle, which has a colourful and bloody history and is well worth a visit.

The hotel itself has seven bedrooms and is rather expensive, but a good range of food is offered, and whereas the dinner menu is perhaps a little highly priced for a family budget, the light lunch menu is enterprising and gives good value. You can eat your lunch in one of the lounges or, if there is space, in the dining room or its adjacent conservatory. From here you have views of the castle.

On warmer days you might well head for the garden, which is partly paved and partly lawned, and has a goldfish pond.

If you need to change a baby the Ladies is spacious and equipped with chairs and plenty of tissues.

LIGHT LUNCHES (12.30–2.30pm) £1–5: salad Mimosa, mussel & onion stew, chicken & veal Basquaise, cold poached salmon;
DINNER (7–9.30pm) £15: halibut terrine, soup, loin of venison, pudding or cheese
Children: own menu, half portions

Open all year except 5 days in Jan Access/AmEx/Diners/Visa
No music One high chair only
P – own car park

Diss, Norfolk — map 8

WEAVERS WINE BAR, Market Hill – ☎ Diss (0379) 642 411.

R

In the town centre.

This building, which dates from the 15th century, was once the chapel of a weavers' guild and has had a varied history since then: butcher's shop, grocery, gents' outfitters, for example.

The current owners completely refurbished the building a few years back and you can now see the original timber structure. Families are made extremely welcome and the staff are flexible in their approach to children's food: baby food will be heated for you, for example, and feeding cups are available.

You can certainly cope with a baby in the Ladies, since a changing mat can be provided.

LUNCH £1–6: lasagne, steak & kidney pie, Suffolk ham, curried lamb, Torbay sole;
DINNER £14: venison & pork & chestnut terrine, steamed Scottish salmon, pudding or cheese
Children: small portions

Open 12–2pm & 7–9.30pm. Closed on Sunday
• Ale – Adnams P – on street

Please let us have reports – good or bad – on any establishments listed in the Guide as soon as possible after your visit.

Ditchling, East Sussex map 4

THE BULL HOTEL, 2 High Street – ☎ Hassocks (07918) 3147.

P

On the B2116.

This very attractive village, not far from Brighton and close to Plumpton race course, has a pub to match. The Bull sits on the corner of the High Street and its considerable character has, thankfully, been retained.

It is a 14th century, black and white building, bedecked with bright flowers. The main bar is handsome: the ancient wooden beams and pillars complement the large open fireplace, and a lovely carved wooden settle and a long wooden table add to the overall effect.

The separate family room is also in character, with another huge fireplace, a beamed ceiling and wooden furniture. There is plenty of space for families to settle here. If the sun shines the large lawned garden, with plenty of bench tables, is the place to be; and there are more tables on a terrace.

BAR MEALS (12–2pm & 7–9.30pm) £1–6: poached salmon, cauliflower cheese, braised lamb chop, cottage pie
Children: smaller portions

• Ale – Flowers, Eldridge Pope, Marston's
P – own car park

Dorchester, Dorset map 2

POTTER IN, 19 Durngate Street – ☎ Dorchester (0305) 268 649.

R

Opposite Boots in the centre of town.

Set in a narrow street of terraced houses, the old grocery shop windows of the Potter Inn display a tempting variety of home-made wholefood cakes; and inside there is an attractive array of salads (19 varieties) and quiches, which change daily. The owner does all the cooking and the delicious smells filter out from the kitchen at the back. The menu is displayed on a blackboard behind the servery.

The 300 year old building is painted green and white and is pleasantly furnished with pine tables, chairs, and settles and has a tiled floor.

The craft shop upstairs also has a few tables. The Ladies is up there too, and you might just about change a baby there – possibly on the window ledge.

There is a small, walled patio with seating for about twenty people, and this is the only place where smoking is permitted, although this is under review.

£1–3: soup, salads, pizza, stuffed aubergines, lasagne
Children: own menu, small portions

Open 10am–5pm Mon-Sat Closed Xmas & Bank Holidays
Access/Visa No smoking
P – public car parks nearby No music

Dowlish Wake, Nr Ilminster, Somerset map 2

NEW INN – ☎ *Ilminster (0460) 52413.*

P

The village is south-east of Ilminster. Head for Kingstone and it is nearby.

This very appealing village has many fine stone buildings and a lovely church, but is probably most notable as the home of Perry cider, and the mill is well worth a visit.

The New Inn is a well-proportioned stone building with a very pleasant and quite spacious bar: the beams are decorated with hops, there is good wooden furniture including some old settles, and a large ingle-nook fire-place with a seat in it alongside the iron stove.

The family room is at the back of the pub, relatively new, and with wide windows which look out to the lawned garden which stretches back along-side the skittle alley. There are plenty of bench tables on the grass, and a wooden climbing frame.

(12–2pm & 6.30–9.30pm) £1–7: whitebait, lasagne, ham & eggs, plaice & chips, sirloin steak
Children: smaller portions

• Ale – Butcombe, Wadworth's P – own car park

Downham, Lancs map 9

ASSHETON ARMS – ☎ *Clitheroe (0200) 41227.*

P

Two miles off the A59.

Situated in one of Lancashire's loveliest villages, the pub was built in the 16th century from local stone. It sits opposite the village church and has a row of handsome stone cottages alongside, as well as some old pillory stocks.

Inside, the pub is a real gem, with three separate but connected rooms which still have their original oak beams. The rooms are furnished with excellent wooden tables, chairs and settles, and a huge central fireplace dominates the bar. Behind this is the area where families are welcome to park themselves – it is separated from the bar, and has a hatch through to the kitchen and through which food is served. There is a wide range of food on offer here, and the cooking has a very good local reputation.

For warmer days there are tables and chairs on the cobbles at the front of the pub. There is a holiday cottage which can be rented, with one bedroom only, but several sofa beds so that a small family can be accommodated.

This is a really fine pub in a delightful part of the Lancashire countryside.

(12–2pm & 7–10pm) £1–9: grilled ham & free range eggs, chicken Cordon Bleu, steaks, Morecambe Bay prawns, whole lemon sole
Children: own menu, half portions

• Ale – Castle Eden, Marston's   P – own car park

Dullingham, Cambs — map 8

KINGS HEAD – ☎ Stetchworth (063 876) 486.

P

On the B1061 about four miles south of Newmarket.

This is a delightful and quiet village a few miles from horse racing's headquarters, Newmarket, and by the village green you will find this attractive pink-washed pub. The children's room is smallish and neatly furnished and had a good quota of families in there when we visited. At weekends families can spread themselves into the Loose Box across the car park. Outside is a small terrace, and on the other side of the pub, quite a large grassy garden with swings and a climbing frame.

A very extensive menu is available each day in the two cheerful bars and the prices are very reasonable. Not surprisingly this is a very popular pub, so you should either plan to arrive early or book a table.

(12–2pm & 6.30–10pm) £2–8: Manor House smokies, steaks, ham & eggs, pork Mexican, lasagne
Children: own menu, small portions

• Ale – Tolly   No music
P – own car park

Dumgoyne, Central — map 11

BEECH TREE INN – ☎ *Kilbarn (0360) 50297.*

P

On the A81 north of Glasgow.

This white-washed, cottagy inn has an excellent position on the path of the West Highland Way, which goes along the route of an old railway line past the pub. A walk up the nearby Hump of Dumgoyne, 700 feet high, will certainly sharpen your appetite and you will be rewarded with lovely views to Loch Lomond.

Families are welcome to use a conservatory room and the adjoining dining room. French windows lead out to extensive lawns which surround both sides of the building. There are trees here, plenty of tables, a duck-pond (with ducks) and a patio area.

The Beech Tree is open throughout the day from May to the end of August.

(12–2.30pm & 5–9.30pm) £1–7: paté, smoked local salmon, Trossacks veal, roast beef, fried scampi
Children: own menu

P – own large car park

Nr Dunoon, Strathclyde — map 11

COYLET INN, Loch Eck – ☎ *Kilmun (036 984) 426.*

P

On the A815.

A friendly welcome awaits you at this 17th century coaching inn. There is a small lounge where you may take the children and, on busy days, the dining room with dark oak tables and chairs is also put to use for families. You have a good view of the loch from this room, which is decorated with old china pieces and copper pans, and has a dresser.

Alongside the road is an attractive grassy garden surrounded by trees and across the road the splendid Loch Eck with towering hills behind.

(11.30am–2pm & 6.30–10pm) £1–6: chicken liver paté, ploughman's, langoustine prawns, trout
Children: half portions

• Ale – Younger's, McEwan's   P – own car park

Durham, Co Durham — map 10

ALMSHOUSES, Palace Green – ☎ Durham (091) 386 1054.

R

On the edge of Palace Green.

Strategically placed between the castle and the cathedral, this is a useful place to know if you need a sustaining cup of tea and a snack after a bout of sightseeing.

The self-service restaurant is indeed housed in a converted almshouse of 17th century origin, and offers an enterprising range of food, including many vegetarian dishes, organic wines and beers, and a good choice of teas and coffees.

There is nowhere official to change or feed a baby, but the staff toilet area is available for mothers.

£1–7: tofu & olive & walnut paté, lamb kebab, fennel & carrot mousse, red mullet, rogan josh
Children: half portions

Open 9am–8pm summer, 9am–5pm winter No credit cards
Licensed P – public car parks

UNDERCROFT RESTAURANT – ☎ Durham (091) 386 3721.

R

In the cathedral, through the cloisters.

The restaurant is actually part of the cathedral itself – located through the cloisters next to the bookshop and opposite the cathedral treasury. As you might expect parking is not too easy around here, particularly in summer, and it is best to use the multi-storey which is well signposted on the approach to the city from the motorway. It's only a short walk and Durham is a nice place to browse.

The restaurant has light pine furniture with fine stone walls. Food is available here all day with a number of daily specials for lunch and always a vegetarian dish.

The facilities for mothers and babies have been improved with the provision of a shelf, a chair and paper towels in the Ladies, and a baby can be changed there. And a further improvement is that the restaurant is now wholly a non-smoking one.

There's no garden here as such and the lawns in the middle of the cloisters are out of bounds, but there are several places where you can sit and relax and enjoy the surroundings. And the Cathedral is a majestic sight.

£1–4: soup, quiche, daily specials, cold buffet
Children: half portions

Open 9.30am–5pm Mon-Sat (11am–5pm Sun) Closed Xmas and Good Friday
No credit cards Licensed
No smoking No music
P – public car parks

Eaglescliffe Village, Cleveland — map 10

POT AND GLASS – ☎ *Eaglescliffe (0642) 780 145.*

P

Just off the A135, north of Yarm.

You may have a bit of fun trying to find this odd little pub set right at the back of this pretty village with its fine 11th century parish church. Your best bet is to follow the boundary wall of the church round by the village green and you will locate the Pot and Glass in a dead end which is in fact opposite the back gate to the churchyard!

Your perseverance will be well rewarded for this is an establishment which is gloriously different, not least for its unlikely situation hidden away on the end of a smart avenue of very middle class houses.

It's deceptively spacious inside with the main bar serving a cosy tap room at one end and a larger lounge bar at the other. Drinks are also dispensed through a glass hatch to a central area with some wonderful red and black Victorian-style floor tiles. The family room is on the right hand side of the main corridor just in from the front door. It has been refurbished recently with some very comfortable powder blue upholstered bench seats which blend in well with the old black-stained beams and panelling.

Through the back of the pub, you will find a small patio with some bench tables and a climbing frame. It's a well-maintained little spot with plenty of greenery and flora.

As befits a 200 year old building, there are plenty of relics from the past adorning the walls, including horse brasses and local items of interest.

The Sunday lunch is a bargain at under £5 (half portions depending on age).

BAR MEALS (12–2pm) £1–3: lasagne, quiche, steak pie, ploughman's
Children: half portions

• Ale – Bass
P – own car park (but very limited)

Easingwold, North Yorks map 10

TRUFFLES, Spring Street – ☎ Easingwold (0347) 22342.

R

In the main street.

This bright and cheerful coffee shop and restaurant is an agreeable place to take the children and it is a firm favourite with local residents who drop in for a morning coffee or a mid-afternoon snack, which is recommendation in itself.

The restaurant has been extended but unfortunately there are no baby changing facilities.

The menu is wide ranging – from home made cakes and scones to excellent value meals. A number of main dishes are available around lunchtime only but snacks can be had all day. There is also a delicatessen and wine shop attached.

£1–4: spinach roulade, savoury pasta, mixed hors d'oeuvres, mushroom Stroganoff
Children: own menu

Open 9.30am–5pm (from noon on Sundays); 7.30–9pm, Wed to Sat
Closed Sun. Open all year
No credit cards accepted No smoking at several tables
One high chair only Licensed
P – street parking

East Grinstead, West Sussex map 3

THE COFFEE POT, 39 High Street – ☎ East Grinstead (0342) 315 284.

R

In the centre of the old town.

This restaurant moved over the road a year or two ago and is now an extension of a bread and pastry shop, Sarah's Pantry. It is a bright and cheerful place on two levels, with a predominantly white decor and good wooden tables. It has the great merit of being a no smoking restaurant and offers snacks throughout the day, as well as more substantial meals at lunchtime.

The owner stressed to us that everything is freshly prepared on the spot and that no additives or artificial colourings are used.

You can change a baby in the Ladies, which has a pull-down shelf.

£1–4: pasta & tuna bake, chicken & broccoli pie, vegetable lasagne, nut roast
Children: half portions

Open 9.30am–5.30pm Mon to Sat
One high chair only Licensed
P – public parking No music

East Ilsley, Berks — map 3

CROWN & HORNS – ☎ East Ilsley (063 528) 205.

P

Off the A34.

This agreeable 18th century pub is well worth a short detour from the busy A34 not far north of Junction 13 of the M4. The village is in 'horsey' territory and the sport of kings motif is prevalent in the pub, with lots of prints of famous jockeys on the walls, horse brasses on the beams, and so on. Some of the customers arrive by horse and there are stables alongside the pub.

There are two rooms where children may go: a small one facing the main bar and a larger one to the side, and both are well provided with wooden tables and chairs. There is also a small dining room.

The old stable yard with its paved floor and chestnut trees has a colourful array of umbrellas over the tables, and during the summer a cold table is set up, and barbecues are done.

(12–2pm & 6–10pm) £1–10: fish pie, braised venison, plaice & chips, Barnsley chop
Children: half portions

• Ale – Wadworth's, Morland's, Fuller's, Bass, Theakston's
P – own car park

East Lulworth, Dorset — map 2

WELD ARMS – ☎ West Lulworth (091 941) 211.

P

On the B3070 a few miles south west of Wareham.

It is pleasant to recommend this traditional pub, which has, thank goodness, not been modernised. The Weld Arms is an agreeable 17th century thatched building with three rooms which contain old wooden settles, some easy chairs and flagstoned floors.

A small, oak beamed room is available for families, and it has its own entrance. Although a bar protrudes into it, it is not used to dispense alcohol. Families are well looked after with the provision of two high chairs; and a table in the Ladies for baby changing.

The garden is spacious and from the picnic tables on the lawn you have fine views of the Purbeck Hills. There are several swings and a slide on which the children can play.

There are some interesting dishes on the menu, including vegetarian, and it is heartening to report that chips are not served.

(12–2pm & 7–9.30pm) £1–8: ratatouille, mushroom roulade, venison & cranberry pie, Polynesian pork, goulash
Children: own menu

• Ale – Devenish P – own car park

East Preston, West Sussex — map 3

OLD FORGE RESTAURANT, The Street – ☎ Rustington (0903) 782 040.

R

Off the A259 and in the centre of the village.

Housed in this 17th century brick and flint cottage, with ivy clad walls, you will find a most attractive restaurant, with a wealth of oak beams. The emphasis is very much on fresh food, and especially fish; you will often have a choice of locally caught lobsters, scallops and crab. We think the three-course lunch offers particularly good value.

The Ladies is spacious and a baby can be changed in comfort on the work top, and there are several high chairs available.

LUNCH (12–2pm) £9: seafood salad, liver Provencale, pudding or cheese;
DINNER (7–10pm) £18: lobster bisque, chicken Waldorf, pudding or cheese
Children: own menu, half portions

Closed Sun dinner/all day Mon Access/AmEx/Diners/Visa
Licensed P – own car park

Eastmoor, Derbyshire map 7

HIGHWAYMAN – ☎ Chesterfield (0246) 566 330.

P

On the A629 out of Chesterfield.

Up on the moors, four miles outside Chesterfield, this large, recently modernised pub is a useful stopping off point for families heading for Chatsworth House, particularly since the pub is open throughout the day.

Great care has been taken to provide facilities for children including both indoor and outdoor play areas – there's Lego inside and slides and swings outside – and even separate boys' and girls' toilets.

The family room which is through the main bar is split level and has comfortable seating. A bonus is that there are changing facilities in the disabled toilet.

The pub dates back to 1620 and, as the New Inn, is mentioned in a Sherlock Holmes mystery. It has unrivalled views of some beautiful countryside through large picture windows.

(12–10pm) £1–6: Fisherman's platter, fried scampi, roast chicken, gammon steak, Cumberland sausage
Children: own menu

• Ale – Whitbread P – Own car park

If you wish to recommend an establishment to the Guide please write to us – report forms are at the back of the book. We need your help to extend and improve the guide.

Easton Grey, Nr Malmesbury, Wilts — map 2

EASTON GREY GARDEN RESTAURANT – ☎ Malmesbury (0666) 840 345.

R

Off the B4040 three and a half miles west of Malmesbury.

After you enter the delightful grounds of Easton Grey follow the signs for 'Boutique' and you will find the restaurant.

It's a cool and pretty garden room, decorated in pale green with wooden lattice work over the walls and with pink tablecloths. There's a big skylight window and lots of mirrors and illustrations of birds, and great bowls of ferns hang from the ceiling. It's very restful especially as you gaze at the expanses of manicured garden.

The menu is comprehensive: from scones to chicken à la créme. A mother would be able to change or feed a baby in the Ladies, where there is a chair, a shelf and paper towels.

£1–5: smoked salmon, toasted sandwiches & salad, dish of the day, lasagne.
Children: smaller portions

Open 9am–5pm Mon-Sat Closed Sun & Xmas
Access/Visa Licensed
P – own car park No music

Edburton, West Sussex — map 3

TOTTINGTON MANOR – ☎ Steyning (0903) 815 757.

P

North of Shoreham, off the A2037 and A281.

This attractive pub and hotel sits in lovely Sussex countryside. You can sit in the spacious lawned garden and gaze at the low and gentle hills around you. There are good walks to be done on the downs, and a bridle path connects with the South Downs Way.

The handsome building is 16th century in origin and behind the black and white front there is a section built from brick and timber in an attractive herringbone design.

Inside, families are welcome to use a separate room off the entrance hall. It has a large open fireplace and is set out as a small family dining room. There is also a very comfortable residents' lounge with a number of easy chairs. You should take a look at the miniature Ford Model T and the grand piano, which are made from icing sugar.

One of the owners, David Miller, was a chef at the Ritz and we are not surprised to hear that the food is gaining an excellent reputation.

(12–2.15pm & 7–9.15pm) £1–9: taramasalata, salmon mousse, moussaka, spicy home-made sausages, sirloin steak
Children: half portions

• Ale – Adnams, Bateman's, Fuller's, King & Barnes
P – own car park

Edinburgh, Lothian — map 11

GALLERY CAFE, National Gallery of Modern Art, Belford Road – ☎ 031-332 8600.

R

North west of central Edinburgh about half a mile from St Mary's Episcopal Cathedral.

This very pleasant café, within the National Gallery of Modern Art, is decorated in grey and white with blue plastic seats. It is a bright and appealing place, with its large windows and clever use of mirrors behind the trellis work. There is a large terrace, which can seat about seventy people, and this is open during the summer.

The restaurant has a wide range of snacks, both savoury and sweet, and the food is made on the premises. The Ladies is spacious with a shelf on which a baby can be changed.

£1–3: quiche & salad, filled baked potatoes, cheesy egg croissant, chicken & steak pie
Children: half portions

Open 10.30am–4.30pm Mon-Sat, 2–4.30pm Sun
Open all year exc. Xmas & New Year   No credit cards
No smoking in half the restaurant   One high chair only
Licensed   No music
P – large car park for Gallery

Never use an out-of-date Guide. Many places are excluded because their standards have dropped or their policies towards families have changed. Many new establishments are added each year.

HELIOS FOUNTAIN, 7 Grassmarket – ☎ 031–229 7884.

R

On the west side of the Grassmarket.

The building originally housed the Bank of Glasgow, which went bankrupt in 1900. Now the first thing to greet you is a shop which is crammed with books on alternative health and medicine, with jewellery, toys and crafts, candles and all sorts of trinkets. Keep a close eye on the children, here.

At the back there is a small and airy vegetarian restaurant with about nine tables and with benches around the walls. The kitchen is open plan, which is always reassuring, and there are fresh flowers on the tables.

Changing a baby is not easy since the lavatory is quite small, but breast-feeding mothers need have no inhibitions in this friendly restaurant – and the shop is great fun.

£1–3: carrot & celery soup, tomato & peanut pasta, savoury loaf, tofu pie
Children: smaller portions

Open 10am–6pm, Mon to Sat. Open until 8pm and from 11am–5pm on Sundays during the Festival.
Access/Visa Unlicensed
No music No smoking
One high chair only P – on street

HENDERSONS SALAD TABLE, 94 Hanover Street – ☎ 031-225 2131.

R

Off Princes Street and on the corner of Thistle Street and Hanover Street.

A shop, wine bar, and restaurant are encompassed by Henderson's, which is much more spacious than you would guess from outside, and is a real warren of rooms and alcoves. On the ground floor, fruit and veg and wholemeal bread from their own bakery is sold; and down the stairs you will find an attractive self-service vegetarian restaurant with pine tables. The choice of food is comprehensive with a very large range of salads, and the sensible owners offer half portions to adults as well as children.

There is also a very pleasant, spacious, low-ceilinged wine bar, a separate no-smoking room, and two very snug alcoves with arched roofs (the old pavement cellars).

If you need to change or feed a baby, a chair will be put in the Ladies.

£1–3: vegetable curry, cauliflower cheese, ratatouille, mushroom savoury, stuffed aubergine
Children: half portions

Open 8am–11pm Mon-Sat. Closed Sundays, Xmas and New Year
Access/AmEx/Visa • Ale – Belhaven
No smoking in wine bar and restaurant
P – difficult, meters only

SUNFLOWER COUNTRY KITCHEN, 4 South Charlotte Street – ☎ *(031) 220 1700.*

R

First opening off Princes Street at West End.

This excellent restaurant, primarily but not totally vegetarian, has been in and out of the Guide over the years, depending on the availability of a high chair. At the moment it has one; it used to have several; and occasionally it has none at all.

It is a busy and well-organised place, and the food is fresh and interesting, and includes local organic produce. It is a self-service restaurant and the constituents of the various meals are described in detail.

You could certainly change a baby in the Ladies, since there is plenty of space, and there is a padded bench to make the process easier.

£1–4: various salads (mixed bean, beansprout, lettuce with date & apples, etc), roast ham, tuna paté, Welsh rarebit
Children: half portions

Open 8am–7pm, Mon to Sat (and 10am–6pm on Sundays during the Festival)
No smoking in half the restaurant No credit cards accepted
P – on street (meters) One high chair only

Egton Bridge, North Yorks — map 10

THE HORSE SHOE – ☎ *Whitby (0947) 85245.*

P

Two miles off the A171, east of Whitby.

Although this small village is only a few miles from the coast, the most rewarding direction to approach from is over the wonderfully scenic North Yorkshire moors. The village is dominated by this sturdy stone-built pub which is just off the road.

There is a cosy lounge bar with wooden settles and cream painted walls from which hang various pictures. The family room is on the side of the bar towards the back of the building and is itself divided into two halves by a three quarter wall. Both sections are fairly small but there are plenty of tables and chairs and the place is nicely decorated. There are a couple of high chairs on the premises.

Outside there are some white tables and chairs on the front lawn and a further lawn at the side of the pub to which you walk via a bridge over the stream which runs merrily past.

BAR MEALS (12–2pm & 7–9pm) £1–6: soup, egg & bacon flan, stuffed turkey, sirloin steak, steak & kidney pie
Children: own menu

• Ale – Theakston's, Tetley's P – own car park

Elgin, Grampian map 12

THUNDERTON HOUSE, Thunderton Lane – ☎ *Elgin (0343) 548 767.*

P

Off the High Street.

This house has had a long and interesting history. As long ago as the 14th century, the palace of the Earl of Moray stood on the site; and some of the building which now stands dates back to the 17th century.

It is a lovely old building, and the ghost of Bonnie Prince Charlie is said to haunt the bedroom which he occupied before the Battle of Culloden in 1746. The bar is friendly enough and comfortable, and adjoining it is a family room. It is furnished with sturdy wooden tables and chairs, and has plenty of space.

It's a very good pub, where families are made welcome; and has the great advantage of being open all day, with food available at all times. It is good to see that there is a good selection of real ales – a rarity in Scotland.

(11am–7.45pm) £1–8: haddock & hash browns, barbecue ribs, rainbow trout, grilled chicken, steaks
Children: half portions

• Ale: Belhaven, Caledonian, Greenmantle, Heriots and guests
P – on street

Places included in the Guide must offer the following basic facilities:
Pubs – a separate area or room for families where alcohol is not served;
Restaurants – high chairs and special menus/reduced portions.

Elkstone, Glos **map 2**

HIGHWAYMAN, Beech Pike – ☎ Miserden (028 582) 221.

P

On the A417 seven miles or so north of Cirencester.

This 16th century stone pub is a busy and appealing roadside inn, and you can't miss the old stagecoach which stands in the car park. Inside you will find a large bar with stone walls and beamed ceilings, and the large firelaces have log fires in winter.

It's very welcoming and so is the family area, which is at the back of the bar and is comfortably furnished with plenty of tables and chairs. There is also a separate room off the bar, with several tables and padded benches.

There is a very attractive restaurant (Turpins) which opens in the evenings from Tuesday to Saturday, and it is also available to families on Saturday mornings and on Sundays.

Through a door is a grassy, enclosed garden with bench tables. There is also a separate play area for children, with swings and a slide, in a pretty wooded spot on the far side of the car park.

With an excellent choice of food on the various menus, this is a splendid pub for families.

(12–2.15pm & 6–10.15pm) £1–7: mushroom dip, chicken Cordon Bleu, pizzas, seafood pancake, steak Chasseur

TURPINS £2–13: game soup, smoked salmon, beef in ale pie, lemon sole, steaks

Children: own menu

• Ale – Arkell's P – own car park

Elslack, North Yorks **map 9**

TEMPEST ARMS – ☎ Harby (0282) 842 450.

P

On the A56, close to its junction with the A59, 3 miles south of Skipton.

An attractive stone-built pub, situated close to the main road but enjoying some fine views of the beautiful countryside which marks the beginning of the Yorkshire Dales area.

Apart from the obvious attraction of some very well-kept real ale, the food here is also a high spot as one would imagine with a French landlord!

Exposed stonework dominates the pub's interior with a superb open fire a feature of the main lounge. There is comfortable bench seating all around and an interesting collection of curios and hunting prints adorning the walls.

Families can use a room right at the far end of the pub, through the smaller of the two bar areas, up a couple of stairs. It is light and airy, well furnished with tables and chairs and is mainly designed for those who are dining.

This is a good place to know if you are heading for the Dales or visiting nearby Skipton, with its ancient castle, and its excellent shopping.

(11.30am–2pm & 6.30–10pm) £2–5: fish & mushroom pie, fresh salmon & mayonnaise, deep fried scampi, Brockwurst sausage

• Ale – Tetley's, Thwaites, Younger's
P – own car park

Elstead, Surrey — map 3

WOOLPACK – ☎ *Elstead (0252) 703 106.*

P

On the B3001, the Farnham to Milford road.

Situated in a pleasant Surrey village, this pub looks very smart with a cream-painted lower storey and a tile hung upper floor. You enter a large and comfortable bar area with wooden pillars and beams; it is very well furnished and well carpeted, and there is an abundance of tables and chairs and padded wooden settles.

At one end of the pub there is a spacious and bright restaurant and at the other end a bright and functional family room with several wooden benches and pews. It leads out through French windows to a lawned garden with bench tables: and there is a climbing frame and a slide for the children.

The bar food shows real imagination and there is a wide choice of hot and cold food including an excellent range of salads.

(12–2pm & 7–9.45pm) £1–7: hummus & pitta bread, chickan satay, cod & prawn pie, lamb curry, pork casserole
Children: own dishes

• Ale – Friary Meux & guests   No music
P – own car park

Elsted, Nr Midhurst, West Sussex **map 3**

ELSTED INN – ☎ Midhurst (073 081) 3662.

P

Off the A272 three miles West of Midhurst.

The pub has changed its name on occasions. It used to be The Ballards, and long before that the Railway Inn. If you consult your dictionary you will discover that a ballard is a bald headed man or an ancient musical instrument rather like a large xylophone.

Whatever the merits of the various names, real ale enthusiasts will certainly be interested in this pub, which has its own brewery in what were the old stables. The owner is trying to maintain the Victorian character of the place with small grates, sash windows etc. There is certainly a homely and pleasant atmosphere, and an excellent family room. It is a cosy one with partly panelled walls, a fitted carpet, its own toilet facilities and its own entrance to the garden.

The garden is a long enclosed grassy one with fruit trees and plenty of bench tables. There are tree swings, a boule pitch, a barbecue; and a very sensible idea, a separate area for young children is kept free of dogs.

The menu changes each day and everything is cooked on the spot from local ingredients. The one exception is a locally made pork pie.

(12–2pm & 7–10om) £1–9: mussels in garlic, beef in beer, local trout, salmon fillets, spatchcock in lemon & ginger
Children: own menu, half portions

• Ale – Ballard's, Greene King, Marston's and guests
P – own car park

Elsworth, Cambs **map 7**

GEORGE & DRAGON – ☎ Elsworth (095 47) 236.

P

Off the B1040 south of St Ives.

In a small farming village, with medieval origins, this 17th century pub shows a modest exterior to the world, but inside you will find a delightful inn of several rooms.

The large bar area has dark panelled walls and lovely oak settles gathered at one end around a fireplace with a long wooden mantle. The landlady's collection of copper kettles cluster on the ceiling beams and a blackboard shows the daily "specials".

The separate children's room is really splendid, spacious and light and well-furnished with cane furniture, so that the parents can relax as well –

as the owners pointed out. The owners have quite rightly declared this a no-smoking area. This opens out to a stretch of grassy garden, with two patio areas, and there are swings, a slide, and a climbing frame.

A very enterprising range of bar food is always available; and there is now also a handsomely furnished restaurant which is open most lunchtimes and evenings.

All in all, a splendid pub for all the family.

(12–2pm & 7–10pm) £1–10: trout & salad, coquilles St Jacques, chicken Normandy, steaks, Hungarian goulash
Children: own menu

• Ale – Greene King, Ruddles, Webster's
P – own car park

Ely, Cambs **map 8**

OLD FIRE ENGINE HOUSE, 25 St Mary's Street – ☎ Ely (0353) 662 582.

R

In the town centre – on the A10.

Hard by the superb cathedral, you will find this handsome 18th century building, which, at the turn of the century, really did house the town's fire engine.

Its attractive rooms now house an art gallery on the upper floors as well as a restaurant, and the dining room, a pleasant, well-proportioned room with a tiled floor and good oak tables, looks out to a delightful walled garden, with a smooth lawn and several shady apple trees.

The cooking is English in emphasis and local ingredients are used whenever possible. If you need to change or feed a baby, there is a bathroom and a sitting room upstairs.

LUNCH (12.30–2pm) £14: Loch Fyne herrings, gigot of lamb, apple pie & cream;
DINNER (7.30–9pm) £15: smoked salmon paté, casserole of pigeon, syllabub
Children: half portions

Open 10.30am–9pm
Closed Public Holidays, 2 weeks from 24 Dec., Sunday evenings
No credit cards accepted No music
• Ale – Adnams P – at side and on street

Empingham, Nr Oakham, Leics — map 7

WHITE HORSE INN, Main street – ☎ Empingham (078 086) 221.

P

On the A606.

Very close to Rutland Water with its many facilities, this pub began life as a courthouse in the 17th century, and is a long, well-proportioned stone building, with white shutters.

Families are welcome to use a nicely decorated room up some stairs from the bar; there are several tables and comfortable seating, and it is good to report that this is a no smoking area.

At the side there is a small enclosed lawned garden; and a terrace at the front with plenty of rustic tables and chairs, and enlivened by the climbing plants and bright flowers. The main bar is spacious and comfortable, and broken up into sections by stone pillars and a central fireplace.

Morning snacks and afternoon teas are also served, and this is a useful pub for families since it is open all day.

(12–2pm & 6.30–10pm) £2–8: seafood stir fry, beef & vegetable pie, sirloin steak, lasagne, red bean & pepper pie
Children: half portions

• Ale – Courage, John Smith's P – own car park

Eskdale Green, Cumbria — map 9

KING GEORGE IV INN – ☎ Eskdale (09403) 262.

P

Off the A595 east of Ravenglass.

A very attractive, whitewashed Lakeland inn of 15th century origins, which is only a stone's throw from the famous Ravenglass and Eskdale railway, known to most people as the "Ratty".

It is situated in magnificent countryside and if you are feeling particularly brave you can drive here from the Ambleside side over the spectacular and daunting Hard Knott Pass. On the way you will see the Roman fort which was built at about the same time as Hadrian's Wall.

The pub was built on a Roman watering site and the well still lies under the cellars. The Eskdale Hunt also leaves from here several times a year.

A pleasant family room, with a profusion of wooden beams, has several tables and wooden pews around the wall. There is a games room, with bar skittles and a pool table, off the family room. There is also a beer garden, where ducks sometimes congregate.

(12–2.30pm & 6–9.30pm) £1–4: salads, local trout, cheese & onion flan, Westmoreland pie, steaks
Children: own menu

• Ale – Bass, Stone's, Theakston's, and guests
P – own car park

Exmouth, Devon — map 2

ROUND THE BEND, 53 The Strand – ☎ Exmouth (0395) 264 398.

R

In the centre of the town.

The restaurant is housed in an attractive old building, which used to be used by a grain merchants and is located on one of the main squares of the town.

Downstairs you will find a pleasant coffee shop, with pine furniture, and this is open throughout the morning. A little patio at the back of the building has a few tables and chairs.

Upstairs the restaurant (open from 12 to 2pm) is a most attractive room with a high ceiling and brick walls. The emphasis is on wholefood vegetarian dishes.

At present there is nowhere to change a baby with any ease.

£1–3: houmous with pitta bread & salad, homity pie, mixed vegetable pie, rice & vegetable bake
Children: half portions

Open 9.30am–2.30pm Mon-Sat, 7–10pm Fri & Sat
Open all year   No credit cards accepted
P – public car park nearby   Licensed

Faringdon, Oxon — map 3

THE BELL, The Square – ☎ Faringdon (0367) 20534.

P

Centre of town on the A420.

This is very much a traditional inn in the centre of town. It was built in the 16th century and the bar retains some of its historic past. At the back of the pub is a quiet courtyard with bench tables and in summer it is strewn with trailing roses and flowers grown in old Thames boats.

Food is served in the bar and in the restaurant all week, and traditional Sunday lunches are also served. You will usually find an enterprising and keenly priced special bar meal in the evenings: perhaps moules marinières or a tray of hors d'oeuvres with crusty bread and a bottle of wine for under a tenner for two people.

The children's room is actually the residents' lounge – a room off the entrance hall – and it is furnished with comfortable bench seats, with a variety of old prints on the walls.

BAR SNACKS (12–2pm & 6–9.30pm) £1–6: steak & Guinness pie, fish & chips, curry Madras, casserole of lamb
Children: half portions

• Ale – Wadworth No music
P – own car park at rear

Also recommended in the Family Welcome Accommodation Guide.

Feock, Nr Truro, Cornwall **map 1**
PUNCH BOWL & LADLE INN – ☎ Truro (0872) 862 237.

P

On the B3289 south of Truro.

A marvellous job has been done in renovating this fine old pub, which looks so smart and appealing with its white-painted walls under a thatched roof. There is masses of space inside, and it is nicely arranged in various rooms and alcoves. The wooden beams and pillars and wood panelling are very much in character and there are good wooden tables and extremely comfortable armchairs and sofas scattered about.

Families are welcome to use three alcove rooms, which are all well away from the bar. They are very attractive, with their full complements of low black beams and thick plaster walls, and all are comfortably furnished with padded bench seats and easy chairs. Outside there is a terrace with a few tables and chairs.

It's a most attractive pub which also offers a good selection of food, which is available for most of the time that the pub is open.

✕ (11.30am–2.30pm & 6.30–10pm) £1–7: smoked salmon, halibut, lamb chops, pie of the day, steak teriyaki
Children: own menu, half portions

• Ale – Devenish P – ample

TRELISSICK GARDEN – ☎ Truro (0872) 862 090.

R *Just off the B3289 south of Truro. Well signposted.*
The beautiful house and garden of Trelissick were given to the National Trust in 1955 and the various walks radiate out from the house, which is not open to the public.
You do not have to pay the entry fee to enjoy the restaurant, which is housed in a huge barn with the wooden roof beams criss-crossing above. There is a good range of food on offer at the self-service counter and it is a pleasant place for a meal or a snack. Sunday lunches are also available and you should book in advance.
There is a shelf in the disabled lavatory and a baby could be changed there.
Near the restaurant there are an interesting gift shop, a garden shop and a Gallery which sells art and craft goods of excellent quality.

✕ £1–5: bean & pepper soup, cauliflower & pasta in cream cheese sauce, lamb casserole, salads
Children: small portions

Open: 11am to 6pm early March to end of October; from 1pm to 6pm on Sundays.
P – own car park

Also recommended in the Family Welcome Leisure Guide.

Fletching, East Sussex — map 4

GRIFFIN INN – ☎ Newick (082 572) 2890.

P

This 16th century inn is situated in a decidedly pretty vilage, which recently won the accolade of "best kept village" in Sussex. It is on the edge of Ashdown Forest and Sheffield Park and close to the Bluebell Steam Railway.

The pub has several comfortable rooms including a large, well-furnished lounge with oak-panelled walls, heavily beamed ceiling, and a crackling log fire which had a contented dog in front of it when we visited in the Autumn. It has half a dozen tables and may sometimes be called into use as a subsidiary dining room.

Food is available every day, and the owners emphasize that it is home-made from fresh local ingredients. Traditional Sunday lunches are served during the winter – three courses for around £8 – and a barbecue is set up on Sunday evenings in summer. There is an excellent range of beers available.

Outside is a gravelled patio and a long grassy garden which overlooks the rolling beauty of the South Downs.

(12–2pm & 7–10pm) £1–9: fish & herb terrine, leek & bacon & cheese bake, roast poussin, savoury pancake, steaks
Children: half portions

• Ale – Harvey's, Ruddles, Hall & Woodhouse
P – own car park

Flichity, Highland — map 12

GROUSE AND TROUT – ☎ Farr (080 83) 314.

PR

On the B851 between Farr and Croachy.

Situated in Upper Strathnairn this bar and restaurant is well worth the drive down a dozen miles or so of winding road south of Inverness. Once a farm, the lovely stone buildings, low and deep- roofed, have been superbly converted and form an open square. From the attractive walled garden you can see the gentle hills all around.

The interior is very well designed and a conservatory has been added to the dining room, from where you have splendid views of the countryside. There is also a comfortable sitting area where you can take the children, and the Ladies is fine for breast-feeding and nappy-changing, and there are two high chairs.

There are four rooms in the hotel, one of which is a family room, and fourteen chalets in the grounds. These are functional with clean and bright and well-furnished interiors; patio doors lead to little gardens. There is a hard tennis court for guests and bicycles can be hired.

The bar is open throughout the day and you can get some sustenance at most times; there is just the occasional gap of half an hour or so when the kitchen staff can catch their breath.

BAR MEALS (12–2.30pm & 6–9pm) £1–12: Orkney herring, steaks, plaice & chips, haggis;
DINNER (7–9pm) £13: smoked salmon, beef Stroganoff, baked apple pie
Children: own menu, half portions

Open all year Access/AmEx/Diners/Visa
P – own car park Licensed

Fochabers, Grampian **map 12**

BAXTERS – ☎ Fochabers (0343) 820 393.

R

On the A96.

The self-service restaurant is part of the visitor centre run by the famous Scottish food manufacturers. It is a bright and well-furnished place, which offers excellent value for money. There is a very good choice of fresh foods, a marvellous cup of tea, and lovely views of the Spey Valley through the wide windows.

The Visitor Centre is well-designed with shops which sell speciality foods, cooking utensils and craft goods. There are also guided tours of the factory at regular intervals.

There are several high chairs on the premises; and good facilities in the Ladies for dealing with babies – chairs, tables, and paper towels, for example. There is a patio area, and several picnic areas in the landscaped gardens.

This is a very well-organised and pleasant place to visit, with very friendly and helpful staff.

£1–5: soup, filled jacket potatoes, Lossiemouth scampi, grilled Spey salmon, Baxters pancakes
Children: own menu, half portions

Open 10am–5pm, Mon to Fri; from 11am at weekends
No smoking in part of restaurant   No credit cards
P – own car park

Fonthill Bishop, Wilts — map 2

KING'S ARMS – ☎ Hindon (074 789) 523.

P

On the B3089 west of Salisbury.

This is a charming pub in lovely surroundings. It is deceptively spacious inside, with a pleasant bar area with plush seats and benches, and up the stairs is another section which also houses a pool table and a dart board.

The family room is off the bar, has several tables and chairs, and has a good view to the lawned and enclosed garden with its bench tables.

(12–2pm & 7–10pm) £1–6: ham & eggs, haddock & chips, chicken Kiev, steaks, vegetable curry
Children: own menu

• Ale – Wadworth's & guests   P – own car park

Ford, Nr Chippenham, Wilts — map 2

WHITE HART – ☎ Castle Coombe (0249) 782 213.

P

Just off the A420 west of Chippenham.

An archetypal 16th century village inn which is built of stone and has a steeply pitched roof. It is a busy and popular pub and inside you will find a pleasant bar with a large iron stove at one end.

At the other end of the bar there is a long spacious buttery bar, and families are welcome to settle in here to eat or drink. Adjoining the buttery there is a very large restaurant.

There is a small forecourt outside the front door, and across the road a large paved terrace, with plenty of bench tables. From here you can see and hear a stream rushing by below.

🍴 (12–2.15pm & 7–9.30pm) £1–7: chicken Madras, lamb hot pot, haddock & chips, liver & onions
Children: small portions

• Ale – Fuller's, Marston's, Ruddles, Wadworth's
P – own car park

Ford, Nr Shrewsbury, Shropshire — map 6

CROSS GATES HOTEL – ☎ Shrewsbury (0743) 850 332. *Pot Luck*

P

On the A458 just west of Shrewsbury.

This pub has been altered greatly over the last few years. It began life as a farmhouse in the 18th century, and just across the road has its own bowling green.

The interior has a large and comfortable main bar, well carpeted and decorated and with some of the original beams still in place. The family room is off the bar and is set up with plenty of tables and chairs.

Across the car park is a lawned garden with bench tables and garden furniture. There is plenty of play equipment for children including an old tractor, a swing, a slide, a climbing frame and some ropes hanging from a tree.

🍴 (12–2pm & 7–10pm, not Tues pm) £1–6: scampi & chips, beef & onion pie, plaice & chips, rump steak, salads
Children: own menu, half portions

• Ale – Davenport's, Wem P – own car park

Fordwich, Nr Canterbury, Kent — map 4

FORDWICH ARMS – ☎ Canterbury (0227) 710 444.

P

In the centre of the village opposite the town hall.

This very popular pub is in a most attractive village a couple of miles north east of Canterbury. It is a large and attractive mock Tudor inn, which was built in the 'thirties, and is opposite the ancient town hall. It is a smartly furnished pub with lots of oak panelling in evidence and an open fire in the bar.

The large and sedate family room also has its quota of wood panelling and is similarly well-furnished with plenty of tables and chairs. It overlooks a terrace and a large lawned garden, which runs down to the River Stour where lots of boats can be seen. Centuries ago, sea-going ships used to come this far up the river. It is now safely fenced off to protect the children and there are plenty of tables and benches scattered about. There is a flagged terrace as well where you can sit.

(12–2pm & 6–10pm, Mon to Sat) £1–6: paprika beef & rice, cauliflower & broccoli cheese, cassoulet, bacon & onion pudding
Children: half portions

• Ale – Boddington's, Fremlins, Marston's
P – own car park

Fownhope, Hereford & Worcs **map 2**

GREEN MAN INN – ☎ *Fownhope (043 277) 243.*

P

On the B4224 in the village.
This excellent pub is set in the beautiful Herefordshire countryside, and close to the lovely River Wye. It is a classic 15th century inn with most of the essential attributes: a black and white, part-timbered facade, a low-beamed bar, and above all a friendly atmosphere. One of its most celebrated landlords would not have had any trouble with drunken customers

– he was Tom Spring, bare-knuckle heavyweight champion of England.

You will always find food on the go here, and the dining-room, housed in an old barn, is a lovely sight – very spacious, with black beams and pillars, and an outlook on one side to a very large grassy garden with lots of trees and flowers. There are swings and a climbing frame for the children.

The children's room, off the main bar, is also the Buttery and is a spacious room, well-furnished with wooden settles and polished tables. Its windows overlook part of the garden.

(12–2pm & 7–10pm) £1–7: plaice & chips, grilled trout, Tom Spring's steak sandwich, steaks, lasagne verdi
Children: half portions

• Ale – Hook Norton, Marston's, Sam Smith's
No music P – own car park

Also recommended in the Family Welcome Accommodation Guide.

Framfield, East Sussex map 4

BAY TREES RESTAURANT, The Street – ☎ Framfield (0825) 890 636.

R

On the B2102 just east of Uckfield.

This 17th century building, with its partly tile hung, brick facade, used to be the village store. It is now a spacious restaurant, and the dining room has brick pillars, wooden beams and copper artefacts on the walls.

A great bonus is the presence of a swimming pool in the garden, and you can sharpen your appetite with a swim before lunch. You can of course eat around the pool or in the beautifully kept, lawned garden alongside.

If you need to change a baby you could cope by using the vanitory unit in the Ladies.

LUNCH £8, 2 courses: gravadlax, coq au vin;
DINNER £9: seafood cocktail, turkey fricasée, pudding or cheese
Children: own menu, half portions

Open 12.30–2pm & 7.30–9pm Access/Visa
Licensed P – own car park

Frensham, Surrey map 3

MARINERS HOTEL, Mill Bridge – ☎ Frensham (025 125) 2050.

R

On the A287 South of Farnham, and close to Frensham Ponds.

You cannot miss this large Victorian building, painted white with a blue trim, on the main road south. The name of the pub suggests definite nautical connections, and the story is that the original house, which burnt down in the last century, was used as a depot for smugglers en route between the south coast and London.

It is a very spacious and cheerful place with a large bar area. Off to one side is a room with a vaulted ceiling and plenty of wooden tables and families are welcome to park themselves here. There are several high chairs available and the Mariners is open all day from Monday to Saturday.

There are two large patios on each side of the pub and a small lawned area with bench tables.

(12–2pm & 6–10pm) £2–12: canelloni, pizzas, plaice & chips, chicken Hawaii, fillet steak
Children: own menu

• Ale – Bass, Gale's, Marston's and guests
Access/AmEx/Diners/Visa P – own car park

Fyfield, Oxon map 3

WHITE HART – ☎ Oxford (0865) 390 585.

P

Off the A420, seven miles from Abingdon.

It would be difficult to nominate a better pub than the White Hart with its delightful atmosphere and wide choice of real ale and excellent food. It is impossible to name a better family pub.

There are no less than four rooms in which children are welcome with their adults: a pretty gallery, which overlooks the main bar; a spacious, well-furnished room down some stairs; and yet another room on the ground floor with tables, a large open fireplace and ancient wooden walls. On Sunday lunchtimes a fourth area, a lovely room with wooden beams and pillars, which is normally the restaurant, is also pressed into service. What with the large grassy garden for summer days, you will always find somewhere to park yourselves and your children.

The pub, built in the 15th century as a charity house, is actually owned by St John's College, Oxford, and any academic would feel at home in the bar with its high and handsome vaulted ceiling – and a handsome selection of real ales too.

You will find an imaginative and wide-ranging selection of food on tap as well. It's home-made, and even the bread is baked on the premises. There is a table and chair in the Ladies to help with changing or feeding of babies, and there are two high chairs on the premises.

The White Hart is an exceptional pub in every way, where the whole family is made welcome.

(12–2pm & 7–10pm) £1–8: avocado prawn, steaks, moussaka, chicken Strasbourg, local trout, braised pigeon
Children: half portions

• Ale – Boddington's, Morland's, Ruddles, Theakston's, Wadworth's & guest beers
P – own car park

Galashiels, Borders **map 11**

SANDERS RESTAURANT, 94a High Street – ☎ Galashiels (0896) 56055.

R

On the A72 the town centre.

This is a surprising little place, tucked away behind the shops of the High Street. It was once a tailor's shop and its past is remembered with prints of old sewing machines on the walls and collages of buttons. There are a few tables outside the front of the restaurant, and a delightful garden with a small lawn, trees, flower beds and benches and tables.

The toilet area is too small for you to attempt to change a baby, but the staff room can be used if you ask.

£1–3: paté, garlic mushrooms, steak pie, haddock & chips, lasagne
Children: half portions

Open 10am–3pm Monday; 10am–9.30pm, Tues to Sat; 4–7pm Sunday
Closed Xmas & New Year Access/Diners/Visa
Licensed One high chair only
P – public car park opposite

Galmpton, Nr Brixham, Devon — map 1

MANOR INN – ☎ Brixham (0803) 842 346.

P

Just off the A379, between Brixham and Paignton.

Terraces and little patios, with plenty of bench tables, surround this smartly decorated pub, and one of them is partly covered and barbecues are held there during the summer.

The facade of the pub is mainly painted white, but one wall has been left with its original pink tinged stone. Inside there is a spacious family room with plenty of tables at which you can enjoy a drink or a meal together, and the landlord provides a high chair, too. There is a wide choice of food on the various menus.

The pub also has three self-catering flats, which are let on a weekly basis.

The village was once the home of Agatha Christie.

(12–2pm & 7–9.30pm) £1–7: garlic mushrooms, steaks, Brixham plaice, ratatouille, turkey & ham pie
Children: own menu, half portions

• Ale – Ind Coope Burton   P – own car park

Gargrave, North Yorks — map 9

THE ANCHOR – ☎ Skipton (0756) 749 666.

P

On the A65, just outside the village.

A massive investment by new owners Whitbread has completely transformed this well-known roadside inn which now trades (God help us) under the company's Brewer's Fayre banner.

Anyone who likes real pubs will lament the passing of yet another of Britain's inns of character but there is little doubt that the Anchor's new format draws in the lager drinkers.

Nevertheless, the Anchor provides outstanding facilities for families. The lawned garden with its bench tables and play equipment has actually been improved with some welcome safety precautions added, notably soft landing areas around some of the slides etc.

It is very sad to tell that the pub's ancient beams and exposed stonework have disappeared, to be replaced by pine wood fittings, tables and chairs and yards of deep pile carpet.

The menu is standard Brewers Fayre food and a childrens' menu is available. The Ladies has good facilities for baby-changing. Families can use a special area to the side of the building, around the corner from the bar and there is a play room for small children. The pub is of course open all day, including Sundays (by dint of its restaurant) and there are plenty of high chairs.

(11.30am–10pm daily) £1–7: hot mushrooms, gammon steak, fillet of plaice, Cumberland sausage, salads

• Ale – Boddington's, Castle Eden, Marston's
P – own car park

Gifford, Lothian — map 11

TWEEDDALE ARMS, High Street – ☎ Gifford (062 081) 240.

P

Six miles or so south of Haddington, on the B6355.

Pubs where families are welcomed are hard to find in this area, and so we are happy to recommend this attractive 17th century coaching inn situated in a very pleasant village. It is a long, white-painted building, smartly furnished and the baskets of dried flowers hanging on the walls and ceilings add a cheerful touch.

Families are welcome to use a comfortable and attractively furnished lounge, and on summer days you might head for one of the two pretty walled gardens, where there is plenty of space and the added bonus of a climbing frame, a swing and a trampoline for the children. There is also a huge stretch of village green at the front of the pub.

There is an excellent choice of food on the bar menu, as well as a full restaurant menu in the evenings and at Sunday lunchtimes. In common with most of the pubs and hotels in Scotland, the bar is open throughout the day.

(12–2pm & 7–9pm) £1–5: smoked salmon, lamb Madras & rice, fried haddock, fricassee of chicken, lasagne
Children: half portions

• Ale – McEwan's P – on the street

Glamis, Tayside — map 11

STRATHMORE ARMS, Main Street – ☎ Glamis (0307) 84248.

R

In the centre of the town.

Two adjoining buildings make up this restaurant and hotel, the one houses a spacious bar and the other a restaurant done out in traditional style with Regency striped chairs set around tables with crisp white tablecloths.

The food is varied and enterprising and the lunch menu offers remarkably good value. Children are offered smaller portions of the available dishes, rather than the inevitable fish fingers and chips.

If you need to change a baby there is plenty of room in the Ladies.

This is a well-run establishment, where families are welcomed and where excellent service and value for money is provided.

LUNCH £8: prawn & mackerel salad, loin of pork, pudding or cheese
DINNER £15: roast duck & avocado, medallions of veal, pudding or cheese
Children: half portions

• Ale – Alloa P – own car park

Goodwick, Nr Fishguard, Dyfed — map 5

FARMHOUSE KITCHEN, Glendower Square – ☎ Fishguard (0348) 873 282.

R

Off the A40. Take the sign to Goodwick, and the restaurant is next door to the Hope & Anchor pub.

This pretty two-roomed restaurant is a couple of hundred yards from the main road and close to the ferry terminal. It offers freshly cooked food at reasonable prices – a two course lunch at around £5, and Sunday lunch for around £7. Morning coffee and afternoon teas are also served, with an à la carte menu in the evenings, and there is a good vegetarian selection.

The restaurant is neat and attractive with polished wood floors and sturdy wooden furniture and a comfortable little room to one side houses a bar, a couple of sofas and a rocking chair. The owners will find space upstairs for a mother who needs to change or feed a baby.

LUNCH £5, 2 courses: egg mayonnaise, Welsh lamb hot pot;
DINNER £10: cockled avocado, pork tenderloin, pudding
Children: own menu, half portions

Open 10.30am–4pm & 7–9.30pm Tues-Sat; 12–2pm & 7.30–9.30pm Sun; 7–9.30pm Mon (and closed Mon in winter)
No credit cards Licensed

P – public car park at rear   One high chair only

Goose Eye, West Yorks — map 9

THE TURKEY INN – ☎ Keighley (0535) 681 339.

P

On minor roads two miles from Oakworth.

To find the village follow the B6143 through Oakworth; turn off at the Golden Fleece pub and turn left at the next junction; then you will pick up the signs to Goose Eye.

The pub was originally converted from a row of weavers' cottages, and has been in business for over 200 years. The interior, with its stone floors and heavy beams, has a traditional pubby look and there are various alcoves off the bar were you can sit and enjoy your Turkey bitter, which is brewed over the road. Families are welcome to use a cheerful room off the bar and it has plenty of tables and bench seats.

Off the car park, across the road, is a stretch of lawn with several statuettes posed here and there, including a pair of delightfully smug stone lions.

(12–2pm & 6.30–9pm, not Mon) £2–7: giant Yorkshire puddings, haddock & chips, egg & tuna mayonnaise, steaks, vegetable au gratin
Children: own menu

• Ale – Tetley's and guest beers
P – own car park

Grange, by Errol, Tayside — map 11

FARMHOUSE BUTTERY at WATERYBUTTS – ☎ (08212) 228

R

On a minor road (the B958) south of the A85 between Perth and Dundee.

This traditional stone farmhouse is a couple of miles east of Errol, and you should watch out for the sign to "Scotherbs"; the production of herbs is one of the branches of the business.

The farmhouse is a Victorian building, but it stands on the site of a 12th century monastery. The buttery is in the original dining room of the house and overlooks a large and grassy garden with several picnic tables, and a 14th century dovecote.

The food is all home cooked and of course features many of the fresh herbs, and there is quite a selection of herbal teas. You are welcome to wander around the farm, and it is a good opportunity to replenish your stocks of culinary herbs.

£1–3: carrot & coriander soup, courgette & cheese quiche, open sandwiches, salads
Children: half portions

Open 10.30am–4pm, mid-April to mid-October
No credit cards One high chair only
Unlicensed P – own car park

Grasmere, Cumbria — map 9

TRAVELLER'S REST – ☎ Grasmere (096 65) 378

P

On the A591 north of the village.

This long white pub is reputed to be the oldest building in Grasmere. Flanked by spectacular views of the Langdale Pikes, Helvellyn and the Fairfield Horseshoe it provides a handy resting place for walkers and travellers.

There is a large car park which makes access easy on this busy road. There is lots of space to eat outside either in the beer garden or on the tables at the front of the pub. The interior has its fair share of oak beams and log fires and families can either use the dining room, which has a nice oak dresser, or the games room, which has a pool table and dart board. Facilities can be made available for baby changing: ask the helpful staff.

In summer the pub is open all day, except on Sunday.

(12–2.30pm & 6–9.30pm) £2–8: goulash, chicken supreme, scampi, Cumberland sausage
Children: half portions

• Ale – Courage, John Smith's

BALDRYS – ☎ Grasmere (09665) 301

R

In the Red Lion Square, near the centre of the village.

You'll find this plain and simple tea room close to the centre of Grasmere village. The walls are neatly decorated partly with Laura Ashley wall-paper and partly with pine; and old prints on the walls and lace table-cloths on the tables add to the charm.

Everything is home-made by the owners who even manage to bake their own bread despite having three small children of their own. There is no children's menu as parents are encouraged to let their children choose half portions of the wholefood on offer.

Mothers wishing to breastfeed their babies are encouraged to do so. It is possible to change a baby in the Ladies where paper towels are supplied.

Quiches and cakes are available to 'take away' for anyone wishing to picnic in the glorious countryside. Eighteen varieties of teas are on offer and customers are advised to let the pot brew for at least three minutes. The more adventurous may care to sample a bottle of gooseberry champagne.

£1–4: avocado paté, home pickled herring, chicken & mushroom pancakes, fish pie
Children: half portions

Open 9.30am–5.30pm daily (closed Thursdays from Oct to Whitsun)
No credit cards accepted Licensed
No smoking throughout
P – two public car parks nearby

Grassington, North Yorks — map 9

DEVONSHIRE HOTEL – ☎ Grassington (0756) 752 525

P

On the main square.

This large, stone-built building dominates the attractive cobbled market square of Grassington where tourists flock daily to explore its many shops and attractions.

After browsing in the village's many nooks and crannies a visit to this friendly pub is just the thing to revive the inner man.

There's a cosy central bar area with stone pillars and wooden settles while the functional family room, located just up a couple of stairs, has wood-panelled walls, and plenty of bench seating.

There are a few seats outside on the cobbled front. The pub is open throughout the day (Monday to Saturday) during the summer months.

BAR MEALS (12–2pm & 5.30–9.30pm) £2–6: chicken & chips, ham & eggs, fillet steak, Wharfedale trout
Children: own menu, half portions

• Ale – Younger's P – on square (limited)

Great Baddow, Essex **map 4**

SEABRIGHT'S BARN – ☎ Chelmsford (0245) 478 033.

PR *Just south of Chelmsford off the A12 or B1007.*

This is a very busy and popular pub and restaurant which caters very well for the family market. It is contained within a huge converted barn, where the exposed beams and timber are used to good effect.

It is all very well organised and families can settle down together in the conservatory, with its pleasant cane furniture, in the various lounges or in the restaurant, where plenty of high chairs are made available.

On summery days you can head for the large terrace and the garden. The children can amuse themselves in the play area, well-equipped with swings, climbing frames, nets, a see-saw, etc. There is also a small aviary, some goats and rabbits.

If you need to change a baby there is a wide shelf in the Ladies.

(12–3pm & 6–11pm) £1–10: chicken satay, seafood crepe, steaks, ratatouille, lasagne
Children: own menu, half portions

Access/Visa
• Ale – Adnams, Greene King, Ridley's
P – own car park

Great Bridgford, Staffs **map 6**

THE MILL AT WORSTON – ☎ Seighford (0785) 282 710.

PR *Just off the A5013 West of Stafford. Turn off at the sign for Izaac Walton's cottage.*

This is a marvellous place for a family to visit. It is an interesting building: an early 19th century mill which rises up through its three floors to an attic, and all the old mill machinery and equipment is displayed on the upper floors.

Children will be delighted by the huge grassy garden which has a play area with swings, a slide and a climbing frame. There is an island in the middle of a large pond with a rope bridge across it and another commando-style play area nearby. Throughout the garden boards with wild life information have been set up, and children are encouraged to identify insects, birds, and so on. They can also feed the many swans, ducks and geese.

Benches and tables are scattered about the garden and alongside the little river which bounds the garden.

Families can also use a spacious conservatory at the front of the pub, and there is a museum gallery up a spiral staircase on the first floor.

The bar areas are nicely decorated and furnished with wooden tables and chairs and the old mill wheel is still in place at one end of the bar. Beyond it is a very pleasant restaurant, and there are plenty of high chairs available here.

The Mill is a splendid pub/restaurant which sets out to cater for families and succeeds admirably.

BAR MEALS (12–2pm & 7–10pm) £1–5: jacket potatoes, lasagne, mixed grill, chicken Kiev;
RESTAURANT (12–2pm & 7–10pm) £10: garlic mushrooms, chicken chasseur, pudding
Children: own menu, half portions

Access/Visa P – own car park
• Ale – Flowers, Marston's, Whitbread

Great Budworth, Cheshire map 6

COCK O' BUDWORTH, Warrington Road – ☎ Northwich (0606) 891 287.

P

On the A559 North of Northwich.

This large pub is a real mixture of building styles, but its origins lie back in the 16th century. Long ago a poet called Barnaby drank himself to death here and legend has it that he still haunts the place.

In the past few years or so it has been altered, and there are now two rooms at the back of the pub where families are welcome. A pleasant and bright room with bench seats and several tables leads out to a delightful conservatory with white painted furniture and a tiled floor. It is good to report that it is designated as a no smoking area.

The conservatory leads on to a patio with several bench tables, and there is a large lawned garden, safely enclosed, beyond. It is ringed with trees, has many bench tables, swings and a see-saw.

There is plenty of space in the pub, which is geared up to provide a good range of food. There is a dining room as you enter and another agreeable eating area up the stairs. The bars are on two levels, and there are alcoves here and there. There are several high chairs on the premises.

An excellent family pub.

(11.30am–2.30pm & 6.30–10pm) £1–9: scampi & chips, beef curry, vegetarian stir fry, lamb kebabs
Children: own menu, half portions

• Ale – Greenall's P – own car park

Great Langdale, Nr Ambleside, Cumbria — map 9

STICKLEBARN – ☎ Great Langdale (09667) 3560

P

Off the B5343.

A four mile drive along the valley from Skelwith Bridge is well rewarded by a visit to the Sticklebarn. Nestling below the Langdale Pikes and near to Dungeon Ghyll Waterfall is this old barn made of lakeland slate and local limestone.

The upper floor houses a large cafe with checked tablecloths, pine ceiling with large cross beams, white walls and random stone. These original features are somewhat marred by the juke box and amusement machine, not to mention the inflatable fried egg perching above the self service food counter.

The lower floor is a cheery pub with a large slate patio with plenty of benches and breathtaking views. Tarry a while and enjoy watching hikers scramble across the fells. There is a room off the main bar where families can sit.

Food is available throughout the day from breakfast at 8.30am. The menu is the same in both eating areas and specials are available in the bar.

(8.30am–11pm) £1–9: cheesy baked potato, Cumbrian shepherd's pie, burgers, chicken tikka, lasagne
Children: own menu

• Ale – Ruddles, Webster's P – own car park

Grindleton, Lancs — map 9

THE BUCK INN – ☎ Clitheroe (0200) 41248 — *Pot Luck*

P

One mile off the A59 in the village.

If you have been out walking in the countryside around Pendle Hill, you can revive the inner man at this traditional village pub. A family room was recently added and is pleasant enough with its stone flagged floor

and large patio windows. There is a pool table in here.
Old photographs of village life are on the walls and there is a piano opposite the bar which the landlord says customers are quite welcome to play – providing they know how! In the winter real coal fires add to the atmosphere,and there is a small beer garden for summer days.

(12–2.30pm except Mon & 7–10pm, Thurs-Sat) £1–5: seafood pancake, beef & mushroom casserole , liver & onions, lasagne
Children: half portions

• Ale – John Smith's P – own car park

Groombridge, Kent — map 4

CROWN – ☎ Langton (0892) 864 742

P

On the B2110 west of Tunbridge Wells.
Opposite the village church this very handsome brick and tile-hung 16th century inn stands in a row of houses of the same vintage and overlooks a small triangular village green. You can laze there or sit at the bench tables on the long terrace in front of the pub. There is a rambling garden at the back with a few apple trees.
The interior is splendidly in character with massive black beams, wood panelling, oak settles, and with a big inglenook fireplace in the main bar. A fine collection of pewter tankards and jugs hangs from the ceiling and there are prints and horse brasses on the walls.
Families can use a cosy little room up some stairs; it has wood panelled walls and beams and a collection of old bottles, plates and jugs. An alternative is the spacious and comfortable dining room.
There is quite an emphasis here on food which is all freshly cooked and more interesting than the usual pub food. A traditional Sunday roast is served for around £5 and you can also tuck into a three course evening meal for around £11.

(12–2pm & 7–9.30pm) £1–5: braised lamb, poached salmon, roast duck, plaice & chips, chicken curry
Children: half portions

• Ale – Harvey's, Marston's, Brakspear's and guests
P – own car park No music

Haddington, Lothian **map 11**

WATERSIDE BISTRO & RESTAURANT, Waterside – ☎ Haddington (062 082) 5674.

R

Not far from the town centre, close to the municipal golf course.

This bistro and restaurant was constructed from several 18th century cottages, and the conversion was done skilfully and with style. The restaurant is on the first floor and has antique chairs and tables, lots of interesting pictures and plates on the walls, and fresh flowers on the tables. From here you have a good view of the River Tyne and of St. Mary's Church. The bistro takes up the ground floor, and the prices are aimed more at a family budget.

There is a small garden at the side of the building, with well-kept flower beds, and it overlooks the river.

The Ladies is reasonably spacious if you need to change a baby and is equipped with a chair, two basins and plenty of tissues.

LUNCH £9: fresh mussels, chicken Rossini, pudding or cheese;
DINNER £12: smoked salmon, braised venison, pudding or cheese
Children: half portions

Open 12–2pm & 6.30–10pm Access/AmEx/Diners/Visa
• Ale – Belhaven, Greenmantle P – own car park

Hail Weston, Cambs **map 7**

THE ROYAL OAK – ☎ Huntingdon (0480) 72527.

P

Off the A45 north of St Neots.

A fine 17th century pub in a small village, it is painted white, with dormer windows set in a steeply pitched thatched roof; and cheerful window boxes and baskets of flowers adorn the walls. The inside is very much in keeping with oak pillars and splendid beams and a huge inglenook fireplace – a smart and agreeable bar.

There are two areas where familes are welcome: a small "snug" with a few tables and bar billiards; and a comfortable room at the back of the pub, with a darts board.

The garden is safely enclosed and the large lawn has plenty of tables and chairs with sun umbrellas and a 9 hole putting green. Behind a row of firs, the play area has swings, a slide, a climbing frame and an adventure play unit. There is also a patio area with several tables. The sensible landlord prohibits dogs from the garden.

✕ (12–2pm & 7–9.15pm, not Sun and Mon pm) £1–6: egg mayonnaise, plaice & chips, vegetable curry & rice, rump steak, lasagne
Children: own menu

• Ale – Wells P – own car park

Hallow, Hereford & Worcs — map 6

THE CROWN – ☎ Worcester (0905) 640 408.

P

On the A443 north-west of Worcester.

This sprawling roadside pub is smartly painted cream, and families are welcome to park themselves in the lounge area cum entrance hall. There is plenty of space here and an abundance of tables under the oak beams.

On summer days the garden will surely attract families. It is huge, and the enclosed lawns have plenty of bench tables, a big wooden fort, slides and swings, and a barbecue which comes into play at weekends.

There is a good range of food including a good choice of salads available every day, and a carvery at £8.45 (£4.25 for under 12's). There are two high chairs.

✕ (12–2pm & 5.30–10pm) £1–5: salads, stuffed jacket potatoes, Madras curry & rice, beef Italian
Children: own menu, half portions

• Ale – Younger's P – own car park

Hamble, Hants — map 3

BETH'S, The Quay – ☎ Southampton (0703) 454 314.

R

Go through Hamble till you see the sea.

By the shore in this charming village where the yachting set gather, the restaurant is housed in a delightful two-storey brick house in the Queen Anne style. The well-proportioned lounge has comfortable chairs and a small bar, and on the other side of the entrance there is a small dining room. The main dining areas are upstairs.

A great bonus, especially for families, is the barbecue garden at the back of the restaurant. This opens in summer whenever the weather permits:

every night of the week except Wednesday, and at lunchtimes on Saturday and Sunday. It is enclosed by a brick wall, and much of it is covered by a cheerfully striped awning.

If nappy-changing or breast-feeding is on the agenda, the owners can sometimes offer a spare room upstairs, and will certainly find somewhere for the job to be done.

BARBECUE £1–7: deep fried whitebait, steaks, large prawns, spiced chicken, doner kebab;
RESTAURANT £17: fresh pasta, breast of duck, pudding
Children: half portions

Open 12–2pm & 7–9.30pm Closed 2 weeks in January
Access/AmEx/Diners/Visa Licensed
P – public car parks across road

Happisburgh, Norfolk — map 8

THE HILL HOUSE – ☎ Walcott (0692) 650 004.

P

On the B1159 due east of North Walsham.

The pub stands back from the main road and is a handsome building of 15th century vintage, with tables set out in front. It has its full quota of wooden beams inside, and above all you will find a relaxed and friendly atmosphere in the long and comfortable bar. It has a place in literary history since Sir Arthur Conan Doyle is said to have written "The Dancing Men" while staying here.

There is a functional family room with comfortable dining chairs around the tables; and the toys and a football machine will keep the children amused. At the back of the pub there is a really charming garden, with lots of roses and other flowers, and several tables.

All the food is freshly cooked on the premises, and the restaurant opens every evening.

(12–2pm & 7–9.30pm) £1–15: whitebait, garlic mushrooms, steak & kidney pie, lasagne, moussaka
Children: own menu, half portions

• Ale – Adnams, Greene King, Woodforde's and guests
P – own car park

Harberton, Nr Totnes, Devon — map 1

CHURCH HOUSE INN – ☎ Totnes (0803) 963 707.

P

Off the A381 south of Totnes.

This handsome inn, parts of which date back to the 13th century, is a cheerful sight: a long, two storey, stone building, with baskets of bright flowers offsetting the white-painted walls. It sits alongside a very fine village church and is said to be haunted by a monk.

The interior is very much in character. Heavy black beams hold up the ceiling and there is an open fireplace at one end of the open plan bar and an ancient oak screen at the other. Nice old wooden settles and a varied collection of wooden tables complete the picture.

Behind the old oak screen there is a spacious family room with several large tables and a high chair.

It's a most appealing pub and there is an enterprising choice of food from which to choose.

(12–1.45 & 7–9pm) £1–8: cauliflower au gratin, fresh salmon ploughman's, prawn curry, lamb cutlets, lemon sole
Children: own menu

• Ale – Bass, Courage   P – own car park

Hardington Mandeville, Somerset — map 2

MANDEVILLE ARMS – ☎ West Coker (093 586) 2418.

P

Off the A30 between Crewkerne and Yeovil.

This pub has been enlarged and completely refurbished and very smart and comfortable it looks. The use of genuine old wooden beams lends it considerable character.

A new family room and restaurant has been built and the landlord likes the parents to stay with their children, and not to leave them to their own devices while they prop up the bar.

There is a delightful garden at the front of the pub. It is surrounded by a small stone wall and looks very cheerful with its collection of sun umbrellas and colourful flowers.

Food is served every day from a wide-ranging and enterprising bar menu, and in the winter a three-course Sunday lunch is available for around £6.

(12–1.45pm & 7.30–10pm) £1–9: scallops provencale, spicy pork in ginger, chilli Mexicana, lamb curry, steaks, vegetable gratin
Children: own menu, half portions

• Ale – Butcombe, Flowers, Marston's
P – own car park

Harlech, Gwynedd **map 5**

PLAS RESTAURANT, High Street – ☎ Harlech (0766) 780 204.

R

In the town centre.

A smart and pleasant café in what was once an inn and then the summer house of the Earl of Winchelsea. His second son (later to be played by Robert Redford in Out of Africa) probably ran in and out with his bucket and spade. The exterior is stone, freshly white painted with attractive awnings over the bow windows.

The restaurant stretches the full width of the building, clean and cool with cream walls and seating about forty people. Beyond this is verandah which has been enclosed in glass and has cane and pine furniture and a lovely display of plants and flowers. From here, and from the delightful garden, you have views of the bay, the golf course and the famous and very imposing castle.

There is a craft shop attached to the café.

(9am–8.30pm) £1–7: herring salad, plaice & chips, lasagne, sirloin steak
Children: own menu, half portions

Closed early Nov to mid-Mar   Access/Visa
Licensed   P – public car parks

Places included in the Guide must offer the following basic facilities:
Pubs – a separate area or room for families where alcohol is not served;
Restaurants – high chairs and special menus/reduced portions.

Harome, Nr Helmsley, North Yorks **map 10**

STAR INN – ☎ Helmsley (0439) 70397.

P *Off the A170 south east of Helmsley.*

This fine old building with its steep thatched roof dates back to the 16th century and has an interior to prove it – oak beams and low ceilings hung with old glass bottles, dark wooden tables and padded settles; in short all the characteristics of a classic English hostelry.

The attractive dining room, with an extraordinarily low ceiling, can be used by families; but even better for children is the coffee lounge at the top of the building. There are plenty of board games to amuse them.

In addition there is a delightful garden with several fruit trees at the rear of the pub, or you can sit at the front on the terrace. There is an enterprising and wide-ranging menu, which includes an excellent choice of vegetarian dishes, and a good selection of real ales.

(12–2.15pm & 7–9.30pm) £2–4: best end of lamb, chicken en croute, hot leek & walnut parcels, steak & oyster pie, nutty ham

Children: half portions

• Ale – Bateman's, Timothy Taylor's, Tetley, Theakston's

P – own car park

Harrogate, North Yorks map 10

BETTYS CAFÉ TEAROOMS, 1 Parliament Street – ☎ Harrogate (0423) 502 746.

R

Off the A61 near the town centre and opposite Montpellier Gardens.

This is certainly not a place to be missed if you have children and are visiting the decidedly upmarket shopping centre in Harrogate. It is a rare opportunity for parents of young children to relax in a stylish, high quality eating establishment. You can enjoy one of the café's delicious savoury snacks including the well-known rarebits, or take your pick from one of the many freshly made cakes.

The Harrogate Bettys gives a terrific welcome to families; it provides excellent service and an interesting children's menu including double decker sandwiches, Bettys clown or Bettys banana boat.

Like the other cafés in the Bettys chain (York, Ilkley and Northallerton), the Harrogate café offers unbeatable facilities for mothers and babies; changing mats, playpen, potties, bibs and beakers are all made available, plus a great number of high chairs.

The kitchens will also supply a range of baby foods. It is also worth noting that Bettys has no objection to discreet breast feeding in the restaurant – a policy which all breast feeding mums will surely welcome.

£1–7: scrambled eggs with smoked salmon, haddock & prawns au gratin, rarebits, omelettes, rosti with bacon
Children: own menu, half portions

Open 9am–9pm all week
Access/Visa Live piano music
Half the restaurant is no smoking Licensed
P – street parking

Harwich, Essex map 4

THE PIER AT HARWICH, The Quay – ☎ Harwich (0255) 241 212.

R

If you are catching a boat from Harwich, give yourself enough time to have a meal at this appealing fish restaurant: follow the signs for the Quay and there it is.

The attractive listed building, which dates from 1874, houses two restaurants, both brightly decorated, and the one upstairs, with a wonderful view of the sea, is the more expensive. The 'Ha'penny Pier' downstairs, however, is perhaps more suited to the family budget – a main course of fish and chips is around £5 and a three-course children's menu of soup, fish and chips and ice-cream costs just under £4. This offers excellent value.

✕ HA'PENNY PIER (12–2pm & 6–9.30pm) £1–6: Pier haddie, whitebait, Ha'penny pie, lasagne;
LUNCH (12–2pm) £9, 2 courses: pork & chicken liver terrine, escalope of halibut & salmon;
DINNER (6–9.30pm) £20: fresh lobster bisque, steamed fillet of sea bass, pudding or cheese
Children: own menu, half portions

Closed Xmas Day evening & Boxing Day Access/Visa
• Ale – Adnams P – own car park

Also recommended in the Family Welcome Accommodation Guide.

Haskayne, Lancs map 6

THE SHIP INN – ☎ *Halsall (0704) 840 572.*

P

Turn off the A5147 opposite Haskayne signpost.
If you are heading for Southport or the coast you could break your journey at this large white-walled pub which really caters for families.
The family room is spacious and has loads of tables and chairs and rather a lot of amusement machines. Large patio windows open on to a play area full of swings, slides, a Wendy house and a large play boat.
The main rooms of the pub are comfortable and smartly furnished, with naval artefacts much in evidence, model ships, life belts, brass instruments and so on.
Another garden overlooks the Leeds/Liverpool Canal, which is mostly used now by pleasure boats. The menu is inexpensive and concentrates on traditional pub food.

✕ (12–2pm & 5.30–9.30pm) £1–3: steak pudding, gammon & chips, hot pot pie, haddock & chips
Children: own menu

P – own car park

Hatherleigh, Devon — map 1

GEORGE HOTEL, Market Street – ☎ Okehampton (0837) 810 454.

P

On the A386 in the village (on a bend).

This delightful 15th century coaching inn began life as a monk's retreat and is a splendid, rambling pub whose blackened wooden beams and huge open fireplaces attest to the great age of the place. The family room, which is off the main bar, is very much in character, with wooden beams and solid oak tables. It is spacious and comfortable, but why on earth have the licensees seen fit to put a pool table in there. From our observations, this inevitably seems to attract men with sleeveless T-shirts, which don't quite cover their lager bellies.

There are bench tables at the back of the pub and a swimming pool, which is opened during the summer months.

The pub is open throughout the day on Monday and Tuesday, which are market days.

(12–2pm & 6.30–9pm) £2–7: whitebait, George 'fry up', chicken & mushroom pie, spinach & mushroom roulade, steaks
Children: half portions

• Ale – Bass, Greene King, Wadworth's
P – own car park through arch

Hatton, Nr Warwick, Warwicks — map 7

THE COUNTRY CAFE, Hatton Craft Centre – ☎ Claverdon (092 684) 3350.

R

A couple of miles north west of Warwick off the A41. Look for the sign.

The thriving Hatton Craft Centre has many attractions including a garden centre, a farm shop, a pick-your-own fruit park, and a large picnic area. The craft shops are numerous and include a toy shop, and special events (clay pigeon shoots, sheep shearing, archery and so on) are held through the summer.

The coffee shop is housed in a spacious converted barn and is nicely furnished with wooden chairs and tables. The patio overlooks a really splendid play area with a rope bridge, a wooden pirate ship, etc, and there is plenty of space for children to run. Very sensibly the owners prohibit dogs from this area.

There is a baby changing table in the disabled toilet area.

£1–4: soup, filled jacket potatoes, salads, lasagne
Children: small portions

Open 9am–5.30pm Closed Xmas day to end January
No credit cards   No smoking
One high chair only   Unlicensed
P – ample

Hay-on-Wye, Powys map 2

THE GRANARY – ☎ Hay-on-Wye (0497) 820 790.

R

The café is situated near the clock tower in this appealing town, whose position on the borders of England and Wales has ensured more than its fair share of bloody mayhem over the centuries. It's quite peaceful now and the town has become a notable centre for second-hand books.

The restaurant certainly was a granary, as the machinery and pulleys which are still in place will confirm. It's a relaxed and welcoming place, with an excellent choice of freshly cooked food available, including an extensive vegetarian menu.

If you need to change or feed a baby, there is an upstairs room with a table and a chair.

£1–4: vegetable soup, aubergine paté, houmous and pitta bread, rogan josh, steak & kidney pie
Children: half portions

Open each day 10am–5pm, to 9pm during Easter and summer holidays
Closed Xmas Day   Access/Visa
• Ale – Bass, Hancock's
P – plenty of street parking except Market Day (Thursday)

Henborough Post, Nr Blackawton, Devon map 1

SPORTSMANS ARMS – ☎ Blackawton (080 421) 231.

P

On the B3207 west of Dartmouth.

You cannot miss this large roadside pub, cream painted with dark brown shutters, near Dartmouth. Tubs and baskets of flowers enliven the front of the pub, and there is also a terrace running across its width.

Inside there are two spacious and cheerfully decorated bars, with a couple of open fireplaces, and a pleasant dining room. There is also plenty of space in the family room, which is up some stairs at the side of the pub. It is a functional room, with several tables, a blackboard for children to scribble on and two high chairs.

A good sized enclosed garden is alongside the pub, with bench tables on the lawn, a scattering of bright flowers, and some climbing frames for the children.

The pub is open all day throughout the summer, and food is available at all times, apart from an occasional break of half an hour.

✕ (12–10pm) £1–7: lemon sole, cauliflower tuna, moussaka, rump steak
Children: own menu, half portions

• Ale – Bass, Flowers P – ample

Hessenford, Cornwall — map 1

COPLEY ARMS – ☎ Hessenford (050 34) 209.

P

On the A387.

You will find this smart looking pub at a point midway between St Germans and Looe. The old stones of the facade are covered in creeper and roses, with many tubs of bright flowers adding to the fun.

The River Seaton runs through the grounds of the pub and you can sit on the bench tables alongside the water. Alongside there is a sizeable play area with swings, a see-saw, a slide and some climbing frames.

The long and spacious lounge bar has plenty of tables and chairs, and booths with wooden settles. There are prints on the walls and an iron stove. The family room is comfortable and opens on to the patio area at the side of the pub. We noticed a couple of high chairs in the family room, and a buffet is also set up in there.

The pub is open throughout the day during the summer months.

✕ (12–1.45pm & 7–9.30pm) £1–7: fisherman's pie, moussaka, Mexican chicken, cod & chips, curry
Children: own menu

• Ale – Hicks, Tinner's P – own car park

Hevingham, Norfolk — map 8

MARSHAM ARMS, Holt Road – ☎ Hevingham (0605) 48268.

P

On the B1149 north of Norwich.

This appealing inn, smartly decorated under its tiled roof, stands in the countryside about seven miles from Norwich and was originally a hostel for farm labourers, and built in the 19th century. The wooden beams and large open fireplace survive from the original design.

The building has been extended over the years and especially to provide better facilities for families who are welcome to use a spacious and nicely furnished room away from the bar. It is good to report that it is a no smoking area.

An alternative, when the sun shines, is the beer garden; a paved terrace with garden furniture and wooden benches. Alongside there is a children's play area, which is surrounded by trees.

There is a good choice of real ales at the Marsham Arms and of bar food, and there is also a spacious restaurant with several high chairs provided.

(12–2pm & 6–10pm) £1–9: lasagne, cod bake, beef pie, cold buffet, steaks
Children: own menu, half portions

• Ale – Adnams, Bass, Greene King, Woodforde's
P – own car park

Also recommended in the Family Welcome Accommodation Guide.

Hewish, Nr Weston-super-Mare, Avon — map 2

THE FULL QUART – ☎ Yatton (0934) 833 077.

P

On the A370 east of junction 21 of the M5.

Tubs of colourful flowers brighten the front of this large, white-washed roadside inn, and inside the cosy atmosphere has been kept by dint of the low beamed ceilings, stone fireplaces, wooden settles and copper and brass artefacts on the walls.

There is a separate room set aside for families, and quite a range of food to choose from, including a Jolly Roger menu at 99p for under 7's. A traditional Sunday lunch is served at just under £6 for adults (£3.75 for children).

On summer days the spacious garden is a pleasant place to sit, with plenty of tables on the wide lawn. A sand pit and a climbing frame are in place for the children.

(12–2.30pm & 6.30–10pm) £1–9: spare ribs, mixed grill, steaks, plaice, chicken Cordon Bleu.
Children: own menu

• Ale – Bass, Butcombe, Flowers
P – own car park

Hexham, Northumberland **map 9**

BLINKERS COFFEE HOUSE, The Old Grammar School Stables, Hallgate – ☎ Hexham (0434) 606 656.

R

Next to the Old Hexham Gaol, now a museum with a tourist information centre attached.

The restaurant is housed in what used to be an old stable, and it has been nicely renovated. You will receive a friendly welcome from the mother and daughter who own the place, and there is a pleasant atmosphere even if the tables are quite close together.

The enclosed patio area relieves the pressure a bit, and is very safe for children. The owners are content for mothers who need to change or feed a baby to use the staff room.

£1–3: apple & cheese & prawn bowl, filled jacket potatoes, ham & peach salad, savoury vol au vents
Children: small portions

Open 9.30am–5pm Mon to Sat Unlicensed
One high chair only P – public nearby

Highcliffe, Nr Christchurch, Dorset **map 3**

HINTON OAK – ☎ Highcliffe (0425) 271 040.

P

On the A337 east of Christchurch.

This large, rambling pub is really what used to be called a roadhouse, and the interior has been sympathetically converted by the owners, Bass. Don't be put off by the large amusement machine which confronts you as you enter.

The bar is broken up into alcoves and separate sitting areas, and the advantage for families is the presence of a very large conservatory at the back of the pub.

It is well decorated with padded cane furniture and there is a fine display of hanging and standing plants and palm trees. Adjoining the conservatory there is a special children's lavatory and it contains a changing mat. The conservatory overlooks an enclosed garden which has a play unit with a slide, a climbing frame, etc.

(12–2pm & 7–9pm) £1–8: leek & bacon pie, swordfish steak, lentil crumble, tricolour pasta, plaice & chips
Children: small portions

• Ale – Bass P – own car park

Higher Burwardsley, Cheshire **map 6**

PHEASANT INN – ☎ Tattenhall (0829) 70434.

P

Off the A534 or A41 west of Nantwich.

This lovely old pub, built in the 17th century, is part sandstone and part half-timbered and is about ten miles from Chester. It sits on the Peckforton Hills and you have splendid views across Cheshire to Wales. The bar is a pleasant place to be, with its low ceilings and exposed beams and with lots of brass and china decorating the walls. It is notable also for a log fire which is open on two sides.

There is a small family room or sun room, which was once a part of the

yard and has a stone-flagged floor, a couple of tables, a settle and some chairs. An alternative at lunchtimes only is the dining room, a pleasant room with cream walls and oak beams, and by now a conservatory should also be in use. On warmer days you can sit at the bench tables on a large grassy area alongside the pub and enjoy the views, which will also include the landlord's Highland cattle in the adjoining fields.

(12–2.30pm & 7–9.30pm) £2–6: game pie & salad, moussaka, smoked salmon, chicken & Stilton roulades, sirloin steak
Children: half portions

• Ale – Bass P – own car park

Holmfirth, West Yorks map 6

THE WRINKLED STOCKING – ☎ Huddersfield (0484) 681408.

R

On the main road through the town.

This small town is busily cashing in on its fame as the location for "Last of the Summer Wine" so it's not difficult to understand why they chose such an odd name for this small tea room which is actually next door to Norah Batty's cottage.

You'll certainly enjoy half an hour in this pleasant, airy place, which is brightly decorated and has attractive cream furniture. The matching crockery adds that little touch as well. Tea, coffee and snacks are on the go all day and you can also get more substantial meals such as salads and quiches. There is a good choice of teas, ranging from Yorkshire to Lapsang Souchong.

Mothers will find the Ladies comfortable and spacious enough to change or breastfeed a baby, since there is a handy ledge and also a chair.

There is a gift shop on the ground floor underneath the tea room.

£1–4: cream teas, salads, fresh sandwiches
Children: smaller portions

Open 9.45am–5.30pm Closed at Xmas
One high chair only No credit cards
P – on street Unlicensed

Please let us have reports – good or bad – on any establishments listed in the Guide as soon as possible after your visit.

Holne, Devon — map 1

OLD FORGE – ☎ Poundsgate (036 43) 351.

R

Holne is well-signposted off the A38 near Ashburton. The Old Forge is by the church.

You will find this attractive café sitting in front of the village church. The walls of the Old Forge are crisply painted white and offset the black beams on the ceiling. The bellows and anvil which were used by the last smith, Fred Pearse, are still here.

When we called in one cold Spring day it was a pleasure to sit by the roaring fire; and families receive a warm welcome here and food is available throughout the day. It's virtually all home made, too, and it's good to report that chips are emphatically not on the menu. The children have a good range of snacks from which to choose.

At the front of the old Forge there are some bench tables in the courtyard and some of these are under a pretty wooden canopy which is hung with flowers.

The café also has some local crafts for sale.

£1–4: full breakfast, quiche & salad, burgers, jacket potatoes, cream tea

Open 11am–6pm every day Easter to end-Sept; 1–5pm Oct; 2–5pm Sat & Sun in Nov
Closed Nov-Mar No credit cards accepted
Unlicensed No music
P – own car park

Hopton Wafers, Nr Cleobury Mortimer, Shropshire — map 6

CROWN INN – ☎ Cleobury Mortimer (0299) 270 372

P

On the A4117 west of Cleobury Mortimer.

It is as ever a delightful surprise to find this old stone inn, covered in Virginia creeper, and nestling so close to the famous Clee Hill, from where you have a marvellous view of the shires rolling beyond, although the beacons burn no longer.

The family room is spacious and smart with plenty of tables and comfortable chairs. For summer days there are two patios, and a lovely country garden with a sloping lawn which is edged by a small brook. All very relaxing.

The food is enterprising and almost all home-made; and, apart from the

excellent choice of bar snacks, the restaurant offers a full lunch and dinner menu, including a Sunday lunch at around £9.

BAR SNACKS (12–2pm & 7–10pm) £2–8: chicken curry Madras, plaice & chips, lasagne, sirloin steak
Children: own menu, half portions

• Ale – Flowers, Jolly Roger, Wadworth, Wood's
P – own car park

Horringer, Suffolk — map 8

BEEHIVE – ☎ Horringer (028 488) 260

P

On the A143, just south of Bury St Edmunds.

The simple flintstone front of this 18th century pub gives no clue to the roominess of the interior. There are several rooms, pleasantly intimate under the low ceilings, gathered around a central bar area; they include two delightful small rooms at one side, with wood panelling and excellent furniture, and families with children are welcome there.

The food is very enterprising, and is available at every session except Sunday evening. If the weather is warm you might enjoy the food on the smartly furnished patio, or on the lawn alongside. These areas are floodlit in the evenings.

(12–2pm & 7–9.30pm, not Sun pm) £1–7: scrambled egg with smoked salmon, taramasalata with pitta bread, local venison steak, Arbroath smokies
Children: half portions

• Ale – Greene King P – own car park

Howgate, Nr Penicuik, Lothian — map 11

OLD HOWGATE INN – ☎ Penicuik (0968) 74244

P

On the B7026 by the A6094 turning.

Rebuilt in 1743 to serve the Edinburgh to Dumfries coaches, this attractive pub has a lovely fresh feel to it rare in such an old building.

Families can use two delightful low-ceilinged rooms, which are fairly small and are mainly used by customers for pre-meal drinks and post-meal coffees. The restaurant can also be used, and it is an unusual one since it specialises in smorrebrod – Danish open sandwiches – and there are over fifty varieties.

A small back garden leads off the restaurant, and there is a slide for the children. There is one high chair on the premises; the Ladies has a table and a stool, so a baby can be changed or fed.

(11.30am–2.30pm & 6–10pm) £1–5: smorrebrod – Danish herring, smoked eel with scrambled eggs, chicken liver & brandy paté, ham, chicken with asparagus
Children: half portions

Closed Xmas and New Year's Day
• Ale – McEwan's, Theakston, Belhaven and guests
P – own car park No music

BURNSIDE – ☎ Penicuik (0968) 78341.

R

On the A701 between Howgate and Leadburn.

The restaurant and bistro is housed in a converted barn, which was once a creamery. It's an appealing building and has the advantage of an attractive setting; you can sit on the large paved patio at the side of the restaurant and look across the car park to a wood with a burn running through it.

The interior of the restaurant is simple and comfortable, and there is a wide range of food on offer, and even some real ale to sample.

Baby changing facilities are not, unfortunately, provided. You must do the best you can in the Ladies.

£1–8: smoked haddock mousse, fresh salmon en croute, chicken diablo, beef curry, vegetarian crepe Mornay
Children: half portions

Open 11.30am–10pm
• Ale – Belhaven, Theakston's P – own car park

Hurdlow, Nr Buxton, Derbys — map 6

BULL I' THE THORN – ☎ Longnor (0298) 85348

P

On the A515 about five miles south of Buxton.

This fine old pub sits in the expansive Derbyshire countryside on the old Roman road between Buxton and Ashbourne. Once a farmhouse, the building became a pub in the 15th century. On a massive beam over the

entrance are three marvellous wood carvings – the eponymous bull in the thorn bush, an eagle and some hounds. The bar is superb: a long room with a stone-flagged floor, wood-panelled walls, a wonderfully carved upright chair, wooden settles and a grandfather clock.

The children's room at the back is unpretentious but cheerful and it opens on to a paved terrace and a lovely, big lawn encompassed by a stone wall. There is a swing here too. During the summer a big function room is also opened for the use of families.

The food is served at all times and is good value; children's meals cost £1.

(11.30am–2pm & 6.30–9.30pm) £1–5: cottage pie, sirloin steak, roast beef, plaice & chips
Children: own menu, half portions

• Ale – Robinson's P – own car park

Never use an out-of-date Guide. Many places are excluded because their standards have dropped or their policies towards families have changed. Many new establishments are added each year.

Hurn, Nr Bournemouth, Dorset map 2

AVON CAUSEWAY HOTEL – ☎ Christchurch (0202) 482 714

P

At the Hurn roundabout on the B3073 follow signs to Avon and Sopley. This interesting pub was made out of a railway station on the Bournemouth line, and a large yellow hand will point your way to it off the road. You drive through the railway gates and across the huge car park and there it is: a smartly painted building with a part of the old platform still attached. White fencing, a canopy, hanging flower baskets, old platform seats and a Pullman carriage which is now a restaurant complete the picture.

The open plan bar is large and bright, with comfortable seating and a fine selection of railway memorabilia on the walls. The family room has a separate entrance and there is certainly no feeling of travelling second class. It is very smartly decorated, and has padded furniture, a tiled floor and masses of greenery including imitation coconut trees. Great fun. The room also has its own toilet areas.

French windows lead out to a lawn and a patio and there is a play area which includes a wooden train and an assault course.

(12–2pm & 6.15–9.30pm) £1–8: smoked salmon, grilled trout, mixed grill, Welsh rarebit, steaks
Children: own menu

• Ale – Eldridge Pope, Marston's, Ringwood, Wadworth's
P – own car park

Hurst Green, Lancs map 9

WHITEHALL, Warren Fold/Avenue Road – ☎ Stonyhurst (025 486) 456

R

Turn off at the Shireburn Arms Hotel on the B6243 and onto Warren Fold.

An attractive stone building houses this restaurant and craft centre. The small front patio has a stone table with flagged seats and inside the traditional decor of wooden tables and stone floor has much charm. The freshly prepared food is inexpensive and the owner will provide feeding and changing facilities for babies.

The craft centre is on the upper floor where painting classes are also run by a local artist and informal classes about the local countryside are regular features.

(11am–5.30pm) £1–5: sandwiches, Hungarian lamb casserole, pizza, lasagne
Children: half portions

Closed every Mon & Tues and all Jan No music
Unlicensed No credit cards
P – on street

Huxley, Nr Tarporley, Cheshire map 6

FARMERS ARMS – ☎ *Huxley (0829) 781 342*

P *West of Tarporley, and can be reached from the A51 or A41.*

The pub is housed in a long and low brick building, which is painted black and white and has an attractive little porch. It has been many things in the past: a Post Office, butcher's shop, and even, it is claimed, a hospital during the Civil War.

Inside you will find old beams supporting the ceilings and, since some rebuilding was done, some new ones. Brasses both ancient and modern hang on the walls. Families are welcome in two rooms; both have low-beamed ceilings and are cheerfully decorated, and offer comfortable seating. There is a high chair available.

Outside there is a small patio, and a lawned garden with rustic furniture plus a children's play area with swings, climbing frame and a see-saw. There is a barbecue area and you can even arrange to take your own food along for a family barbecue.

(12–2pm & 6–9.30pm) £1–7: plaice & chips, chicken curry, lasagne, vegetarian moussaka, steaks
Children: own menu

• Ale – Greenall P – own car park

Ickham, Kent map 4

DUKE WILLIAM – ☎ *Canterbury (0227) 721 308.*

P *Off the A257 about five miles east of Canterbury.*

Set in a pleasant village, this roomy and attractive 17th century pub has a cheerful air, and the style is set by the ebullient and friendly landlord who was a professional chef for twenty years or so, and produces a good choice of freshly cooked dishes, both at the bar and in the spacious restaurant. Families can take advantage of a room at the back of the pub, which leads out to a delightful lawned garden, crowded with plants and flowers, or of the conservatory which was built last year and is a no smoking area. To one side is a patio and some swings; and there is more patio with goldfish ponds at the back, and this is all lit up on summer evenings. From here you look out on rolling farmland.

(12–2pm & 7–10pm, not Sun pm or Mon am) £1–5: Duke William brunch, plaice & chips, crab salad, Lincolnshire sausage, chilli con carne
Children: small portions

• Ale – Adnams, Fuller's, Shepherd Neame, Young's and guests
P – ample street parking

Ilkley, West Yorks **map 9**

BETTYS CAFÉ TEAROOMS, 34 The Grove – ☎ Ilkley (0943) 608 029.

R

In the town centre.

Bettys has a deserved reputation for its style, excellent service and exceptional quality.

Like the other Bettys (in Harrogate, York and Northallerton) the Ilkley tearooms welcomes families, provides an interesting children's menu and superb mother and baby facilities, with a playpen, changing mat and chair in the Ladies and six high chairs in the restaurant.

The restaurant has the atmosphere of a bygone age, with its palms and delightful display of teapots. Like the others in the chain, it offers a splendid selection of teas and coffee, a wide choice of mouth- watering cakes, chocolates, scones and muffins all of which are freshly prepared on the premises.

£1–4: rarebits, scrambled eggs with smoked salmon, cheese & herb paté, haddock & chips, bacon muffins
Children: own menu, half portions

Open 9am–7pm Mon-Thurs, 9am–9pm Fri-Sun
Access/Visa Licensed
No smoking in most of café P – public car park at rear

Ingliston, Nr Edinburgh, Lothian — map 11

NORTON TAVERN – ☎ Ingliston (031) 333 1275.

R

On the A8 west of Edinburgh.

As you travel along the main road look out for the Norton House Hotel, and you will find the pub and restaurant right next door. It has been constructed in the old stables, and many of the original features have been retained: for example the old stalls have been incorporated into the restaurant area.

The conversion has been carried out with some style; there are interesting pictures on the oak-panelled walls and a splendid stone fireplace, oak tables and chairs and wooden settles. The large windows look out to the patio. A large walled garden has plenty of bench tables and a play area for the children.

Although the restaurant has several high chairs, there are no facilities for baby changing.

The menu has an American theme, from 'Kentucky Derby' to 'Mississippi Mud Pie'.

This is a pleasant pub and restaurant which sets out to welcome and provide for the whole family. Like many Scottish pubs it is open all day from Monday to Saturday and provides food at all times.

✕ (12–9.45pm) £1–6: prawn & sweetcorn parcels, burgers, supreme of chicken, sirloin steak, lamb kebabs
Children: half portions

Access/AmEx/Diners/Visa
P – own car park

Ironbridge, Shropshire — map 6

THE MALTHOUSE, The Wharfage – ☎ Ironbridge (095 245) 3712.
Pot Luck

R

Main road out of Ironbridge towards Shrewsbury.

The pub, with its cream-painted brick and black woodwork, overlooks the river from the main street of the town, well-known for the Ironbridge Gorge Museum.

The interior of the pub is spacious and comfortable – but without a family room – so we are highlighting the Buttery as a good place for a family meal. The large room offers self-service food from a large counter at one end, and the food is all home-made and is offered at reasonable prices.

There are a few tables outside the pub. The Ladies is spacious and you could change a baby there.

(12–2.30pm & 7–10pm) £1–4: garlic mushrooms, plaice & chips, cold buffet, steak & mushroom pie.
Children: half portions

Open all year Access/Visa
• Ale – Davenport's , Wem P – own car park

Keenthorne, Somerset map 2

APPLE TREE INN – ☎ Nether Stowey (0278) 733 238.

R

On the A39 west of Bridgwater.

This cream-painted building has a splendid sign on its walls, and a cheerful aspect helped by the stretch of lawned garden with parasols over the tables. There is also a small patio at the side, and a grassy area at the back with some swings.

The restaurant itself is comfortable and nicely decorated, and there is another area set up for teas and snacks, and this looks through wide windows on to the patio.

Help can normally be offered to a mother wishing to feed or change a baby; for example a vacant bedroom might be made available.

BAR SNACKS (12–2pm & 6.30–9pm) £2–9: trout paté, seafood Mornay, lemon sole, steaks;
DINNER (6.30–9.30pm) £11: whitebait, roast rack of lamb, pudding or cheese
Children: own menu, half portions

Open all year Access/AmEx/Visa
Licensed P – own car park

Keeston, Nr Haverfordwest Dyfed map 5

KEESTON KITCHEN – ☎ Camrose (0437) 710 440.

R

On the main A487 – not in the village.

Converted from an old farm cottage, this roadside restaurant is cosy and welcoming and has a little sheltered terrace by the front door. Coffee is served from about 10.30am and a good selection of reasonably priced snacks is served at lunchtime. There's plenty to suit a young palate and, if required, half portions are available as they are for dinner, although the owners prefer that the dining room is clear of smaller children in the evenings, so that the adults can enjoy themselves.

The owners can find some space in their own accommodation where a mother could feed or change a baby.

The owners now have two self-catering flats available in the house next door, and these can be booked for single nights as well as longer periods.

LUNCH (12–2pm) £1–5: Welsh rarebit, vegetarian moussaka, Indian samosas & salad, sweet & sour pork, salade Nicoise;
DINNER (7–9.30pm) £12: prawn cocktail, Turkish lamb kebab, banana split
Children: own menu, half portions

Access/Visa • Ale – Bass
P – own small car park

Kendal, Cumbria — map 9

FLAVOURS OF KENDAL, 3 Stramongate – ☎ Kendal (0539) 720 341.

R

In one of the main streets.

This refreshing restaurant decorated in shades of green with scatterings of flowers painted on the walls is open every day. Access with a push chair is easy and mothers may feed their babies in the booths with high backed settles. There is a table in the Ladies for changing nappies.

All the food is home made and the many delights are listed on the blackboard featuring a large proportion of vegetarian dishes. Part of the restaurant is non smoking.

A take away service for packed picnics, pizzas and quiches is available.

£1–5: cauliflower bake, bean & vegetable casserole, chicken in lime, pizza
Children: own menu, small portions

Open 9am–8.30pm, June to October; 9am–4.30pm otherwise
P – public car park nearby Licensed

NUTTERS COFFEE HOUSE, Yard 11, Stramongate – ☎ Kendal (0539) 25135.

R

Off Stramongate near Market Square.

Down from the Market Square tucked away in a small yard off Stramongate is this genuine 17th century building. It is now an eating house serving home made food from local suppliers using organic produce wherever possible.

The lower floor hints of a bygone age with an old black cooking range and free standing beams supporting the second eating area. The polished staircase and floor enhances the exposed stonework.

You can get full meals all day here and there are also snacks, cakes, and a constant supply of tea and freshly ground coffee.

There's a chair in the Ladies if you need to change a baby.

£1–3: soup, steak & kidney pie, chicken paté with apple sauce, baked potatoes with various fillings
Children: half portions

Open 10am–6pm (later on Fri & Sat) Closed Sunday
No credit cards No smoking upstairs
Licensed One high chair only
P – nearby car park

Kentallen, Highland **map 12**

THE HOLLY TREE – ☎ Duror (063 174) 292.

R

On the A828 three miles south of Ballachulish Bridge.

This restaurant and hotel has a unsurpassed position on the shore of Loch Linnhe with beautiful views across the water and to the mountains of Ardgow beyond. The grounds extend alongside the loch and it is a lovely place to relax in peace and tranquillity.

The restaurant was created from a railway station which was built at the turn of the century and many of the original features, which leaned heavily on the Art Nouveau style, have been retained

You can sit in the dining room and have the same unrivalled views of the loch, and the floor at the back half of the room has been raised so that other guests do not miss out on the scenery.

Alasdair and Jane Robertson have achieved an excellent reputation for their restaurant. A part of that success is the use of fresh local produce: beef, lamb and venison, excellent seafood, and herbs and salad from the garden.

LUNCH (12.30–2pm) £14: cottage cheese & pineapple salad, fillet of local sole, chocolate rum mousse;
DINNER (7.30–9.30pm) £22: peach & Stilton salad, soup, roast loin of lamb, sticky toffee pudding
Children: own menu, half portions

Open all year except Xmas & New Year
Acess/AmEx/Visa licensed
No smoking in dining room P – own car park

Also recommended in the Family Welcome Accommodation Guide.

Kildrummy, by Alford, Grampian map 12

THE MOSSAT SHOP & RESTAURANT – ☎ Kildrummy (09755) 71355.

R

On the A97 where it meets the A944.

This is a well designed little craft shop and café complex of the sort which is so welcome in Scotland. The dining room is simply and attractive decorated and has pretty tablecloths and curtains.

The owners offer splendid value for money, and a fair choice of food, high teas for example which include a hot dish plus tea, toast, scones and cakes – and all for around £4. Terrific value. Baby changing is difficult – but might be done in the Ladies.

The shop sells some lovely locally-made goods – superior to the normal run of 'craft' goods. This is a good place to stop in an area of great beauty.

£1–7: tuna mayonnaise, fried fish, mixed grill, liver & onions, sirloin steak
Children: half portions

Open 10am–6.30pm, Easter to November; weekends only in winter. Closed in January
Access/Visa Licensed
P – own car park

Killearn, Central **map 11**

OLD MILL INN – ☎ Killearn (0360) 50001.

P

On the A875.

From the road this pub looks like a row of cottages, but it was a weaving mill and was built in 1774. There is the feeling of a genuine pub here, reinforced by the comfortable interior with dark wooden tables and chairs, a complex web of beams across the ceiling, a huge stone chimney with a wood-burning stove, and the original oil paintings on the walls.

Families are welcome to use a large room separated from the bar area by some double doors. This room gives on to the patio and the garden, which has upturned barrels as tables and tree stumps to sit on.

The pub is open all day, 11am to 11pm from Monday to Friday, and until midnight at the weekend.

(12–2pm & 6–9pm; 12–9pm Sat & Sun) £1–4: scampi, chicken & chips, omelettes, pizzas, gammon steak
Children: own menu

P – own car park

Kilmahog, by Callander, Central — map 11

LADE INN – ☎ Callander (0877) 30152.

P

On the A821 one mile north of Callander.

Just outside the attractive town of Callander you will find this agreeable country pub. It is spacious inside, with plenty of seating, and families are welcome to use a light and airy room which is down a few steps from the main pub and looks directly out to the garden. This has several tables and is bordered with shrubs, tubs of flowers, a pretty little rockery and a fountain. A congenial place to be on a summer day.

You will receive a friendly welcome from the staff and the home-made food is freshly cooked, served in hearty portions and is very good value. Just the thing to set you up either before or after exploring the Trossachs. There is a high chair on the premises.

(12–2pm & 5.30–9pm, 12–9pm Sunday) £1–7: platter of prawns, haddock, chicken & mushroom pancake, lasagne, sirloin steak
Children: half portions

• Ale – Ruddles, Webster's   P – own car park

Kincraig, Highland — map 12

LOCH INSH BOAT HOUSE – ☎ Kincraig (054 04) 272.

R

Off the B9152 (it's parallel to the A9 north of Kingussie). Follow the signs to Loch Insh Watersports.

This restaurant, built from natural stone and old telegraph poles, has a superb position on the shore; and since Loch Insh is a great centre for watersports, the customers have a lot of fun watching, from the balcony or through the windows, the various antics on the water.

There's a grassy and sandy area by the water's edge or you can seek the shade in the woods behind where tables are also set up. The picnic area is banned to dogs – another very sensible idea.

There's a good choice of fresh salads on the menu and the children's menu includes a drink and ice cream. Barbecue stands are available and you can use them in the woods or on the shore. The Ladies is quite small, but you could just about change a baby in there.

£1–9: filled jacket potatoes, hamburger, sirloin steak, venison casserole, lasagne
Children: own menu, half portions

Open 10am–10pm, Jan to end Oct
Closed end Oct-end Dec Access/Visa
Licensed One high chair only
P – own car park No smoking in dining area

King's Lynn, Norfolk map 8

FARMERS ARMS – ☎ King's Lynn (0553) 675 566.

P

At the intersection of the A148 and the A149 just east of King's Lynn.

The pub is part of the Knights Hill Village and is constructed from the old stables and a grain store, the original carrstone walls make an attractive frame for a very well-designed and roomy pub. There is a restaurant at one end, with brick and stone walls and a high vaulted roof. Adjoining this is another eating area, and then a long bar area with loads of wooden tables and chairs scattered about.

Families are of course welcome in the restaurant, and high chairs are available, but if you merely require a drink or a snack, there are a couple of delightful alcove rooms off the bar.

Outside there is a big grassy area with a number of bench tables – a bit noisy because a main road is nearby, but pleasant enough on summer days.

We were most impressed with the care that has gone into this project – and it is a particularly useful place for families since the pub is open throughout the day and food is always available.

(10am–10pm) £1–8: burgers, farm & field pie, lemon sole, garlic chicken, steaks
Children: half portions

• Ale – Adnams, Bass, Ruddles P – own car park

The hotel alongside, the Rising Lodge, is recommended in the Family Welcome Accommodation Guide.

Kingscote, Glos — map 2

HUNTER'S HALL – ☎ Stroud (0453) 860 393.

P

On the A4153 west of the junction with the A46.

An impressive old coaching inn of mellow stone which stands alone, opposite the turning to Kingscote Village. Children are welcome in an area between the bar and the restaurant; it is comfortably furnished with easy chairs and a few tables. But you will have a lot more room upstairs in a large and very pleasant room where families would be very comfortable. It is on two levels, well furnished with pine tables and nicely decorated. You can even overflow at busy times into a beamed function room alongside.

The garden is really delightful; it is huge with an immaculate lawn and is beautifully laid out with bushes and small trees. There are lots of tables; and a play area with swings, a mini assault course, and a fort. Barbecues are held here at weekends.

Food is served every day and the enterprising landlord, with a family of his own, has two high chairs available.

You should be aware of the evening opening hours: 6.30pm from the May to the August Bank Holiday and on Friday and Saturday all year, but otherwise 7pm.

✕ (12–2pm & 7–9.45pm) £2–8: beef crumble, steak & kidney pie, rump steak, cold buffet, vegetable pie
Children: own menu

• Ale – Bass, Hook Norton, Uley, Wadworth's
P – own car park

Also recommended in the Family Welcome Accommodation Guide.

Kingskerswell, Devon — map 1

BICKLEY MILL INN – ☎ Kingskerswell (0803) 873 201.

P

In the minor roads off the A380 south of Newton Abbot.

The pub is not so easy to find but is very close to Stoneycombe quarry. It's a very large pub which was renovated to provide comfortable and spacious bar areas and a large restaurant. The aim is of course to attract families in this busy holiday area, and the family room has therefore got plenty of space, with several tables, padded benches and a couple of amusement machines.

The 17th century building was indeed once a mill, and is now very smartly turned out. There are tables and chairs set out here and there around the outside of the pub.

(11.30am–2pm & 6–10pm) £1–8: garlic mushrooms, grilled trout, seafood Mornay, salads, steaks
Children: own menu

• Ale – Bass, Eldridge Pope, Wadworth's
P – ample

Kingsteignton, Nr Newton Abbott, Devon — map 1

OLD RYDON INN, Rydon Road – ☎ Newton Abbot (0626) 54626

P

Just north of Newton Abbot. If you follow the road to Teignmouth (A381) you will see the Bell Inn. Turn there and follow your nose for a few hundred yards.

Once a farmhouse, this is a handsome building, parts of which date back to the 13th century. A steeply pitched roof overhangs the building at the back, and the front is beautifully proportioned, white-painted, and with wisteria clinging to it.

Inside are a series of small rooms with hugely thick walls and black ceiling beams. Up some stairs above the bar is a room where families are welcome to go: it was once the hayloft, and is a lovely room with plenty of tables at which to park yourselves. There are alternatives at lunchtimes and on Sundays and Mondays for families: the restaurant and dining room are also available, and again are very pleasant and cosy rooms. In the restaurant there is a table with a glass centre and below it you can see an old well – that should interest the children.

There is plenty of space outside for warmer days, with a large covered patio on two levels, with greenery and flowers trailing all over the awnings, a terrace with some tables, and a pretty lawned garden with a swing.

A wide range of enterprising food is always available and all of it is freshly prepared and cooked; and there is a high chair. So close to the South West end of the M5, and only a short detour off the A38, this is a pub which is well worth seeking out.

(12–2pm & 7–10pm) £1–6: egg & smoked salmon mayonnaise, seafood casserole, beef & mushroom pie, butterbean & vegetable gratinée, Tandoori chicken
Children: own menu

• Ale – Bass, Wadworth's, Old Rydon
P – own car park

Kingston, Nr Lewes, East Sussex map 4

JUGGS, The Street – ☎ Lewes (0273) 472 523

P

South of Lewes and signposted south of A27 towards Newhaven.

This delightful pub, with a half tiled facade, dates from the 15th century and the splendid bar with a low beamed ceiling and a big open fireplace confirms this. The owners emphasise how they try to cater for a wide spectrum of people, including families, and the pub is so busy that they obviously succeed.

The sizeable family room is particularly attractive with brick floor and walls, lots of wood in view and with wide windows to a patio. And it is a 'family' room – the owners wish the children to be supervised by their adults. Outside is a long terrace with trestle tables; there is also a patch of garden with a climbing frame.

(12–2pm & 6–9.30pm) £1–6: spaghetti Bolognaise, Hawaiian rarebit, haddock & chips, taramasalata & pitta bread, steak & chips
Children: half portions

• Ale – Harvey's, King & Barnes No music
P – own car park

Kingston Upon Thames, Surrey map 3

CLOUDS CAFE, 6/8 Kingston Hill – ☎ 01 546 0559

R

On the old Kingston to Putney road just before Kingston Hospital.

This is an appealing, well-run restaurant with efficient and cheerful staff. The decor, centred on wooden tables, old advertising signs and hanging plants, is simple and effective; and the food, although of the "fast" variety, is as fresh and healthy as possible with pasta, salads, jacket potatoes and a few vegetarian dishes on the menu, while artificial flavourings are avoided.

You would not be able to change a baby in the Ladies, but the staff can find a quiet corner upstairs.

£2–11: vegetarian salad, pasta, barbecued chicken, steaks, burgers
Children: own menu

Open 11am–11.30pm Open all year
Access/Visa P – on street

Kingsworthy, Nr Winchester, Hants — map 3

CART & HORSES – ☎ Winchester (0962) 882 360

P

At the junction of the A33 and A3090 just north of Winchester.

This agreeable roadside pub dates back to the 17th century and is a popular and busy place. An old cart is on display in front of the pub, which is smartly painted white under a tiled roof. Inside, tradition is maintained with a low beamed ceiling and old oak tables and chairs and settles.

Families are welcome to use the eating area or the paved terrace at the back of the pub. An alternative in winter is the old barn which has been converted to a skittle alley and function room, and is a comfortable and pleasant room with its white-washed walls and beamed ceiling.

The terraced lawn, with plenty of picnic tables and a barbecue area, is a popular spot in summer, and up a few steps there is a children's play area which is safely enclosed. There are Wendy houses, a slide, swing boats, a mini assault course and some trampolines.

(12–2.30pm & 6.30–10.30pm) £1–7: cold buffet, vegetable & bean curry, lasagne, seafood platter, baked cod
Children: own menu

• Ale – Marston's No music
P – own car park

Kingussie, Highland — map 12

TAYLOR'S BAR & RESTAURANT – ☎ Kingussie (0540) 661 251.

R

In the centre of the town.

This restaurant, which used to be in the Guide under another name, has been completely refurbished. There is plenty of space in the restaurant, an attractive room with wood panelling, open stonework and large ceiling fans.

The bar is open all day and has an unusual feature: half a boat, beautifully restored and painted, is incorporated into the decor.

If you need to change a baby the staff will find some space for you. The space is limited in the toilet area, although the facilities may be extended sometime this year.

£2–7: burger & salad, lasagne, shepherd's pie, trout, chilli con carne
Children: half portions

Open 10am to 9.30pm Licensed
No smoking in part of the restaurant P – on street

Kinver, Staffs **map 6**

WHITTINGTON INN – ☎ Kinver (0384) 872 496.

P

On the A449 near Kinver.

You enter this splendid pub, very smart with its black beams and white-painted brickwork, through a huge studded oak door. The spacious rooms have fine oak panelling, and children are welcome in one of the alcove rooms. At the back is a big patio with a fish pond and a delightful lawned garden enclosed by a wall.

The upstairs wine bar is now open only at weekends and families are also welcome there. It is a lovely room with a big vaulted ceiling and white-washed brick walls. There's a good choice of food (a good range of salads, for example) at reasonable prices. Lady Jane Grey spent some time here when it was owned by the Whittington family, and still appears, it is said, on the staircase; but, mercifully, with her head intact.

This is a real oasis of food and drink for families in this area, which is poorly represented in the Guide.

(12–2.15pm & 7–10.15pm) £1–4: salads, pizzas, lasagne, chicken chasseur, fisherman's pie
Children: half portions

Open all year
• Ale – Courage, Marston's, Flowers P – own car park

Knebworth, Herts **map 3**

STATION PUB – ☎ Stevenage (0438) 812 224 *Pot Luck*

P

Right opposite Knebworth Station you will find this large pub, which is very much geared up for family custom. There is plenty of room in the pub itself, with a spacious bar, and an eating area at one end.

For families, there is a good-sized conservatory with a tiled floor and plenty of tables and chairs. This looks out to the garden which has plenty of equipment with which to amuse the children – a slide, climbing frame, and several swings. It is pleasant for the adults, too, with a large lawned area with bench tables.

The pub is open all day from Monday to Saturday, and by now a refurbishment programme will have been completed

(12–2pm & 6–9pm, not Sun pm) £1–7: whitebait, steaks, grilled trout, chicken Kiev
Children: own menu

• Ale – Brakspear's, Flowers, Marston's, McMullen's
P – own car park

Knutsford, Cheshire **map 6**

DAVID'S PLACE, 44 King Street – ☎ Knutsford (0565) 3356

R

In the centre of the town.

This restaurant has moved to new premises which used to be a wine bar – and jolly smart it is, too. It is now designed on three levels, with quite a lot of green in the decor against cream walls, and nice wicker chairs on one level and wheelback chairs on another. Large pots contain trailing plants. It's attractive and relaxing.

Children can still have smaller portions of the various dishes and the lunch menu, as before, offers pretty good value. There are several high chairs but, alas, nowhere to change or feed a baby.

LUNCH (12–2pm) £11: humous & pitta bread, home-made fish cakes, pudding or cheese;
DINNER (7–10pm) £18: avocado & salmon terrine, loin of lamb, pudding or cheese

Closed Sun & bank holidays Access/AmEx/Diners/Visa
Licensed
P – public car park or street parking

Lacock, Chippenham, Wilts **map 3**

CARPENTERS ARMS – ☎ Lacock (024 973) 203

P *Just off A350, two miles south of Chippenham. In the village, close to the church.*

You can leave your car on the outskirts of this famous medieval village, and a short walk will take you past the Abbey, and back in time 400 years. The Carpenters Arms, like its neighbours, is built of ancient and solid stone and the interior has been furnished in a style which reflects the origins of the building. There is plenty of space and the pub is broken up into a series of connecting rooms with brick and partly wood-panelled walls, pine clad pillars and pine furniture.

As you enter there are two rooms on the right, and families are welcome to settle there. They are charming little rooms with wooden beams, a few tables and padded pews and chairs, and one of them has an open fire. There is a small walled patio at the back of the pub. The restaurant is very smart and most attractive under its vaulted wooden roof with its wooden cross beams.

(12–2pm & 7–10pm) £1–9: lasagne, vegetable crumble, Lacock pie, beef Wellington
Children: own menu

• Ale – Usher's, Ruddles, Webster's P – in front of the pub

Landscove, Devon **map 1**

LIVE AND LET LIVE – ☎ Staverton (080 426) 663

P *Two miles from the A38.*

After the speedy A38 you must take a narrow, winding lane with sudden, panoramic views of the countryside.

It is a neat and compact village pub with a smallish family room, with a few tables and chairs, at the back. The Stable Room, a separate room at the rear of the building, is also opened whenever the pub gets busy, at weekends in summer, for example.

At the front of the pub is a small lawned garden with a few bench tables and opposite and behind the car park is a pretty orchard where you may sit and the children may play.

Food is available every day, with cold dishes only on Sunday evenings.

You can count on a generous plateful, and, on the evidence of our meal last Spring, the home-baked ham is as good as ever.

(12–2.30pm & 7–10.30pm) £1–8: salads, cod & chips, steaks, pork chop
Children: own menu

• Ale – Landscove, Ind Coope Burton
P – own car park opposite

Langham, Leics — map 7

NOEL ARMS – ☎ *Oakham (0572) 722 931*

P

Off the A606 in the centre of the village.

If you fancy some Ruddles, head for this pub since it is only a stone's throw from the famous brewery itself. It is an attractive and spacious pub with a small patio by the front entrance.

You enter a long, low-ceilinged bar furnished with good wooden furniture: an oak chest, settles and nice tables. Families are welcome to occupy one end of this room, where they are well away from the bar area. But there is also a pleasant and spacious coffee room on the other side of the pub. There was a very enticing cold buffet on display when we last visited. A traditional Sunday lunch is served for around £8.

The pub is open from 11am to 11pm from Monday to Saturday, and also offers breakfasts from 10 o'clock onwards – so it is a useful pub for families.

(11am–2pm & 7–10pm) £1–6: devilled whitebait, beef & veg pie, smoked salmon, plaice & chips
Children: half portions

• Ale – Marston's, Ruddles P – own car park

Langley, Nr Macclesfield, Cheshire — map 6

HANGING GATE INN – ☎ *Sutton (02605) 2238*

P

Off the A54 Congleton/Buxton road at signpost for Langley.

This comfortable and traditional pub, smartly painted white, stands on a hillside and parts of it date back to the 16th century. It was once a farm, and the owners keep to tradition since they have geese, hens and goats in part of the garden.

There are small terraces, one with a small lawn, on three sides of the pub and you have superb views of the Cheshire plains and the Pennines. On a clear day you can see past the Jodrell Bank telescopes to the Wirral.

The same views can also be seen from the family room, which is down some stairs from the bar and has an open fireplace and pine tables and stags' horns on the wall. In addition there is a charming, little room where families are welcome. This is the Blue Room with a couple of wooden tables, a beamed ceiling and horse brasses on the wall. You can book this for small parties, but not at weekends.

Food is served every day and includes a good selection of daily specials.

(12–3pm & 7–10pm) £1–6: local trout, plaice, lasagne, cottage pie, sirloin steak
Children: own menu, small portions

• Ale – Marston's, Border P – own car park

Lanreath, Cornwall — map 1

PUNCH BOWL INN – ☎ Lanreath (0503) 20218

P

Off the B3359 north-west of Looe.

This pub was first licensed in 1620, and sits in the centre of the village opposite an interesting farm museum; it is notable for a wrought-iron sign designed by Augustus John. It's a big, rambling pub whose several rooms have low beams, wood-panelled walls, stone flagged floors, a formidable collection of horse brasses – all the traditional impedimenta of an historic inn, which indeed it is.

The long, wedge-shaped family room is operational mainly during the summer season and the owners prefer children to be supervised by their adults. The children's menu is displayed on a blackboard here. Paved patios with plenty of tables and chairs stretch around the inn and end up at a small lawned garden.

There is an extensive menu including lots of seafood and this is always available (but less choice out of season), as are traditional Sunday lunches at just under £6 for three courses.

(12–2pm & 7–9.30pm) £1–4: whitebait, plaice & chips, curry of the day, chicken & chips
Children: own menu

• Ale – Bass, Bateman's, Theakston P – own car park

Launcells, Nr Bude, Cornwall — map 1

RED POST INN – ☎ Bridgerule (028 881) 305

R

On the A3072 where it crosses the B3254.

As you bowl along the main road towards Bude and the coast, you cannot fail to spot the Red Post Inn, a thatched building painted a curious shade of yellow. It is said that a pub has stood at this crossroads since the 9th century, and nowadays it has a restaurant attached to it – made from the old stables. It is bright and welcoming under the vaulted and beamed ceiling and you will find food available throughout the day from 9am – and breakfast starts at 7am on Saturdays.

There is a very wide choice of food, and mothers will be pleased to find plenty of space in the Ladies with a table top for changing nappies, a nappy disposal unit, and a chair.

There is a patio outside with plenty of bench tables and a large lawned area with swings.

£2–10: salads, plaice & chips, mixed grill, steaks
Children: own menu, half portions

Open 9am–10pm every day Easter-mid Oct, and Fri-Sun in winter; 9am–4pm Mon-Thurs in winter Access/Visa
P – own car park Licensed

Launceston, Cornwall — map 1

GREENHOUSE WHOLEFOOD RESTAURANT, Madford Lane – ☎ Launceston (0566) 3670

R

Near the town centre.

The self-service restaurant concentrates on wholefood vegetarian dishes, and almost all the ingredients are organically grown. As well as vegetarian meals (and the cheese used, by the way, is also vegetarian) there is a good range of cakes and pastries.

It is housed in a light and airy room with side windows on to the street, and with green and cream decorations and pine-clad walls. There are lots of plants, and prints on the wall.

It's a pleasant place to eat, with a friendly atmosphere. If you need to change or feed a baby the owners can offer facilities upstairs: there are a table, a chair and paper towels.

The Greenhouse also has a branch at the Launceston Steam Railway. The same excellent vegetarian menu is served and high chairs are provided.

£1–3: salads, pizzas, nutburgers, aduki bean pie, courgette & tomato bake
Children: half portions

Open 10am–4pm Mon to Sat Closed for 3 weeks in Nov
No smoking Licensed

Lechlade, Glos **map 3**

TROUT INN, St John's Bridge – ☎ Faringdon (0367) 52313.

P *On the A417 one mile east of Lechlade.*

Next door to St John's Bridge, which is the first lock down river from the source of the Thames, sits this fine Cotswold stone pub, originally a 13th century almshouse which became a pub a couple of centuries later.

The bar has a flagged floor, low-beamed ceiling and wooden settles, and to one side is a well-furnished and airy children's room with old maps and photographs on the walls, and a large fish tank.

There's a marvellously big and grassy garden overlooking the Thames, and indeed the inn still has fishing rights to two miles of trout and coarse fishing water. There are plenty of bench tables scattered about and, during the summer, a marquee is set up and there are weekend barbecues.

You will find a varied menu here seven days a week, and the pub has a high chair. On Saturday during the summer months the pub is open all day.

(12–2pm & 7–10pm) £2–10: seafood crumble, local trout, rump steak, vegetarian crumble
Children: own menu

• Ale – Courage P – own large car park

Ledsham, West Yorks **map 7**

CHEQUERS INN – ☎ South Milford (0977) 683 135.

P *Two miles off the A1 signposted Ledsham and Selby.*

You will be surprised how quickly the hustle and bustle of travelling along the A1 can be forgotten at this delightful pub at the heart of the tiny village of Ledsham. You enter the pub through the immaculately kept walled garden where in summer you can sit on the patio shaded by large umbrellas.

The interior is furnished and decorated in traditional style, from the timbered bar to the small family room off one of the lounges. It is delightful to report that no music spoils the conversation in this excellent pub, nor are those so-called amusement machines tolerated!

As a legacy of the past history of the pub, it does not open on Sundays. The church-going wife of the local squire disapproved of the local lads' fondness for hops on a Sunday. However the pub is open all day on Saturday.

✕ (12–2pm & 6–8.30pm) £1–4: Yorkshire ham, ploughman's, lasagne, smoked salmon scramble
Children: half portions

Closed Sundays No music
• Ale – John Smith's P – own car park

Lee, Nr Ilfracombe, Devon map 1

GRAMPUS INN – ☎ *(0271) 62906.*

P

Off the B3231 west of Ilfracombe.

Situated between Ilfracombe and Bull Point, this is a delightful 14th century inn, which was originally a farmhouse. Its white-washed rough cast walls are cheerfully decorated with hanging baskets of flowers. The surrounding area is owned by the National Trust, so there is little fear of the peace and tranquillity of this pretty little hamlet being endangered. The beach is only a few minutes away, so a bathe might sharpen your appetite for a snack and a glass of Flowers.

The main bar is a most attractive place, its low-beamed ceiling complemented by the wooden settles around the walls, and with an original inglenook fireplace with a large stove. Through the back there is a pool room; and on the other side there is a smallish family room with several tables and chairs (and a high chair).

There is a patch of lawned garden and a larger stretch of terrace, with plenty of bench tables and some swings for the children. It is all surrounded by sloping ground covered with oak and beech trees.

✕ (12–2pm & 7–9.30pm) £1–8: pheasant paté, braised beef in Guinness, red hot bean pot, steaks
Children: own menu

• Ale – Flowers P – own car park

Letheringsett, Norfolk — map 8

KING'S HEAD – ☎ Holt (0263) 712 691.

R

On the A148 just West of Holt.

A well-proportioned, four-square brick building houses this popular pub, and alongside is a huge, lawned garden with lots of bench tables. It's a good place to be on a summer's day.

The restaurant is attached to one side of the pub and is an L-shaped, beamed room, pleasantly decorated and with white walls. Children can have half-portions of any of the dishes on the menu; and babies could be changed in the Ladies.

Incidentally the pub is open throughout the day, from Monday to Saturday, during the summer months.

£1–7: steak & kidney pie, plaice & chips, salads, steaks
Children: half portions

Open 12–2pm & 6–9pm No credit cards accepted
• Ale – Greene King, Bass, Adnams and guests
P – own car park

Lewiston, Inverness-shire, Highland — map 12

LEWISTON ARMS HOTEL – ☎ Drumnadrochit (045 62) 225.

P

Just south of Drumnadrochit off the main A82.

In between your searches for the elusive local monster you might renew your strength with a pint and a meal at this handsome, white-painted, 18th century inn.

The interior is well laid out and welcoming and families can head for the small and comfortable lounge with smartly upholstered chairs. The dining room is just as pleasant, roomy and light, and furnished with wheelback chairs. It looks out through French windows to the sheltered garden with its large lawn and encircling flower beds and trees.

There is a high chair and bar snacks are available every day.

(12.30–2.30pm & 6.30–8.30pm) £1–4: fried haddock, pork & salad, scampi, lasagne
Children: small portions

P – on street No music

Linton, North Yorks — map 10

THE WINDMILL – ☎ Wetherby (0937) 62209.

P

One and a half miles off the A661.

A 17th century pub in a strikingly pretty village, the Windmill is surely worth a visit if you are in the Wetherby area. It has all the qualities you look for in a classic English inn. Note the ancient espalliéed pear tree by the entrance.

It has a lovely, cosy interior with exposed stone walls, ancient timbers and some excellent antique furniture, notably a superb grandfather clock in one of the bars. There are also various paintings, brasses etc, adorning the walls plus a selection of stuffed animals, including a pair of ferrets which eye the customers from a handy vantage point.

Just off the dining room is a delightful conservatory which families can use. It is well-furnished with a carpet and attractive tables and chairs, and a profusion of plants and creepers make it a nice spot to relax over a few drinks. In the evening lantern lights are put out to give a really pleasing effect.

The conservatory leads down some steps to a sloping grassy garden with weeping willow and other greenery where there are bench tables and seats. At night there are some floodlights to keep the garden in view.

Families also have the use of another small room adjoining the bar.

BAR MEALS (12–2pm & 6.30–9pm, not Sun pm) £1–7: seafood risotto, lasagne, smoked trout, steaks, chicken Kiev
Children: own menu

• Ale – Younger's, Theakston's P – own car park

Linwood, Nr Ringwood, Hants — map 3

HIGH CORNER – ☎ Ringwood (0425) 473 973.

P

Off the A338.

Never mind the potholes in the track which leads to this pub; it is well worth the effort to visit this delightful old place, a rambling, 17th century building with dormer windows and a big chminey at one end. It is a lovely woodland setting with a large garden which has a marvellous play area for the children – slides, swings, ropes, climbing frames and a Wendy house.

Families are well catered for with several areas where they can park themselves. The conservatory connects the pub to the Stable bar and the barbecue area. It can be reached directly from the garden, and you can of course keep a beady eye on your children as they enjoy the play area. The Stable bar is also designated as a family area, and is housed in an attractive old barn. Finally there is another area where families can sit together called the Lego Room: there are three Lego play units to keep the children amused.

The various lavatories are spacious and well equipped, and the Ladies has a tiled table top and a changing mat for babies, plus a bin underneath for disposable nappies.

There's a wide and enterprising choice of food available at all times; there are barbecues on summer weekends; and Sunday lunch at around £7. The pub also owns three high chairs. It is a welcoming and very well organised family pub.

✕ (12–2pm & 7–10pm) £1–8: curry, fried plaice, grilled Avon trout, chicken Malabar, salmis of pheasant
Children: own menu

• Ale – Flowers, Wadworth's, Whitbread
P – own ample car park

Also recommended in the Family Welcome Accommodation Guide.

Little Gaddesden, Herts — map 3

BRIDGWATER ARMS – ☎ Little Gaddesden (044 284) 2408.

P

Off the A4146 north-west of Hemel Hempstead.

An unusual pub in that it is the ground floor of a Georgian mansion, the rest of which is split into flats, it's a long spreading place with a large and well-furnished family rooms at both ends of the pub. The enclosed grassy garden has several bench tables. The pub is in the middle of National Trust land and Whipsnade Zoo and Dunstable Downs are just up the road.

We were told that the public bar was restored a few years ago when the church-wardens complained that there were no facilities for darts, cribbage and dominoes for the local farm labourers and foresters. The Sunday lunchtime carvery is deservedly popular with families. It costs under £10 for three courses for an adult, half price for under 14's, while under 5's can eat free. High chairs are provided, too.

(12–2pm & 7–10pm, not Sun pm) £1–5: lasagne, chilli con carne, vegetable biryani, cottage pie, ploughman's
Children: own menu

• Ale – Courage, John Smith's P – own car park

Little Washbourne, Nr Tewkesbury, Glos — map 2

HOBNAILS INN – ☎ Alderton (0242) 620 237.

P

On the A438 six miles east of Tewkesbury.

This low-slung, white-painted inn with its heavy stone roof dates back to the 15th century and has been in the same family for over 200 years. There's a delightful bar, beamed and low-ceilinged, as you enter and a bigger bar alongside.

Children are welcome in the big skittle alley which has loads of tables and chairs. It is sometimes booked for private functions in the evening, but there are also two dining rooms where families are welcome.

The food (available every day) is based on baps with a multitude of different fillings; and you can combine them at will. There is a "Puppy Menu" and miniature baps for children and the enterprising landlord has no less than three high chairs (the restaurant opens in the evenings). In addition there are other hot dishes and an excellent vegetarian choice.

There is an enclosed garden, part patio and part lawn, alongside the pub. There are bench tables and a good display of flowers, and some swings for the children.

(12–2pm & 7–10pm) £1–4: baps (steak, egg & mushroom, gammon & eggs, liver & onions, etc), lasagne, cashew nut & mushroom loaf
Children: own menu, half portions

• Ale – Flowers, Wadworth's No music
P – own car park

Litton, Somerset — map 2

YE OLDE KING'S ARMS – ☎ Chewton Mendip (076 121) 301.

P

On the B3114 West of Midsomer Norton.

A superb 15th century pub not far from the famous Chew Valley Lake with all its bird life. The pub has some water too – a small stream in its delightful garden with beautifully kept lawns, masses of split-log benches and tables, a slide and six swings, and some fine yew trees.

The pub has several inter-connecting rooms, with stone walls, some wood panelling and black oak beams and all well-furnished with wooden tables, pew seats, etc. The family room is in character, with oak-panelled walls, a big open fire, and nice wooden tables.

There is quite an emphasis on food here, and as well as a bar menu, there is a restaurant and a carvery. It is a busy pub and you are advised to book for the restaurant.

(12–2pm & 7–10pm) £2–8: salads, grilled trout, ham & eggs, lasagne
Children: own menu

• Ale – Butcombe, Bass, Courage, Wadworth's
P – own car park

Llangadfan, Nr Welshpool, Powys — map 6

CANN OFFICE HOTEL – ☎ Llangadfan (093 888) 202.

P

On the A458 west of Welshpool.

This pub, with its unusual name, is busy and popular and is housed in a pleasing building, which is painted white with black woodwork.

The bar is small and cosy; and families can make use of the lounge off the hall. It is primarily used as a dining area but you can just have a drink there if you so wish.

The garden, at the back of the pub, is safely enclosed by high hedges and has picnic tables set out on the lawn.

(12–2pm & 7–9.30pm) £2–8: plaice & chips, lasagne, chilli con carne, steaks, gammon
Children: own menu, half portions

• Ale – Marston's P – own car park

Llangollen, Clwyd — map 6

GALES, 18 Bridge Street – ☎ Llangollen (0978) 860 089.

R

In the town centre.

A picturesque town which houses the renowned international Eisteddfod each year. It is in the Dee valley in the heart of lovely hilly country and is guarded on one side by the famous Horseshoe Pass.

This restaurant has a catholic mixture of tables and chairs, some stout and splendid; and pews from a church in the back room and from a chapel in the front. The rooms are panelled, with an even board floor and oak pillars and beams. It is all very appealing, and classical music plays softly; and there are prints for sale on the walls.

The patio is enclosed by brick and trellis and there is a vine-covered arbour, with wooden benches and tables.

The building dates from 1775, thought some parts are a bit older. It has great charm and atmosphere, and the food is reasonably priced. A mother could use a spare bedroom if she needs to feed or change a baby.

(12–2pm & 6–10.15pm) £1–5: mushroom & trout Mornay, tuna & tarragon mousse, beef & paprika pie, Hawaiian pork, spicy vegetable casserole
Children: small portions

Closed on Sundays Access/Visa
One high chair only Licensed
P – 5 spaces and on street

Llantilio Crossenny, Gwent map 2

HOSTRY INN – ☎ Llantilio (060 085) 278.

P

Off the B4233 East of Abergavenny.

This appealing country pub was built in the mid 15th century, and its ancient stone walls are now painted white. We were told that since then it has been owned by only four different families. Situated in lovely countryside between Monmouth and Abergavenny, it is an unpretentious place, with a good "pubby" atmosphere in the bar. Down a couple of stairs is a fair-sized room with a bow window, with a few tables and chairs, padded window seats, a piano and an open fire. Families, of the well-behaved kind, are welcome to use this pleasant room.

Outside is a good sized lawned garden, with bench tables, and a swing. There is also a small terrace at the front of the pub, and you will not be too bothered by passing traffic.

(12–2pm & 7–10pm) £1–5: beef casserole, faggots & peas, vegetable chilli, roast lamb, lasasgne
Children: small portions

• Ale – Smiles and guests

P – small car park and on road

Llwyndafydd, Dyfed **map 5**

CROWN INN – ☎ New Quay (0545) 560 396.

P *Off the A487 or the A486 near New Quay.*

This is a very popular pub especially on summer days when the terrace is packed with families having food and suitably long drinks. Above all, the children can have a lot of fun in the playground with its slides, swings, climbing frame, and a little "magic roundabout" for younger children.

Your eye will be caught by the good proportions of this long and low building, smartly painted white with black trimmings. There is plenty of space, too, in the family room which is off the main bar and has a good quota of tables, benches and so on.

An enterprising choice of food is available, and the pub is now open seven days a week.

(12–2pm & 6–9pm) £1–9: garlic mushrooms, haddock, steaks, beef Wellington, pizzas
Children: own menu

• Ale – Bass, Flowers P – own car park

London **map 3/4**

BRITISH HOME STORES, 101/111 Kensington High Street, W8 – ☎ (071) 937 0919.

R *This store was refurbished a couple of years ago and now contains various stores from within the group: Mothercare, Blazer, Habitat, etc.*

The restaurant on the first floor is spacious and cheerful and offers pretty good value among the hot meals at lunchtime and the snacks through the rest of the day. There are plenty of high chairs.

There are two mother and baby rooms here. One is a part of the disabled toilet area close to the restaurant, and the other is on the ground floor near Mothercare.

£1–4: steak & kidney pie, lasagne, stir-fried quorn, cod & chips
Children: small portions

Open 9am–5.45pm, Monday to Saturday   Licensed
P – public car parks nearby   Access/Visa

CRANKS, two branches at: 8 Marshall Street, W1 – ☎ (071) 437 9431 and 9–11 Tottenham Street, W1 – ☎ (071) 631 3912.

R *The Marshall Street branch of the well-known vegetarian restaurant is in a pleasant modern building quite close to tired and tawdry Carnaby Street. They have high chairs but nowhere to feed or change a baby. There's a good range of salads, hot vegetarian dishes, baked potatoes and so on.*

The best plan is to order your salad or hot savoury dish and ask for a separate empty bowl for your small child.

The Tottenham Street branch, just behind Goodge Street underground station, has essentially the same menu as the Marshall Street branch. There is one high chair and a shelf has been installed in the Ladies to facilitate the changing of babies.

LUNCH (from 11.30am) £1–4: salads, baked potato, pizzas and quiches, hot dishes of the day (e.g. casserole of broccoli & black-eyed beans in cheese sauce)

Open 8am–8pm, Mon-Sat. Closed Sun and Bank Holidays
Access/AmEx/Diners/Visa   Licensed
No smoking in part of the restaurant

CUMBERLAND HOTEL (THF), Marble Arch, W1 – ☎ (071) 262 1234.

R *The Coffee Shop, busy as it is, is a welcome haven from the horrors of Oxford Street. It is a bright and comfortable place, on two levels and with several no smoking tables. It is open from 6.30am to midnight (except for an hour's break at 10am) and offers a whole range of snacks, grills, burgers, pastries or just tea and toast if you wish.*

The Ladies in the main foyer has space in which to change or feed a baby.

(6.30–10am) – Breakfasts
(11am-midnight) £1–7: soup, prawn cocktail, grilled lemon sole, salads, hot and cold buffet
Children: own menu, half portions

Access/AmEx/Diners/Visa   Licensed

D H EVANS RIVER RESTAURANT, Oxford Street, W1 – ☎ (071) 629 8800.

R

The theme of the restaurant, on the sixth floor, is the Thames and it is divided into three sections – Embankment, River Park, Tower – with each suitably decorated. Children will like the River Park where you eat in a bandstand surrounded by a mural of Guards in red uniforms and bearskins. The Tower and the Embankment are no smoking areas.

There are various self-service counters offering a varied choice of food throughout the day, starting with breakfast at around £3.

The mother and baby room is on the second floor in the children's department.

£1–6: fish, roast of the day, salad bar, filled jacket potatoes, pasta, daily specials

Open Mon-Sat 9.30am–5.30pm (7.30pm Thur)
Access/AmEx/Diners/Visa Licensed
No smoking in half of restaurant

GARDEN CAFE, White House Hotel, Albany Street, NW1 – ☎ (071) 387 1200.

R

Opposite Great Portland Street Underground station.

This spacious, comfortable and pleasant coffee shop is within the White House Hotel, close to Regent's Park and not far from Madame Tussaud's and London Zoo. It was refurbished last year and looks as cheerful as before, although the carpet clashes something rotten with the patterned upholstery of the chairs.

It is open all day and serves an eclectic choice of snacks, salads, grills and dishes of the day at reasonable prices, as well as a three-course set menu at around £12.

Mothers will find space to change or feed a baby in the powder room, where there are chairs, a counter on which to change a nappy, and plenty of paper towels.

£2–12: Yorkshire rarebit, fish & chips, chicken korma, lamb Italienne, steaks
Children: half portions

Open 7am-11pm Mon-Sat & 7.30am–10.30pm Sun
Access/AmEx/Diners/Visa Licensed

GEALE'S FISH RESTAURANT, 2 Farmer Street, W8 – ☎ (071) 727 7969.

R

Behind the Gate Cinema at Notting Hill Gate.

This lively and ever-popular fish and chipper was opened by the present owner's grandfather in 1939 – two days after war was declared on Germany. What an act of faith. It is good to report that the standards never waver here; you will invariably eat excellent food at reasonable prices.

A choice of fishy starters is followed by marvellously fresh fish at prices ranging from £3 and upwards according to size and availability.

If a mother needs to change or feed a baby, the friendly staff will find a spot for her upstairs, and there are no less than five high chairs on the premises.

£1–8: crab soup or fish soup, prawn cocktail, deep-fried clams, fish, puddings (e.g. apple crumble & cream)
Children: smaller portions

Open Tue-Sat 12–3pm & 6–11pm. Closed Mon & Sun & 2 weeks at Xmas, Easter week, and mid August for 2 weeks.
Access/Visa • Ale – Brakspear's
No music

L S GRUNTS, 12 Maiden Lane, WC2 – ☎ (071) 379 7722.

R

Quite close to the Covent Garden Piazza, this big and busy Chicago pizza pie restaurant lies back from the street. The range of pizzas is large and so are the portions, which range from 'regular' to elephantine, which would feed half a dozen people. There is a small pizza, too, 'son of a Grunt'.

The children are given balloons, and cartoons on the large screen video, and there are nappy-changing facilities in the Ladies.

£2–11: garlic mushrooms, pizzas, salads

Open 12–11.30pm Mon-Sat and 12–9pm Sun
Access/Visa   Licensed

HAMLEY'S, Regent Street, W1 – ☎ (071) 734 3161.

R

This famous toy shop has a restaurant in the basement. It is a self-service snack bar, cheerful and open-plan, and very busy indeed. We visited it at lunchtime at half-term one year and the queue was about the length of a cricket pitch. Many of the children no doubt anticipated one of the array of fanciful ice-creams on the menu.

The mother's room is still on the fourth floor.

£1–4: sandwiches, baked potatoes, lasagne, chilli con carne

Open 9.30am–6pm Mon-Sat (till 7.30m Thurs) & later in the period before Xmas
No credit cards accepted   Unlicensed

HAND IN HAND, 6 Crooked Billet, SW19 – ☎ (081) 946 5720.

P

This is a very busy and popular pub, especially at weekends. By the west side of Wimbledon Common, it's a real haven for parents who have been enjoying the Common with their children: walking, or flying a kite, can be thirsty work.

Inside you will find a cheerful open-plan pub with a few alcoves on the one side. Families are welcome to use a room just by the main entrance. It has a few tables and chairs, and a dart board occupies one end of the room. There is a courtyard at the front with a few benches.

Pub food is available throughout opening hours, and this pub is open all day from Monday to Saturday.

(12–9pm) £1–9: chilli con carne, shepherd's pie, pizzas, steaks, vegetable bake

• Ale – Young's, Ruddles No music
P – on street

HARRODS, Brompton Road, SW1 – ☎ (071) 730 1234.

R *There are several self-service restaurants in the store and the Dress Circle on the first floor and the Upper Circle on the fourth are the most suitable for families because they have high chairs available and no smoking areas. You will always find a good spread of salads, quiches, pastries etc.*

The Georgian Restaurant is also on the fourth floor and offers a good range of starters, a carvery, an excellent cold buffet and some à la carte dishes. The new Terrace Bar is alongside but does not cater for children.

Nearby, on the fourth floor, is a Ladies cloakroom with a separate little room for breast-feeding and nappy changing. There is another mother and baby room on the first floor in the children's clothes department.

DRESS CIRCLE AND UPPER CIRCLE (9am–5.45pm, 6.45pm Wed) £1–5: salads, quiche, open sandwiches, Tandoori chicken, goujons of plaice
GEORGIAN RESTAURANT (12–2.30pm) £18: vegetable terrine, ribs of beef & Yorkshire pudding, apple fritters with apricot sauce
Children: half portions

Access/AmEx/Diners/Visa Licensed
No music

JOHN LEWIS, THE PLACE TO EAT, Oxford Street, W1 – ☎ (071) 629 7711.

R *This exceptionally bright and well organised self-service restaurant on the third floor has seven different sections offering different kinds of food – Breakfast All Day, Crock Pot, Patisserie, Cold Table, Crêperie, Seafood and the Soda Fountain. Something as you see to suit most palates and at reasonable prices – nothing above £7. The Cold Table has an excellent range of salads, and the Crock Pot offers various daily specials. The staff are extremely helpful and seem to take a great pride in the place. It gets very busy though – the best advice is to lunch before 12. The Coffee Shop also has high chairs and serves light meals all day, as well as lunchtime specials.*

There is an excellent mother and baby room, or perhaps it should be called a parents and baby room, since fathers are not denied access. It has separate breast feeding and nappy changing areas, a bottle warming facility, and plenty of space. It is on the fourth floor, near the children's shoe department, and is accessible by lift.

RESTAURANT £1–7: salads, lamb hot pot, chicken chasseur, seafood Mornay;
COFFEE SHOP £1–3: croissant, soup, salads
Children: own menu in Place To Eat

Open Mon-Sat 9.45am–5pm, Thurs to 7.30pm
No credit cards accepted Licensed
No smoking in any part of the store
No music

MILBURNS at the VICTORIA & ALBERT MUSEUM, Cromwell Road, SW7 – ☎ (071) 581 2159.

R

A couple of years or so ago, after many delays, Milburn's opened their new restaurant in the Henry Cole Wing of the museum. It was worth waiting for because it is a lovely spot – very spacious with a York stone floor, some nice exposed brickwork, and good wooden tables. It is usually busy at lunchtimes, but don't be put off because the queue seems to move quickly.

The menus concentrate on salads, quiches, etc., and a hot dish of the day, and the serve-yourself salads are good.

You can change or feed a baby in the Ladies – there is a chair and a substantial table.

LUNCH (12–2.45pm) £1–3: soup, baked potato, salads, quiche, hot dish of the day

Open Mon to Sat 10am–5pm, Sun 2.30–5.30pm
No credit cards accepted Licensed
No music

NEW SERPENTINE RESTAURANT, Hyde Park, W2 – ☎ (071) 402 1142.

R

All the catering in Hyde park is now in the care of Prue Leith, and the New Serpentine Restaurant sits alongside the Lido. It is housed in a building which is part conservatory – wooden framed glass panels – and part marquee – a tent forms the roof. It is a temporary structure, and an attractive one, especially since it looks out over the water and the park.

The restaurant provides food throughout the day and you can pop in for

breakfast or a cup of tea, as well as enjoy a full meal. We had an excellent lunch from the short and interesting menu and were well looked after by the efficient and friendly staff.

Situated in the middle of a royal park the restaurant is designed to attract a wide cross-section of customers, including families. Although there are two high chairs there are no facilities for mothers to change a baby's nappy. The lavatories are spacious and could easily contain a changing table, but what a pity that the manager whom we questioned on this point seemed noticeably uninterested in providing this basic amenity.

£3–10: courgette & mint soup, warm sesame chicken & salad, pork & Welsh leek sausages, olive & artichoke pie, spicy lamb meatballs
Children: own menu

Open 10am to 10.30pm, every day
Licensed   Access/Visa
P – own car park (but usually full)

PALMS, 3–5 Campden Hill Road, W8 – ☎ (071) 938 1830.

R

At the Kensington High Street end of Campden Hill Road.

This restaurant is a lively and welcoming place, which is done out in a functional and agreeable style. The prices are reasonable, the pasta is fresh, and the service is relaxed and friendly. There are a few tables on the pavement and sliding doors give an airy feel to the restaurant.

However, the music is usually too loud. It annoys many customers and the rest don't even hear the racket around them. Far better, in our opinion, to hear the much more acceptable sound of people chatting to each other. That's the only background a restaurant needs.

The restaurant has several high chairs, but you would struggle to change a baby in the Ladies.

£2–7: gazpacho, spaghetti alle vongole, fettucine al pesto, lasagne, dish of the day
Children: small portions

Open 12–11.30pm   Open all year
Access/Visa   Licensed

PALMS has another outlet in London, with the same basic menu, and high chairs are available at 39, King Street, Covent Garden, WC2 – ☎ (071) 240 2939

PETER JONES, Sloane Square, SW1 – ☎ *(071) 730 3434.*

R

There is a restaurant on the fourth floor – and a Coffee Shop on the fifth floor, in both of which you can get something to drink or eat throughout the store's opening hours.

A splendid mother and baby room is situated on the third floor, with everything you need including a changing table and mats, chairs, paper towels and a baby food warmer.

RESTAURANT, £1–9: club sandwich, omelettes, dishes of the day, roast of the day, chicken Lahore, scones and pastries;
Children: own menu
COFFEE SHOP £2–4: salads, quiche, pizzas

Open Mon-Sat 9.30am–5pm (6.30pm Wed – Coffee Shop only)
Licensed No credit cards accepted
No music No smoking areas

SELFRIDGES, Oxford Street, W1 – ☎ *(071) 629 1234.*

R

Top of the Shop on the fourth floor is a bright, cheerful and roomy restaurant, which offers something to suit the palate at all times of the day – including breakfast right through to lunchtime. The lunchtime meals (between 11am and 3pm) include a good choice of salads and dishes of the day, plus cakes, sandwiches and snacks at other times.

The children's menu covers the normal burgers, sausages and beans type of meal – portions cost from 30p upwards.

The mother and baby room is on the floor below (third), and here also is the Selfridge restaurant, quiet and comfortable, and with waitress service. You can eat breakfast, lunch and afternoon tea.

In addition there are the Bridge Café in Miss Selfridge and the Gallery Coffee Shop on the ground floor.

There are plenty of high chairs available.

TOP OF THE SHOP £1–6: paté, salads, plaice & chips, steak & kidney pie, daily specials;
SELFRIDGE RESTAURANT – lunch (11.30am–2.30pm) £10: prawn cocktail, roast chicken, creme caramel & cheese
Children: own menu

Open Mon-Sat 9.30am–6pm (Thur 8pm) Licensed
Access/AmEx/Diners/Visa Mostly no smoking

SIMPSON'S PICCADILLY RESTAURANT, 203 Piccadilly, W1 – ☎ (071) 734 2002.

R

From breakfast through to tea there's always something hot available at Simpson's lower ground floor restaurant. For break-fast you have a wide choice from coffee & croissant at just over £1, to a traditional English breakfast for about £4. At lunchtime there's a wide choice between dishes of the day, the cold buffet, the carvery, or the quick lunch menu.

There's an excellent choice of sandwiches, omelettes, savouries and pastries for tea, and the tea is made with water from the store's own artesian well.

You could cope with a baby in the nearby Ladies – though there's no special mother's room.

BREAKFAST & SNACKS (9.30–11.30am & 3.30–5.45pm) £1–6: egg, bacon & mushrooms, scrambled eggs, omelettes, Welsh rarebit;
LUNCH (12–2.30pm) £2–16: potted shrimps, Irish stew, plaice, roast of the day, Dover sole
Children: half portions

Access/AmEx/Diners/Visa One high chair only
Licensed No music

VERITABLE CREPERIE, 329 King's Road, SW3 – ☎ (071) 352 3891.

R

Less than a mile down the King's Road from Sloane Square, this crêperie has plain brick walls, a wooden floor and round tables under a high ceiling. There is a pleasant atmosphere, enhanced by the wide windows, the quiet classical music, and the cheerful staff.

The savoury crêpes are really galettes, a speciality of Britanny made with buckwheat flour, and there is a very wide-ranging choice – as there is of the sweet variety – and you can devise any number and combination of fillings.

Children can share one between two or an extra plate can be provided. A baby would have to be changed on the floor of the Ladies.

£2–5: savoury galettes, sweet crêpes, salads

Open noon-midnight Closed Xmas Day
Access/Visa Licensed

Long Melford, Nr Sudbury, Suffolk **map 4**

CROWN INN HOTEL, Hall Street – ☎ Sudbury (0787) 77666.

P

On the A134 half way down the main street.

This is an exceptionally smart inn and small hotel, which is immaculately maintained both inside and out. It dates back to the 17th century, although some of it was rebuilt when it was burned by rioters in 1885; the Riot Act had to be read from its steps. There is a comfortable and well-furnished reception area, and families are welcome here. The pretty walled garden is bedecked with flowers with a spacious lawn and plenty of bench tables, and some toys for the children.

The inn is open throughout the day (from 8am to 11 at night) and there is a good choice of bar snacks at reasonable prices; afternoon teas are also served.

(12–3pm & 7–10pm) £1–5: plaice & chips, salads, roast lamb, liver Provencale
Children: own menu, small portions

• Ale – Adnams, Nethergate   P – own car park

Also recommended in the Family Welcome Accommodation Guide.

Long Rock, Nr Penzance, Cornwall **map 1**

MOUNTS BAY VINEYARD WINERY & RESTAURANT – ☎ Penzance (0736) 60774

R

Off the A30 just east of Penzance. Follow the signs for Ludgvan.

The vineyard was established in 1984 and now has six acres of vines, and the first wines were made a couple of years ago. You can sit in the bright and airy surroundings of the conservatory style restaurant and look out over the vineyards, and of course sample the wines. The food is all home-made and is cheerfully served. If the sun shines you can head for the gravel patio, where some tables are set up. It overlooks the vineyard, and with many flowers around, is pretty and peaceful. There is a play area for children.

Babies can be changed in the Ladies, where there is a table.

£1–3: pasty & beans, salads, chicken & mushroom pie, chilli tacos, ratatouille
Children: smaller portions

Open 10am–5pm Access/Visa
Licensed One high chair only
P – own car park No music

Longhorsley, Nr Morpeth, Northumberland map 10

LINDEN PUB – ☎ Morpeth (0670) 516 611.

P

On the A697 north of Morpeth.

At the end of a long driveway you will find the Linden Hall Hotel, a glorious Georgian mansion built from local stone in 1812 for a local bigwig and set in three hundred acres of splendid parkland.

Behind the hotel is the delightful Linden Pub, a converted granary which is built of the same stone as the hotel. Inside, the stone walls, decorated with old advertising signs, have been retained along with the exposed beams and there is an open fire.

The large family room has been made under the rafters and the terrace outside has plenty of tables and chairs and a giant draughts board. An excellent range of food is served including a children's menu and half portions.

It is an excellent family pub.

(12–2pm & 6.30–9.30pm) £1–6: kipper paté, leek & pasta crumble, fillet of sole, grilled lamb cutlets
Children: own menu, half portions

• Ale – Theakston's, McEwan's P – own car park

The Linden Hall Hotel is recommended in the Family Welcome Accommodation Guide.

Lower Basildon, Nr Reading, Berks map 3

CROWN, Reading Road – ☎ Upper Basildon (0491) 671 262.

P

On the A329 North-west of Pangbourne.

The pub is situated just outside Pangbourne in a lovely stretch of countryside and looks very smart in its coat of cream paint. There are a couple of roomy bars, including the comfortable "Quiet Bar", where the music can only be dimly heard.

The family room is off the larger bar, and is a bright and airy room; indeed it is mostly windows, looking on to the large garden. Here there are plenty of bench seats, and an adventure playground to amuse the children: tyre swings, a climbing frame, things to crawl through, and a pigsty which has been enterprisingly converted to "Candy Cottage".

(11am–2pm & 6–10pm) £1–5: plaice & chips, sirloin steak, scampi, burgers
Children: own menu

• Ale – Courage   P – own car park

Lower Hardres, Kent — map 4

THE THREE HORSESHOES – ☎ Canterbury (0227) 70333.

P

Off the B2068 south of Canterbury.

This lovely old coaching inn with its flat brick front was built some time around 1700. The friendly landlord has deeds which date back to that time, and he has a further and very important sense of tradition with his varying range of beers available straight from the barrel, and he reckons to have served over 300 different brews in the last ten years.

It's a charming and relaxed 'pubby' pub; as the landlord stresses, a real pub – "untrendy, with no space invader or cigarette machines". Children, who must be supervised, are welcome in a pleasant room overlooking the garden which, in its turn, overlooks mile after mile of open country.

Bar food is served at lunchtimes only at markedly low prices, and mention must be made of the fine collection of English cheeses which is always available.

(12–2pm, Mon to Sat) £1–3: ploughman's, Spanish omelette, smoked mackerel & salad, terrine, pork & apple casserole

• Ale – Young's, and guest beers   No music
P – small car park and street

If you wish to recommend an establishment to the Guide please write to us – report forms are at the back of the book. We need your help to extend and improve the guide.

Lower Woodford, Wilts — map 3

WHEATSHEAF – ☎ *Middle Woodford (072 273) 203.*

P

Off the A360 north of Salisbury.

This delightful old pub began life as a farm in the 18th century and its brick and flint walls are covered in Virginia creeper. It was altered quite substantially a few years ago, but nothing was done to spoil its character. It still has its fair share of wooden pillars and beams and a cheerful open fire. The dining room, where children are welcome with their adults, has the novel feature of a little wooden bridge over a goldfish pond. It is an attractive room with heavy black beams and pine furniture.

A wide variety of food at very good prices is available every day, and unusually for a pub, includes a comprehensive vegetarian menu.

The garden is simply a delight: a large, grassy, enclosed area with a couple of swings and climbing frames and shaded by a huge tree. It is so peaceful.

(12–2pm & 7–10pm) £1–8: smoked salmon, prawn or chicken curry, broccoli bake, veal Cordon Bleu, mushroom & nut fettucine
Children: own menu

• Ale – Hall & Woodhouse P – own car park

Loweswater, Cumbria — map 9

KIRKSTILE INN – ☎ *Lorton (090 085) 219.*

P

Off the B5289 south of Cockermouth.

This 16th century inn has an idyllic situation close to Crummock Water and from the bar you can see the brooding outline of Melbreak Fell in the background. It is very peaceful here, made more so by the splendid old church which is opposite the pub – these two focal points of village society, preaching and pints, are often found to be close neighbours.

Families will find this a very useful pub, since food is available (including breakfast from 8am and afternoon teas) during most of the day, and they can use either a small lounge at the side of the bar, or a room in an adjacent barn, which has a pool table, jukebox, etc. A terrace and a lawn run along the front.

(12–2.30pm & 6–9pm) £1–8: omelettes, Cumberland sausage, haddock & chips, sirloin steak, bean & tomato casserole
Children: own menu

• Ale – Jennings No music
P – own car park

Lowsonford, Nr Henley in Arden, Warwicks **map 7**

FLEUR DE LYS – ☎ *Lapworth (0564) 782 431.*

P

North-east of Henley in Arden and can be reached from the A34 or the B4095.

This long cream-painted pub, whose origins may lie as far back as the 15th century, sits alongside the Stratford-upon-Avon Canal, which joins the Grand Union a bit further north.

You can watch the to-ings and fro-ings of canal life from the large grassy garden, but you would also have to keep a sharp eye on your children. They are safer in the enclosed play area which has a slide, a climbing frame and tyre swings.

The alternative on cooler days is the family room which is in one of the oldest parts of the pub. There is plenty of space in the room, a pleasant spot with its wood panelling, antique dressers, large open fireplace and wooden furniture. A few toys are provided for the children.

It is useful for families to know that this pub is open all day, and food is available for most of the time.

(12–9pm) £1–6: celery & Stilton soup, garlic mushrooms, crab & prawn thermidor, savoury pie
Children: own menu, half portions

• Ale – Boddington's, Flowers, Marston's, Wadworth
P – own car park

Luccombe Chine, Isle of Wight **map 3**

DUNNOSE COTTAGE RESTAURANT – ☎ *Isle of Wight (0983) 862 585.*

R

Off the A3055 south of Shanklin (there is a sign).

The original cottage is an archetypal English building of thatch and stone. The restaurant sits alongside and its interior maintains the cottagey theme with wooden beams and panelling, lots of willow pattern plates on the walls and a fine grandfather clock.

It has a superb garden, with a large expanse of lawn, and an extensive rose garden, all fringed by stately trees. A pair of Anglo-Nubian goats, Mallow and Maple, live at the top of the garden.

The food is conventional tea shop fare, and there are no changing facilities beyond a wooden chest in the Ladies.

£1–4: ploughman's, scampi, cod & chips, chicken & chips
Children: smaller portions

Open 10.30am–5pm. Closed weekdays in winter
One high chair only Access/Visa
P – own car park Licensed

Ludlow, Shropshire map 6

This is a wonderful old town of narrow cobbled streets, packed with Tudor and Georgian houses; John Betjeman thought it one of the loveliest towns in England. There is a fine Norman castle, partly ruined, from which medieval Welsh princes attempted to govern the turbulent Celts; and the Church of St Laurence is one of the biggest parish churches in the land.

ARAGON'S, 5 Church Street – ☎ Ludlow (0584) 873 282.

R

In the town centre, about 100 yards from the castle.

This is a very useful restaurant to know about, since it is open throughout the day and the evening, seven days a week. There is a wide choice of food available, a couple of high chairs, and space to change a baby in the Ladies, where there is a table and a chair.

It is a smart, modern restaurant which is nevertheless housed in an ancient building in this historic town. The owners stressed that they are very much committed to catering for all the family. We can also applaud their stamina since they are open all day and every day.

£1–11: gazpacho, plaice and chips, mushroom Stroganoff, seafood pancake, fresh pasta
Children: own menu, half portions

Open 8am–10pm, every day except Xmas
Access/AmEx/Diners/Visa
P – on street or public car parks

EAGLE HOUSE RESTAURANT, 17 Corve Street – ☎ Ludlow (0584) 872 325.

R

In the main street of the town, on the Shrewsbury to Hereford road.

This 17th century building once housed a coaching inn called the "Eagle & Child", and the Oak Room restaurant, with its original beams and oak panelling, is very appealing. A little courtyard has tables set up for warmer days. The upstairs dining room, the Pine Room, has now become a wine tasting room, since the owners also have a wine business.

You will get a good choice of food here, including several vegetarian dishes, at reasonable prices. If you need to change a baby there are a table and chairs in the Ladies, plus paper towels etc.

LUNCH £1–6: pork & liver terrine, mushrooms in red wine, tomato & aubergine & nut pancake, chicken with mushrooms & bacon;
DINNER £11: vegetarian paté, lemon sole, pudding or cheese
Children: half portions

Open 11.30am–2.30pm & 7–10pm No credit cards accepted
P – own car park One high chair only

Lurgashall, West Sussex — map 3

NOAH'S ARK INN – ☎ Northchapel (042 878) 346.

P

By the village green.

This archetypcal village pub sits alongside the delightful village green and what better than to sit outside, nurse a glass of King & Barnes bitter, and watch some cricket. The pub, in traditional Sussex style, has a tile hung facade, which is bright with masses of flowers in tubs and window boxes.

It is very much a "local" and all the better for it, and inside you will find cricket and football trophies over the fireplace and photographs of the inn from times past. You can play shove ha'penny in one of the bars.

Families are welcome to use a small room with a few tables, and the walls are enlivened by several sporting prints. The alternative is to sit in the sun by the village green.

(12–2pm & 7–10pm) £2–6: ploughman's, ratatouille, liver & bacon, poached salmon trout
Children: half portion

- Ale – Friary Meux, King & Barnes

P – own car park

Lustleigh, Devon **map 1**

CLEAVE – ☎ Lustleigh (064 77) 223.

P

Just off the A382 north of Bovey Tracey. Watch for the sign.

The village is largely composed of lovely thatched granite cottages and is famous for its May Day festival.

This 15th century pub, thatched like most of its neighbours, suits the village perfectly. You can sit at peace in the delightful lawned garden at the front of the pub. It is a secluded spot, sheltered by trees and with a fine array of greenery and flowers all around.

There are two sizeable bars inside and an attractive dining room, and families should head for a pleasant, wood panelled room at the back of the pub. There are several tables, some padded chairs and only one amusement machine.

(12–2pm & 7–9pm) £2–5: cheese & onion flan, chicken curry, lasagne, cauliflower cheese, coq au vin

Children: smaller portions

- Ale – Bass, Flowers, Marston's

P – on street (can be difficult)

PRIMROSE COTTAGE – ☎ Lustleigh (064 77) 365.

R

Opposite the church you will see this restaurant and tea rooms in its coating of primrose paint and with boxes of cheerful flowers adorning its front. Inside there are now two pretty rooms, with beamed ceilings, wide windows, and some antique furniture. The owners also run an antique furniture business from the upstairs rooms.

At the back there is a delightful garden, which is full of plants, small trees and flowers. There are a couple of terraces, with tables and chairs, statuettes here and there and a stream meanders through. The garden slopes down to the River Bovey.

If you need to change or feed a baby, the owners will provide an upstairs room.

£1–5: cream tea, ploughman's, fisherman's pie, cannelloni, creamy vegetable pie.
Children: half portions

Open 10am–5.30pm, 1 March to 30 November
Closed weekdays end-Nov to Mar   No credit Cards
Unlicensed   No music
One high chair only   No smoking
P – street parking

Lyddington, Nr Uppingham, Leics — map 7

MARQUESS OF EXETER – ☎ Uppingham (0572) 822 477.

P

Off the A6003 south of Uppingham.

From the front you will see a well-proportioned 16th-century thatched inn with a stone facade, and with a sign depicting the eponymous Olympic hurdler, made more famous after his death by the film Chariots of Fire.

Behind, however, there is a very large and plushly decorated pub and across the car park a hotel.

There is a spacious bar, as you enter; on one side is the restaurant, on the other side is another good-sized room where families are welcome to park themselves. It is smartly furnished, with plush red coverings on the seats and wooden settles, and copper topped tables. There is also a small patio at the back of the building.

Food is available every day and includes a three-course Sunday lunch for around £9.

BAR MEALS (12.15–1.45pm & 7.15–10pm) £1–8: sirloin steak, coq au vin, fish crumble, moussaka, eggplant & cheese bake
Children: half portions

• Ale – Bateman's, Ruddles, Theakston's, Webster's
P – own car park

Lydford, Devon — map 1

CASTLE INN – ☎ Lydford (082 282) 242.

P

Off the A386 South of Okehampton.

This is a most appealing pub, a pink-washed, 16th century stone building, gaily covered with hanging plants and flowers. It is remarkable because the inside of the pub, delightful to see anyway with wooden settles, nice wooden tables, and open fireplaces, has a fine collection of china plates (over 300 of them), and an equally fascinating display of prints on the walls. The jewel in the crown is their collection of Lydford pennies, minted by Ethelred the Unready, in 1000 AD.

Let us not forget the family room which is a cosy area between the two bars, with two large wooden tables, and all enclosed by high-backed curved wooden settles.

Outside is a small patio, and a most attractive lawned garden ringed by trees and bright with flowers. A children's playground has been built in an adjoining paddock and has a swing and climbing frames.

Up above looms the stern keep of Lydford Castle, which sits on the site of an ancient British hill fort, with the River Lyd on three sides. The castle used to house a court with a prison below, and a local poet wrote in the 17th century:

'I oft have heard of Lydford law
How in the morn they hang and draw,
And sit in judgement after.'

(12–2.30pm & 6.30–9.30pm) £2–4: steak & kidney pie, curry & rice, haddock, cold buffet

• Ale – Courage P – own car park

Please let us have reports – good or bad – on any establishments listed in the Guide as soon as possible after your visit.

Nr Lymington, Hants — map 3

TOWLE'S COUNTRY RESTAURANT, Walthampton Hill – ☎ Lymington (0590) 73113.

R

On the B3054 just east of Lymington.

We spotted this lovely collection of brick farm buildings while we were en route to Beaulieu, stopped and found a most attractive restaurant.

You enter through a courtyard, where you can sit on summer days and no doubt you will be addressed by the parrot who stands guard.

The restaurant has a long bar on one side and on the far side opens out under the vaulted roof of what was once a hay loft. It is decorated and furnished in very agreeable style and there are a couple of high chairs on the premises.

It is not an inexpensive place if you go for the à la carte menu, but the bar meals offer a reasonable alternative.

If a baby has to be changed, the shelf and the chair in the Ladies will help you.

BAR MEALS £2–7: ploughman's, salads, scampi & chips, smoked salmon;
RESTAURANT £18: smoked salmon, beef Stroganoff, pudding or cheese

Open noon–1.45pm & 7–9.30pm. Closed Sun pm & Mon
Access/AmEx/Diners/Visa Licensed
• Ale – Eldridge Pope P – own car park

Lytchett Minster, Dorset — map 2

SLEPE COTTAGE, Dorchester Road – ☎ Morden (092 945) 281.

R

On the A35, between Poole and Dorchester.

An archetypal, whitewashed 16th-century thatched cottage which is approached by a red brick path. Inside, the attractive and homely atmosphere is maintained amid the whitewashed walls, black beams, and small windows which are set in the thick cob walls. The owners also offer a traditional Sunday lunch at around £5.

Nappy-changing can be achieved, just about, in the Ladies.

£1–3: honey roast ham & salad, ploughman's, home-made soup, shepherd's pie, cream tea

Open 10.30am–5.30pm (5pm in winter). Closed December
Licensed   No credit cards accepted
One high chair only   No music
P – own car park

Lytham St Anne's, Lancs   map 6

TIGGIS, Express Buildings, Wood Street – ☎ Lytham (0253) 711 481.

R

Tucked away off the main town centre street.

This bustling Italian restaurant is, like its sister restaurant in Preston (q.v.), usually busy. In the early evenings, especially at weekends, the restaurant is inundated with families wanting to dine out together.

The restaurant caters well for young children and even babies, providing plenty of high chairs and of course half portions of the delicious pastas made in the busy open plan kitchens. Tiggis provides typical Italian food, concentrating on a wide variety of pizzas and pastas, but it also features some excellent 'blackboard specials'.

With a family you would be well advised to ask specifically to sit downstairs where all the action is. Upstairs is quieter and there is also a very large bar.

£1–10: lasagne al forno, cannelloni, chicken cacciatore, scampi Provencale
Children: half portions

Open 12–2pm & 6–11pm
Access/Visa   Licensed
P – street parking nearby

Maentwrog, Gwynedd   map 5

THE GRAPES HOTEL – ☎ Maentwrog (076 685) 208.

P

Just off the A487 as you turn into the village.

Wooded hills rise steeply across the road from this grey stone building dating from 1853, though the cellars are 15th century, and hanging baskets and pretty window boxes brighten the grey facade. At the back the large veranda, safely railed along the front, overlooks a pretty garden with trees, shrubs and a small pond with a fountain. Alas the garden is private but the verandah is ideal for summer eating.

The family room is just off the verandah and is a sizeable one since it runs the depth of the building and is comfortably furnished with pine tables and chairs and padded settles.

This pub has elected to open all day (except Sunday) and food is available most of the day. In the afternoon during summer cold food is available on the verandah. The two bars have a lovely ambience with their solid wooden tables, prints and copper artefacts on the stone walls, and a stag's head surveying everything.

(12–2.15pm & 6–9.30pm) £1–7: plaice & chips, lamb Madras, spaghetti Bolognese, steak au poivre, seafood Mornay
Children: own menu, half portions

P – own car park • Ale – Bass, Stone's

Nr Maidstone, Kent map 4

BULL, Penenden Heath – ☎ Maidstone (0622) 752 888.

P

North of Maidstone, off the A249.

This large and busy pub faces Penenden Heath, and has been a hostelry for a couple of hundred years. The heath offers all sorts of sporting facilities – cricket, tennis, bowls, etc – plus a children's playground.

The Bull is deservedly popular with families, and has a large room for their use off the main bar. It is a comfortable, wood panelled room with several tables, upholstered benches, and building blocks and a blackboard for the children.

The garden at the back of the pub is safely enclosed and has plenty of bench tables and a children's play area with a wooden slide with wood chippings on the ground to ensure a safe landing. There are several apple and willow trees which attract the squirrels, and a patio which attracts the adults.

The pub is open all day from Monday to Saturday.

(12–2pm & 6.30–10pm) £1–8: plaice & chips, steaks, trout, lamb chops, burgers
Children: own menu

• Ale – Flowers, Fremlins P – own car park

Marlborough, Wilts map 3

An attractive town with a broad main street (you can park in the middle) with many Georgian houses and a couple of fine churches. It's a good centre for tourists; Savernake Forest is close and there are many Roman sites nearby.

GREEN DRAGON, High Street – ☎ Marlborough (0672) 512 366.
Pot Luck

P

On the main street.

This functional pub in the busy main street of the town has an attractive Georgian facade, with bow windows on the ground floor and brick above. You enter a large open-plan bar and there is a small family room, with several tables, on the floor below. Beyond the family room is a large lounge area, with a stone floor, and a table football game.

There is a patio at the back with bench tables, and a pool room in an outhouse.

(12–2pm & 7–8.30pm) £2–4: terrine, stuffed breast of lamb, moussaka, scampi
Children: small portions

• Ale – Wadworth's
P – on street

POLLY TEA ROOMS, High Street – ☎ Marlborough (0672) 512 146.

R

In the main street opposite the Castle and Ball.

A traditional English tea shop which really looks the part with an abundance of beams holding up the ceilings, old photographs and prints on the walls and always a good display of cakes and scones, large vats of jam and so on – and friendly, helpful staff. You can pile into a full, heart-stopper breakfast until 11.30 in the morning and then lunch takes over until about 3 o'clock and in between times there are the snacks, gateaux and ice creams.

If you need to change a baby there is ample room in the Ladies, plus a table and a chair.

£1–5: soup, ham & chestnut en croute, chicken Mexico, locally smoked trout, plaice & chips
Children: small portions

Open 8.30am–6pm Mon-Fri (7pm at weekends)
Access/AmEx/Diners/Visa Licensed
No smoking in half the restaurant No music

P – in the main street

Marsh Gibbon, Bucks — map 3

GREYHOUND – ☎ Stratton Audley (086 97) 365.

P *Off the A41 east of Bicester.*

This well-proportioned, spacious stone building was re-built in the mid-18th century and houses a very attractive pub. You enter a most handsome long bar with stone walls and a tiled floor with open fireplaces at either end, one of them particularly substantial. At one end is a restaurant and, alongside, a small family room with a few tables, padded bench seats and partly panelled walls.

On summer days you might head for the large grassy garden at the back of the pub: there are bench tables among the many small trees and bushes, and a climbing frame. The small front garden is a delight, with masses of flowers and creepers climbing over the front wall of the building.

(11am–2.30pm & 6–8pm, not Sun pm) £2–9: whiting with salad, crispy Mexican pancake, venison pie, seafood risotto, roast beef & Yorkshire pudding
Children: half portions

• Ale – Fuller's, Greene King, Hook Norton, Theakston's
P – own car park

Mary Tavy, Devon — map 1

MARY TAVY INN – ☎ Mary Tavy (082 281) 326 — *Pot Luck*

P *On the A386 about three miles north of Tavistock.*

This is a useful pub to know in this popular tourist area; handily placed on the road north of Tavistock.

It has two spacious bars and a fairly basic family room which runs along the front of the pub. It's actually a covered veranda with bench tables running down its length.

There is a beer garden, which has a few tables and chairs.

(12–2.15pm & 7–10pm) £1–5: turkey & mushroom pie, local trout, plaice & chips, salads
Children: own menu

• Ale – Usher's, Hicks, Ruddles P – own car park

Matlock, Derbyshire **map 7**

STRAND RESTAURANT, 43 Dale Road – ☎ Matlock (0629) 584 444.

R

Near the town centre, and on the A6.

This nicely decorated restaurant has echoes both of a teashop and a brasserie, with its tiled floor, pot plants and wooden tables and chairs. It is on two levels, with a gallery running round the edges of the high-ceilinged room.

All the food here is freshly-cooked by the owners who took over the restaurant a couple of years ago. Youngsters are very welcome at lunchtimes, and also during the early evening, but must not outstay that welcome at night.

You could just about manage to change a baby in the Ladies.

£1–9: cheesy potato bake, steak & kidney pie, hunter's pie, cauliflower Mornay, sirloin steak
Children: half portions

Open 10–2pm & 7–10pm, Tues to Sat No credit cards
Licensed One high chair only
• Ale – Marston's
P – own car park

Matlock Bath, Derbyshire **map 7**

LA CAVERNA – ☎ Matlock Bath (0629) 55635.

R

On the main street, the A6.

This Italian restaurant has a cheerful and welcoming air, with its white walls and checked tablecloths and a lively smell of garlic. Through the windows to one side you can see the steep stone walls which line the main street.

The restaurant sits in a courtyard which also contains a number of shops – and, of course, a fountain. When the weather is kind you can enjoy a drink under the colourful parasols.

£1–7: fresh sardines, spaghetti Bolognese, tortellini, sirloin pizzaiola, lemon sole
Children: half portions

Open 11am–2pm & 6.30-10pm (11pm Fri, Sat, Sun). Closed Mondays

Access/AmEx/Diners/Visa Licensed
P – on street

Mawnan Smith, Cornwall **map 1**

RED LION – ☎ Falmouth (0326) 250 026.

P

In the minor roads south of Falmouth.

This is the archetypal village pub. It was built in the 15th century and its thatched roof sits above stone walls which are smartly painted white.

It is a comfortable pub with a large public bar and a pleasant lounge area. Like the lounge the separate family room has a high ceiling and is a pleasant and functional room. The licensees can provide a high chair, and serve a traditional Sunday lunch at just over £4.

The adults will perhaps enjoy the fresh fish which is on offer each day, while the children will no doubt be pleased with the range of ice creams.

(12–2pm & 7–9.15pm) £1–10: ham & eggs, gammon steak, catch of the day (e.g. John Dory, Torbay sole), steaks
Children: own menu, half portions

• Ale – Devenish P – own car park

Melmerby, Cumbria **map 9**

VILLAGE BAKERY – ☎ Langwathby (076 881) 515.

R

On the A686.

This is a most enterprising and picturesque restaurant. Housed in an 18th century converted barn, it is set in some spectacular Cumbrian countryside where you will find some marvellous views.

The restaurant has stone walls, a stone-flagged floor, good wooden tables and chairs, and a Welsh dresser against one wall. There is a small and elegant conservatory on the front of the building. Upstairs there is a craft gallery with an excellent range of products.

The food is baked in the restaurant's own wood-fired brick oven and the bread, pie and pizzas use wholemeal flour ground at a local water mill. Many of the vegetables are grown organically on a smallholding at the back of the restaurant. The menu is comprehensive: you can enjoy breakfasts, lunches, savoury snacks, and cream teas, all at very reasonable prices.

Mothers with babies can feed and change them in the Ladies, where there is a pull-down shelf and a changing mat.

There is no garden here, but the whole of the village green stretches outside the front door.

£1–6: Inverawe kippers, Lakeland char, spinach & nut pasty, Cumberland sausage
Children: half portions

Open 8.30am–5pm (Tue-Sat) 9.30am–5pm (Sun) 8.30am–12 (Mon)
Closed from Xmas Eve to Easter   No music
Access/Visa   No smoking
P – own car park

Mentmore, Bucks **map 3**

STABLE YARD TEA ROOM – ☎ Cheddington (0296) 668 660.

R

Off the B488 South of Leighton Buzzard.

In the splendid village of Mentmore, a sustaining cup of tea or coffee and an economically priced snack can be found in this tea room. The old stables house a craft centre and gallery, a guest house, and the tea shop. The cobbled courtyard is partly used for parking; but on a warm day you can park yourself at the bench tables outside and enjoy the atmosphere.

The tea shop shares a part of the stables with the craft shop under the high wooden ceiling. With all the craft items on display it is an interesting place to have a snack, and the tables are attractively laid with flowered table cloths. A good display of sandwiches, pies, rolls and cakes greets you, and there is a fair choice of light lunch dishes.

You can change a baby on a table in the Ladies, which is located in the adjoining guest house.

✗ (10am–6pm, Tues-Sun) £1–3: quiche, pizza, lasagne, cauliflower cheese
Children: half portions

Closed Xmas & Boxing Day   No credit cards accepted
Licensed   One high chair only
P – in courtyard

Metal Bridge, Nr Gretna, Cumbria **map 9**

METAL BRIDGE – ☎ Rockcliffe (022 874) 206.

P *Just off the A74 – watch for the sign to Metal Bridge.*
This well-organised pub was enlarged in a very successful way by using an old sandstone barn to house a large restaurant. It has a couple of high

chairs but is now only open in the evenings. There is plenty of room to deal with a baby in the Ladies.

The pub has a number of rooms to choose from, and children are welcome in the conservatory (with an array of solid cane chairs) off the main bar. It overlooks the River Esk, as does a small terrace with a couple of bench tables. Bar food is available every day and a traditional Sunday lunch is also served at around £5.

BAR MEALS (12–2pm & 6–9.30pm) £1–4: soup, Lockerbie haggis, haddock, salads;
Children: own menu, half portions

Open all year • Ale – Younger's
P – own car park

Milngavie, Strathclyde **map 11**

THE FAMOUS COFFEE HOUSE, Findlay Clark Garden Centre, Boclair Road – ☎ Balmore (0360) 20700.

R

On the B8049 just south of junction with A807; look for the Findlay Clark Garden Centre.

The largest garden centre in Scotland houses an excellent coffee shop in a conservatory, which is smartly decorated with trellis and curtains on the walls, pictures (for sale), basket weave chairs, and naturally lots of potted plants. The place has been extended but retains its agreeable atmosphere. The whole place, with vast gift and garden accessory area indoors, is laid out in a spacious and attractive way.

There are no facilities in the Ladies to assist a mother to change a baby, but the disabled toilet can be used.

£1–4: ratatouille, spicy bean hot pot, open sandwiches, chicken exotica
Children: half portions

Open 10am–5pm Closed Xmas and New Year
No credit cards Unlicensed
P – own car park

If you wish to recommend an establishment to the Guide please write to us – report forms are at the back of the book. We need your help to extend and improve the guide.

Milton Abbas, Dorset — map 2

TEA CLIPPER – ☎ Milton Abbas (0258) 880 223.

R

Off the A354.

You will find this appealing tea room in this very interesting village. It was one of the first model villages, planned in the 1700s by the Earl of Dorchester, whom Horace Walpole described as 'the most arrogant and proud of men, with no foundation but great wealth'. Well, he knew a thing or two about architecture, and his village is well worth a visit.

The L-shaped room is neat and pretty with a good array of wooden tables of various shapes and sizes, and all covered in flowery tablecloths. These are complemented by the stripped wooden pillars and beams and an inglenook fireplace.

At the back there is a craft shop; and a walled and paved area which will seat about forty people. The owners have two flats to rent in a converted barn at the back of the restaurant.

All day you will find a snack or a home-made cake to eat, and the cream teas are quite a speciality here. But there is nowhere to change or breastfeed a baby, although the lavatories are reasonably spacious.

✕ £1–3: jacket potatoes, pizzas, smoked salmon, omelettes, cream teas
Children: half portions

Open 10.30am–6pm (weekends only in Nov)
Closed Mon & Dec to Mar Unlicensed
No credit cards accepted No music
One high chair only P – roadside

Milton Street, Nr Alfriston, East Sussex — map 4

SUSSEX OX – ☎ Alfriston (0323) 870 840.

P

Watch out as it's easy to miss: take the road to Alfriston off the A27, turn left on the road to Litlington and left again to Milton Street.

This secluded and traditional country pub is set in lovely Sussex countryside near the picture postcard village of Alfriston. It has a pleasant and spacious family room on two levels and it's well furnished with solid wooden tables and a toy cupboard. There is another room where families are also welcome, the "pig-sty", because that is what it used to be. It has solid pine furniture and a brick floor, and looks out to the garden and the South Downs beyond.

The friendly landlord encourages young families to visit his pub, and the huge garden, with its views of gentle Sussex hills, is a great attraction. There is a large wooden climbing frame, swings and Wendy house, a children's bar, and a slide.

Food is available every day and the menu changes to suit the seasons. There is a notable range of home-made soups available. Barbecues are held on Fridays and Saturdays during the summer.

(12–2pm & 7–9.30pm) £1–6: garlic mushrooms, vegetable bake, grilled trout, rabbit pie, steaks
Children: own menu, half portions

• Ale – Harvey's and a guest   No music or machines
P – own car park

Mintlaw, Grampian map 12

COUNTRY PARK INN – ☎ Mintlaw (0771) 22622.

R

On the A950 on the west side of the town.

This was once the Station Hotel and is an attractive white-washed building which is close to the disused Mintlaw Station.

Through the spacious bar and lounge you will find a pleasant restaurant with fresh flowers on the tables, comfortable seats and some alcove areas. There is also a function suite at the side of the inn and this comes into play for the busy Sunday lunch period.

You can sit in the restaurant and eat either from the bar lunch or the à la carte menu, and children can have half portions at half price. It is all very relaxed and the genial owner keeps it that way.

If you need to change a baby the upstairs bathroom provides adequate space.

(12–2pm & 7–9.30pm) £1–5: ratatouille, chicken curry, beef steak pie, herring in oatmeal, tandoori chicken & salad
Children: half portions

Access/AmEx/Diners/Visa   Licensed
No smoking in restaurant   P – own car park

Misterton, Nr Crewkerne, Somerset **map 2**

WHITE SWAN – ☎ Crewkerne (0460) 72592.

P *On the A356 south of Crewkerne.*

Your first impression of this 18th century roadside pub is the mass of colour from the many window boxes and hanging baskets that festoon its stone walls and the long stone barn that stands beside it.

It is a pleasant and friendly pub, and the various bars and alcoves, with low ceilings and beams, give it a cosy atmosphere. This includes the comfortable family room, and a high chair is made available. There is a wide choice of food to be had, including a vegetarian section.

Across the road is a large enclosed lawned garden which overlooks houses and rolling countryside beyond. For the children there are swings, a see-saw and climbing frame.

(12–2pm & 7–9pm) £1–6: salads, salmon steak, venison in red wine, lemon sole, vegetarian goulash, steaks
Children: own menu

• Ale – Gibbs No music
P – own car park, across the road

Mitchell, Cornwall map 1

PLUME OF FEATHERS – ☎ *Mitchell (0872) 510 387.*

P

On the A30 between Bodmin and Camborne.

The pub is housed in a 17th century listed building, to which John Wesley was a frequent visitor. It sits alongside the A30 and a couple of years ago was refurbished. The changes were made with great care and there are now several lounge and eating areas grouped around a central bar. There are plenty of wooden chairs and tables dotted about, and during the renovations an old well was uncovered, and this is now quite a feature, covered in glass and illuminated.

Families are welcome to use a comfortably furnished area away from the bar, or the adjacent food bar. There is a garden off the car park with a good children's play area, which includes a climbing frame, a slide, a wooden fort and a pets corner.

(12–2pm & 6–9.30pm) £1–6: whitebait, steaks, plaice & chips, salads, pasties
Children: half portions

• Ale – Devenish   P – own car park

Mithian, Cornwall map 1

THE MINERS ARMS – ☎ *St Agnes (087 255) 2375.*

P

Near St Agnes, two miles off the A3075.

Parts of this pub date back to the 16th century and it presents a cheerful face to the world, with a facade that is partly unadorned stone, partly slate and partly white-painted stone. In between the walls there is a small cobbled courtyard with a few seats.

There are two delightful, low-ceilinged bars and families can use the small cellar lounge, a white-washed room with a timber roof and padded seats all around the walls. A half door leads out into a small lawned garden. A delightful lounge can also be used by families. It has a splendid decorative ceiling and during the conversion of the room (it used to be a dining room) a lovely painting of "The Blue Boy" was discovered.

(11am–2pm & 6.30–10.30pm) £1–8: cottage pie, seafood lasagne, steak, game pie, red devilled layer
Children: own menu

• Ale – Devenish   P – own car park

Mitton, Nr Whalley, Lancs — map 9

OLD STONE HOUSE EATING ESTABLISHMENT, Mitton Road – ☎ Stoneyhurst (0254) 86544.

R

Two miles off the A59.

Set in its own attractive grounds this is a restaurant which has managed to retain its country house feel. Although an extension has been added, the best tables are in the large central dining room complete with huge fireplace, original oak panelling and carved shields on the wall. Recently part of the old outbuildings has been turned into a pub – "Owd Neds" and hotel accommodation is also being offered.

The menu is largely Italian – you can watch your pizzas being made in the open kitchen – although there is always a number of specials displayed on blackboards.

There is plenty of space to change and feed a baby in the Ladies lavatory, which has a chair and table.

£1–8: salade Nicoise, marinated herrings, pizzas, spaghetti Bolognese, chicken à la crème
Children: own menu

Open 12–2.30pm, not Mon or Tue; 7–10.30pm Mon to Fri and 6.30–11.30pm, Sat; 12–10.30pm Sun   Licensed
Access/AmEx/Visa   P – own car park

Moffat, Dumfries & Galloway — map 11

BLACK BULL HOTEL, Station Road – ☎ Moffat (0683) 20206.

P

In the town centre.

This famous pub opened its doors in 1568, and now looks very smart in its coat of white paint, with black edgings and shutters for the windows. It is a rambling building, long and low, and inside you will find a couple of large and comfortable bars. One of them is more of a brasserie bar these days and families are welcome to eat in there together.

In addition, there is a family room away from the bar. This is the Burns Room, where both the walls and the ceilings are panelled in wood; there are a few tables, banquettes around the walls, and a couple of amusement machines. The poet used to frequent the Black Bull and indeed inscribed one of his poems on a window pane, but it is said that the window is in a Moscow museum.

An alternative is another lounge which has recently been redecorated and refurnished. It is warm and cosy with books on display and its character is much enhanced by the lovely decorative Jacobean ceiling.

(11.30–2.15pm & 6.30–9.15pm) £1–7: fish pie, haggis, cheese & potato hot pot, trout, steaks
Children: own menu

• Ale – McEwan's, Theakston's
P – small car park or on street

Also recommended in the Family Welcome Accommodation Guide.

Monksilver, Somerset — map 2

NOTLEY ARMS – ☎ Stogumber (0984) 56217.

P

On the B3188, south of Williton.

This attractive white-walled village pub has a light and clean family room, well-furnished with tables and chairs and plenty of toys. The relaxing and comfortable bar has some good wooden tables and wood burning stoves at either end.

There is a delightful and large garden, with plenty of tables and chairs, lovely shrubbery and flower beds and, to add to the interest, a stream running through.

The pub offers a good choice of freshly-made, home-cooked dishes, which are more enterprising than normal pub food and very reasonably priced. Their ice cream is also home-made. The pub has one high chair, and the Sunday roast, served during the winter, is around £3.

(12–2pm & 7–9.30pm) £1–4: vegetable curry, whole prawns, poorman's pocket, shepherd's purse & richman's pouch (pitta bread with various fillings), pork & veg goulash with rice
Children: half portions

• Ale – Usher's, Ruddles P – own car park

Never use an out-of-date Guide. Many places are excluded because their standards have dropped or their policies towards families have changed. Many new establishments are added each year.

Mouldsworth, Nr Chester, Cheshire — map 6

GOSHAWK, Station Road – ☎ Manley (09284) 302.

P

On the B5393 between Northwich and Chester.

This brick pub, like many others, arrived with the railway and is opposite the station. It is a big, rambling place and off the main bar is the family room, a big room with cream-painted walls and well furnished with wooden settles and tables and comfortable chairs.

The garden is very safe, completely fenced in, and well equipped with rustic climbing frames, swings and climbing ropes. There is plenty of open space. It is an ideal place to take the children, especially with a children's menu at under £2.

(12–2pm & 6–8.30pm) £1–6: chicken & mushroom pie, plaice & chips, gammon & egg, sirloin steak
Children: own menu

• Ale – Greenall's P – own car park

Nailsworth, Glos — map 2

WEIGHBRIDGE INN, Avening Road – ☎ Nailsworth (045 383) 2520.

P

On the Avening/Tetbury road B4014, and not far from Amberley and Minchinhampton Common.

We have fond memories of this pub – the first we entered with our baby daughter of a few weeks. We were directed to their excellent family room – and naively thought that there were thousands of pubs like this where families are welcome.

It is a delightful white-painted building with an interior of rough stone walls and good wooden furniture. Families are well catered for with two rooms where children are welcome; a small one off the bar with a large, open fireplace, oak tables and a settle; and upstairs a superb high-ceilinged beamed room with an array of polished oak tables and chairs. It leads out to a grassy, sloping garden and a patio with several bench tables, and sun umbrellas.

There is an excellent choice of food at reasonable prices, and the owners do not fry any food at all. Neither is there music in the pub nor any of those obnoxious 'amusement' machines. What a wonderful haven for all the family.

(12–2pm & 7–9.30pm) £1–4: two-in-one pie (steak & mushroom pie with cauliflower cheese), cheese & asparagus flan & salad, lasagne, vegetable and lentil crumble
Children: half portions

• Ale – Wadworth's, Courage No music
P – own car park

Nancenoy, Nr Helston, Cornwall map 1

TRENGILLY WARTHA – ☎ *Constantine (0326) 40332.*

P

Off the B3291 between Constantine and Gweek.

Along the narrow country lanes east of Helston you will eventually espy this long, cream-painted building, with a garden room at the front. This is in fact the family room and has a couple of long tables at which to park yourselves and the family. Alongside is an entrance hall with a pool table.

The long bar is relaxing and comfortable and the eye of real ale fans will certainly be drawn to the row of barrels behind the bar. The beers are varied on a regular basis.

At the far end of the bar there is an attractive lounge where families are also welcome. It is comfortably furnished and has an open fire. The restaurant is an attractive room and when we ate there we were very impressed by the standard of the cooking.

(12–2pm & 6.30–9.30pm) £1–8: smoked salmon trout, dressed crab salad, Trengithy sausage, sirloin steak
Children: small portions

• Ale – a varying choice No music
P – own car park

Also recommended in the Family Welcome Accommodation Guide.

Nantwich, Cheshire map 6

CAFE CONTINENTAL, Pepper Street – ☎ *Nantwich (0270) 628 451.*

R

In the town centre.

This is a fairly new, self-service restaurant in a traffic free area in the centre of Nantwich. It looks clean and fresh with 1920 style prints on the walls, and a mottled marble floor. Tables and chairs are put outside on warmer days.

The owners certainly welcome children, who are usually much in evidence, and there is even room for push chairs inside. Babies can be changed in the upstairs toilet area, where there is a table and a changing mat.

£1–3: pizzas, savoury & sweet crêpes, omelettes, salads
Children: small portions

Open 8am–5.30pm Mon to Sat. Closed on Sunday
No smoking in most of the café Licensed
P – public car park nearby

CHURCHE'S MANSIONS, Hospital Street – ☎ *Nantwich (0270) 625 933.*

R

On the east side of the town on the A52.

A magnificent oak-framed mansion which was built in 1577 for a wealthy landowner in the traditional Elizabethan black and white style. The interior, lovingly restored, is all oak panelling, heavy beams and fine fireplaces. The furniture, also oak and mainly 16th and 17th century, adds to the whole pleasurable effect. At the back there is a very pretty lawned garden, with trees and flowers, and it is beautifully kept.

It is open most of the day, since coffee is served from 10am and teas from 2.30 to 4.30 pm.

The menus are enterprising and imaginative, and offer excellent value.

Sorry – nowhere to change or feed a baby.

LUNCH (12–2pm) £9: herrings in sour cream, hare casserole, pudding
DINNER (7–9.30pm) £17: fish chowder, stuffed pepper, roast pheasant, pudding.
Children: small portions

Access/Visa Licensed
P – own car park No music

Please let us have reports – good or bad – on any establishments listed in the Guide as soon as possible after your visit.

Needingworth, Nr St Ives, Cambs — map 7

PIKE AND EEL HOTEL – ☎ St Ives (0480) 63336.

PR

Go into the village and look for the sign to the pub on the main street.

This is a delightful place for a family outing. There are acres of space around the pub, which is right on the banks of the River Ouse. It is a big and attractive stone building, partly Tudor, once owned by Ramsey Abbey and was the site of an old chain ferry. Long lawns sweep down to the river's edge with lovely trees all around, and a good array of small boats, moored at the pub's marina, to look at.

Inside there is a spacious bar and two rooms which children can use. Both are heavily beamed and low-ceilinged in the original Tudor part of the inn and very comfortably furnished. A very large garden room restaurant has been attached to the front of the pub, and families are welcome to eat here. It is nicely laid out and is very bright and cheerful, with rows of windows looking out to the garden and the river. Several high chairs are provided.

(12–2pm & 7–10pm) £2–12: pickled seafood, roast of the day, carrot & almond loaf, trout, steaks
Children: small portions

• Ale – Bass, Greene King, Adnams   P – plenty

Also recommended in the Family Welcome Accommodation Guide.

Nettlebed, Oxon — map 3

WHITE HART – ☎ Nettlebed (0491) 641 245.

P

On the A423 north-west of Henley-on-Thames.

Built in the 17th century from brick and flint, this solid coaching inn sits on the roadside under its steeply pitched roof. Inside is a large and relaxing bar on two levels; there are open fires, a varied selection of nice wooden tables and the wooden pillars attest the age of the building. A cold buffet is set up every lunchtime in the summer, and a Sunday roast can be had for about £8, and high chairs are available.

Families are very welcome in this pub and apparently arrive in force for Sunday lunch. At other times they can use a couple of alcoves off the bar downstairs. One is a pretty little room with padded bench seats and it leads on to a paved patio, well provided with rustic tables and benches. There is also a large enclosed garden with bench tables set out on the lawn, and a swing. From here you can peer over the fence at the local bowls players.

(12–2pm & 7–9.45pm) £2–9: moules mariniere, lamb kebabs, baked trout, chicken curry, sirloin steak
Children: small portions

• Ale – Brakspear's No music
P – own car park

New Quay, Dyfed **map 5**

BLACK LION HOTEL – ☎ New Quay (0545) 560 209.

P

Follow the one way system to "Harbour and Beach".
Of 17th century origin, but rebuilt in 1830, this stone hotel is close to Newquay harbour, down a narrow road. You can walk straight into one of the bars off the street and very welcoming it is with oak beams, lots of brassware and two fireplaces – one used as a 'sit-in' area, the other housing a wood-burning stove. This bar leads to a well-worn and comfortable family room.
The beer garden, with a few bench tables, has a fabulous position overlooking Cardigan Bay, the beach and the harbour, all ringed by protective hills. There is a children's slide here and an "enchanted tree".
During the months of June, July and August the pub is open all day from Monday to Saturday.

BAR SNACKS (12–3pm & 6–9.30pm) £1–6: brunch, plaice & chips, burger, pork fillet in cider & cream, salads
Children: own menu

• Ale – Webster's, Ruddles, Flowers P – own car park

Also recommended in the Family Welcome Accommodation Guide.

THE HUNGRY TROUT, 2 South John Street – ☎ New Quay (0545) 560 680.

R

In the town centre.
The restaurant has an excellent elevated position, and from the bay windows you can look out over the harbour and the sweep of Cardigan Bay. The building which was once a post office has a black and white facade,

and there is bench seating outside: it's a pleasant spot on warmer days.

There is a great variety of dishes available here; they range from beans on toast to a full à la carte dinner menu. You could eat a modest lunch for around £2, or spend over £10 on an evening meal. The roast of the day, with all the trimmings, represents very good value at just under £3, and there is, as you would predict, plenty of fresh fish on the menus.

There is nowhere, at present, to change or feed a baby.

£1–8: crab salad, burgers, plaice & chips, poached scallops, veal Marsala, steak Diane
Children: own menu, half portions

Open 10am–10 pm March to Nov; weekends only in winter
Access/Visa Licensed
No music One high chair only
P – public car parks

Newbridge-on-Wye, Powys map 6

NEW INN – ☎ Newbridge (059 789) 211.

P

In the centre of the village.

This hotel was converted from a row of 19th century cottages, and the long and low building looks very smart in its coat of white paint with black woodwork. The owners have completely refurbished the inn over the last few years.

Families are welcome to settle in a comfortable lounge which is well provided with sofas and easy chairs. An alternative on summer days is the small lawned garden.

There is plenty of choice on both the restaurant and bar menus and they include special dishes of the day.

(12–2pm & 7–9pm) £2–12: cottage pie, beef Bourgignonne, fillet of plaice, sirloin steak, chicken casserole
Children: half portions

• Ale – Marston's P – own car park

Also recommended in the Family Welcome Accommodation Guide.

Newcastleton, Borders map 11

THE COPSHAW KITCHEN, 4 North Hermitage Street – ☎ Liddesdale (03873) 75250.

R

On the east side of the main street, the B6357.

This restaurant used to be a grocer's shop and is now divided into two parts: the plain and simple tearoom and the restaurant, which is also an antique shop. There is a huge old dresser on one side and shelves on the other, all inundated with antique china and bric-a-brac. The menu is the same in each but you pay a bit more in the restaurant – but the prices are very reasonable.

At the front is a shop where there are further antiques and second-hand goods for sale and more antiques up the stairs. The snack menu and children's menu serve as one and the same; quite right – why should the children always get the fish fingers.

The proprietor will provide a chair in the small Ladies for a mother wishing to breast feed a baby.

£1–6: egg mayonnaise, haddock & chips, steaks, lasagne, chicken curry & rice
Children: own menu, half portions

Open 9.30am–6pm every day; 7.30–9pm Wed to Sat
Closed Jan & Feb
Access/Visa Licensed
P – own car park

Newgate Street, Nr Hertford, Herts map 3

COACH AND HORSES – ☎ Cuffley (0707) 872 326.

P

At one end of the main street.

This is a charming old village pub which, we are glad to report, rarely changes over the years. It is brick, part covered in black boarding and with an ivy-covered porch overhung by dormer windows and a steeply pitched roof.

At the back there is a charming grassy garden with some fine trees. There are wooden chairs and tables, and a swing and climbing frame for children to amuse themselves while the adults amuse themselves with a few draughts of the amber fluid.

The L-shaped bar, with stoves at either end, is long and low with oaken beams and stone flags at one end. There is a fine collection of pewter tankards over the bar. The children's room, spacious and wood-panelled, and decorated with old cycling posters doubles as a club room in the evenings (the local cycling club still meets there for instance).

(12–2pm & 6–9pm, not Sun) £1–4: potted shrimps, chicken & mushroom pie, smoked haddock pasta, mushroom & nut fettucini, beef in red wine

• Ale – Adnams, Benskins, Ind Coope Burton
P – own car park

Newport, Isle of Wight — map 3

GOD'S PROVIDENCE HOUSE – ☎ Isle of Wight (0983) 522 085.

R

In the middle of the town, by St Thomas's church.

The unusual name, so the story goes, refers to the luck of its inhabitants in escaping the ravages of the Plague. Some parts of the building date back before 1665, although it is a charming mixture of styles, with Georgian windows, for example.

Three rooms make up the restaurant, all nicely furnished with oak tables and wheelback chairs; and one room looks out on to the pretty square, with its church and small shops.

The staff are friendly and welcoming and there are four high chairs available. You can change a baby in the Ladies, where there is a wide shelf and a chair can be put in there, too.

£1–5: roast of the day, steak pie, wholemeal quiche, roast chicken
Children: half portions

Open 9am–5pm (11.30am–2pm on Sunday)
No credit cards   Licensed
P – on the street

Newton, Lincs — map 7

RED LION – ☎ Falkingham (052 97) 256.

P

In the village.

This delightful pub, long and low and built of stone, is a real find in a county which is very short of places we can recommend.

Children are welcome in three rooms in the pub: in the food bar, notable for its penny farthing in one corner; in a very smartly furnished family room with a nautical theme and big open fireplace; and in another lovely room at the garden end of the pub. It is furnished with padded wooden settles, a little dresser and plenty of wooden tables.

The garden itself is enclosed and immaculate with a long smooth lawn, a swing, a small paved patio with white furniture, and bags of bright flowers.

The food is based on a comprehensive cold buffet: lots of fresh salads, prawns, pies and an array of meats. The landlord serves small, normal or large portions and to tackle the large plate you would have to be in the gargantuan class.

An unusual feature of the pub is the presence of a squash club with two courts, and visitors can play here if they book in advance.

(12–2pm & 7–10pm) £1–7: soup, paté, cold buffet
Children: own menu, half portions

• Ale – Bateman's P – own car park

Newton on Ouse, North Yorks — map 10

DAWNAY ARMS – ☎ Linton-on-Ouse (03474) 345.

P

Well sign-posted from the A19 north west of York.

A reader who, with her 14-month-old, was given a warm welcome told us about this pub. It is a smart black and white 17th century listed building standing on the roadside.

Inside are two comfortable bars, a darts alcove and a large dining room which doubles as the family room. It overlooks the beautiful grassy garden which slopes down to the Ouse. You'd need to keep a watch on your children near the river, but they will be able to play in safety in the children's playhouse. It is close to the pub and to the small patio just outside the dining room.

The pub has two high chairs and a children's menu, and the landlord likes children to leave by 8.30pm. Our reader reports that she had a lovely lunch and that families were clearly made very welcome here.

(11.45–1.45pm & 6.45–9.45pm) £1–7: whitebait, Barnsley chop, plaice, lasagne, chicken Kiev
Children: own menu

• Ale – John Smith's, Tetley P – own car park

North Berwick, Lothian — map 11

HARDING'S RESTAURANT, 2 Station Road – ☎ North Berwick (0620) 4737.

R

By the station – follow the British Rail signs.

Christopher Harding has built up an excellent reputation in the three years or so since he opened his eponymous restaurant in an Edwardian tea room, which has been restored to its original form. It has a simple, white wood panelled interior with checked tablecloths, Indian rugs on the walls and an old dresser. It is a bright and welcoming place.

The food is firmly based on the fresh ingredients which are available on the day, and this is also a place to find some excellent Australian wines.

LUNCH £9: avocado vinaigrette, breast of chicken, pudding or cheese;
DINNER £15: warm pheasant terrine, steamed fillet of turbot, pudding or cheese
Children: small portions

No credit cards One high chair only
Licensed P – on street

North Bovey, Devon — map 1

RING OF BELLS – ☎ Moretonhampstead (0647) 40375.

P

Off the B3212 near Moretonhampstead.

It's worth a detour along very narrow roads to see this classic English village of thatched houses clustered around a small green.

The pub is a delightful 13th century building with a wonderful low-beamed bar, spiral staircases, and a notable grandfather clock which is built into the wall. Families are welcome in the lounge, which has a large open fireplace with an iron stove, or in the dining room.

You will always find some food at the pub, and that includes an evening menu and Sunday lunch.

There is a grassed and paved area which can seat about 100 people, and a salad bar is open during the summer months.

(12–2pm & 6.30–9.30pm) £4–6: lasagne, chilli con carne, curry, steak & kidney pie
Children: half portions

• Ale – Ind Coope Burton, Tetley, Wadworth
P – street parking

North Curry, Somerset **map 2**

THE RISING SUN, Knapp – ☎ Taunton (0823) 490 436.

P *Between the A361 and the A378 east of Taunton. Look for the North Curry sign.*

It is well worth the effort to seek out this 16th century inn, which was once licensed for cider only. If you head for North Curry, you will find some well-placed signs just outside the village to point you to the pub.

It has been renovated and expanded, and very smart it looks in its coat of white paint, and with baskets of bright flowers and honeysuckle adorning the front walls. Inside there is a most attractive bar with comfortable arm chairs, and a huge stove set in a mammoth fireplace. There are some fine wooden beams and pillars in the various rooms, and off the bar is a pretty dining room.

The family room, with its stone walls and old oak panelling is a delight. There are padded settles and several tables and another huge walk-in fireplace with an iron cooking range.

There is an excellent choice of food at this welcoming family pub in lovely countryside – seek it out and enjoy it! But please note that the pub is closed all day on Monday.

(12–2pm & 7–9.30pm, not Mon) £1–7: Brixham plaice, ploughman's, steaks, cauliflower cheese, lasagne
Children: own menu, half portions

• Ale – Bass, Exmoor P – own car park

North Gorley, Nr Fordingbridge, Hants **map 3**

ROYAL OAK – ☎ Fordingbridge (0425) 652 244.

P *Just off the A338, four miles North of Ringwood.*

Originally a hunting lodge, this spruce-looking 17th century thatched pub is in a lovely setting and has a fine oak tree at the front. Just off a busy road and into New Forest territory it is surrounded by common land and overlooks a large duck pond. A picket fence protects the customers from inquisitive donkeys and there is plenty of wild life on the pond to watch. It is just the place to take a family for a drink or a meal.

At the back of the pub, the rather functional family room has a partly glassed roof and doors on to the garden, a large, enclosed area with well kept lawns and borders, and plenty of tables with sun umbrellas. There are also some swings, a climbing frame, and a rocking horse at the side of the pub.

(12–2pm & 6.30–9.30pm) £1–7: salads, chicken curry, poached cod, steak
Children: own menu

• Ale – Flowers, Marston's, Ringwood
P – own car park

Northallerton, North Yorks — map 10

BETTYS CAFE TEAROOMS, 188 High Street – ☎ Northallerton (0609) 5154.

R

On the main street.

You will find a civilised and charming atmosphere at this café, the smallest of the celebrated chain of Bettys. The standards are extremely high and the welcome for families is whole-hearted.

Northallerton is a pretty market town with plenty to do and Bettys makes a fine stopping off point for you to catch your breath.

There are changing facilities in the Ladies (and a playpen) upstairs and, as well as high chairs, nappies, bibs and beakers will be provided. The infants' and children's menu shows real flair and imagination.

If you find it hard to resist home-made cakes this is the place and there is also a wide range of savouries, grills and sandwiches. There is also an excellent range of tea and unusual blends of coffee. If you haven't time to stop, the pastries are for sale in the shop at the front of the restaurant.

£1–5: rarebits, haddock & prawns au gratin, omelettes, plaice & chips, scrambled egg with smoked salmon

Open 9am–5.30pm, from 10am Sundays   Access/Visa
No music   Licensed
No smoking in café
P – on street and car park nearby

Northwich, Cheshire map 6

THE MOORINGS, Anderton Marina – ☎ Northwich (0606) 79789.

R

Just off the A533 North of Northwich.

It is difficult to believe that a quarter of a mile after passing the grime and bustle of the I.C.I. factory alongside the Trent and Mersey canal, you can find the tranquillity of this bright, clean restaurant which overlooks moorings for some forty boats. It has a clean-cut look with plain cream walls, plain blue carpets, flowers and plants and cane furniture. There is a small, enclosed patio with bench tables, and this overlooks the marina.

It's a pleasant place to visit and the Sunday lunch at around £7 is deservedly popular.

The Ladies is spacious, and the staff will put a chair in there if a mother needs to change or feed a baby.

£1–4: prawn cocktail, steak & kidney pie, plaice & chips, chilli con carne, lasagne
Children: own menu, half portions

Open 10am–10pm Tue-Sat, 10am–6pm Sun Closed Monday
Open all year Access/Visa
Licensed P – own car park

Norton, Shropshire map 6

HUNDRED HOUSE HOTEL – ☎ Norton (095 271) 353.

P

On the A442 between Bridgnorth and Wellington.

This hotel and pub has been renovated and adapted with great style by the Phillips family, who used to own the Greyhound at Marsh Gibbon (q.v.). You enter a bright and airy reception area, with a tiled floor, exposed brick walls, doors with stained glass panels, and bunches of dried flowers and herbs hanging from the ceiling.

The style is continued in a lovely high-ceilinged room, with a Colebrookdale cast-iron range. Families are welcome to park themselves here, and there are windows on to the sizeable garden, shaded by trees. The two donkeys, Gerrard and Susan, are still on hand to crop the lawns.

The large bar has cast-iron cooking pots and other utensils hanging from the beamed ceilings – a suitable reminder of the old industries of this region, where nearby Ironbridge is regarded as one of the cradles of the Industrial Revolution. The museums there are well worth a visit.

The bar is on two levels, and families can relax at the tables in the eating area which is notable for a huge fireplace. There is a great emphasis on food here, and the menu certainly looks enticing. Some of the produce will come from the hotel's vegetable garden: mange-tout and asparagus perhaps, as well as the herbs.

By this summer the pub will be open all day from 11am to 11pm and you should note that breakfast can also be had from 7.30 to 11am.

It's a delightful spot where families are properly looked after throughout the day.

BAR MEALS (11am–11pm) £2–10: fresh vegetable terrine, salmon kedgeree, seafood pie, grilled saddle of rabbit, beef olives
Children: own menu

• Ale – Flowers, Marston's, Phillips and guests
P – own car park No music

Also recommended in the Family Welcome Accommodation Guide.

If you wish to recommend an establishment to the Guide please write to us – report forms are at the back of the book. We need your help to extend and improve the guide.

Norton St Philip, Somerset — map 2

GEORGE INN – ☎ Faulkland (037 387) 224.

P

On the A366.

A magnificent and classic old inn dating from the 13th century and possibly even earlier, where little has been done to spoil an oak-beamed and wood-panelled interior with its old tables and wooden settles. The landlord, thank goodness, has no music in the pub nor any of those ghastly games machines with their hideous electronic noises.

Children are welcome in one of the lounges which is large and very much in character with a good array of tables and chairs, and a huge stone fireplace. Another children's room comes into play at the weekend when the 'Dungeon Bar', which held a group of the rebel Duke of Monmouth's men prisoners in 1685, is open. Take a look at the splendid wooden ceiling. The 'Monmouth Room' is also available at times for families.

On sunny days you can sit in a small courtyard, with a part-paved, part-cobbled floor, and surrounded by thick stone walls and heavy roofs. Alternatively there is a pretty lawned garden with several apple trees, and from there you look out across playing fields to the local church.

There is a good choice of hot and cold food available, both at the bar and in the restaurant, and a traditional three-course lunch is served on Sundays for around £8. There are two high chairs available.

(11.30am–2pm & 6.30–10pm) £1–4: ploughman's, hot pasty, vegetarian lasagne, baked potato with ham & cheese
Children: small portions

• Ale – Bass, Wadworth's No music
P – own car park

Nuthurst, West Sussex — map 3

BLACK HORSE – ☎ Horsham (0403) 891 272.

P

On a minor road off the A281 south east of Horsham.

This is a very appealing village pub; housed in what was once part of a row of cottages and is now a long, low, red-brick building. Inside the rooms are very smart with pine-clad walls, low beamed ceilings, an abundance of good wooden furniture, paved stone floors, with a big open fire in one bar and a substantial wood-burning stove in the other. There are two other rooms in the same style and children are welcome in the one furthest from the bar. It's very well furnished and you can see the structure of the old walls.

Food is served in the bar every day except Sunday evenings when, if the weather relents, a barbecue is held. This is a busy pub but when we visited the food was served up with commendable efficiency.

There is a patio at both the front and the rear of the pub with plenty of bench seats, and a pretty lawned garden, well shaded by tall trees and with a cheerful stream swooping through it.

(12–2.30pm & 7–10pm) £1–7: cottage pie, ploughman's, mixed grill, stuffed trout
Children: own menu, half portions

• Ale – Benskin's, Hall & Woodhouse, King & Barnes, Tetley's, Young's
P – own car park

Oakwood Hill, Nr Ockley, Surrey — map 3

PUNCH BOWL INN – ☎ Oakwood Hill (030 679) 249.

P

Off the A29 south of Ockley – the last turn before the Sussex border.

An attractive, tile-hung pub which is surrounded on all sides by long vistas of countryside. Part of the building is over 600 years old, and the bar is a splendid sight with its stone floors, black beams, wooden pew, and a magnificent inglenook fireplace.

The family room upstairs doubles as a function room and is actually housed in the old village hall. From its wide window you look across to Leith Hill with its tower, built by an 18th century eccentric. An alternative at lunchtimes is the delightful, low-beamed dining room. On summer days you can head for the patio with its many bench tables and a large, business-like barbecue – which is usually in operation on summer weekends. There's also a good choice of real ales and always some guest beers on offer.

(12–2pm & 7–10pm) £1–6: curried chicken with rice, ham & egg, chips & peas, plaice & chips, steak & kidney & Guinness pie, steaks
Children: own menu

• Ale – King & Barnes, Hall & Woodhouse, Young's and guests
P – own car park

Old Deer, by Mintlaw, Grampian — map 12

SAPLINBRAE HOUSE HOTEL, Saplinbrae Sporting Estate – ☎ Mintlaw (0771) 23515.

R

On the A950 west of Mintlaw.

The new owners welcome families to their bar and restaurant and have added a bistro to the available facilties. The lounge is pleasanty busy and noisy, with enough space between the tables for carry-cots, etc. The friendly staff will gladly find somewhere for a mother to change or feed a baby.

The hotel is housed in a former dower house, built in 1756, and is set in 400 acres of grounds. There is accommodation here but the owners have set their marketing cap at "the more lucrative business market".

(11am–11pm) BISTRO AND BAR £2–9: rollmop herring, roast pheasant, prawn salad, steak Rossini, roast beef & Yorkshire pudding
Children: half portions

• Ale – Theakston's Access/AmEx/Diners/Visa
P – own car park

Onecote, Nr Leek, Staffs — map 6

JERVIS ARMS – ☎ Onecote (053 88) 206.

P

On the B5053, east of Leek.

This attractive old pub, of 17th century vintage, has been extended and now boasts two family rooms. One of them has its own entrance and has plenty of tables and chairs available; alongside is the original family room with low beams, copper-topped tables and padded wooden settles. The Ladies has baby changing facilities, and high chairs are also available.

The large lawned garden is delightful, with a little stone bridge over a meandering stream – it's actually the River Hamps. But you must watch your children because the garden is unfenced. There are plenty of bench tables, and a climbing frame, a slide, and a wooden play house for the children.

This is an excellent family pub in the lovely surroundings of the Peak National Park. There is self-catering accommodation in a converted barn alongside the garden.

✕ (12–2pm & 7–10pm) £1–6: plaice, fillet steak, chilli con carne, homity pie, savoury cheesecake
Children: own menu

• Ale – Bass, Ruddles, Stone's, Theakston's
P – own car park

Osmington Mills, Nr Weymouth, Dorset — map 2

SMUGGLERS INN – ☎ Preston (0305) 833 125.

P *Off the A353 north-east of Weymouth.*

The partly thatched 13th century inn has a delightful setting in a valley on the Dorset coastal path. It has recently been renovated with great care by the licensee; although the interior is now open plan, there are plenty of nooks and crannies to keep it cosy. Huge old timbers have been used and the black panelling has been retained. There is a restaurant at one end of the pub.

The family room is housed in a thatched extension and has a pool table, video game and a piano. It is comfortably furnished and one of the seats is made from an upturned rowing boat, and there are a couple of small saddles (on secure stands) for children to sit on.

On warm days you can sit on the paved terrace and keep a watch on the children while they enjoy the swings and the slide.

✕ (12–2pm & 7–9.30pm) £1–13: lasagne, meat & vegetable pie, plaice & chips, steaks, rack of lamb
Children: own menu

• Ale – Courage, Ringwood   P – own car park

Oswaldkirk, North Yorks — map 10

THE MALT SHOVEL – ☎ Ampleforth (04393) 461.

P *On the B1363, south of Helmsley, three miles off the A170.*

This attractive pub was built as a manor house in the 16th century and became a coaching inn 200 years later. It sits in a sleepy village set snugly between the Ampleforth Forest and the beautiful Vale of Pickering.

The interior of the pub is made up of several different rooms with the bar serving two of them. The family room is directly off the car park, and is fairly spacious with wood panels and a large inglenook fireplace. The snug bar is also very attractive with wooden settles and horse brasses. Another feature of the place is a superb oak staircase in the main hallway. There are lots of interesting pictures and other bric-a-brac on the walls.

The garden at the rear is also a lovely place to pass the odd hour or two. The patio with its white tables and chairs looks out onto a carefully maintained miniature box hedge maze. Next door to this is an enclosed lawn with bench tables.

BAR MEALS (12am–2pm & 7–9pm) £1–8: salmon roulade, chicken Aphrodite, Moorland chop, venison steak, fresh fish of the day
Children: own menu, half portions

• Ale – Sam Smith's P – own car park

Over Peover, Cheshire — map 6

WHIPPING STOCKS, Stocks Lane – ☎ Knutsford (0565) 812 332.

P *On the A50 South of Knutsford.*

This large pub, built of dark red brick, and enlivened by rows of flower boxes, has several rooms off the large main bar where families are welcome, and they are usually packed with children and their adults, all tucking into their food.

French windows open on to a large enclosed garden which has plenty of bench tables on the lawn – a relaxing place to be on a summer day.

(12–2pm & 7–9.30pm, not Sun or Mon pm) £1–6: rollmop herring, steak & kidney pie, chilli con carne, haddock
Children: own menu, half portions

• Ale – Samuel Smith's P – own car park

Oving, West Sussex — map 3

GRIBBLE INN – ☎ Chichester (0243) 786 893.

P *Between the A27 and the A259 just east of Chichester.*

This was Rosa Gribble's cottage and she lived in it for nearly a hundred years. It became a pub as recently as 1980 and there have been additions, for example a large eating area and a kitchen. The whole pub maintains the same delightful style, with bare brick walls, ancient exposed timbers, old church pews and wooden settles and tables.

There is plenty of space in the bar and the eating area, and just as well because this is a very busy and popular place, and deservedly so. The family room is also spacious and relaxing, with several cushioned settles, stools and sturdy tables. Alongside is a another smaller room. It leads out to a large and very pretty lawned garden, with an abundance of trees, bushes and bright flowers.

It is good to report that there is a no smoking area in this excellent pub. By now the pub's own brewery should be in operation – yet another good reason for a visit.

(12–2.30pm & 6.30–9.30pm, not Sun pm) £1–7: whitebait, turkey & ham pie, seafood special, sirloin steak, vegeburger
Children: smaller portions

• Ale – Hall & Woodhouse, Palmer's, Gribble
P – own car park No music

Owslebury, Nr Winchester, Hants **map 3**

THE SHIP INN – ☎ Owslebury (096 274) 358.

P

In the village south east of Winchester.

This is a smashing old pub in the minor roads quite close to the famous Marwell Zoo. Above the white rough cast walls, the facade is hung with tiles, and big tubs of flowers give a welcoming look to the place.

The bar is broken up into various alcoves, with a low ceiling and an inglenook fireplace, and the black wooden pillars and beams confirm the 17th century origins of the building.

Children, as long as they are accompanied by an adult, are welcome in a small and comfortable room off the bar; it has a few tables and a piano.

Roses and honeysuckle clamber over rustic open fencing which surrounds the large flat garden with a climbing frame, swings, and bench tables; and fine views of the surrounding countryside. It's a delightful spot.

(12–2pm & 7–9pm, not Sun pm) £2–8: plaice & chips, scampi & chips, chilli con carne, sirloin steak, beef Stroganoff
Children: own menu

• Ale – Marston's P – own car park

Oxenhope, West Yorks **map 9**

WAGGON AND HORSES – ☎ Haworth (0535) 43302.

P *Half a mile out of town on the A6033 towards Hebden Bridge.*

For the traveller on the Brontë trail, this large roadside pub offers a welcome break from the souvenir shops of the sadly commercialised town of Haworth nearby.

In keeping with the area's literary tradition, the bar snack menu reads like a book, extending to no less than six pages. Not for nothing does the pub claim to offer the most comprehensive bar menu for miles around.

The dining room to the side of the bar serves as a family room and although there are no half portions, extra plates will be provided to split normal portions.

(12–2pm & 7.30–10.30pm) £1–6: fish & chips, curries, clam fries, liver & bacon, salads, steaks

• Ale – Theakston's, Tetley's, Webster's

P – own car park

Oxford, Oxon **map 3**

EAGLE AND CHILD, St Giles – ☎ Oxford (0865) 58085.

P *Near the city centre.*

This lovely old pub stretches back in a series of narrow wood panelled rooms with many old photographs on the walls. It has interesting literary associations, since it was the "local" of C.S. Lewis and J.R. Tolkien. As you enter there are two or three cosy little alcoves, which can only accommodate half a dozen people in any comfort, and then two more rooms.

The last of these is a conservatory with a few tables, and is the most suitable for families, especially because it is a no smoking area. Through the glass doors there is a little patio with a few bench tables and it is safely enclosed.

The Eagle & Child has a really pleasant atmosphere, offers a good choice of pub food at reasonable prices, plus a selection of real ales. A pretty good formula, especially since families are made thoroughly welcome by the licensees and staff.

(12–2pm every day, and 6–8pm Mon-Fri) £1–4: lasagne, vegetable pot, pizzas, chilli con carne, lasagne

Children: small portions

• Ale – Arkell's, Ind Coope Burton, Wadworth's
P – on street or in nearby car parks

BLUE COYOTE, 36-37 St Clements – ☎ Oxford (0865) 241 4319

R

Near Magdalen Bridge, on one of the main roads in and out of Oxford (it's a continuation of the A40).

The bright blue canopy and facade of the Blue Coyote will ensure that you cannot miss it, and inside you will find a lively and cheerful restaurant. The blue coyote theme is carried through in the decor, and the menu has a definite American slant, although a traditional roast is available on Sundays.

There is plenty of room inside, with plain wooden tables and chairs, and potted plants here and there. When we last visited we had lunch here one Sunday and were impressed by the way the staff coped efficiently and very cheerfully with a very full house.

There are several high chairs, but no facilities for changing a baby.

£2–11: hot crab fritters, tagliatelli, Texas smoked beef chilli, T-bone steak, sea bream
Children: smaller portions

Open 12-11pm Mon to Thurs; 12–12 Fri to Sat; 10am–11pm Sunday
Access/Visa Licensed
P – on street or at rear of the restaurant

BROWNS, 5–9 Woodstock Road – ☎ Oxford (0865) 511 995.

R

On the A34 close to its junction with the A423 and just north of the city centre.

This big, bustling restaurant has a simple and effective decor of bentwood chairs and wooden tables, and lots of plants and mirrors. A large skylight gives a spacious effect to the place, as does the bar area which, on warmer days, opens out on to the pavement.

The menu concentrates on salads, pasta and grills, and offers plenty of things to appeal to a young palate. There are lots of high chairs available; and a mother and baby room provides a folded changing table. The staff make a real effort to welcome parents with young children; indeed people of all ages find a warm welcome.

By now the restaurant will have been extended and the extra room will include a larger no smoking area.

✕ £1–9: spaghetti, fisherman's pie, venison steak, burgers, chicken pie
Children: own menu, small portions

Open 11am–11.30pm, every day (from noon on Sundays)
Closed at Xmas   No credit cards accepted
No smoking on one side of restaurant • Ale – Adnams
P – on street

SWEENEY TODD'S, 6–12 George Street – ☎ Oxford (0865) 723 421.

R

In the city centre.

Parking can be difficult in the centre of Oxford (one of the more hostile towns for the motorist, we find) but this restaurant is a relaxing, cool place with reasonably-priced fast food.

On the ground floor you will find a smallish bar area with a few wooden tables; and up the stairs, the main restaurant is on two levels. The first level, with white decor and plenty of space, is connected by an open staircase to a balcony area. It is pleasant and rather stylish.

There are several high chairs on the premises, but no facilities for baby changing.

✕ (12–11pm) £1–8: crudités, pizzas, chef's salad, burgers, barbecued meats
Children: own menu, half portions

Open all year   Access/Visa
Licensed
P – small car park round the corner

Nr Parbold, Lancs — map 6

THE FARMERS ARMS – ☎ Parbold (02576) 2074. — *Pot Luck*

P

On the B5246, follow the Rufford sign off the A5209. The pub is actually closer to Rufford than to Parbold.

At the foot of Parbold Hill, a popular spot with walkers and motorists alike, this spacious pub and restaurant is an excellent spot to relax in attractive surroundings.

Bar meals are available both lunchtime and evenings and the family room off the main bar is nicely furnished with red velvet seating and wooden tables.

A large grass play area has swings, a slide and a climbing frame and several bench tables, so that parents can watch their children.

The adjoining restaurant also welcomes youngsters, especially for Sunday lunch and it is open all day on Sundays. There is a special menu and several high chairs are available. It has a timbered ceiling and large picture windows which overlook well manicured lawns and the countryside beyond.

BAR SNACKS (12–2.30pm & 5.30–10.30pm) £1–8: Pangang satay, salmon mayonnaise, pizza, steaks, plaice & chips
Children: own menu

• Ale – Burtonwood P – own car park

Parkmill, Nr Swansea, West Glamorgan — map 1

GOWER INN – ☎ Bishopston (044 128) 3116.

P

On the A4118, west of Swansea.

This stone pub has loads of room, including a couple of areas where families are welcome to sit. Up a few stairs from the large bar area there is a comfortable, well-furnished lounge, which overlooks a small patio. On the same level as the bar, but well away from it, you will find another spacious lounge, well provided with tables and chairs.

There is a good selection of food on offer here, including a Sunday lunch at under £6, and high chairs are available. Please note that the Sunday lunch is not served in the very busy period of July and August.

On summer days you can head for the sizeable patio, which has plenty of bench tables.

During the summer months the pub will be open throughout the day (June to September).

(12–2.30pm & 6.30–9.30pm) £1–8: lasagne, sirloin steak, beef carbonade, chicken casserole, lentil crumble
Children: own menu, half portions

• Ale – Bass, Hancock's P – own car park

Peebles, Borders — map 11

CRINGLETIE HOUSE HOTEL – ☎ Eddleston (072 13) 233.

R

Two and a half miles north of Peebles on the A703.

This is a most appealing and distinguished sandstone country house, built in 1861 and rather Gothic with its high windows, half towers and tall chimneys. It is set in nearly thirty acres of lovely gardens against a backdrop of soft rolling hills. There is a play area for children, with a swing and a climbing frame. The two dining rooms are elegant, well-proportioned and beautifully furnished; and decorated with an abundance of fresh flowers.

There is an enterprising choice of food and the lunch menu offers good value. Testimony to the quality of the food is the inclusion of the hotel in the "Good Food Guide" for twenty years, and you can be sure that the food will be fresh, because there are a couple of acres of kitchen garden.

A baby could be fed and changed in reasonable comfort in the Ladies.

LUNCH (1–1.45pm) £12: tomato & mozzarella salad, poached salmon, lamb, pudding or cheese;
DINNER (7.30–8.30pm) £20: hot mushroom mousse, carrot & orange soup, baked monkfish, pudding or cheese
Children: half portions

Closed Jan & Feb   Access/Visa
Licensed   No music

P – own car park

Also recommended in the Family Welcome Accommodation Guide.

Pembridge, Hereford & Worcs — map 6

NEW INN – ☎ Pembridge (054 47) 427.

P

On the A44 between Kington and Leominster.

This is now a quiet and rather delightful village in lovely surroundings, and this marvellous, black and white 14th century inn, which was once a courthouse, suits it admirably. Considering its proximity to the Welsh border it is perhaps surprising that it survived all the violent mayhem which afflicted this part of England centuries ago.

Inside is a marvellous public bar, which looks as though it hasn't changed since the inn first traded, with a flag-stoned floor, huge open fireplace, black beams and a curved wooden settle. The lounge where children may be taken is large and comfortable with inviting armchairs and sofas and some nice wooden tables. There's no garden – just a couple of picnic tables outside on the cobbled front.

You will find some interesting bar snacks here, plus a Sunday lunch for around £6; and there is a high chair on the premises. Some friends of ours who usually stop here on their way to and from Hereford races have given us enthusiastic reports of the food.

(12–2pm & 7–9.30pm) £1–6: mussels in lemon butter, poached salmon, crispy duck salad, fillet of pork in cider apple & cream, steak sandwich
Children: half portions

• Ale – Flowers No music
P – own car park

Also recommended in the Family Welcome Accommodation Guide.

Pendoggett, Cornwall — map 1

CORNISH ARMS – ☎Port Isaac (0208)) 880 263.

P

On the B3314 north of Wadebridge.

This attractive old pub has an exterior partly covered by slate and the floors inside are of the same material, no doubt from the local Delabole quarries.

As you enter there are three low-ceilinged rooms adjoining each other, and they are all comfortably furnished in attractive style. The smallest of them has a padded settle curving around the walls, and the Coffee Room is a delightful and cosy room, with padded benches around its walls.

Families with children are welcome to use the Coffee Room at lunchtimes, and the restaurant is also available to them in the evenings.

For the unencumbered adult drinker the spacious back bar, with more padded settles and a good array of wooden tables, is the place to be. There's a good, friendly atmosphere here in which to sup a couple of glasses of the strong Pendoggett Special.

✕ (12.30–2pm & 7–9.30pm) £2–9: lemon sole, beef Bourgignonne, trout Cleopatra, tuna fish salad

• Ale – Bass, Pendoggett Special P – own car park

Perranuthnoe, Cornwall — map 1

VICTORIA INN, Church Town – ☎ Penzance (0736) 710 309.

P

Off the main A394 Helston to Penzance Road.

An appealing pub, which is situated in a small and quiet village, only a couple of minutes' walk from the sea. This is a lovely stretch of coastline, not far from St. Michael's Mount, and there are splendid walks.

The pub, which is very popular with local people, has lots of old photographs on the walls and displays the various menus on pieces of slate attached to the walls.

The family room is well away from the bar and has tables and chairs on one level and padded benches and tables on a higher level. There is also a pool table and a dart board. It leads out to a small patio. There is also a small flower garden across the road at the front of the pub.

✕ (12–2pm & 6–9.30pm) £1–8: filled jacket potatoes, spare ribs, chicken curry, fresh trout, salads, steaks

Children: own menu, half portions

• Ale – Courage, John Smith's

P – own car park, and on street

Pewsham, Nr Chippenham, Wilts **map 2**

LYSLEY ARMS – ☎ Chippenham (0249) 652 864.

P *A couple of miles east of Chippenham on the A4 at the junction with the A342.*

This very large and busy roadside inn is smoothly painted white under its steep roof with dormer windows. A long bar greets you as you enter and on the other side of a large fireplace there is a very comfortable sitting room with a sofa and some easy chairs in front of a huge log fire.

The other end of the pub comprises an eating area and off this is the Garden Room, and families are welcome to use this to eat together or just to have a drink. It's really a large conservatory and it leads out to an enclosed and secluded garden. Alongside is another very large garden with plenty of bench tables and a children's play area which includes slides, swings, a climbing frame and a see saw. There is loads of space for everyone to relax on those long summer days.

The pub is open all day during the summer months (June to September) from Monday to Saturday, and cream teas are served during the afternoons.

(12–2pm & 6.30–10pm) £2–9: garlic mushrooms, local trout, vegetable gratin, swordfish, steaks
Children: own menu

• Ale – Bass, Wadworth's P – own car park

Piercebridge, Co Durham **map 10**

THE GEORGE – ☎ Darlington (0325) 374 576.

P *Just off the A67 and on the B6275, west of Darlington.*

This fine old pub was refurbished a couple of years ago and now includes a very wide choice of food both from the bar and the restaurant menus. There are several high chairs on the premises.

The family room is located in the middle of the pub, a handsome room with oak panelling and an inglenook fireplace. At the back of the pub there is a lawn with a few tables and chairs set out, and you have a pleasant view of the River Tees from here.

BAR MEALS (12–2pm & 7–10pm) £1–9: home-made paté, whitebait, chicken in Stilton sauce, cod & chips, steaks
Children: half portions

• Ale – John Smith's P – own car park

Pisgah, Nr Aberystwyth, Dyfed — map 5

HALFWAY INN, Devil's Bridge – ☎ *Capel Bangor (097 084) 631.*

P

On the A4120.

One of the finest views, of the Rheidol valley surrounded by hills, awaits you at this appealing old pub – a long, white-painted two-storey building. Just down the road are the well-known Mynach Falls, and it is a lovely part of the world.

Even lovelier for real ale drinkers when they walk to the end bar, a stillage holds a dozen or so barrels, from which you help yourself. The licensee will serve around 65 different ales during the course of a year. It is a nice bar too, with a slate floor, stone walls, and good wooden tables and benches.

The family room is quite spacious and has plenty of tables and comfortably padded bench seats, and through a window you can see the trickle of a small waterfall. A small snug, with one table, is off to one side.

There are tables outside the pub, and up above it a long grassy terrace with a play area for the children, and a paddock for passing pony trekkers. The views from here will delight you.

Please note that this pub does not open on Sunday evening during the winter (October to May).

(11am–3pm & 7–11pm) £1–7: lasagne, fisherman's pie, chilli con carne, ploughman's, sirloin steak
Children: own menu

• Ale – Felinfoel and a range of 65 brews – always 13 on tap
P – own car park No music

Plumley, Cheshire **map 6**

SMOKER INN – ☎ Lower Peover (056 581) 2338.

P *On the A556 Chester-Nantwich road, about two and a half miles from junction 19 of the M6.*

This is an immaculately maintained white-painted part-thatched inn dating from Elizabethan times on a busy main road close to the M6. It has an excellent lawned garden with plenty of tables and chairs at the side – albeit a bit noisy alongside the main road.

Inside are several smart, low-beamed rooms including one between the bar and the restaurant where children are welcome. It is comfortable and furnished with padded benches and tables, and an alternative for families is a lounge to the right of the entrance. The landlord and his wife are welcoming to families, but have no hesitation in asking the parents of noisy or badly behaved children to leave. More power to their elbow.

The pub offers an excellent bar menu from Monday to Saturday (sandwiches only on Sunday); the restaurant serves a range of roasts and grills with a table d'hote menu at just over £10. There are three high chairs available.

BAR SNACKS (11.30am–2.30pm & 6.30–10pm) £1–6: Cumberland sausage, plaice & chips, halibut steak Mornay, kofta curry, moussaka
Children: own menu, half portions

• Ale – Robinson's P – own car park

Places included in the Guide must offer the following basic facilities:
Pubs – a separate area or room for families where alcohol is not served;
Restaurants – high chairs and special menus/reduced portions.

Plush, Dorset **map 2**

BRACE OF PHEASANTS – ☎ *Piddletrenthide (030 04) 357.*

P

Signposted from the B3143 near Piddletrenthide.

This is a super pub in every way and well worth a short drive along country lanes. In fact you can reach it very easily from Cerne Abbas if you turn into Piddle Lane and go straight across country.

It is a most attractive building, made by amalgamating two cottages and the village forge, and now sits under its thatched roof. The bar takes up one side of the pub, and is a long room with a beamed ceiling and an open brick fireplace at one end and a wood burning stove at the other.

The family room, the old kitchen, is to one side of the bar and is a bright and cheerful place, with chequered tablecloths on the tables.

To add to the pleasure of a visit here, the garden is really lovely with a sloping lawn against a backcloth of trees, a rockery and an iron seat encircling a large tree. A children's play area has also been installed with a climbing frame, etc.

The food (available every day) is enterprising and you can have a traditional Sunday lunch here too for less than £6 (three courses).

It's a lovely spot – but please note the opening hours – which in the evening is often 7pm, especially in winter.

(12–2pm & 7–10pm) £1–9: soft herring roes in garlic butter, bouillabaisse, liver with bacon & onions, rosettes of lamb, fish pie
Children: own menu

• Ale – Bass, Charrington No music
P – own car park

Polbathic, Cornwall **map 1**

HALFWAY HOUSE – ☎ *St Germans (0503) 30202.*

P

Just off the A374 east of Looe.

A 16th century coaching inn which is handily placed midway between Plymouth and Looe. The front of the pub is close by the main road, and is bright with hanging baskets and tubs of flowers, and the unpainted stone at the back of the building testifies to the age of the building.

From the small bar area, a door leads through to a lounge which is furnished with dark oak tables and chairs.

The family room is through an archway and there are several pine tables.

Up the stairs there is an attractive restaurant and from here a door leads out to an enclosed garden. There is a flat area of lawn with bench tables, and the rest of the garden slopes up to some trees and bushes. There is a climbing frame for the children.

The pub provides a comprehensive choice of food including a three-course Sunday lunch at around £5 – good value.

(12am–2.30pm & 6–10.30pm) £1–9: plaice & chips, vegetable curry, chicken Kiev, steaks, nut & mushroom fettucine
Children: own menu

• Ale – Courage   P – own car park

Pontargothi, Dyfed **map 5**

CRESSELLY ARMS – ☎ Nantgereid (0267) 290 221.

P

On the A40 between Llandeilo and Carmarthen.

This appealing pub is very smartly turned out in its coat of white paint with black trimmings, and sits alongside the River Cothi. One of the bonuses of visiting the pub is that you can sit in the lovely garden alongside the river. The children are well catered for, too, with a safely enclosed play area with swings and an enchanted tree.

Inside you will find a very pleasant bar area, with a small restaurant to one side. Up some stairs from the bar there is another attractive room, comfortably furnished with well padded seats and copper topped tables, and families are welcome to settle here.

The landlord emphasized that families are very welcome in his pub and form an important part of his trade. Another of the advantages here is that food is available for most of the opening hours, and there is always a good selection of fish.

(11am–2.15pm & 6–10pm) £1–6: plaice & chips, beef curry, lasagne, steak & kidney pie, hake & chips
Children: small portions

• Ale – Flowers and guests   P – own car park

Please let us have reports – good or bad – on any establishments listed in the Guide as soon as possible after your visit.

Poole, Dorset **map 2**

CLIPPER RESTAURANT, 100 Dolphin Centre – ☎ Poole (0202) 683 334.

R

On the first floor of the Dolphin Shopping Centre in the centre of Poole. The restaurant, like the shopping centre itself, has been revamped in the last couple of years. It is a bright and airy place, attractively decorated and furnished. The restaurant has been re-designed into a number of self-service counters: vegetarian, salads, hot meals, drinks and so on. The food is excellent and the alterations have clearly not affected the quality.

The Ladies room of the Clipper is large, and has chairs and a counter for changing a baby, and a supply of paper towels. One of the lavatories is completely self-contained with a hand basin and counter for complete privacy.

(9.30am–5.30pm, Mon to Sat) £1–6: prawn & salmon cocktail, roast turkey, plaice, cheese & oatmeal roast
Children: own menu, half portions

Open all year No credit cards
P – multi-storey in the Centre Licensed

Portmellon, Cornwall **map 1**

RISING SUN – ☎ Mevagissey (0726) 843 235. *Pot Luck*

P

Just South of Mevagissey.

You reach this village through the narrow streets of Mevagissey, and you will find this large, white-painted pub on the water's edge. There is a sand and shingle beach which is a bit overawed by a new housing development.

The whole of the first floor of the pub is at the disposal of families with a games room and a family room, clean, functional and well organised. You have the great bonus of lovely views across the water.

There is plenty of choice on the menu, and the prices are in tune with a family budget.

Please note that this pub opens only during the summer season – from Easter through to September.

(12–2pm & 6.30–9.30pm) £1–7: toasted sandwiches, jacket potatoes, chicken & chips, plaice & chips, salads
Children: own menu

Closed Autumn to Spring
• Ale – Hicks, Wadworth's P – own car park

Portpatrick, Dumfries & Galloway map 11

THE CROWN HOTEL, North Crescent – ☎ Portpatrick (077 681) 261.

P

Follow the main road into Portpatrick and turn right when you reach the harbour.

Do not be deceived by the ordinary appearance of this pub, set in a row of houses in this very attractive little port which is ringed by low hills. You will find a real pub with a warm and welcoming atmosphere. The cream walls are set off by the dark furniture, old pictures, and stone fireplace; there are three small rooms, one of which is separate from the bar and where families are welcome to park themselves.

The restaurant at the back of the pub is absolutely delightful. The walls are partly panelled in wood and above are decorated tiles with mirrors at intervals; all this, with the tiled floor and bentwood chairs gives the place the look of a brasserie. You go up some steps into a smaller area, and then into a most attractive conservatory, with masses of plants and this overlooks a sunken patio area with white furniture. It's a bustling, friendly place and the food is excellent and excellent value (especially the fish).

(12–2.30pm & 6–10pm) £1–6: moules mariniére, salads, beef hot pot, haddock & chips, scallops in red wine, whole plaice
Children: half portions

P – on the harbour front

Preston, Lancs map 6

TIGGIS, 38/42 Guildhall Street – ☎ Preston (0772) 58527.

R

Off Fishergate – one of the main streets.

Despite the name of the street this restaurant is a good five to ten minutes' walk from the Guild Hall, but is handily placed in the centre of town. As you enter enticing wafts of garlic confirm that you are about to savour Italian cooking. It is a big and bustling place and the staff are friendly and efficient. The attractive decor of tile floors, marble tables and lots of potted plants stays true to the style of the Italian trattoria.

The kitchens are open plan and you can see, and particularly hear, the chefs at work. The menu concentrates on pasta, and pizzas, and favourites such as steak Pizzaiola.

The staff will happily arrange half portions of any dishes for children: and there is a shelf in the Ladies to facilitate nappy-changing.

(12–2pm & 6–11.30pm, not Sun) £1–7: calamari, bresaolo, lasagne al forno, chicken Kiev, linguine alle vongole
Children: half portions

Access/Visa Licensed
P – multi-storey car park by the bus station

Preston Bagot, Warwicks — map 7

CRABMILL INN – ☎ Warwick (0926) 843 342.

P

On the B4095 west of Warwick.

The building's origins lie back in the 16th century and, as the name suggests, it was once an apple press. The brewery has opened the pub out, and it now contains a series of connecting but separate rooms and bars, and they include a couple of areas, well away from the bars, where families can sit.

An alternative on warmer days is the lawned garden with its wooden tables and chairs; and there is a tree house with swings and a slide for the children. The pub is now open throughout the day from Monday to Saturday.

(12–2pm & 7–9.30pm, not Sun pm) £1–8: salmon steak, grilled gammon, Cumberland sausage, steaks, plaice
Children: own menu

• Ale – Flowers, Wadworth's, Marston's
P – own car park

Queensferry (South), Edinburgh, Lothian — map 11

HAWES INN – ☎ Edinburgh (031) 331 1990.

P

On the south side of the Forth Bridge Road, the inn is almost underneath the Forth Rail Bridge; follow the 'Boat Ride' signs.

This fine old pub was built in the 16th century and is famous for its associations with Robert Louis Stevenson, who dreamt up the plot of "Kidnapped" in one of the rooms. The inn has a very comfortable family room with lots of tables and chairs, a mini-rocking chair and a high chair and it is reserved for customers with families until 8pm. We are delighted to record that the family room is a non-smoking one. The food is varied and sensibly priced, and two high chairs are available.

Behind the pub is a pleasant garden with a few tables and chairs, a swing and a slide. Trains occasionally rumble by on the bridge above.

In common with many Scottish pubs the Hawes Inn is open throughout the day, and food is available from noon onwards. There is a good selection of dishes including a range of Mexican food.

BAR SNACKS (12–9pm) £1–9: fried haddock, spiced minced lamb, escalope of pork Holstein, burgers, steaks
Children: half portions

• Ale – Arrol's, Ind Coope Burton P – own car park

Rampisham, Dorset — map 2

TIGER'S HEAD – ☎ Evershot (093 583) 244.

P

Off the A356 south-east of Crewkerne.

An old photograph shows the original village pub with flint walls and a thatched roof, but it burned down in 1915 and was replaced by this well-proportioned stone building. It is set in a picturesque village through which runs the river Frome.

The family room is just off the main bar and the kindly landlady used to provide children's books and board games. Many of these books have been torn apart and pieces stolen from the board games – another instance of the hooligan minority spoiling things for the rest of us. O tempora, o mores.

At the back is a lovely walled garden which is a mass of flowers in summer, and a stream.

Food which is always fresh and home-cooked is served every day and that includes a traditional Sunday lunch at under £6 for three courses and coffee. There is an excellent choice of vegetarian meals.

(12–2pm & 7–9.30pm) £1–7: rabbit pie, Cerne Valley trout, venison casserole, lentil crumble, spicy bean casserole
Children: small portions

• Ale – Butcombe's, Greene King, Wadworth's

P – own car park No music

Richmond, Surrey map 3

REFECTORY, 6 Church Walk – ☎ *(01) 940 6264.*

R

Park either in the Paradise Road multi-storey or in Sheen Road. Street parking is easy on a Sunday.

We paid a visit, en famille, to this restaurant last Spring and enjoyed ourselves as much as ever. The restaurant is in a quiet corner by the parish church and you can sit in the paved courtyard by the entrance if the weather is kind. Inside, the dining room is simply and agreeably furnished with good wooden furniture, and the atmosphere is friendly and welcoming.

We like this restaurant because it is one of the few in the London area which offers a genuine welcome to all the family: apart from the high chairs, the owners provide a changing table in the Ladies, and will find a quiet corner for breast feeding mothers. But this is also a real restaurant with freshly cooked English food and splendid vegetables and puddings, generously served. Above all the prices are sensible: a rare happening in the London area. There is an unusual wine list, too, with English and Australian wines.

This is a popular restaurant and booking ahead is advisable; it is also open for coffee from 10am to noon and for afternoon teas from 2 to 5pm, Tuesday to Saturday.

LUNCH (12–2pm Tue-Sun) £8: prawns in cream cheese, Exmoor lamb casserole, steamed jam sponge
Children: smaller portions

Closed Mondays & Xmas, New Year and Easter Sunday
Access/Visa Licensed
P – street or public car park No music

Risely, Beds map 7

FOX AND HOUNDS – ☎ *Bedford (0234) 708 240.*

P

North of Bedford off the A6 or B660.

This spacious pub sits in a village which is neatly placed between the two important arteries of the A1 and A6. It is painted smartly in white under a steeply pitched roof and the front is embellished with tubs of bright flowers. The original building dates back to 1550.

Inside there is a comfortable bar area and families are welcome in a large room to one side. It has heavy ceiling beams, and is comfortably furnished with padded chairs and wooden tables, and a huge fireplace forms a wall between this room and the bar and now houses the charcoal grill. This is very much in use since you are asked to choose your own steak (you are charged by weight) and this is then served up with salad. There is also a separate restaurant, which opens in the evening.

At the back there is a patio, and a huge grassy area to loll upon on summer days. There are plenty of tables and chairs, some children's games and a slide, and the landlord will be adding more play equipment for the summer.

(12–2pm & 7–10pm, not Sun pm) £1–10: chicken curry, steaks with salad, lasagne, fisherman's pie
Children: half portions

• Ale – Wells   P – own car park

Romsey, Hants — map 3

LUZBOROUGH HOUSE, Botley Road – ☎ Romsey (0794) 523 816.

P

On the A27 to the east of Romsey.

This lovely old house was once a gamekeeper's cottage and was also occupied by Lord Mountbatten's private secretary, and the idea of converting it to a pub must have appalled many people. But it has been done with skill and with sympathy for its origins.

A new wing houses a large, open plan lounge bar and there is a separate food counter and plenty of comfortable seats. Beyond this there are several other rooms, one of which was a kitchen in the 16th century; it has a huge inglenook fireplace with a wood burning stove, and has a fine collection of exposed wall beams. Alongside is a similar room, with its own inglenook fireplace, and families are welcome to use this; it is also used as an overflow dining area.

If you go through the elegant dining room, which is of 18th century vintage, you will come to another family room, a conservatory done in a Victorian style, and with a tiled floor, bamboo furniture and tubs of flowers.

From there you can step into the spacious walled garden with its lawns well provided with bench tables. There is also a play area with a Wendy house, slide, rocking horses, seesaws, and a bouncy castle.

It is a splendid place for families, and especially so since it is open all day except Sunday, and food is available at all times.

(12–10pm) £1–9: smoked salmon, chicken Kiev, plaice & chips, mixed grill, fillet steak
Children: own menu

• Ale – Flowers, Strong's, Boddington's
P – own car park

COBWEB TEA ROOMS, 49 The Hundred – ☎ Romsey (0794) 516 434.

R

Close to the centre of the town and opposite the entrance to Broadlands.

The Cobweb Tea Room is housed in a cottage with an 18th century front, and is true to tradition with black beams. The building is 500 years old in parts and is close to the main shopping area. The facade is freshly painted and is cheerfully decorated with an abundance of bright flowers which grow in tubs and hanging baskets.

The owner is happy to welcome families, and would make her private accommodation available to mothers who need to attend to babies.

You can have snacks throughout the day, and light lunch dishes from noon; and all the food is home-made.

There is an attractive walled-in garden and a terrace with a few tables.

£1–3: soup, toasted sandwiches, chicken curry, goulash, beans on toast
Children: half portions

Open 10am–5.30pm, Tue-Sat   No credit cards

No smoking at two tables No music
Licensed One high chair only
P – public parking 100 yards away

Ross-on-Wye, Hereford & Worcs map 2

MEADER'S HUNGARIAN RESTAURANT, 1 Copse Cross Street – ☎ (0989) 62803.

R

In the town centre.

This bright, modern restaurant has an appealing decor of cream and green floral wallpaper and curtains, and it all looks fresh and inviting.

Coffee and snacks are served from 10am and the daily menu offers very good value; there are several vegetarian dishes on the menu, as well as "chef's specials" every day. The evening menu has a fair choice of grills and fish, as well as Hungarian specialities (one of the owners comes from there). The friendly owners, with children of their own, will find somewhere for a mother to feed or change a baby.

DAY MENU £1–7: vegetable curry, Hungarian goulash, scampi & chips, paprika potatoes, sirloin steak
DINNER £10: mushroom paté, pork goulash, pudding
Children: own menu

Open 10am–2.30pm, Mon to Sat; 7–9.30pm, Thurs to Sat; also Tues/Wed pm during holiday season
Closed Sundays & Xmas No credit cards accepted
One half is no smoking One high chair only
P – difficult

Rowarth, Cheshire map 6

LITTLE MILL INN – ☎ New Mills (0663) 743 178.

P

Off the A626 Marple-Glossop road. There is a turning on the south west side of the village of Charleworth and then you will find signs to Rowarth and the Little Inn.

The pub is situated in marvellous rolling countryside – the drive to it across the hills is a delight, and we were lucky enough to do it on a sunny Autumn day. The original building was an 18th century mill and photographs inside show how the mill wheel was swept away by a flood in 1930.

The family room is off the bar and is charmingly furnished with seats and tables from a railway dining car and has a good collection of train pictures, including the Flying Scotsman. The carriage itself is at the back of the pub and now houses three bedrooms and it's called the Derbyshire Belle Motel. The bar is most attractive with its stone pillars, wooden beams and padded settles, and there is a lovely old fireplace too. There is a small pool room off the bar.

The children will be delighted with the garden because it has four swings, a climbing frame and a tree house with a slide which takes you right across the mill stream to the other side. Great fun. The adults can watch from the terrace at the front of the pub.

The pub is open all day and you will find food on offer throughout opening hours. There is a high chair on the premises.

(12–10.30pm) £1–5: Bury black pudding, grilled trout, curries, salads, plaice & chips
Children: small portions

• Ale – Banks, Robinson's, Ruddles, Bateman's
P – own car park

Rowsley, Nr Matlock, Derbys — map 7

CAUDWELL'S COUNTRY PARLOUR – ☎ Matlock (0629) 734 374.

R

Signposted off the A6 between Matlock and Buxton.

This is a wonderful place to bring the family for an afternoon out with a difference. The small but immaculate cafe is part of the Caudwell's Mill Craft Centre complex. This features a working 19th century flour mill, driven by a water wheel and five craft workshops open to the public where glassblowers, wood turners and potters keep alive dying traditions.

The food is almost entirely vegetarian with all the flour used having been ground at the mill and everything is prepared freshly every day.

The complex is surrounded by lawns and a mill stream idles its way past. It is a peaceful haven away from the commercialism that has blighted so much of beautiful Derbyshire.

You can change a baby in the disabled toilet where there is a pull-down shelf.

£2–4: tuna & anchovy tart, savoury crumble, pizza, lasagne
Children: half portions, own menu on request

Open 10–6pm, winter until 4.30pm. Closed Xmas Day, Boxing Day.

Weekends only January/February No credit cards
No smoking Unlicensed
P – own car park

Rye Foreign, East Sussex — map 4

HARE AND HOUNDS – ☎ Rye (0797) 21483.

P

On the A268 just North of Rye.

This probably started life as a farmhouse in the 16th century and is now an attractive roadside pub; it is painted white, with a tile-hung upper floor, square windows standing out from the facade, and lots of bright flowers in tubs and window boxes. There are a couple of bars, under the beamed ceilings, and an inglenook fireplace.

Off the main bar is a pool room and next to it the brightly decorated family room, with bench tables, a fish tank and a juke box, a blackboard and children's toys. It overlooks the large garden, whose lawns are enclosed by hedges, with trees here and there, bench tables, and a play area for children, with swings, a slide, a Wendy house, a climbing frame and a scramble mat.

There is a high chair on the premises.

(12–2.15pm & 6.30–9.30pm) £1–9: burgers, tortellini, chicken curry, steaks, beef Stroganoff
Children: own menu, half portions

• Ale – Courage, Greenall's P – own car park

Ryton-on-Dunsmore, Warwicks — map 7

RYTON GARDENS – ☎ Coventry (0203) 303 517.

R

On the B4029 east of Coventry. It is signposted from the A45 and the A428.

This restaurant is part of the National Centre for Organic Gardening, which opened a couple of years ago. In a wooden building, which also contains a shop, the restaurant has a bright and neat interior, and outside is a large paved patio with plenty of tables and chairs.

From there you look out to the Centre's twenty acres of gardens, which include a rose garden, a herb garden, a wild flower meadow, a picnic area and a children's play area with a wooden climbing frame and some swings. There is a table and chair and paper towels in the Ladies, if a baby needs to be changed.

The food is mostly grown on site, and the menu changes on a daily basis. It's good healthy stuff and reasonably priced. You can also sample a comprehensive choice of organic wines from France, Germany, Italy and England.

£1–3: salads, soup, broccoli quiche, Hungarian pancakes
Children: small portions

Open 10am–5pm (till 4pm, Oct to March)
Open all year Access/Visa
Licensed No smoking
No music One high chair only
P – own car park

St Davids, Dyfed map 5

CARTREF RESTAURANT, Cross Square – ☎ *St Davids (0437) 720 422.*

R

This is a busy and enterprising family restaurant in the centre of the town, and is built around a 17th century stone cottage. The four rooms have rough stone walls, ceiling beams, and varnished pine furniture, and it adds up to a welcoming atmosphere.

The range of food on offer is very wide and you will find something to your taste at any time of the day from snacks and sandwiches to a fillet steak, and it is also good to see some interesting vegetarian dishes.

There is a patio at the back of the restaurant, with a self-service bar, which looks out to the Cathedral. If a baby needs to be changed or fed the helpful staff will find space upstairs. More space will by now have been added with the opening of the Sycamore Room, which offers snacks and children's meals.

£1–12: crab mayonnaise salad, poached lemon sole, steaks, chicken Kiev, lentil & cheese roast
Children: own menu, half portions

Open 10am–9.30pm (Sunday 11am–9pm)
Open Easter to end of Oct
Licensed Access/AmEx/Diners/Visa
No smoking in one room
P – car park near Cathedral

Sabden, Lancs **map 9**

THE WELLSPRINGS – ☎ Clitheroe (0200) 23870.

P

Two miles off the A59.

Set hundreds of feet above sea level, close to the summit of Pendle Hill in the heart of Lancashire witch country, the place enjoys some really panoramic views of the Ribble Valley and rural countryside beyond. On a clear day it is well worth the effort to drive up to this spectacular spot and take in the view from the picture windows. This will include the skiers on the artificial slopes alongside and an occasional hang glider.

It really is a huge pub, and the family room, though adequate, is dwarfed by the other rooms. Children are welcome at lunchtimes and in the early evening but must take their leave by 8.30pm.

(12–2.30pm & 6.30–10pm) £1–7: eggs Madras, haddock & chips, lasagne, steaks, pizzas
Children: own menu

• Ale – John Smith's P – own car park

Salisbury, Wilts **map 3**

This city has a lot of car parking space and a sensible and helpful traffic control system. The city's Cathedral is magnificent (Pepys was guided 'all over the Plain by the sight of the steeple') and the town has many other fine buildings and is an excellent tourist centre.

HAUNCH OF VENISON – ☎ Salisbury (0722) 22024.

P

In the town centre.

This extraordinary pub was once the churchhouse for the adjoining St. Thomas's Church; its black and white upper floors overhang the street and inside you will be aware of the age of the building as you see the black and ancient timbers on the walls and the beamed ceilings.

The bar is small and gets very busy, and up the stairs is another small room where families are welcome. It is a splendid room with the same dark panelling, wooden settles against the walls and a marvellous open fireplace. At lunchtimes you can eat bar snacks in part of the restaurant on the first floor, and there is much more space here.

(12–2pm & 6–10pm) £1–10: game pie, ham & mushroom pie, savoury pancakes, turbot, steaks

• Ale – Courage   No music
P – public car parks nearby

OLD CASTLE, Castle Road – ☎ *Salisbury (0722) 28703.*   *Pot Luck*

P

Opposite Old Sarum, on the A345, a couple of miles from the city centre.

Standing on a hill on the outskirts of the city, this roadside pub was a farm 150 years ago. Across the road is Old Sarum, the original site of Salisbury and before that a Roman camp and Iron Age fort.

There is masses of space inside the pub, but it is broken up into interconnected rooms, with alcoves here and there.

Families are welcome to settle in the Garden Room which is off the main bar. It is a large conservatory and has a touch of the British Raj with its tiled floor, plants, an overhead fan, and old-fashioned radiators. It is light and bright and attractive. The Ladies has a large powder room with a counter and baby changing mat and another shelf on which to lay a baby.

The garden has lawns on various levels, with picnic tables and umbrellas, and overlooks Salisbury and a wide valley. There is a bouncy castle in one part of the garden.

(12–2pm & 7–9pm) £1–6: lasagne, moussaka, steak & kidney pie, savoury lamb
Children: own menu, half portions

• Ale – Courage   P – own car park

HARPERS RESTAURANT, Market Place, – ☎ *Salisbury (0722) 333 118.*

R

In the city centre.

Look for the dark green paint and Harpers sign above the row of shops in the market square, on the Guild Hall side.

This is a smart upstairs restaurant, light and airy with brown and white decor, modern cane furniture and attractive Tiffany lamps. You can get a variety of well cooked fresh food with or without the delicious spicy sauces.

Unfortunately the Ladies is up another flight of stairs and is not very large, so baby-changing is difficult.

LUNCH (12–2pm) £7: hot mushrooms with bacon, roast of the day, treacle tart with cream;
DINNER (6.30–10pm) £13: Sicilian fish soup, New Forest venison, pudding or cheese
Children: own menu, half portions

Open 12–2pm & 6.30–10pm (10.30pm on Sat) Mon to Sat
Access/Diners/Visa One high chair only
P – large public car park (Market Place)

MICHAEL SNELL, 8 St Thomas's Square – ☎ Salisbury (0722) 336 037.

R

In the city centre.

On the other side of St Thomas's from the Haunch of Venison, you will see this well-proportioned building in its pale green paint. A shop takes up part of the ground floor with two tea rooms on either side. The smaller one leads out to a patio with several tables; and the larger one is a bright, airy room with pristine white-washed walls, and pine furniture. The tall windows remind you that this was once St Thomas's School.

There's a welcoming, busy atmosphere, helped by the smart and pleasant staff. A children's menu is good and healthy: ham and green salad for example, or cheese and a baked potato. If you need to change a baby there is a small shelf in the Ladies, and paper towels are provided.

All the food here is made from fresh ingredients, and chocolate lovers should know that Michael Snell has his own chocolate factory at the top of the building.

£1–6: soup, mushroom flan, beef curry & rice, turkey & ham pie, moonraker vegetable pie
Children: own menu

Open Mon-Sat 9am–5.30pm Closed Sunday
No credit cards accepted Open all year
Unlicensed No music
No smoking areas in both rooms P – public car park

Places included in the Guide must offer the following basic facilities:
Pubs – a separate area or room for families where alcohol is not served;
Restaurants – high chairs and special menus/reduced portions.

PLAYHOUSE RESTAURANT, Malthouse Lane – ☎ *Salisbury (0722) 20117.*

R

In the town centre.

On the ground floor of the Playhouse Theatre, which you cannot fail to see from the public car park at the back, this is a plain and simple restaurant, pleasantly furnished with pine tables. You can drop in for a snack or a light lunch, and the display of cold food (quiches, salads, etc) looks very appetising, and is very good value. It is a popular place for parents who are out shopping.

The restaurant opens in the evenings when there is a performance: from 6pm from Monday to Saturday. Facilities to change a baby are meagre – just a couple of chairs in the Ladies.

£1–2: soup, quiche, pizza, egg mayonnaise, salads
Children: small portions

Open 10am–2pm & 6pm onwards Mon-Sat   Access/Visa
Open all year   Licensed
No smoking area   No music
One high chair only
P – vast public car park at rear (free after 6pm)

Sandford, Nr Wareham, Dorset — map 2

WOODS EDGE RESTAURANT – ☎ *Wareham (0929) 556 959.*

R

On the A351, north east of Wareham.

This agreeable restaurant is tucked into the dense trees alongside the main road, and the bright green awnings over the windows give it a cheerful air.

It is a sunny and appealing place with masses of space: an open-plan design incorporating three eating areas. The cream walls, Laura Ashley curtains and the greenery to be seen through most of the windows adds up to a pleasant place to have a meal. There is also a small lounge area with comfortable settees. Outside is a smart little patio with sun umbrellas over the tables.

The Ladies is spacious and includes a table where a baby can be changed; and there is a supply of paper towels.

This is an excellent family restaurant, which we are happy to recommend.

£2–11: vegetable lasagne, fish & chips, roast of the day, chicken Chasseur, steak Bordelaise
Children: own menu

Open 10.30am–2.15pm & 6–9pm Mon to Sat; 10am–10 pm Sun
Open all year Licensed
No smoking in part of the restaurant Access/Visa

Sapperton, Nr Cirencester, Glos **map 2**

DANEWAY INN – ☎ *Frampton Mansell (028 576) 297.*

P

Off the A419 Cirencester-Stroud road past Sapperton Village. Go down the hill to the Old Canal Bridge.

This large white-washed stone inn was originally built 200 years ago to house the navvies digging the long Canal Tunnel, and later the "leggers" used to collect here for hire. They were the men who pushed the barges through the tunnel – lying prone and propelling the barges by pushing with their legs on the roof of the tunnel. Tough work.

Inside you will find a comfortable bar with a handsomely beamed ceiling, horse brasses here and there and padded settles. A notable feature is the massive carved wooden fireplace which came from Amberley Hall. Alongside the bar is a compact, low-ceilinged room where families can settle. There are a few assorted tables and chairs, a high chair, and a few toys to amuse the children.

At the front of the pub is a terrace with bench tables and below it a large grassy garden with plenty more bench tables. You are surrounded by fields and wooded slopes – it's very peaceful.

(12–2pm & 7–9.30pm) £1–4: lasagne verde, steak & kidney & Guinness pie, vegetarian nut roast & salad, salads, mushroom crèpe

• Ale – Archer's, Wadworth's, and guest beers
P – own car park

Scaftworth, Notts **map 7**

KING WILLIAM INN – ☎ *Doncaster (0302) 710 292.*

P

In the village off the A631 Bawtry to Everton road. Sign easily missed.
You might struggle a little to find this red brick pub but once you have

done so you'll find it's worth the effort. The owners go out of their way to encourage and cater for families, providing no less than three separate family rooms – one using milk churns as seats.

There is a huge garden with an excellent children's play area with swings, a slide, a climbing frame and playhouses. The adults can relax in the garden too or on the terrace and also enjoy the company of the many ducks, hens and peacocks.

They even stage special events during the year including a midsummer festival with Morris men and a Punch and Judy show. For the real ale buff with a family this could be the perfect pub as there are several guest beers, all well kept.

The bar menu is extensive and the children have their own Mister Men menu. Late night supper snacks are also available after 10pm (9.30pm Sun).

(12–2.30pm & 7–10.30pm, except Mon night) £1–6: beef in ale, chicken curry, mixed grill, crab salad, vegetarian crumble
Children: own menu, half portions

• Ale – Everard's, Castle Eden, Marston's, Tolly and guests
P – own car park

Seatown, Chideock, Dorset — map 2

ANCHOR – ☎ Chideock (0297) 89215.

P

Turn off the A35 in the middle of Chideock, opposite the Church and Castle Inn; follow the road for three quarters of a mile to Seatown.

A large encrusted anchor from a ship wrecked on the infamous Chesil beach in 1748 and raised by fishermen in 1985 appropriately sprawls across the lawn of this well situated 17th century white-washed pub. It stands with a cluster of other cottages on the edge of the beach in a valley between Golden Gap and Doghouse Hill. The wide expanse of the coastal scenery can be enjoyed from the tables on the terrace of the small square family room, which is across the corridor from the main bar.

The sloping, lawned garden is to one side of the pub and the famous anchor and a rowing boat provide unusual play equipment for the children. Another stretch of garden goes down to the beach.

During the summer months (Whitsun to September) the pub is open all day and food is available at all times, so it's a useful pub for families.

(12–9.30pm in summer; 12–2pm & 6.30–9.30pm in winter) £1–8: seafood platter, salads, curry & rice, whole local plaice, rump steak, pizzas
Children: half portions

• Ale – Palmer's P – space for 20 cars

Selling, Nr Faversham, Kent **map 4**

WHITE LION – ☎ Canterbury (0227) 752 211.

P

South of Exit 7 of the M2.

This attractive 18th century inn was refurbished last year and a smartly decorated restaurant was added. The two main bars have a delightful atmosphere, partly due to the heavy beams on the ceilings, the large open fires, and wooden tables and settles. They are smartly decorated with Liberty fabrics and plenty of plants and flowers.

The family room is off one of the bars and also has its own entrance from the car park. It is a pleasant and comfortable room, with an open fire and a few tables and chairs. The pretty lawned garden, with its rose trees and silver birches, is the place to be on a summer day. The children can play on the old farm machinery and the haycart, and there is also an aviary.

There is a good range of food here, including several vegetarian dishes, and a three-course Sunday lunch for just over £8.

(12–2pm & 7–10pm) £2–11: crab paté, plaice & chips, okra curry, steaks, beef pudding
Children: half portions

• Ale – Shepherd Neame P – own car park

Semley, Nr Shaftesbury, Dorset **map 2**

BENETT ARMS – ☎ East Knoyle (0747) 830 221.

P

Off the A350 north of Shaftesbury.

The pub was built from the local Chilmark stone in the 18th century by a local landowner, who wanted a village pub in which his estate workers could enjoy themselves. It has stood the test of time and is a handsome sight, situated, as is right and proper, on the village green close to the church, and with a small garden to the rear.

Families are welcome to use an eating area which is up several steps from the bar. There is excellent bar menu at reasonable prices, and a restaurant for more elaborate meals. Most of the food is cooked on the spot from fresh produce which might include fresh fish from Poole and salmon shipped overnight from Scotland.

(12–2pm & 7–10pm) £1–7: scampi royale, trout, steaks, Wiltshire ham with egg & chips, lasagne
Children: smaller portions

• Ale – Gibbs Mew   P – own car park

Also recommended in the Family Welcome Accommodation Guide.

Shave Cross, Nr Bridport, Dorset **map 2**
SHAVE CROSS INN – ☎ Broadwindsor (0308) 68358. *Pot Luck*

P

Off the B3162 North of Bridport.
This attractive pub is tucked away in the Marshwood Vale – another bit of hidden rural Dorset. Built in the 14th century of cob and flint and with a thatched roof, the inn was a lodging house for travelling monks.
The children's room is at one end of the pub and is housed in an old con-

verted store. It has tables and chairs, but it is a bit cut off from the rest of the pub and is also a through route to the lavatories. The stone, thatched skittle alley is also pressed into service during the summer months.

The pub is in a delightful spot, so perhaps it's best to choose a fine day and take advantage of the lovely walled garden where wisteria rambles; there is also a wishing well and a pond and solid wooden tables and chairs; and an adventure playground.

Please note that the pub is shut every Monday, except on Bank Holidays.

(12–2pm & 7–9.30pm, not Mon) £1–8: haddock & chips, Dorset paté, lamb & apricot pie, steaks, moussaka
Children: own menu, half portions

• Ale – Eldridge Pope, Bass, Hall & Woodhouse
P – own car park No music

Shenington, Oxon map 3

THE BELL – ☎ Edge Hill (029 587) 274.

P *One mile off the A422 west of Banbury.*
This delightful 17th century pub sits in an exceptionally pretty and quiet

village in which the houses (and the pub) are built from the honey-coloured local Hornton stone. The village green is opposite the pub, and is a lovely spot to relax on a summer's day; and you might be pressed into service as an auxiliary fielder if a family game of cricket gets going.

You enter straight into a pleasant beamed bar with stone walls and open fireplaces; and the family room is small and pine-panelled, with a few tables and chairs and with plates and prints on the walls.

There is an enterprising menu, and all the food is prepared from fresh ingredients. You can have a Sunday lunch here for just under a fiver. We also noticed that the Hook Norton looked in excellent condition.

(12–2.30pm & 7–11pm, not Sun pm) £2–7: hake, lamb & almond casserole, pork vindaloo, chicken with honey sauce, steak & kidney pie
Children: half portions

• Ale – Hook Norton, Courage No music
P – roadside

Also recommended in the Family Welcome Accommodation Guide.

Shepperton, Middlesex — map 3

THAMES COURT, Ferry Lane – ☎ *Walton-on-Thames (0932) 221 957.*

P

Head for the river from the B375.

This large handsome pub is in a terrific spot on the Thames, and you can sit and watch the river from the lawned garden with its big trees. You must pick your time though, because it's an extremely popular pub, especially when the sun shines.

The inside is well done, particularly the main bar with its gallery, wooden panelling and settles. There's lots of room for families both in the entrance hall and the buffet room, where the usual pub food is on offer every day at lunchtimes; and from May to the end of September in the evenings.

(12–2.15pm & 6–9pm) £1–6: sandwiches, ploughman's, salads, filled jacket potatoes, roast of the day

• Ale – Bass, Charrington P – own car park

Sherborne St John, Hants map 3

SWAN, Kiln Road – ☎ Basingstoke (0256) 850 165.

P *Off the A340, north of Basingstoke.*

Outwardly this fine village pub is still the same as when we first saw it years ago, its deep-red brickwork covered in ivy and topped with a thatched roof. But, a few years back it was ripped asunder and completely redesigned to make the maximum use of space.

The family room is particularly attractive: a large, bright and comfortable conservatory with marble topped tables and a tiled floor. It overlooks a patio and a spacious lawned garden with masses of bench tables and a wooden play area which incorporates a slide, swings, climbing frame, etc.

It is a popular pub and gets very busy at weekends; if you want Sunday lunch here, it is advisable to arrive early. The pub stays open all day from Monday to Saturday.

(12–10pm) £1–6: plaice, salads, burgers, scampi
Children: own menu

• Ale – Flowers, Wethered P – own car park

Shere, Surrey map 3

PRINCE OF WALES – ☎ Shere (048 641) 2313.

P *In the main street – Middle Street.*

On warm summer days the bench tables in the small garden are usually fully occupied by families eating and drinking together. For not so nice days there is a completely separate family room alongside the garden. It is a wooden cabin, functional but comfortable enough with plenty of tables and chairs, a box of toys, and a high chair. Barbecues are held in the garden on Saturday evenings and Sunday mornings – weather permitting.

The village is extremely attractive and this large and well-proportioned pub is one of the few in Surrey which makes any effort to welcome families. The brewers and most of the publicans seem to have forgotten that it is not all Jags and gin & tonics and expense account lunches.

(12–2pm & 7.30–9.30pm, not on Sun or Mon evenings) £1–4: grilled trout, salads, prawn curry, gammon, scampi & chips
Children: small portions

• Ale – Young's No music
P – own car park

Shipton Gorge, Bridport, Dorset — map 2

NEW INN – ☎ Burton Bradstock (0308) 897 302.

P

In the centre of the village, on the A35.

This is a small and attractive village with many stone buildings, and the pub, also built of stone in the 18th century, stands in the centre.

Do not arrive as a coach party because the rooms are small, and particularly the family room, a cosy place with a beamed ceiling, and with table skittles in one corner. Up some steps is a small restaurant with half a dozen tables. The main bar is notable for its huge stone fireplace with a massive oak cross-beam, and this is complemented by a wooden settle, oak stools and wooden window shutters.

There are two small patches of garden at the front and the rear of the pub.

(11.30am–1.30pm & 7.30–9pm) £1–7: rabbit & pigeon pie, mixed grill, seafood salad, trout, steaks.
Children: own menu

P – own car park • Ale – Palmer's

Shrewsbury, Shropshire — map 6

GOOD LIFE, Barracks Passage, Wyle Cop – ☎ Shrewsbury (0743) 50455.

R

This excellent vegetarian restaurant offers a warm welcome to families, and has no less than four high chairs available. You can also cope with changing a baby, since a chair is provided in the Ladies.

The restaurant is housed in a fine 14th century timbered building just around the corner from the Lion Hotel, and there are two very attractive rooms in which you can settle to enjoy the wholefood cooking. All the dishes are prepared on the spot, and there is always a hot dish of the day and a good range of salads from which to choose.

£1–2: golden pea & mint soup, five bean cheese pot, spinach moussaka, vegetable curry
Children: smaller portions

Open 9.30am–3.30pm Mon–Fri, 9.30am–4.30pm Sat. Closed Sun
No credit cards accepted No music

No smoking downstairs **P** – public car park nearby
Licensed

Sibton, Nr Saxmundham, Suffolk — map 8

WHITE HORSE, Halesworth Road – ☎ Peasenhall (072 879) 337.

P

Off the A1120 West of Yoxford.

Despite its postal address this pub is very close to Yoxford, and there is a smallish sign to the pub in the village of Peasenhall.

The well-proportioned 16th century pub is in a very quiet spot, with an enclosed, lawned garden, which has a children's slide. There is also a lovely grassy area, about three acres in extent, at the back of the pub – intended for a limited number of caravans, but also a good spot for children to play.

Inside you will find a handsome beamed bar, with a large fireplace complete with wood-burning stove; up some stairs is the Gallery, where families are welcome. Nicely furnished with wooden settles, it looks out over the garden.

Please note that the pub is closed at lunchtime on Monday (except Bank Holidays).

(12–1.30pm & 7–9pm, not Sun pm) £2–5: plaice & chips, lasagne, curry, coq au vin
Children: own menu

• Ale – Adnams, Ruddles **P** – own car park

Sicklinghall, North Yorks — map 10

THE SCOTTS ARMS – ☎ Wetherby (0937) 62100.

P

Two and a half miles off the A661, at the centre of the village.

You can be sure of a warm welcome at this attractive and inviting white-washed country inn which was made from three cottages and an old ale-house. The spacious dark-beamed, stone-walled interior has a profusion of brass ornaments, pictures and other curios with several stone fire-places adding a warming touch. Families can use two side rooms which are located at either side of the main bar, one of which has a pool table and amusement machines.

In fine weather you will enjoy sitting out in the very pretty gardens. Two areas contain wooden bench seats and tables and there is also a children's slide and climbing frame and an attractive wooden horse and pig.

Bar meals are served at lunch and evening times, seven days a week and there is also a special Sunday lunch at around £8. This is available in the adjoining restaurant, which has two high chairs.

(12–2pm & 6.30–9pm) £1–4: salads, steak & kidney pie, scampi, lasagne, haddock & chips
Children: half portions

• Ale – Younger's, Theakston's P – own car park

Sidford, Devon **map 2**

BLUE BALL – ☎ Sidmouth (0395) 514 062.

P *On the A3052.*

This big and busy roadside pub looks as smart as ever with its white walls gleaming under the thatched roof. It was actually built in the 14th century, and has been run by the same family since 1912.

Inside is a cheerful long bar with a full quota of black beams and pillars as befits a pub with a history dating back so far. The family room, 'the Stable', is spacious and well cared for, with an abundance of tables and chairs.

By the side of the pub is a very neat grassy garden enclosed by a wall and hedgerow; and a bigger lawned garden at the back with bench tables, some swings, a see-saw and a Wendy house. Here there is a patio with an under-cover barbecue area, and this goes into action on any summer day when the weather is kind.

You will find some food every day here and that includes a Sunday roast at under £5, and breakfasts from 8.30 a.m.

It's a delightful and well-run family pub in a busy holiday area.

(10.30am–2pm & 6.30–10pm) £1–8: prawn & egg mayonnaise, steaks, chicken Mornay, vegetable moussaka
Children: half portions

• Ale – Devenish No music
P – own car park

Nr Sidmouth, Devon — map 2

THE BOWD INN – ☎ *Sidmouth (0395) 513 328.*

P

On the A3052 at Bowd Cross (junction with the B3176).

This is a classic English pub, with a thatched roof crowning its smartly painted white walls, and with tubs of bright flowers around the entrance. Inside the archetypal style of an old inn is continued with black beams and pillars, wooden settles, bow windows, huge open fireplaces and copper pans and horse brasses.

The family room is off the main bar through some glass doors and is in the same style as the rest of the pub: there is good wooden furniture and prints on the walls. An alternative for families is the very attractive dining room on the other side of the pub.

The garden has loads of space with plenty of bench tables, some of them under wooden canopies. There is an excellent play area with slides, see-saws and climbing frames.

The pub stays open throughout the day during summer and is a welcoming spot for families.

(11am–2.30pm & 6–9.30pm) £1–10: plaice & chips, steaks, lamb curry, venison chilli, chicken & courgette pie
Children: own menu

• Ale – Bass, Devenish   P – own car park

Skipton, North Yorks — map 9

WATSON'S TEA ROOMS – ☎ *Skipton (0756) 700 267.*

R

In the Craven Court Arcade off the main shopping street.

This delightful restaurant sits on the balcony of a well designed arcade which has been recently built on the site of an old department store. Watson's, like the rest of the shops in this beautiful arcade, has style. Yet, it is a most relaxing place to stop for tea and a bite to eat, well away from the hustle and bustle of the market stalls on the main shopping street.

The restaurant has a summer and winter menu offering an array of substantial meals and snacks. The children have their own menu offering the inevitable chips which come with jumbo sausage or sea stars, plus a selection of home-made biscuits, desserts and cakes. Feeding cups are available as well as high chairs and there is sufficient space in the Ladies to change and feed a baby.

£1–3: jacket potatoes, Yorkshire pudding with onion gravy, lasagne, haddock & chips, pies in a pot
Children: own menu

Open Mon to Sat 9am–5pm Access/Visa
No smoking in most of the restaurant Licensed
P – public car park nearby

Skirmett, Bucks **map 3**

KING'S ARMS – ☎ Turville Heath (049 163) 247.

P

Off the A4155 between Henley and Marlow.

This smartly painted pub, parts of which date back to the 16th century, is situated in a quiet village in the Hambleden Valley. There is a paved terrace at the front with a few tables and chairs, and a pretty and enclosed garden at the side with plenty of bench tables and a superb weeping ash. The attractive countryside spreads out before you.

There are three main rooms within: an attractive restaurant, the main bar with a beamed ceiling and an open fire, and the Bistro where children are welcome. It's a charming room with a high-vaulted ceiling and a pool table.

Sunday lunches are available at £8.50 for three courses, and the set meals at £8 including a glass of wine seem to be excellent value.

(12–2pm & 7–10pm, not Sun pm) £1–4: spare ribs, cottage pie, haddock & chips, garlic prawns, steak & kidney pie
Children: own menu

• Ale – Adnam's, Brakspear's, Flowers, King & Barnes, Ruddles
P – own car park

Snettisham, Norfolk — map 8

ROSE AND CROWN INN, Old Church Road – ☎ Dersingham (0485) 541 382.

PR

Just off the A149 on the north side of the village.

This ancient pub, of 14th century origin, presents a lively face to the world, with a wealth of bright flowers adorning its front. You wouldn't guess that there is so much space inside, but there are three lovely bars, an attractive restaurant and a very large family room.

The front bar is a delightful room with heavy black beams, which have an array of cooper's and carpenter's tools, a tiled floor and a huge open fireplace. Another smaller bar leads through to the pleasantly decorated restaurant; and there is a very comfortable back bar with a large brick fireplace.

Off the back bar is a really splendid family room. A lounge area leads up to a very spacious eating and drinking area which also contains a barbecue. The room is light and bright, with a wooden vaulted ceiling, tile floors and bentwood furniture. French windows open on to a spacious terrace with plenty of bench tables and an immaculately lawned garden, safely enclosed by a wall. To one side there is a large play area under a weeping willow. There are swings, a wooden hut and a wooden Wendy house, and a safe surface of wood chippings.

It is good to report that the Ladies has a surface on which a baby could be changed.

This is a superb family pub, which we singled out for an award in the first edition of the Family Welcome Guide, and it is better than ever.

(12–2pm & 6.45–10pm) £1–10: smoked salmon, salads, steaks, ham 'n' eggs, scampi Provencale, lamb chops
Children: own menu

Access/Visa Open all year
• Ale – Adnams, Greene King, Woodforde's, Wells
P – own car park

Somerton, Somerset **map 2**

WHITE HART – ☎ Somerton (0458) 72314.

P *In the centre of the village.*

This is a very smart and attractive village, full of stone buildings, and with many pubs. One of the most pleasant is the White Hart, and particularly so for families, who can use a room on the left as you enter.

It is clearly marked as a family room and is an agreeable rectangular room with stone walls, a heavily beamed ceiling, several wooden tables and an alcove with a dresser in it.

There are two spacious and pleasant bars and another room off the bar where a family could also sit for a meal. At the back of the pub you will find some tables laid out in a courtyard which is bright with tubs of flowers.

(12–2pm & 7–9pm) £1–7: smoked mackerel, burgers, steaks, salads, steak & kidney pie
Children: half portions

• Ale – Courage, Wadworth's, John Smith's
P – on street

South Harting, West Sussex **map 3**

WHITE HART INN, – ☎ Harting (0730) 825 355.

P *In the centre of the High Street.*

This quiet and unspoiled village in the South Downs is well matched by this 16th century inn, which retains its character with oak beams and inglenook fireplaces.

The charm of the interior is enhanced by the oak and mahogany tables, and the walls are decorated with plates, pewter pots and old photographs of Harting and its inhabitants.

Families are welcome to use a sizeable room up to 8 p.m. It is also used as a public bar, but while families are there the bar remains shuttered. There are tables around the sides of the room, a pool table in the middle and a large chest filled with children's toys.

A large walled garden is an added attraction on summer days. It has an ornamental pond with goldfish, a swing and a slide, and some rabbits and ducks in enclosures. It's a very pleasant spot.

(11am–2pm & 7–9.45pm, not Mon pm) £1–4: garlic mushrooms, tuna bake, Lancashire hot pot, lamb with rosemary
Children: own menu, half portions

• Ale – Ind Coope Burton   P – own car park

South Zeal, Devon — map 1

OXENHAM ARMS – ☎ Okehampton (0837) 840 244.

P

Off the A30 east of Okehampton, and near Sticklepath.

The thickness of the walls around the windows point to the great age of this superb inn, and indeed it was built in the late 12th century. The stone front is covered in Virginia creeper and you enter through a fine, arched doorway. The main bar is L-shaped with bench seats in alcoves, a splendid fireplace, and an abundance of black beams.

On the far side of the bar is a family room with a couple of tables. It's rather small and basic but carpeted and comfortable, and notable for the presence of a prehistoric stone set in the wall.

At the back of the pub is a small patio and a lovely grassy sloping lawn with a rockery, and several bench tables. It's enclosed by a rough stone wall and looks out on one side to a field.

(12–2pm & 7–9.30pm) £1–5: local trout, cod & chips, salads, steak & kidney & mushroom pie, spaghetti Bolognese
Children: half portions

• Ale – St Austell's, Tinner's, Bass
P – on street and some outside pub

Southwold, Suffolk — map 8

RED LION, 2 South Green – ☎ (0502) 722 385.

P

Close to the centre of town, off Queen Street.

The pub is situated in a charming part of this pleasant town – on the corner of the Greens, open spaces which overlook the sea and were formed when the town was rebuilt after a fire in 1658.

The pub is housed in a building of that vintage, and the main bar has a nautical theme. The family room is spacious and comfortably furnished with several tables, chairs and settles, and it has an open fire for the cooler months.

The landlord told us that the pub is very busy at weekends and during the summer season, and so it is advisable to arrive early if you intend to eat.

There are a few tables at the front of the pub, but no garden as such – the Greens provide ample space on warmer days.

(12–2pm & 5.30–9pm, not Friday pm or Sunday pm) £1–6: cold buffet

Children: own menu, half portions

• Ale – Adnams P – own car park

Sowerby Bridge, West Yorks — map 10

THE MOORINGS, Canal Basin – ☎ Halifax (0442) 833 940.

P

Just off the A58. On the canal!

You find pubs in some interesting places and this one, in a converted canal warehouse, is an ingenious piece of enterprise. The buildings date from 1790 and form part of the once major inter-change moorings between the Rochdale canal and the Calder and Hebble Navigation. Today it is a marine leisure centre in its own right with several shops and is a base for a fleet of narrow boats which are available for hire.

The big picture windows in the pub offer fine views over the canal and if the weather is fine you can sit on the terrace and watch the array of colourful barges which populate the waterway.

The interior is decked out with scrubbed pine settles and tile-topped tables and children can use a special room off the main bar lounge with the same super views.

The landlord is rightly proud of his beer and various rosettes and certificates for real ale line the walls. There's a restaurant upstairs which opens in the evenings and for Sunday lunches. We visited the pub on a Sunday lunchtime when it was packed and we were struck by the cheerful and friendly atmosphere. The customers included plenty of families and people of all ages and the staff coped with them all in splendid and efficient style. The food we had was excellent.

BAR MEALS (12–2pm & 6.30–9.30pm) £1–5: Bargee plates with salads, haddock & prawn crumble, Murphy's pie, baked potatoes, spinach & mushroom lasagne.

Children: own menu

• Ale – Younger's, McEwan's, Moorhouses, Theakston's & guests

P – on the wharf

Speldhurst, Kent **map 4**

THE GEORGE & DRAGON INN – ☎ Tunbridge Wells (0892) 863 125.

P

Off the A26 North of Tunbridge Wells.

This marvellous pub can be dated back to 1212 when it was a manorial hall, and as is right and proper, it is opposite the village church. It is a solid half-timbered building, and the main bar has a heavily beamed ceiling, a fine flagged floor, and a huge fireplace.

The room where children are welcome is a smaller version of the same with a few tables and chairs and a magnificent stone fireplace. There's a cold table every lunchtime (and very tempting it looks too) and bar snacks morning and evening.

There's a smart little garden ringed with bright flowers and with several white tables.

(12–2.15pm & 7–10pm) £1–7: paté, salads, calves liver & bacon, plaice, fresh salmon
Children: own menu, half portions

• Ale – Harvey's, Larkins, Marston's, King & Barnes
P – own car park No music

Spetisbury, Nr Blandford Forum, Dorset **map 2**

MARIGOLD COTTAGE TEAROOMS – ☎ Blandford Forum (0258) 452 468.

R

On the A350 south of Blandford Forum.

You will first be struck by the immaculate condition of this lovely 16th century English cottage, painted white below the thatched roof. The interior confirms one's first impressions, and on summer days you should head for the pretty garden, with its shady apple trees. There are also extra tables in a summer house alongside a collection of colourful caged birds.

There is plenty to choose from on the menu and it is all home-made and very good value, with English breakfasts available up to 11am, lunch from 12 to 2pm, afternoon teas, and a variety of snacks available at any time.

The Ladies has adequate space if a baby needs to be changed.

✕ £1–5: cheese on toast, cream teas, various roasts with vegetables, fried plaice
Children: small portions

Open 9.30am–5.30pm, Tues to Sat; 7.30–9.30pm, Fri & Sat
Closed Mondays and from 25 Dec to 1 Feb
Access/Visa   Licensed
One high chair only   No music
P – 15 spaces

Staines, Surrey — map 3

SWAN HOTEL, The Hythe – ☎ Staines (0784) 452 494.

P

Close to Staines Bridge where the A30 meets the A320.

Close to the centre of Staines, this fine old inn sits alongside the River Thames. It is a well-proportioned building, and on the river side a gallery runs along the white-painted facade.

There are lovely views of the river from the lounge bar and from the family room. The latter is a spacious and comfortable room with plenty of tables, padded seats and settles, a huge open fireplace and wide windows looking out to the river. There is also a long paved terrace with the same views of the Thames and the boats that pass by.

You should note that the pub is open all day from Monday to Saturday from May to August inclusive.

✕ (12–2pm & 6–10pm) £1–6: spicy chicken, black pudding, beef Madras, Lancashire hot pot, lasagne
Children: smaller portions

• Ale – Fuller's   P – spaces at the front

Stanton St John, Oxon — map 3

STAR INN – ☎ Stanton St John (086 735) 277.

P

Just off the B4027 east of Oxford. There is a sign to the pub.

The original part of this pleasant stone pub dates back to 1720, and a modern addition combines well with it. Inside you cannot really see the join.

The pub has a large lounge bar with a flagstone floor and a large inglenook fireplace. Down the stairs in the older part there is a comfortable public bar, and alongside you will find a new and spacious family room, which is a no smoking area.

A great asset is the sizeable enclosed garden which has a sand pit and some swings. On the verge of the car park there is another large grassy area where children can play.

It is a charming and civilized pub with no fruit machines or juke boxes, and the music is kept at an unobtrusive level; there is a choice of real ale and of freshly cooked food, including vegetarian dishes.

(12–2pm & 7–10pm) £1–7: crispy garlic courgettes, chicken Kiev, pork in beer, winter vegetable casserole, sirloin steak
Children: own menu, half portions

• Ale – Hall & Woodhouse, Wadworth's
P – own car park

Staple Fitzpaine, Somerset — map 2

GREYHOUND – ☎ Hatch Beauchamp (0823) 480 227.

P

South of Taunton off the A358.

This fine old stone pub, built as a hunting lodge in the 17th century, is at its most handsome in the autumn when the Virginia creeper is at its colourful best. The place has been altered over the years, but the delightful main bar and a couple of adjoining rooms remain as they have for decades and have a lovely atmosphere.

Children are welcome in two large rooms at the back of the pub, in the care of their adults, if they intend to eat. If it is merely a quick drink or two that is needed, the spacious entrance hall is the place to go. There is a garden with plenty of tables and chairs, and slides and a climbing frame for young children.

There is a great emphasis on food in the pub, with some interesting dishes always on the menus. All the pasta and bread are made on the premises, and there is always an extensive vegetarian menu. The Sunday lunch, roast and a pudding for around £6, is very good value. It is an ideal place for a family to stop for a meal or a snack, or just a drink. You will find the staff welcoming and helpful.

(12–2pm & 7–10pm) £1–6: devilled whitebait, fettucine, gigot of lamb, mixed game casserole, liver & bacon & mushroom pie
Children: half portions

• Ale – Flowers, Golden Hill, Marston's

P – own car park

Steyning, West Sussex **map 3**

STAR INN – ☎ Steyning (0903) 813 078.

P

In the centre of the village.

This pleasant village pub was built of brick in the 18th century and was originally a home, run by the Quakers, for waifs and strays.

It is a comfortable and welcoming place, with low-beamed ceilings, wheelback chairs and log fires in winter. It is popular with the local people as well as visitors, and families can use an area which is partitioned off from the main bar by old beams and a stable door. It will seat a dozen or more people at its dark oak tables.

The pretty garden at the side of the pub has a high flint wall with climbing plants on one side and a little stream on the other. In between there is a paved area and some lawn with tables and chairs. Across the car park there is another enclosed, grassy area with more seating.

The pub is open throughout the day from 11am to 11pm on Saturdays.

(12–2pm & 7.30–9.30pm) £1–4: ham & cheese & mushroom pasty, jacket potatoes, steak & kidney pie, trout crumble
Children: small portions

• Ale – Flowers, Castle Eden P – own car park

Sticklepath, Devon **map 1**

DEVONSHIRE INN – ☎ Okehampton (0837) 840 626. *Pot Luck*

P

On the A30 just East of Okehampton.

This pleasant 16th century roadside pub is on a fairly busy road with the large car park on the other side of the road – be very careful. There's a small room where children are welcome, just off the bar, and there are several wooden tables there. Basic pub grub is on the menu here.

The bar is in character, low-beamed with wooden pews, and at the back, over a fast-running stream, is a little patch of garden with bench tables.

(12–2.30pm & 6–9.45pm) £1–7: pasty & chips, burgers, salads, chicken & chips, sirloin steak
Children: own menu

• Ale – Usher's, Ruddles P – own car park

Stockbridge, Hants **map 3**

GREYHOUND HOTEL – ☎ Stockbridge (0264) 810 833.

P

In the main street.

The Greyhound looks every inch the traditional English coaching inn, standing in its smart coat of paint in the main street of this attractive and historic market town. The pub has exclusive fly fishing rights to 300 yards of the famous river Test which flows immediately behind and you can sit in the adjacent garden.

There are two spacious bars and the lounge bar is very welcoming with its wooden ceiling beams, solid oak tables, wheel back chairs and bench seats, prints of North West Frontier troops, fishing rods and so on. It is very comfortable and relaxing.

Families are welcome to use a separate room, which is also the breakfast room, off the main bar. There are several tables and chairs in here, and a splendid open fireplace. A high chair can be provided here. There is an enterprising and wide ranging menu, with quite an emphasis on fish dishes.

The Ladies is very smart and well equipped and has chairs and a wide counter on which a baby could be changed.

This is a really excellent pub where everyone, including families, is made welcome.

(12–2pm & 7–9.30pm) £2–11: fresh local trout, game pie, steak & oyster pie, fresh lobster, Dover sole

• Ale – Courage P – own car park

Also recommended in the Family Welcome Accommodation Guide.

Stockport, Greater Manchester **map 6**

COCONUT WILLY'S, 37 St Peters Gate – ☎ Stockport (061) 480 7013.

R

In the town centre.

This is a converted double fronted shop, in the centre of Stockport. The decor certainly asks to be noticed with its emerald green ceiling, pink and white stippled walls and a rust fitted carpet. There is mixture of real and artificial plants and hanging baskets everywhere.

The staff are most helpful and pleasant, and stressed that if a mother needed to feed or change a baby she could use the office.

This cheerful vegetarian restaurant offers a good range of wholefoods at very reasonable prices, and welcomes the whole family. There is a remarkable range of bottled beers for the adults to try – all free of chemicals and preservatives – and a good choice of organic wines.

£1–6: onion bhajis, stuffed vine leaves, houmous & pitta bread, salads, wholemeal pizzas, nut roast
Children: half portions

Open 11.30am–10pm, Tues to Sat Licensed
No smoking in one side of restaurant Access/Visa
P – car parks nearby

Stoke-sub-Hamdon, Somerset **map 2**

PRINCE OF WALES, Ham Hill – ☎ Martock (0935) 822 848.

P

Follow the signs for Ham Hill in Stoke-sub-Hamdon.

What a fantastic site for a pub! This ivy covered stone building was once the Quarry Paymaster's house. On a Friday he would pay the Hamstone quarry workers, who also lived up there, and then get the money back in the evenings, by selling them his beer. Good business, eh?

Along one side of the pub, the spacious family room now connects the main bar to the old stone skittle alley which has been transformed into a restaurant with its own bar and gallery. The owners told us that this was once a chapel for the quarry.

Curved and upholstered benches line the walls of the new family room and through the Georgian style windows you can see some of the surrounding countryside. You will get the best views from the Ham Hill Country Park itself, which has provided stone for the buildings in this part of the world for centuries.

The pub itself has a lawned garden with picnic tables, and it is safely enclosed by a wall.

(12–2pm & 7–10pm) £1–11: whitebait, steaks, plaice & chips, vegeburger
Children: own menu, half portions

• Ale – Bass, Usher's, Ruddles, Young's
P – own car park

Stonham Aspel, Suffolk — map 4

STONHAM BARNS, Pettaugh Road – ☎ Stowmarket (0449) 711 755.

R

On the A1120 east of its junction with the A140.

As the name tells you, this welcoming restaurant is housed in a set of converted barns. The two eating areas are light and attractive, with plenty of windows, tiled floors and nice wooden chairs and a conservatory has recently been added.

Everything is home-made (except the bread) and that includes some vegetarian dishes and hot dishes of the day; and these are all on offer at very reasonable prices.

It is part of a garden centre, so you can stock up on your pots and plants here, as well as feed the family. There is a patio outside and a play area with a climbing frame, swings and a sand-pit.

If a baby has to be changed the Ladies is spacious and has a table, a changing mat and paper towels.

£1–5: curried egg mayonnaise, cold buffet, baked potatoes, chicken oat bake
Children: half portions

Open 10am–5.30pm every day   Closed Xmas hols
Access/Visa • Ale – Greene King
P – own car park

Stopham Bridge, Nr Pulborough, West Sussex — map 3

WHITE HART – ☎ Pulborough (079 82) 3321.

P

On the A283 one mile west of Pulborough.

This is an attractive stone pub in a lovely position on the River Arun.

It is even more peaceful now that the road by-passes it. It is made up of a series of small rooms, with wood-panelled walls, and one has an inglenook fireplace. The family room or 'village bar' which was once the public bar, still retains its dart board and is well-decorated and comfortably furnished with plenty of seating for families

On the far side of the road is a charming grassy garden, with some swings, and a climbing frame. It is surrounded by shady trees including a fine willow, and overlooking a gentle stretch of water – alongside is the unique 9th century, arched bridge.

The prices of the food are very reasonable; traditional Sunday lunches are served; and the restaurant concentrates on fish dishes, of which there is a wide choice. Families are welcomed there, too, and there are two high chairs.

(12–2.30pm & 6.30–9.30pm) £1–4: whitebait, meat cobbler, lasagne, prawn & asparagus quiche, fish pie
Children: own menu, half portions

• Ale – Flowers, Strong's P – own car park

Stow Bardolph, Norfolk map 8

HARE ARMS – ☎ *Downham Market (0366) 382 229.*

P

Off the A10, two miles north of Downham Market.

This lovely Norfolk village has a pub to match: a pub which has been a focal point of village life since it was built during the Napoleonic Wars. It is a large and most attractive brick building, partly covered in ivy, and a spacious garden, with plenty of bench tables amongst the flowers and bushes, runs along one side. A smashing place to sit at peace on a summer day.

There is a good-sized conservatory at the front of the pub, and families are welcome to park themselves there. It is a pleasant room with half a dozen tables and decorated with several old advertising signs. Does anyone remember Rajah cigars? Many will remember Wincarnis. The Old Coach House, which is a function room, is also available for family use on Sundays.

Further inside you will find a very attractive, spacious bar, its walls adorned with brass artefacts of all kinds, with china plates and even some hickory shafted golf clubs. Leading off the bar there is the restaurant, a handsome and beautifully proportioned room with some interesting decorations including some portraits on wood of Queen Victoria and other royals.

It's a delightful inn, with an excellent reputation for its food, which includes a traditional Sunday lunch.

(12–2pm & 7–10pm) £1–10: Lynn shrimps, lasagne, game pie, cod Mornay, beef goulash
Children: small portions

• Ale – Greene King **P** – own car park

Stow-on-the Wold, Glos — map 3

UNICORN HOTEL (Crest), Sheep Street – ☎ Stow (0451) 30257.

P

In the town at the junction of the A436 and A429.

A very appealing 17th century stone coaching inn which lies on the main road through this attractive Cotswold town and where it meets the Fosse Way. As you enter there is a sizeable and comfortable lounge with low beams, and families are welcome here.

In addition there is an eating area, the Cotswold Pantry, which provides lunchtime meals and snacks at reasonable prices.

COTSWOLD PANTRY (12–2pm, not Sun) £1–5: smoked salmon, salads, ploughman's, steak sandwich
Children: own menu

• Ale – Bass **P** – own car park

Stratford upon Avon, Warwicks — map 7

CAFE NATURAL, Greenhill Street – ☎ Stratford-upon-Avon (0789) 415 741.

R

Next to Safeways in the town centre.

This cheerful vegetarian café has a strategic position in the busy and tourist-laden town of Stratford only a few doors away from the Teddy Bear Museum. A must on any family itinerary – move over Will Shakespeare.

This is a pleasant place for a family to stop if they are hoofing it around the tourist spots of this famous town. There is a good choice of fresh food, and it is good to report that smoking is banned from the restaurant.

If you need to change a baby the staff will find some space for you.

£1–3: filled jacket potatoes, savoury roulade, salads, mushroom roast, lasagne
Children: small portions

Open 9am–5pm, till 7.30pm Friday Closed Sunday
Unlicensed Access/Visa
No smoking **P** – public car parks

Strathcarron, Highland — map 12

CARRON RESTAURANT – ☎ Lochcarron (052 02) 488.

R

On the A890, south of Strathcarron station.

This charming restaurant overlooks Loch Carron and is loomed over by the West Highland ranges. It is a very attractive cream building next to an old school and with a pottery and gift shop also attached. Inside, the restaurant is smartly and brightly furnished in pine, and there is a good range of food available throughout the day from cakes and snacks to steaks.

A mother might just about change a baby in the Ladies. The owner, rightly, does not like young children (under 5's) in his restaurant after 7pm.

£1–12: paté, smoked salmon, salads, char-grilled steaks, chops, venison
Children: small portions

Open 10.30am–9pm, Mon-Sat   Closed end-Oct to 1st Apr
Access/AmEx/Visa   Licensed
No music   P – own car park

Stretton, Nr Oakham, Leics — map 7

RAM JAM INN – ☎ Castle Bytham (0780) 410 776.

R

On the A1, about 9 miles north of Stamford.

This old pub, familiar to anyone who has travelled up the A1, has been transformed into a smart and "up-market" fast food restaurant and hotel. The stone front of the inn remains but behind it is a restaurant which offers food from 7am onwards. As you enter there is a snack bar, where for example breakfasts are served; down the stairs is a large bar area with a tiled floor, some sofas in one corner, and a glass dome over the centre; and at the far end are two dining rooms, smartly turned out with coral coloured walls, polished wood floors and moulded ceilings.

Off the bar area there is a patio with a few tables and chairs, a stretch of lawn, and the open countryside of Rutland beyond.

The Ladies is spacious and a baby could certainly be changed there, especially since a pull-down shelf has been installed.

(7am–10pm) £2–10: breakfast (until 11am), smoked haddock paté, baked monkfish, burger, leg of lamb, lasagne
Children: own menu, half portions

Access/AmEx/Visa P – own car park

Nr Stroud, Glos **map 2**

OLD LODGE INN, Minchinhampton Common – ☎ Nailsworth (045 383) 2047.

P *Well signposted in the middle of Minchinhampton Common.*

This pleasant pub, which began life as one of Henry VIII's hunting lodges, and at one time was a golf clubhouse, is situated in a wonderful position on the Common. It is surrounded by the golf course, and the clubhouse is now next door.

It is of course very popular with families out for some fresh air, and has a functional family room with doors on to the garden. This is a large area, with a well-kept lawn, tables and chairs, children's toys scattered about, and all enclosed by a stone wall.

There is a strong emphasis on food here, which is cooked by the owners' son. Bar snacks are available throughout opening hours (which seem to vary a bit), while the restaurant is closed on Sunday and Monday evenings. Families will perhaps be interested in the Sunday lunch, which is good value at under £7. Real ale fans will also note the good selection available here.

(12–2.30pm & 6–9pm) £1–5: egg Florentine, filled jacket potatoes, chicken & cider pie, cauliflower au gratin, vegetable casserole
Children: own menu

• Ale – Theakston's, Tetley, Wadworth's and guests
P – own car park

Studley, Warwicks **map 6**

OLD WASHFORD MILL, Icknield Street Drive – ☎ Redditch (0527) 23068.

P *Just off the A435 near Redditch. Follow the sign for Redditch Hospital.*

This is a huge pub, very much aimed at the family market, and with a variety of eating areas within its compass: a wine bar, a carvery, a family fast food area, etc.

It was indeed once a mill and the mill wheel is still in place to prove it. A lawned garden, alongside the River Arrow, has plenty of bench tables and play equipment for the children, plus lots of noisy ducks and swans.

A new family room has been opened since last year. It is a very pleasant place, light and airy with windows on all sides, many of which look over the garden and the stream. There are plenty of wooden tables and chairs and a large curved wooden settle. Fast food is served here at very reasonable prices.

✕ (12–2.30pm & 7–10.30pm) £1–4: pizzas, burgers, salads, lamb chop Chasseur, lasagne;
CARVERY £1–8: steaks, etc
Children: own menu, half portions

• Ale – Bass, Courage, Marston's, Wadworth's
P – own car park

Surlingham, Norfolk — map 8

COLDHAM HALL – ☎ Surlingham (05088) 591.

P

The village is off the A146 south east of Norwich and the pub is signposted in the village.

It is said that the building was once the hunting lodge of Elizabeth I and it has indeed the position which a royal might choose – a delightful setting alongside the water on the edge of the Broads.

You can sit in the garden or on the terrace and enjoy the same view.

Inside, families are welcome to use two areas which flank the main bar but are separated by a partition: the smaller one is mainly an eating area and the larger one has several tables and chairs where you can eat or have a drink.

✕ (12.15–2pm & 7.15–9.30pm) £2–10: ravioli au gratin, steaks, game pie, plaice, smoked Norfolk chicken
Children: half portions

• Ale – Ruddles, Webster's P – own car park

Tal-y-Cafn, Gwynedd **map 5**

TAL-Y-CAFN HOTEL, Llanwrst Road – ☎ Tyn-y-Groes (0492) 650 203.

P

On the A470 north of Llanwrst.

This 16th century coaching inn has great charm as well as an atmosphere of comfort and efficiency. There are dark beams in the older parts of its roomy interior and a feature of the furniture is a quantity of oriental carved pieces.

The children's room, off the hall, is spacious and well furnished, and there is another lounge which families may use (but not at weekends). The large, sunken garden is delightful, with plenty of tables and chairs on the lawn, a rockery, a small pond, a slide and a climbing frame. Just along the way are the magnificent gardens of Bodnant and the Pinetum.

(12–3.30pm & 6.30–10.30pm) £1–5: paté, plaice & chips, butter bean & vegetable gratin, cod Mornay, pizzas
Children: own menu

• Ale – Greenall's P – own car park

Talkin, Nr Brampton, Cumbria **map 9**

HARE AND HOUNDS – ☎ Brampton (06977) 3456.

P

In the centre of the village. Three miles off the A69.

This small black and white village inn is set high in the Cumbrian countryside and close to the picturesque Talkin Tarn. It is a truly unspoiled pub with an interior which has probably not changed much over the years.

The main bar is a cosy affair with black beams, rustic furniture, a fine grandfather clock in the corner and some stained glass coats of arms. The family room, at the back of the pub, has its seating divided into stalls with antique prints on the walls and other curios to ponder.

There is a small walled garden at the side of the pub, with some tables and chairs, sun umbrellas and many flowers.

(12–2.30pm & 7–9.30pm) £1–7: paté, whitebait, fillet steak, rainbow trout, lasagne
Children: own menu

• Ale – Theakston's, Hartley's No music

P – across the road

TARN END HOTEL AND RESTAURANT – ☎ Brampton (06977) 2340.

R

A mile off the B6413, south east of Brampton.

This mid-19th century farmhouse, built of sandstone under a slate and stone roof, has now been converted into a hotel and restaurant overlooking Talkin Tarn. The garden slopes down to the water and it is possible to use the jetty for launching your boat. It is an idyllic spot for windsurferes (bring your own board) and canoes and rowing boats can be hired from the boat house. Pike and perch fishing can be done in the tarn, and you can stroll round the tarn: it is just over a mile.

The pleasant restaurant has delightful views over the lake, as has the bar and restaurant. Bar meals are available at lunchtime, plus morning coffee and afternoon tea; any of which you might enjoy on the hotel lawn.

BAR MEALS (12–2pm) £1–4: crab omelette, Welsh rarebit, steak & kidney pie, trout with salad;
DINNER (7.30–9pm) £14: crayfish salad, loin of lamb, pudding or cheese
Children: own menu, half portions

Access/AmEx/Diners/Visa Licensed
One high chair only No music
P – own car park

Tarrant Monkton, Dorset — map 2

LANGTON ARMS – ☎ Tarrant Hinton (025 889) 225.

P

Just off the A354 east of Blandford Forum. The pub is by the lovely church.

This is a delightful village, and like many of the houses round about, the 17th century pub is thatched with a mixture of flint and brick underneath. The facade is festooned with climbing plants and flowers, and the lawned garden, with bench tables, looks away to open country. A large paved terrace is also a pleasant place to settle on warmer days.

Children are welcome in the large skittle alley at the rear; it obviously doubles as a function room – there are plenty of tables and chairs, a space invader machine, darts, a pool table and an old stove.

The main bar, with its low ceiling and wooden pillars, is pleasantly 'pubby'. There's quite an emphasis on food, and very good value it is too;

the owners also run special food nights and offer a traditional Sunday lunch for just over £7.

(12–2pm & 6–10.30pm) £1–10: lentil & onion soup, chicken & veg curry, fisherman's pie, steaks, plaice
Children: own menu

• Ale – Wadworth's, Eldridge Pope, Hook Norton
P – own car park

Also recommended in the Family Welcome Accommodation Guide.

Tempsford, Beds **map 3**

ANCHOR HOTEL – ☎ Sandy (0767) 40233. *Pot Luck*

PR

On the A1.

This enormous pub is a good one to know if you are belting along the A1 with your family. The restaurant has a carvery with various roasts and a cold buffet, and there is the usual run of bar food available, too. There are plenty of high chairs on the premises.

The children's room is a high-ceilinged, comfortable room which it is sad to see is dominated by a pool table and those ghastly space invader machines. We suggest that you visit on warm and sunny days when you can enjoy the enormous, grassy garden, with its huge trees alongside the

River Ouse, and there are swings, climbing frames, and a slide.
The Ladies' room has space and facilities to change and feed a baby.

(12–2pm & 6.30–10pm) £1–10: steak & kidney pie, chilli con carne, steaks, plaice;
RESTAURANT (12–2pm & 6.30–10pm) £1–10: seafood cocktail, roast of the day, cold buffet, steaks
Children: own menu, half portions

• Ale – Ruddles, Webster's
P – own car park

Testcombe, Nr Stockbridge, Hants — map 3

MAYFLY – ☎ Chilbolton (0264) 860 283.

P

On the A3057 north of Stockbridge.

You would look long and hard to find a more delightful setting than this lovely old brick-built pub. It sits alongside the fast flowing River Test, right by Testcombe Bridge, and you can sit at the many bench tables which are laid out in front of the pub. Surrounded by tall trees, and with the river on one side and open countryside on the other, it's a glorious spot to be on a summer day.

You will not be disappointed with the interior either. The spacious bar, with a low beamed ceiling, has a food servery at one end, and up a few steps at the other end is another large room, with plenty of tables, where families are welcome. Off this room is a very pleasant conservatory with a good view of the river. You are advised to arrive early at weekends if you wish to eat. Not surprisingly it gets very crowded; the lovely setting and the quality of the food ensures the pub's popularity.

(12–2pm & 7–9pm) £2–4: vegetable bake, soup of the day, roast beef & salad, roast pork & salad, chicken Tandoori
Children: small portions

• Ale – Flowers, Strong's, Wadworth's
P – own car park

If you wish to recommend an establishment to the Guide please write to us – report forms are at the back of the book. We need your help to extend and improve the guide.

Thornham, Norfolk **map 8**

LIFEBOAT INN, Ship Lane – ☎ Thornham (048 526) 236.

P

Turn off the A149 towards the church and take the first turning on the left.

This is a cracking old pub in a lovely part of Norfolk, and across the flat landscape you can see the sea in the distance. The attractive interior has everything a rural English inn should have: low ceilings, sloping floors, wooden settles and gnarled pillars. There is a number of rooms clustered around the bar, including a small room where families are welcome. They can also park themselves in the spacious and bright conservatory, which looks out to a walled patio with bench tables and a children's slide.

An interesting choice of home-made food, which changes seasonally, is served and there is a small restaurant too, which is open in the evenings only. There is a high chair on the premises.

As we went to press we learned that some expansion was under way; the restaurant is to be doubled in size, and a dozen bedrooms added to the pub.

(12–2pm & 7–10pm) £2–8: crudités, fisherman's pie, chicken & ham pie, venison sausages, sirloin steak
Children: own menu

• Ale – Adnams, Greene King, and guest beers
No music (except occasional live folk music at weekends)
P – own car park

Thorpe Market, Nr North Walsham, Norfolk **map 8**

ELDERTON LODGE HOTEL – ☎ Southrepps (0263) 833 547.

R

On the A149 between Cromer and North Walsham.

This long building, made of flintstone and with dormer windows, stands on the edge of Gunton Park in a lovely setting. Ahead lies open country and the hotel has its own delightful gardens, too: six acres in all, with lawns and fine trees, and occasional bench tables. Lily Langtree and Edward VII used to dally here when the building was a shooting lodge.

The comfortable, well-decorated restaurant overlooks part of the gardens, and off the large bar is a conservatory where families can eat bar meals, too.

If you need to change a baby the owners would make a bedroom available.

BAR MEALS (12–2pm & 7–9pm) £1–7: paté, salads, omelettes, steaks;
DINNER (7–9pm) £11: fried squid, roast guinea fowl, pudding or cheese
Children: own menu, half portions

Open all year Access/AmEx/Visa
• Ale – Adnams P – own car park

Tideford, Cornwall **map 1**

HESKYN MILL – ☎ Landrake (0752) 851 481.

R

By the A38 west of Saltash. Look for the sign and take the turning to St Germans.

The old mill wheel is still attached to the wall of this beautiful stone building, and inside you can see the rest of the machinery on each floor.

Downstairs there is a small bar and under the low beams a nice mixture of wooden tables, sofas and settles and a wood-burning stove. The restaurant is up the open wooden staircase and is another delightful room, with a mix of differing wooden tables.

You will always find fresh Cornish fish on the menu, and indeed the owners try to use local sources for their food whenever possible.
There is a little terrace by the front door and lawns at the back where you can sit on warmer days.

LUNCH SNACK MENU £2–7: soup, steak sandwich, fish of the day, pasta of the day;
DINNER £16: prawn Waldorf, rosette of lamb, pudding or cheese
Children: small portions

Open 12–2pm & 7–10pm. Closed Sunday and Monday
Access/AmEx/Visa • Ale – St Austell
P – own car park

Tillingham, Essex — map 4

CAP & FEATHERS, 8 South Street – ☎ Tillingham (062 187) 212.

P

In the main street.
This ancient pub, which dates back about five hundred years, has white painted, weather boarded walls and Bulls Eye windows, and is brightly decorated with hanging baskets of flowers. In the bar you should take a look at the curved beam; the story is that this part of the pub used to be an undertaker's, and the bearers did not wish to remove their top hats – hence the need for a curved beam.

The family room has recently been restored and the result is a charming and comfortable room, with a beamed ceiling, a polished floor with a large rug and an open fire. There is seating for nearly twenty people. The small rear garden is safely fenced off from the car park and has a few tables and chairs.

(12–2pm & 7–9.30pm) £2–4: venison in ale, peanut and sweetcorn bake, Surinam pork, lemony lamb, burgers
Children: half portions

• Ale – Crouch Vale P – own car park

Tintinhull, Nr Yeovil, Somerset **map 2**

CROWN & VICTORIA – ☎ Martock (0935) 823 341. *Pot Luck*

P

Off the A303 – follow the signs to Tintinhull House.

The owners of this nicely-proportioned stone pub, with shuttered windows, have children of their own and therefore make due allowance for families, who are welcome in the skittle alley, with its few tables, pool table and piano.

On summery days you would undoubtedly head for the splendid and large garden. There is a lot of lawn on which to relax, with swings and a slide, a climbing frame, and a football net.

Food is served from Monday to Saturday and there is one high chair available.

Nearby is the National Trust property of Tintinhull House with its celebrated gardens.

(12.30–2.30pm & 7.30–9.30pm, not Sun) £1–6: lasagne, trout & vegetables, salads, sirloin steak, chicken in cream & cider
Children: half portions

• Ale – Young's, Butcombe, Courage P – own car park

Never use an out-of-date Guide. Many places are excluded because their standards have dropped or their policies towards families have changed. Many new establishments are added each year.

Tiverton, Devon — map 2

KNIGHTSHAYES COURT – ☎ Tiverton (0884) 254 665.

R

Just off the A396 North of Tiverton.

All the confidence of the Victorian age went into the florid style of this mansion which was built in the 1870's. The gardens are immense and really beautiful, and Knightshayes Court is the home of Lady Heathcoat-Amory, formerly Joyce Wethered, who is reckoned to be the greatest of all lady golfers.

The restaurant was constructed in the old stable block, built in a similar Gothic vein to the main house, and the National Trust shop and a garden shop are also here. The restaurant is spacious and attractively designed: the two rooms have polished brick floors, stone walls with wood panelling, and wooden tables, smartly painted red.

The lavatories are roomy and the Ladies has a chair and plenty of space, alongside the wash basins, on which you can change a baby.

You can get something to eat throughout the day, while lunches are served from 12 till 2pm, and there are plenty of high chairs.

£1–5: Devon paté, beef casserole, ploughman's, salads, cream teas
Children: half portions

Open 11am–6pm, April to October 31 Access/AmEx/Visa
Licensed No smoking
P – plenty – but a walk away No music

Also recommended in the Family Welcome Leisure Guide.

Tivetshall St Mary, Norfolk — map 8

THE OLD RAM – ☎ Pulham Market (037 976) 8228.

P

On the A140, a few miles north of Diss and Scole.

You will easily spot this large roadside pub on the main Ipswich to Norwich road. Under its steep roof, it is smartly painted cream, and a few years ago underwent a complete, and very successful, renovation.

The big bar has a framework of ancient wooden pillars and beams, and a brick floor: a super room which testifies to the 17th century origins of the building. Alongside is a lounge bar with a large fireplace with an iron stove; and beyond that is a family room.

This pleasant area is mostly intended for diners, especially in the even-

ings, but families are welcome to park themselves here, whether they are eating or not. Above the room is an open loft where paintings and craft goods are on display.

Outside you will find a terrace, with a raised area with a good stretch of lawn and several bench tables. There are flowers and small trees scattered about. It's a nice spot to relax on a summer day.

Families will be pleased to note that the pub is open all day, and serves a wide range of food, including vegetarian dishes, from 11.30 in the morning until 10 at night. There's a good range of real ales, too.

(11.30–10pm) £1–11: moussaka, salmon steak, salads, burgers, vegetable gratin, steaks
Children: half portions

• Ale – Adnams, Greene King, Ruddles, Webster's
P – own car park

Tomintoul, Grampian — map 12

GLENMULLIACH RESTAURANT – ☎ Tomintoul (080 74) 356.

R

On the A939 two miles south-east of Tomintoul.

A bright and cheerful building, in beautiful surroundings, and which is run by a family who aim to offer fresh food at reasonable prices. Inside you will find pine tables and benches; and there is a small garden at the front, and a larger grassy area at the side and at the back. From the garden you can hear Conglass Water rushing down the wooded valley ahead.

Although there is no space or facilities for baby-feeding or changing in the restaurant, the friendly owners will find space in their own house for a mother to tend a baby.

The owners certainly offer good value for money with a three-course lunch at just under £4, and children's meals cost around £1.50. New menus now include vegetarian and low fat dishes.

It is a warm and welcoming spot, and is, by the way, on the Whisky Trail (which is signposted for motorists) and the owners have a pets corner with rabbits, guinea pigs, ponies etc.

Last year the owners started a Nordic (cross-country) ski centre: in summer the same area is used for orienteering. There are also mountain bike trails in the hills behind the restaurant.

£1–9: haddock & chips, Scotch mutton pie, venisonburgers, jugged hare, baked Spey salmon
Children: own menu, half portions

Open 8.30am–10pm every day (closes earlier in winter). Closed Xmas Day
Access/Visa Licensed
P – own car park No music

Torbryan, Devon — map 1

OLD CHURCH HOUSE INN – ☎ Ipplepen (0803) 812 372.

P

From the A381 follow signs to Ipplepen and then to the village.

Take a drive through Devon lanes to this ancient pub and see the fine church of Saxon origin opposite and the Saxon oak door embedded in the pub wall. With the history taken care of, you can relax with a drink in the comfortable oak-furnished children's room which is one of the five rooms in this pub of beamed ceilings, dark panelling and stone walls. The pub has recently been extended into the old cellars, and presumably the three ghosts which inhabit the building have no objections to this.

There are a dozen or so real ales on offer and the landlord varies his selection; the menu, which is very comprehensive, includes fresh fish from Brixham and Dartmouth. A three-course lunch is served on Sundays at just over £4.

There is a grassy bank where wild flowers grow and where you may sit on warm days.

(12–2.30pm & 7–10.30pm) £1–9: salads, Dart salmon, Brixham plaice, country pie, steaks, hare & venison pie
Children: half portions

• Ale – Bishop's Tipple, Hall & Woodhouse and umpteen others
P – own car park

Torcross, Nr Kingsbridge, Devon — map 1

START BAY INN – ☎ Kingsbridge (0548) 580 553. *Pot Luck*

P

On the A379 Dartmouth to Kingsbridge road.

We include this old pub with its thatched roof because it is a useful place to know, situated as it is along the huge pebbled sweep of Start Bay. There is a terrace where you can sit and gaze at the sea.

The family room is functional, with plenty of seating, and contains a food bar which serves a good range of pub food, including lots of very fresh fish.

(11.30am–2pm & 6–10pm) £1–9: steaks, plaice, fish pie, crab salad, scallops
Children: own menu, half portions

• Ale – Whitbread, Marston's P – own car park

Tormarton, Avon **map 2**

COMPASS INN – ☎ Badminton (045 421) 242.

P *Half a mile north from Junction 18 of the M4 – take the first right turn off the A46 going towards Stroud.*

This fine old creeper-covered pub of 18th century origin is in a useful spot – only a minute or so from the motorway. The main bar, with a good selection of real ale, leads down to the food bar, and off there is a huge, glass-roofed orangery which is always pleasantly warm, and is bedecked with hanging plants. Children are welcome in the food bar or the orangery. A patio and a pleasant lawned garden offer a pleasant spot to sit on summer days.

There is always a good display of food here, from the cold buffet to the daily specials, and it is served seven days a week. There is also an excellent vegetarian menu, and the pub is open throughout the day. It is good to report that food is available at all times – from 7.30 in the morning until 10.30 at night.

(7.30am–10.30pm) £1–7: soup, salads, fresh poached salmon, chicken curry, dressed crab
Children: own menu

• Ale – Archer, Bass, Wadworth P – own car park

Totnes, Devon **map 1**

SMUGGLERS INN, Steamer Quay Road – ☎ Totnes (0803) 863 877.

P *From the centre of the town, follow the signs to Steamer Quay and the Motor Museum.*

For those visiting the attractive town of Totnes, and especially if you want to see the Motor Museum on Steamer Quay, this busy pub is a very convenient watering hole close to the river. It has masses of room inside, with two family rooms, with plenty of seating.

There's a wide choice of food, and there are four high chairs available. A patio outside has bench seating for about fifty people.

(12–2pm & 7–10pm) £1–8: fried chicken with coleslaw & chips, cottage pie, plaice & chips, mixed grill, steaks
Children: own menu, half portions

P – own car park and public car park across road

WILLOW, 87 High Street – ☎ Totnes (0803) 862 605.

R

At the top of the town, in the Narrows.

This self-service vegetarian restaurant is sited at the top of the hill in the attractive main street of Totnes, a town which is notable for its large number of public car parks. It is a plain and simple restaurant with several nice wooden tables as you enter; a family room with some fairly ancient armchairs at the back; and this leads out to a little patio, with a few tables. It is very peaceful there on summer days.

The dishes are imaginative, and very good value, and are cooked from organically grown vegetables.

The lavatory off the patio has some padded benches on which babies can be changed.

£1–6: broccoli croustade, herb & tofu dip, lentil & vegetable cottage pie, vegetable thali
Children: small portions

Open 10am–5pm Mon-Sat & 6.30–10pm Tues-Sat, July-Sept
10am–5pm Mon-Sat & 6.30–10pm Wed, Fri & Sat, Oct-June
No smoking in restaurant area   Licensed
One high chair only   P – public car park nearby

Trebarwith, Nr Tintagel, Cornwall — map 1

MILL HOUSE INN – ☎ Camelford (0840) 770 200. *Pot Luck*

P

A tricky turn signposted off the road to Trebarwith Strand off the B3263.

This is an ancient and lovely stone building which was once a corn mill, and is situated in a wooded valley close to Trebarwith beach. The bar is very roomy, with polished stone floors and wooden settles, and the family room has plenty of space. There is a good array of pine tables and benches arranged in booths.

It is a pity that a pool table has now been deposited in there, and this may be a sign of the different policies being applied by the new owners. We have already had adverse comment from a reader about the quality of the food and the poor safety aspects of the playground. We have, therefore, put the pub in the Pot Luck category and will look at it again this year.

On summer days you might opt for a seat at one of the wooden tables on the rambling terraced patio with its abundance of plants and flowers. The adventure playground has a model dinosaur and elephant, a climbing frame, swings, sand pits and a soft drinks bar.

(12–2pm & 6.30–10pm) £1–7: steak platter, plaice & chips, beef in beer, lasagne
Children: own menu

• Ale – Flowers   P – own car park

HOUSE ON THE STRAND – ☎ Camelford (0840) 770 326.

R

Right on the Strand.

Changes have been afoot at this welcoming restaurant, which is very close to the beach and you cannot miss the imposing sight of Gull Rock rising from the sea. The restaurant has been greatly extended with the addition of a larger room on the other side of the kitchen. The original café, with its slate floor and pine tables and little terrace, remains.

The food is as interesting as ever and very reasonably priced; there is quite an emphasis on vegetarian dishes and it is good to report that chips never darken the kitchen door. We had a really excellent meal here last summer.

There is no special provision for baby changing but the owners are hoping to fit a shelf in the Ladies.

£2–8: mustardy mushrooms, chunky lentil fritter, seafood croustade, lamb tagine, chicken & sesame koftas
Children: half portions

Open 10am–10pm April to October; in winter 10am–5pm, Mon to Wed; 10am–10pm Thurs to Sat; and 1–5pm Sun
Access/Visa   Licensed
P – two big council car parks nearby

Please let us have reports – good or bad – on any establishments listed in the Guide as soon as possible after your visit.

Trefeglwys, Powys **map 6**

RED LION – ☎ Trefeglwys (05516) 255.

P

On the B4569North of Llanidloes.

Linguists will no doubt be speculating and the answer is that there are indeed three churches in this attractive Welsh village. The pub is neat and square and painted cream, with a pleasant and homely bar with a tiled floor, beamed ceiling and a large fireplace with a stove.

Families should head for the small lounge – an attractive and comfortable room with padded benches and stools and more seating in an inglenook fireplace. There is also a small terrace in a sunny spot at the back of the pub, plus a games room with a pool table.

(12–2pm & 6.30–9.30pm) £1–8: chicken & chips, steaks, plaice & chips, vegetable chilli
Children: own menu

• Ale – Burtonwood   P – own car park

Tregadillet, Nr Launceston, Cornwall **map 1**

THE ELIOT ARMS – ☎ Launceston (0566) 772 051.

P

On the old A30 just to the west of Launceston.

This attractive ivy-clad pub was built in the 14th century and stands on the A30, and to everyone's relief a by-pass has now been opened.

The pub has two names. The other is the Square & Compass: in the early 19th century it was a French Freemasons' lodge, whose members came from amongst former prisoners of the Napoleonic War.

Once past the door you enter a different world. It's like stepping into an old curiosity shop. There are clocks everywhere (61 of them, the landlord told us) – on the walls, and on shelves and even free-standing on the floor. Where there is space there are old prints and photographs, horse brasses and copper objects, and all sorts of memorabilia. To quote "Under Milk Wood": "slow clocks, quick clocks, pendulumed heart knocks, china, alarm, grandfather, cuckoo; clocks shaped like Noah's whirring ark, clocks that bicker in marble ships, clocks in the wombs of glass women, hourglass chimes, tu-wit-tu-woo clocks ... clocks with no hands for ever drumming out time without ever knowing what time it is."

There are two rooms, well away from the bar, where children are allowed and this includes the small and cosy dining room. The other room has bar billiards, bar skittles, a fruit machine and a video game.

The pleasant garden is surrounded on three sides by high hedges and trees, and there are bench tables with parasols, and a wooden Wendy house for children, plus a swing and a climbing frame.

There is an enterprising and very extensive menu, including some house specials.

(12–2pm & 7–9.30pm) £1–8: Cornish crab paté, whole lemon sole, curries, steaks, vegetable moussaka

• Ale – Devenish P – own car park

Tregrehan, Par, Cornwall **map 1**

BRITANNIA INN – ☎ Par (072 681) 2889.

P

On the A390 a couple of miles east of St Austell.

The large and functional roadside pub is a welcoming sight and especially so for a travelling family since it is now open all day (except Sunday) and you will always find some food on the go, with some reasonable choice for children beyond the usual burger and chips.

The spacious family room looks out over a large and pleasant lawned garden with plenty of seating and a play area with swings and a wooden playhouse.

(12–10pm) £1–7: jacket potatoes, cod & chips, sirloin steak, burgers, pork fillet
Children: half portions

• Ale – Bass, Courage, Tinner's P – own car park

Trent, Nr Sherborne, Dorset **map 2**

ROSE AND CROWN – ☎ Sherborne (0935) 850 776.

P

Four miles north-west of Sherborne off the B3148.

A couple of decades ago this was a farmhouse, built from two 15th century stone cottages, which stands up a short drive in this agreeable village. There is a welcoming and "pubby" atmosphere, aided by the simply decorated bar with its tiled floor, open fire, low ceilings, and curved settles. The pub houses a collection of antique brass and copper cooking utensils.

To the right of the entrance you will find a small family room, with a stone-flagged floor, large fireplace and an early Victorian dresser. It can seat about twenty people, and another small dining area has recently been added. There is a varied choice of real ales to be had here, and some very interesting food, especially Creole and Cajun dishes from Louisiana, which was the landlady's home.

Outside the skittle alley borders one side of the garden with plenty of bench tables on the lawn. There is a good display of flowers and you will have a lovely view over the hills of Blackmore Vale, and a sight of the Elizabethan Compton House. The village church is only about fifty yards away, and both the church and Compton House were used as hiding places by Charles II, when he was on the run from Cromwellian soldiers. The story is documented in Samuel Pepys' diaries. The vegetable garden is on the other side of the lawn and the results end up on the menu.

It is agreeable to report that there is a total absence of music and those infernal games machines here – it's a real pub, and long may it remain so.

(12–2pm & 7.30–9.30pm) £1–4: leek & potato soup, cold duck pie & salad, barbecued chicken, Indonesian pork sate with peanut sauce
Children: own menu, small portions

• Ale – Oakhill, Wadworth's and guest beers
P – own car park No music

Troon, Strathclyde **map 11**

THE LOOKOUT, Troon Marina, Harbour Road – ☎ *Troon (0292) 311 523.*

R

Inside Troon Marina.

Within the marina you will see a grey building, which looks like a small industrial unit; but do not despair, go up the concrete stairs and a startling transformation awaits you. On one side there is a big, comfortable bar with a small verandah and this overlooks the marina. On the other side, there is a very attractive restaurant, with a stylish and modern decor. From the windows there are good views of the many boats which crowd the marina.

The staff can provide space for a mother who needs to feed or change her baby.

£1–10: whitebait, seafood crepe, haddock & chips, lasagne, steak
Children: half portions

Open 11am–2.30pm & 5–11pm; all day at weekends
Access/Diners/Visa Open all year
• Ale – Greenmantle P – plenty at the Marina

Trottiscliffe, Kent **map 4**

THE GEORGE INN – ☎ Fairseat (0732) 822 462.

P

Off the A20 turn right at Greenways Hotel.

A very old pub, half white brick and half tiled in the middle of this pretty village. It was originally four cottages; and has low oak beamed ceilings and lots of hanging brass. The main lounge bar has copper topped tables, dark red plush wall seating and stools, and pretty little alcoves.

It is a very smart comfortable pub, and the family room is cosy with several oak tables and chairs, cream painted walls and a video game. They have a patio at the back with white garden furniture; and a lawn at the side with wooden garden furniture, all enclosed and very safe.

(12–2pm & 6–10pm) £1–5: paté, stuffed trout, calamares, salads, game pie
Children: small portions

• Ale – Fremlins P – own car park

Trusham, Devon **map 1**

CRIDFORD INN – ☎ Chudleigh (0626) 853 694.

P

Close to Chudleigh. Can be reached from the B3193.

This is a cracking old pub housed in a Devon longhouse. The main bar is a delightful sight with its ancient wooden beams and pillars, slate floor and wooden tables and settles. The eye is also drawn to the beer barrels set up on stillages behind the bar; apart from the regular ales, there is always a guest beer on tap.

Families are welcome to use another splendid room at one end of the pub. It is used as a restaurant at weekends and in the evenings, and has wooden settles arranged in booths and two large stone fireplaces.

On summer days you can sit out on the terrace at the front of the pub, and children can play in a small enclosed garden at one side. There is a swing and a slide, and some guinea pigs in a cage.

✕ (11.30am–2pm & 7–10pm) £1–5: calamari, grilled sardines, chicken curry, beef in beer, chicken casserole
Children: own menu

• Ale – Bass, Cotleigh, Golden Hill and guests
P – own car park

Nr Turriff, Grampian — map 12

TOWIE TAVERN – ☎ Auchterless (088884) 201.

R

On the A947 at Auchterless, a few miles south of Turriff.

The restaurant has been refurbished over the last couple of years by the new owners, Mr and Mrs Pearson, and has several rooms where families can settle down for a meal.

If you pass through the rather functional bar area you will find two very comfortable lounges and a choice of two dining rooms, both handsomely decorated and furnished in contrasting styles. A great deal of care has gone into the renovations and this is also reflected in the varied and reasonably priced menu, which changes each day.

There are some tables outside the Tavern and a grassy area where children can play. A table and a chair has been placed in the Ladies, and a baby can be changed there in comfort.

This is an excellent family restaurant with good food and a pleasant atmosphere.

✕ £1–5: Buckie prawns, haddock, lentil & spinach pots, lasagne, steaks
Children: own menu, half portions

Open 12–2pm & 6–9pm
Licensed Access/Visa
No smoking in dining rooms No music
P – own car park

Places included in the Guide must offer the following basic facilities:
Pubs – a separate area or room for families where alcohol is not served;
Restaurants – high chairs and special menus/reduced portions.

Tweedsmuir, Borders — map 11

CROOK INN HOTEL – ☎ Tweedsmuir (08997) 272.

P

On the A701 a mile north of Tweedsmuir.

A very scenic drive awaits you, from whichever direction you approach this roadside inn which is said to be Scotland's oldest licensed premises (1604).

A smartly painted building greets you with the curved windows of a 1930's extension on one side. It certainly does not look out of place, nor does the cheerful tartan carpet which covers the ground floor of the inn.

Families can use the large conservatory off the main entrance and it is well furnished with tables and chairs. The adults can also enjoy a superb bar in the old part of the building. It has a stone floor, plastered stone wall and a huge central fireplace. A nice spot for a few draughts of Greenmantle. It is the Willie Wastle bar and a framed copy of the famous poem by Burns hangs in the hall.

Make sure that you visit the Ladies or the Gents before you leave – to see the Art Deco mirrors and tiles which are still in place.

There are two gardens to enjoy on a summer day: across the road a large and shady lawned garden; and alongside the pub another large stretch of lawn with bench tables and a climbing frame.

If you fancy some fishing you can buy a permit at the Inn to fish for trout on the Tweed.

(12–2.30pm & 6–8.30pm, 12–9pm at weekends) £1–8: cruicket eggs, haddock & chips, sirloin steak, Tweed Valley game pie, poached salmon
Children: own menu

• Ale – Greenmantle P – own car park

Twyning Green, Nr Tewkesbury, Glos — map 2

VILLAGE INN – ☎ Tewkesbury (0684) 293 500.

P

Off the A38 three and a half miles North of Tewkesbury.

Once upon a time, when they played cricket on the village green, you could have sat in the shade of the huge plane tree – because in those days of fond memories the summer sun always shone brightly – and cooled the inner man with a few glasses of beer from this pub a few yards away. A handsome pub indeed, long and low and painted cream, and with dormer windows in the steep roof. In the 17th century it was three cottages, one of which was a bakery, and it has an agreeable interior with low ceilings and wooden beams.

The family room is at the back of the bar, is painted cream, and has highly polished tables and bucket seats; just beyond is the skittle alley, which is buffed like the sheen on a guardsman's boots. Outside, a vine covered arbour (with a barbecue at one end) overlooks a beautifully kept, lawned garden, which is enclosed, and has a rocking horse, some other toys for young children, and bench tables. This is a pub of great charm, which suits the attractive village well.

(12–2pm & 7.30–9.30pm) £1–4: plaice & chips, pie, beef Provencale, pork & chicken curry, Twyning sausages
Children: half portions

• Ale – Flowers, Marston's P – own car park

Tyndrum, Central — map 11

CLIFTON COFFEE HOUSE – ☎ *Tyndrum (083 84) 271.*

R

On the A82.

On a main tourist route, this is a busy and efficient restaurant with a shopping area which offers quite a wide range of craft and souvenir goods, clothing, and Scottish delicacies including a wide range of whiskies.

The restaurant is large, well-organised and sparkling clean. The pine ceilings, bright Formica-topped tables and the many plants and flowers add to the welcoming atmosphere.

The lavatories for the disabled have shelves ideal for nappy-changing, and the owner will find a quiet spot for a mother wishing to breast-feed her baby.

There is a good range of food, both hot and cold, served in generous portions. All in all an excellent place for families on the move. A garden and heather centre and an outdoor clothing shop has been added to the facilities.

£1–6: pasta & seafood, fresh salmon salad, pheasant casserole, lamb curry, steak pie
Children: half portions

Open every day 8.30am–5.30pm Closed Jan to mid Mar
Access/AmEx/Diners/Visa No music
Large no smoking area Licensed
P – own car park

Ullapool, Highland — map 12

CEILIDH PLACE, West Argyll Street – ☎ Ullapool (0854) 2103.

R

In the centre of Ullapool just past the Post Office.

This hotel and restaurant started as a coffee shop and a boat house and has expanded over the years to much more. The coffee shop is still there, is open all day, and provides a marvellous selection of home-made food including hot dishes, salads and vegetarian meals. There is now a hotel with twenty-five bedrooms, and a clubhouse which offers basic family accommodation at very reasonable prices.

It is such a friendly and informal place, with many extras such as a picture gallery, an auditorium for music and an excellent book shop with a good selection for children. There is so much to do in this beautiful part of Scotland, including fishing on sea and loch, hill walking and climbing, pony trekking, water skiing and so on.

COFFEE SHOP (10am–10pm) £1–4: carrot & orange soup, fish pie, savoury macaroni, shepherds pie;
DINNER (7–9pm) £15: salmon mousse, lamb & aubergine casserole, pudding or cheese
Children: small portions

Open all year, except 2 weeks in Jan   Access/AmEx/Diners/Visa
One high chair only   Licensed
P – own car park

Uppingham, Leics — map 7

BAINES TEA ROOM, High Street West – ☎ Uppingham (0572) 823 317.

R

In the town centre.

This is a very cosy and appealing tea room which is owned by the cake shop next door, and so there is a good supply of freshly made cakes, scones and pastries. It is essentially a place to stop for a snack and a cup of something, and you will find that the food is generously served – the ploughman's has about half a pound of cheese on the plate.

You can just about cope with changing a baby in the lavatory, and the owners also provide feeding cups and smaller utensils for young children.

£1–2: cheese on toast, ploughman's, soup, salads, beans on toast

Open Mon to Sat 9am–5pm No credit cards
Unlicensed One high chair only
P – on street or public car parks

LAKE ISLE, 16 High Street East – ☎ Uppingham (0572) 822 951.

R

In the centre of the town.

Almost opposite the Falcon, and behind a cheerful green front with wide windows, you will find this pretty restaurant. It has a welcoming air, from the small bar area with its wooden settle and chaise longue, to the spacious dining room with wood panelling, an old dresser, and nice solid wooden tables. We were rather taken by the poem by Ezra Pound on the wall of the bar; it begins:

'O God, O Venus, O Mercury, patron of thieves,
Give me in due time, I beseech you, a little tobacco shop...'

You would probably pick lunchtime for a family outing with the children, and the short menu offers good value. There is also a four-course Sunday lunch for around £13, and a very extensive wine list.

If you need to change or feed a baby one of the bedrooms can usually be made available.

LUNCH £10, 2 courses: smoked salmon & herring terrine, chicken Kiev;
DINNER £16: onion soup, stuffed poussin, pudding or cheese
Children: half portions

Open 12.30–2pm (not Mon); 7.30–10pm, Mon to Sat;
Open all year Access/AmEx/Diners/Visa
Licensed One high chair only
P – street and car parks No music

Walberswick, Nr Southwold, Suffolk — map 8

BELL INN – ☎ Southwold (0502) 723 109.

P

Follow the main street towards the sea.

You can judge the age of this lovely old pub by the deep channels which are worn into the flagstones on the floors. Parts of it are 600 years old and it's a fine sight with the facade covered in roses. There's a great display too in the gardens at the back: there's plenty of room to sit and contemplate the landscape and the sea.

The main bar is dominated by a big, open fireplace and an iron stove around which congregate some fine curved wooden settles, and there's a plusher lounge bar. Families can use a tiny room off the bar and are welcome too in the large dining room and the snack bar at the back of the pub.

Food is served every day except Sunday evenings and this includes a cold buffet at lunchtimes.

(12–2pm & 7.30–9pm, not Sun pm) £1–5: salads, fish & chips, ploughman's
Children: half portions

• Ale – Adnams No music
P – own car park

Welford-on-Avon, Warwicks map 3

THE FOUR ALLS – ☎ Stratford-on-Avon (0789) 750 228.

P

Just off the A439, Stratford to Evesham road.

This is a Whitbread managed house whose interior has been successfully re-structured into a largely open-plan format, with brick pillars and wood panelling here and there and several small alcoves. Families are welcome in areas at either end of the pub which are well away from the bar. The main family area has loads of room and is comfortably furnished; the stone and brick walls and half-panelled walls give it a pleasant ambience, and there is a no-smoking section too. There are also several high chairs available.

A great attraction of the pub is its situation on the river, and there is a landing stage alongside. A large lawned area with plenty of bench tables and a play area with swings and a slide adds to the attractions, and there is an open field beyond.

The pub is open all day from Monday to Saturday, and food is served right through to 10pm.

(12–10pm) £1–8: hot mushrooms, fried plaice & chips, Cumberland sausage, steak, mushroom & nut fettucine
Children: own menu

• Ale – Flowers, Hook Norton, Marston's
P – large car park

Wells, Somerset — map 2

CLOISTER RESTAURANT – ☎ Wells (0749) 76543.

R

In the cloisters alongside the book shop.

Calm and contentment should pervade your soul as you sit in this restaurant which is situated in one side of the cathedral cloisters. The arched roof is beautifully traced in carved stone, and through the mullioned windows, also framed with carved stone, you can see the great cathedral.

The room is long and narrow, and the double row of plain wooden tables, overlooked by memorial plaques on the walls, maintains the ecclesiastical air.

The food concentrates on salads, snacks and hot dishes of the day and there is always a good choice of cakes and pastries. It is all reasonably priced, and the profits go to the cathedral – so dive in.

Unfortunately they have no space for mothers to change or feed a baby – the nearest point of relief is the public lavatories. But at some stage this year a new toilet block will be built and will include space for changing babies.

£1–3: jacket potatoes, quiches, salads, hot dishes of the day
Children: smaller portions

Open 10am–5pm, from 2–5pm Sun; 11.30am–4.30pm Nov to Feb
Closed for 2 weeks at Xmas   No credit cards accepted
Licensed   No smoking
P – public car park   No music

THE GOOD EARTH, 4 Priory Road – ☎ Wells (0749) 78600.

R

On the A371 West of the Cathedral.

When you have uplifted your soul by gazing at the magnificent cathedral in this lovely town, attend to the inner man at this attractive whole food restaurant. It is based in a series of bright and airy rooms with pine floors and solid wooden tables. You can also eat in a little paved courtyard with barrel tables and chairs.

There's a pleasing ambience to this restaurant, and the prices are very pleasing too – a very substantial three-course meal will set you back less than £4. A baby can be changed in the Ladies, where there is a table, and paper towels.

£1–2: soups, pizza, jacket potato with cheese, dish of the day (e.g. mushroom & cashew nut pie, or cauliflower cheese), salads
Children: own menu, smaller portions

Open 9.30am–5.30pm Mon-Sat
Closed Sun Access/AmEx/Visa
Licensed Several no smoking rooms
P – free car park at rear No music

Wendover, Bucks — map 3

RED LION, High Street – ☎ Wendover (0296) 622 266.

P

In the main street of the town.

A rambling, 16th century, black and white coaching inn which sits in the pretty village of Wendover below the Chiltern hills. It has useful facilities for families and children are welcome in the lounge – a large, well-furnished room with a splendid open fireplace – or in a buttery off the main bar (it's a non-smoking area).

There is a good choice of food always available, with dishes on the very large menu which would suit children, and a traditional Sunday roast is also laid on for around £6. There are two high chairs on the premises.

The pub is open all day, 11am to 11pm, from Monday to Saturday.

(12–2.15pm & 6–10.15pm) £1–8: plaice & chips, omelettes, pizzas, Welsh rarebit, steaks
Children: own menu

• Ale – Morland's, Young's, Fuller's, Marston's, Greene King
P – own car park No music

West Bay, Nr Bridport, Dorset — map 2

RIVERSIDE CAFE & RESTAURANT – ☎ Bridport (0308) 22011.

R

Two miles south of Bridport.

This restaurant is about the only reason for visiting West Bay. It is a plain, whitewashed building which also serves as a Post Office but stands out as a white beacon of hope amid the surrounding dross.

The interior is plain and simple, with solid wooden tables, which have fresh flowers upon them, white walls and black beams.

The owners, Arthur and Janet Watson, have been here for twenty-odd years and serve real, beautifully cooked food. No wonder the posh food writers visit the Riverside. The fresh fish is superb and you can see into the kitchen and confirm that every meal is freshly cooked.

Families are made particularly welcome as evidenced by the presence of five high chairs. The lavatories are small and you would change a baby's nappy with difficulty.

£3–10: lobster Thermidor, hake provencale, mussels, sole, haddock, plaice
Children: half portions

Open 10.30am–5.30pm & 6.30–8pm (this can vary)
Closed Mondays and November to February
Access/Visa Licensed
P – on street and in public car parks

West Huntspill, Somerset map 2

CROSSWAYS INN – ☎ Burnham-on-Sea (0278) 783 756.

P

On the A38 just south of Highbridge.

This pub is not very far from the M5 between Bridgewater and Burnham-on-Sea (Junction 22 or 23). Built in the 17th century it is quite a large place and looks very smart with the lower half of the facade painted white and a tiled upper half. Inside there are several rooms around the bar and they have their fair share of wooden beams, exposed brickwork, and wooden tables and settles. There is an open fireplace with a stove at one end of the main bar and an alcove with wooden settles formed into booths.

Families are welcome in a high-ceilinged room with plenty of tables and chairs, and with a skittle alley taking up the other end of the room. There is a high chair available.

For warm days there is a little patio by the entrance, and quite a large enclosed grassy garden with fruit trees and plenty of bench tables.

(12–2pm & 6.30–10pm) £1–4: broccoli & chicken & ham Mornay, curried vegetarian nut roast, beef Stroganoff, smoked salmon
Children: own menu, half portions

• Ale – Eldridge Pope, Butcombe, Flowers and guests
P – own car park

West Pennard, Somerset — map 2

RED LION – ☎ Glastonbury (0458) 32941.

P

On the A361 east of Glastonbury.

Built in the 17th century and once a farmhouse, this pleasant stone pub has recently been restored. You will now find a long and spacious bar with the original flagstone floors and heavy beams, and a large inglenook fireplace.

The separate family room is also spacious and comfortable, with similar stone walls and wooden beams, and plenty of tables and wooden settles. If it is busy, there is yet another room without a bar, the "Parlour", to take the overspill. There is a high chair available.

The L-shaped stone exterior is bright with tubs of flowers and there are a few bench tables here; there are also two small patches of garden with tables and chairs.

(12–2pm & 6–10pm) £1–10: spaghetti carbonara, scampi provencale, chicken princess, beef Stroganoff, sirloin steak
Children: own menu, half portions

• Ale – Bass, Butcombe's, Red Lion Best, Boddington's and guests
P – own car park

West Witton, Nr Leyburn, North Yorks — map 9

WENSLEYDALE HEIFER – ☎ Wensleydale (0969) 22322.

P

On the main street (the A684 Leyburn-Hawes road).

Drivers be warned that the entrance to the car park is tight, and it is very easy to go straight past it. Once inside, however, a roaring log fire ensures a truly warm welcome at this 17th century inn at the heart of Wensleydale. There are a variety of cosy rooms and snug alcoves to choose from and the main family room comes complete with armchairs and antique furniture. There are two high chairs available.

Both bar snacks and bistro meals are available, plus half portions for the children and it is worth looking out for the specials of the day which appear on the blackboard. The pub is open all day from Monday to Saturday.

During the summer the large walled garden is a pleasant place to spend a couple of hours. There is space for the children to play and plenty of tables and chairs for the adults.

(12–2pm & 6–9.30pm) £1–8: green peppercorn & ham terrine, Whitby haddock & chips, cobbler pie, scallop Mornay, fillet steak
Children: half portions

• Ale – Tetley   No music
P – own car park

West Wycombe, Bucks **map 3**

GEORGE & DRAGON – ☎ *High Wycombe (0494) 464 414*

P

In the main street of the village.

The 18th century brick front, with its splendid sign, gives no clue to the spacious lay-out of this well-known coaching inn. As you swing into the courtyard, where the London to Oxford coaches and horses have gone before you, you will find a very large car park and alongside it an equally spacious garden. There is masses of space on the lawn, which is enclosed on three sides and has a lovely display of shrubs and flowers. There are plenty of bench tables at which to perch on warmer days, and the children have a play area with a swing, climbing frame and slide, and a safe bark surface.

From the garden you can see that the back of the pub is much older than the front – it's a rambling black and white building which dates back to the 15th century.

Inside the large bar is comfortably laid out, and heavy wooden cross beams and pillars support the ceiling. Away from the bar there is a charming little room where families are welcome. It has a low ceiling, walls partly panelled in wood, and a few tables and chairs. In a small alcove an antique high chair is stored, alongside an old cash register.

Just along the road you can visit West Wycombe Park, which was the home of Sir Francis Dashwood, who founded the notorious Hell Fire Club in the 18th century.

(12–2pm & 6–9.30pm, not Sun pm) £2–9: game paté, salmon in pastry, vegetable gratin, ham & leek & cider pie, beef Wellington

• Ale – Courage   No music
P – own car park

Weston-on-the-Green, Oxon — map 3

CHEQUERS – ☎ Bletchington (0869) 50319. *Pot Luck*

P

North of Oxford on the A43 near its junction with the A421.

The pub is housed in an attractive, long, low stone building with a thatched roof. A sizeable enclosed garden at the back has a large lawn with plenty of bench tables and a climbing frame.

The interior does not quite live up to the promise of the pub's outside appearance but there is plenty of space, and families are welcome in a large room off the main bar, although this is primarily intended for customers who wish to eat. There is another little room off here, where families can also sit.

(12–2pm & 6.30–10pm) £1–8: burger, fillet of plaice, steaks, mixed grill, ham & chips
Children: own menu, half portions

• Ale – Hall's, Tetley, Fuller's P – own car park

Wetheral, Cumbria — map 9

FANTAILS – ☎ Carlisle (0228) 60239.

R

In the centre of the village.

In the centre of Wetheral on the edge of the village green you will find this 18th century restaurant, built of warm red brick and decorated with hanging flower baskets. Many features remain from its days as a smithy including leaded windows, oak floors, strong beams and whitewashed walls. The main dining room is tastefully furnished and the Dove Room is open at lunchtimes and is full of antique settles and tables.

The extensive menu provides a sophisticated selection but we were assured that fish or chicken is available for children. There is a high chair but perhaps it would be the stouthearted parents of well behaved children or those wishing to treat a teenager who would feel most at home here. If you need to change a baby a small sitting room can be made available.

LUNCH £15: game terrine, lemon sole in puff pastry, pudding or cheese;
DINNER £17: asparagus soufflé, guinea fowl in Calvados, pudding or cheese
Children: small portions

Open 12–2pm & 6.30–9.30pm, Mon to Sat

One high chair Licensed
No smoking at one table P – at front

Wetton, Nr Ashbourne, Staffs — map 6

YE OLDE ROYAL OAK INN, Wetton – ☎ Astonefield (033 527) 287.

P

Off the B5053 or the A52, north of Ashbourne.

This pub is in the delightful Manifold Valley in the Peak District National Park and very close to many tourist attractions such as Dovedale, Hartington and the famous theme park and gardens of Alton Towers.

It is an attractive, 17th century stone building which was once a haunt of sheepdrovers. The bars, with their wooden beams, have an agreeable atmosphere and the family room, with bench seats which can seat about thirty people, is functional and agreeable.

It leads out to a delightful garden, which has bench tables on the lawn, all shaded by flowery cherry, willow and chestnut trees. We sat there one summer evening over a pint or two and enjoyed the peace and quiet immensely.

In addition the pub has space for caravans, and a camping barn for the more hardy holiday makers.

(12–2pm & 7–8.30pm) £1–6: chicken & chips, steak & kidney pie, fresh trout, sirloin steak, plaice & chips
Children: half portions

• Ale – Greene King, Ruddles, Theakston's
P – own car park No music

Weymouth, Dorset — map 2

OLD ROOMS INN – ☎ Weymouth (0305) 771 130.

P

On the south side of the harbour towards South Pier.

This harbourside pub was built in 1667 and has had quite a history. It is reputed to be haunted and a bricked-up tunnel in the cellar suggests that it was used by smugglers.

The original building has been added to and altered over the centuries, and this decade has seen the addition of a family room. Smoked glass patio doors enable you to watch the comings and goings of the ships.

The main bar has a low and heavily beamed ceiling, pine panelled walls and old pine tables and chairs, and nautical paraphernalia decorate the walls. The family room is very much in the same style and on warmer days you can also sit at the picnic tables in the pub's court- yard, and get the same good views of the harbour.

The Old Rooms is open all day from Monday to Saturday, and as one of our readers, Mrs Sarah Hayward, told us is a busy and very friendly pub.

(12–2pm & 7–9pm) £1–6: plaice & chips, chicken Kiev, scallops, pizzas, steaks
Children: half portions

• Ale – Butcombe, Devenish, Marston's and guests
P – public car park nearby

PERRY'S, The Harbourside, 4 Trinity Road – ☎ Weymouth (0305) 785 799.

R

On the harbour side.

This agreeable restaurant is situated in a row of Georgian houses, typical of Weymouth, which overlook the harbour and all its sea going traffic.

Inside you will find a relaxing decor of pine furniture, tiled floors and half panelled walls, which are utilised for a series of exhibitions: prints, paintings and photographs.

This restaurant prepares all its dishes from fresh ingredients, and there is of course an excellent selection of fish – skate, monkfish, turbot, bream; whatever is available at the market.

The Ladies is a mite small if you need to change a baby, but the staff will put a chair in there for you.

LUNCH £11: fish chowder, chicken Provencale, pudding or cheese;
DINNER £14: scallops, turbot, pudding or cheese
Children: small portions

Open 12–2pm Mon to Sat; 7.15–10.30pm every day
Open all year Licensed
Access/Visa One high chair only
P – public car parks

Wheddon Cross, Somerset — map 2

REST AND BE THANKFUL INN – ☎ Timberscombe (0643) 841 222.

P

On the A396 south of Minehead.

This is a well-porportioned, cream-painted building, which looks 18th century but was built a little earlier than that. Inside is a long bar area divided into three sections, and there are two rooms where families are welcome. In the basement there is a large L-shaped room with plenty of tables and chairs, and its own entrance from the patio. On the same level as the bar there is a well-decorated and nicely furnished eating area – and you can sit and have a drink there, too.

In summer the skittle alley is pressed into use as a games room with darts, skittles, and some video games.

Apart from the patio, there is a playing field alongside the pub, with a play area with some swings and slides (owned by the local council).

(12–2pm & 7–10pm) £1–10: chicken & mushroom pie, plaice & chips, steaks, cauliflower cheese
Children: own menu

• Ale – Ruddles, Usher's P – own car park

Whitchurch, Nr Aylesbury, Bucks — map 3

WHITE SWAN – ☎ Aylesbury (0296) 641 228.

P

On the A413 north of Aylesbury.

This attractive village has a pub to match: a charming flat fronted brick building, possibly built in the 17th century, with a partly thatched roof. There are two bars, a small one at the front, and a larger and very pleasant one at the side. It has a lowish beamed ceiling, walls partly panelled in wood, a nice settle and good chairs, including some leather dining chairs, and a grandfather clock. It is a comfortable and friendly place, and you might meet Charlie, the pub's labrador, after whom the bar is named.

Along the corridor is the family room. It has wood panelled walls and several pine tables and is primarily intended for customers to eat their food, but families are welcome to use it to eat or to drink. There is an extensive and reasonably priced range of food on offer.

The large grassy garden at the back is delightful. Surrounded by trees and bushes, with bench tables scattered beween the trees, it looks out to open countryside and next door is the village cricket ground. So, after a few draughts of ale, you might doze a summer afternoon away with one eye on the local cricketing tyros.

(12–2pm & 6–9.45pm, not Sun pm) £1–7: burgers, beef hot-pot, vegetable lasagne, haddock & chips, rump steak
Children: half portions

• Ale – Aylesbury, Bass, Wadworth's P – own car park

Whitewell, Nr Clitheroe, Lancs map 9

INN AT WHITEWELL – ☎ Dunsop Bridge (02008) 222.

P

Off the B6478. Six miles north-west of Clitheroe.

Down the winding lanes of the forest of Bowland you will find this classic country inn alongside the village church. It is a solid stone manor house, parts of which date back to the 14th century, and was once the house of the Keeper of the Forest.

The interior is a mixture of dark antique and country pine furniture, and the east wing of the house is an art gallery, with a studio on the top floor. The enterprising landlord sells high quality shirts, sweaters and shoes; and he is also a wine merchant, which ensures a very comprehensive list. An interesting choice of bar food is always offered here, and is all cooked on the spot; it's jolly good value, too.

There is a comfortable and attractive public bar and families just calling in for a drink or a snack can use a spacious room just in from the main door which has lots of tables and easy chairs and is attractively kitted out with antiques and hunting prints on the walls.

From the rooms at the back of the building and from the garden you have delightful views of wooded hills and the river Hodder below, where the landlord has several miles of fishing.

(12–2pm & 7.15–9.15pm) £1–6: savoury pancakes, Coniston smoked trout, roast rib of beef, fisherman's pie, Cumberland sausage
Children: half portions

• Ale – Moorhouse No music

Also recommended in the Family Welcome Accommodation Guide.

Places included in the Guide must offer the following basic facilities:
Pubs – a separate area or room for families where alcohol is not served;
Restaurants – high chairs and special menus/reduced portions.

Widecombe in the Moor, Devon — map 1

OLD INN – ☎ Widecombe (036 42) 207.

P *North of Ashburton on the minor roads, and can be reached from the A38 or the B3212.*

This famous village has a pub to match. It is part of a row of 14th century stone buildings which also house gift and craft shops. It has several rooms with thick stone walls and lots of oak, and the family room has a large open fire, a floor of worn flag stones, and oak benches and settles.

Children are also welcome in the long and narrow dining room with its several tables and padded bench seats.

The way to the car park is not immediately obvious – take the road to the right of the stone buildings and the car park is on your left. Next to it is a large grassy garden with a tiny brook and with picnic benches, and a terrace.

There's a good choice of food at reasonable prices, with daily specials, several vegetarian dishes and a Sunday lunch for under £4.

(11am–2.15pm & 6.30–10.15pm) £1–8: Moorland smokie, country fish pie, vegetable curry, haggis, steaks
Children: half portions

• Ale – Usher's No music
P – own car park

Wigglesworth, North Yorks — map 9

THE PLOUGH INN – ☎ Long Preston (07294) 243.

P *On the B6478.*

This is busy roadside pub has always been popular with those heading for the Lakes, Skipton or the Yorkshire Dales. Now with the recent addition of a splendid conservatory it is even more of an attraction for those seeking to break their journey.

The half timbered black and white front makes it an easily identifiable landmark and inside there are panelled walls and stone fireplaces. The conservatory, which is used as a restaurant, has pleasant wicker furniture and is full of plants.

The children's room is at the side of the main bar with cushioned bench seats and copper-topped tables. A new garden area overlooking some sumptuous countryside has recently been laid out and is a great place for the youngsters on a sunny day.

(12–2pm & 7–9.30pm) £1–7: savoury pancakes, chicken, scampi, home made pies
Children: own menu, half portions

• Ale – Flowers, Tetley P – own car park

Wighill, North Yorks — map 10

WHITE SWAN INN – ☎ Tadcaster (0937) 832 217.

P *Off the A684. Look for the Wighill sign two and a half miles east of Tadcaster.*

Set in the heart of a picturesque village, it is well worth straying off the main roads to stop off at this ivy clad pub.

It is a delightful pub which is made up from five small low ceilinged rooms, all of which are well-furnished, partly with antique pieces. Two of these rooms can be used by families and one of them is particularly agreeable since it opens on to a patio and the garden.

There is an excellent choice of food here, which includes Sunday lunch for under £8. The pub has a good selection of wines, much wider than most pubs, and of real ales.

(12–2pm & 7–9pm Thurs to Sat) £2–10: garlic mushrooms, fisherman's pot, fresh salmon, lamb Shrewsbury, venison in red wine
Children: small portions

• Ale – Theakston's, Stone's, Tetley, Younger's
P – own car park

Williton, Somerset — map 2

ORCHARD MILL – ☎ Williton (0984) 32133.

R *Off the A39. Look for the signs.*

The fine old building was built in 1616, and sits at the foot of the Quantock Hills. The mill was built of sandstone on three storeys and now houses the restaurant, a craft shop and a museum of agricultural implements.

The restaurant comprises three pleasant little rooms, and the windows have pine shutters. There are a few toys laid out in one of the rooms.

At the front there is a little patch of garden and a rockery, and a couple of tables; and at the side of the building a very pleasant grassy garden with

the tables placed under shady trees. On one side the huge waterwheel still turns. It is a relaxing place to sit and take a snack. The children can enjoy a play area alongside, with a slide, a swing and a climbing frame.

There are no facilities for changing a baby, although the lavatories are spacious, if spartan.

£1–5: cottage pie, trout, lamb & apricot pie, pasta cheese bake
Children: own menu, small portions

Open 10am–5pm, March to December. Closed Mondays; and on Tuesdays March and April, and October to December
P – own car park   Licensed

Wilmington, Devon **map 2**

WHITE HART – ☎ Wilmington (040 483) 226.

P

On the A35 east of Honiton.

A smart, thatched, 16th century roadside inn with a splendid interior. Heavy beams dominate the low ceilings and complement the huge fireplace in the main bar. The landlord has three alternatives for families: a small, smartly furnished lounge off the main bar; at lunchtimes the attractive dining room with its large, old fireplace; and when he is really busy the skittle alley is pressed into use (but not on winter evenings because he runs eight skittle teams).

There is a very pleasant lawned garden, bright with flowers in summer, on one side of the pub and there are several bench tables here. An area above the car park and a small paddock are also made available.

(12–2pm & 7–10pm) £1–9: Cornish pastie, trout, scampi, steaks
Children: own menu, half portions

• Ale – Bass P – own car park

Winchelsea, East Sussex — map 4

NEW INN, German Street – ☎ Rye (0797) 226 252.

P

In the centre of the town.

This old Cinque Port stands on a hill opposite Rye, and it was a thriving port until the 14th century when the harbour silted up. It is a quiet and charming place, and this smart white-painted 18th century coaching inn stands opposite the church of St Thomas Becket which was partly ruined long ago by an invading band of Frenchmen, who soon retired with dented ambitions to their own land.

There is plenty of room inside the well-furnished pub and by the entrance, and well away from the bar, is an area where families are welcome to park themselves; and there are plenty of comfortably padded benches and chairs. Half portions of certain dishes are made up for children, and there is a small "children's choice" menu. There is much emphasis on local fish and their own home-made pies. The Sunday lunch, with a main course at under £5, offers good value.

The walled garden at the back is a delight: its large area is filled with a marvellous display of flowers, with many shady trees and bushes; and there are bench tables and a couple of swings at one end. It is safely enclosed, and the owners do not allow dogs in there; a wise policy in our view.

(12–2pm & 6.30–9.30pm) £1–9: mushrooms in garlic butter, vegetarian platter, fresh fish of the day, pork kebabs, Winchelsea grill
Children: own menu, half portions

• Ale – Courage P – own car park

Wincle, Cheshire **map 6**

WILD BOAR – ☎ Wincle (0260) 227 219.

P

On the A54 between Congleton and Buxton.

This is a traditional, "pubby" pub which stands alone in wonderful moorland countryside. It is a rambling building, made of stone, some of which has been rendered and painted.

There are two rooms where you can sit with your children – one with a games machine, chairs, tables and bench seating and the other is more of a dining room, with several tables with smart check tablecloths.

Reduced portions can be given to children at lunchtimes but no children under 14 are admitted in the evenings.

(12–2pm & 7.30–10pm) £1–7: soup, plaice & chips, sirloin steak, curry
Children: smaller portions

• Ale – Robinson's P – own car park

Wirksworth, Derbyshire **map 7**

CROWN YARD KITCHEN, Market Place – ☎ Wirksworth (0629) 822 020.

R

In the town centre.

The restaurant, a cheerful and bright, glass sided place, is alongside the Heritage Centre, which tells the story of the town's past, and especially the local lead mines and the quarries.

Situated in a small courtyard away from the main road, the restaurant is reached via an incline, so you really will have to push your pushchairs. Inside, there is plenty of space between tables, but no special facilities for baby changing.

£1–3: steak & kidney pie, lasagne, cod mornay, pizza, chicken curry
Children: half portions

Open 9am to 5pm, Monday to Saturday; from 10am on Sunday
Licensed Access/Visa
No smoking during lunch times P – on street

Withington, Nr Cheltenham, Glos — map 2

MILL INN – ☎ Withington (024 289) 204.

P

Off the A436 and the A40. Follow the signs to the Roman Villa.

This ancient, rambling stone pub, its front covered with ivy, is very busy indeed, and especially so at weekends. Nevertheless it is a good proposition for families since there are three rooms where children may go: the first is an attractive high-ceilinged room with one of the biggest inglenook fireplaces we have ever seen, wooden settles and plenty of tables; a delightful little alcove room with a window on to the garden; and a third alcove with a table and some games machines.

The bars are spacious and high-ceilinged, with paved floors, and wooden beams, and there's a sizeable, grassy garden to sit in on warmer days. Watch your children closely, though, a stream runs through it (it's actually the River Coln).

(12–2pm & 7–10pm) £1–8: chicken satay, chicken Kiev, fresh trout, cauliflower cheese, rump steak
Children: half portions

• Ale – Sam Smith's No music
P – own car park

Wolf's Castle, Dyfed — map 5

THE WOLFE INN – ☎ Treffgarne (043 787) 662.

R

On the A40 South of Fishguard.

A delightful stone pub on a busy main route, it looks very inviting with hanging baskets of flowers on the walls. There is a secluded garden at the back, with a lawn and a patio, and surrounded by high banks of flowers and tall trees.

The restaurant, housed in a conservatory, is a very attractive room and families can also use another dining room off the main bar. There is an excellent choice of food both from the bar and the restaurant menus.

The very helpful owners will always make facilities available to mothers who need to change or feed a baby.

BAR SNACKS (12–2pm & 7–10pm) £1–5: smoked trout, plaice, salads, beef Stroganoff, dressed crab;
DINNER (7–10pm) £11: hors d'oeuvres, chicken Chasseur, pudding or cheese
Children: small portions

Access/Visa • Ale – Felinfoel
P – own car park

Wolvercote, Nr Oxford, Oxon — map 3

TROUT INN, Godstow Road – ☎ Oxford (0865) 54485.

P *Take the Godstow road off the roundabout north of Oxford city centre where the A40 and A43 cross. Wolvercote is signposted at the roundabout.*

This ancient and celebrated inn has been a favourite of Oxford dons and undergraduates for hundreds of years. Its origins lie in the 12th century when it was a hospice for visitors to Godstow nunnery, the ruins of which lie across the river.

The lovely stone pub sits in an unrivalled position alongside the River Isis, and the extensive stone terrace provides ample room for customers to enjoy the scene. You may be accosted by one of the many peacocks which frequent the gardens.

There is masses of space inside the pub, which has a series of fine rooms with paved floors and big open stone fireplaces. Families are welcome in the Stable Bar, a superb high-ceilinged room with good wooden tables and a huge open fireplace underneath a massive oak beam. An alternative is the snack bar at the other end of the pub: another spacious room with plenty of tables and chairs.

The pub is open throughout the day from Monday to Saturday and food is available for most of the time.

BAR SNACKS (11am–10pm) £2–5: ploughman's, salads; RESTAURANT (12–2pm & 7–10pm, not Sun pm) £2–8: gravad lax, steaks, cold buffet, stuffed baked trout
Children: half portions

• Ale – Bass P – own car park

If you wish to recommend an establishment to the Guide please write to us – report forms are at the back of the book. We need your help to extend and improve the guide.

Woodbury Salterton, Devon — map 2

DIGGER'S REST – ☎ Woodbury (0395) 32375.

P *Off the A3052 East of Exeter.*

This very smart and cheerful pub, thatched and white-painted, sits in a tiny and attractive hamlet quite close to Exeter and a couple of miles from Junction 30 of the M5.

You will find a busy, well-furnished bar, with black ceiling beams, and it's divided into three sections. At the far end is an area cut off by a black oak screen and families are welcome to sit there, or alternatively, during the busy summer season, they have the more spacious option of the skittle alley up some stairs at the side of the pub. There are plenty of tables and chairs here, plus a pool table.

At the back is an enclosed garden with a good display of flowers.

(12–1.45pm & 7–10pm) £1–6: cheesy jacket potato, hot turkey pie, haddock & chips, vegetable curry
Children: small portions

• Ale – Bass, Flowers No music
P – own car park

Please let us have reports – good or bad – on any establishments listed in the Guide as soon as possible after your visit.

Woodstock, Oxon — map 3

BROTHERTONS, 1 High Street – ☎ Woodstock (0993) 811 114.

R

In the town centre.

This handsome creeper-clad stone house dates from 1627, and tourists with weary feet and a thirst will find something to eat and drink here throughout the day. Lunch runs from noon to 2.30pm and dinner from 6.30 to 10.30pm, with afternoon teas in between.

There are no hard and fast rules about children's portions – an extra plate for a small child to pinch part of an adult meal is not unusual. But the Ladies is too small for baby changing.

It's a pleasant place to sit, with wooden floors, potted plants, old pine tables and chairs, and gas mantles glowing cheerfully on the walls. Very relaxing. The menu is nicely varied: for example there is always a vegetarian dish amongst the daily specials.

£1–10: crudités, Brotherton's smokies, game pie, supreme of chicken, fillet of pork
Children: small portions

Open 10.30am–10.30pm daily Closed Xmas Day
Access/AmEx/Diners/Visa Licensed
P – in market square and behind the Bear Hotel

Woolverton, Somerset — map 2

RED LION – ☎ Frome (0373) 830 350.

P

On the A36 at the junction with the B3110.

A large stone pub set back from the road which was once part of a farm; and long ago the local magistrates' court used to sit here. Outside are two sizeable lawns, with plenty of tables and benches, and shaded by fine spreading trees – an inviting prospect on a hot day.

There's a long, spacious and comfortable bar, and the small children's room is very appealing with its wood-panelled walls, wooden tables and padded benches.

There is quite a range of food available, but no concessions to children in the way of smaller portions – so be prepared to share your plate with your offspring, or to split one meal between two children. The food is based on a wide variety of filled baked potatoes and an equally large range of salads.

It is useful for families to know that this pub is open all day from midday onwards, from Monday to Saturday.

(12–2.30pm & 7–10pm) £2–6: pitta bread with chicken tikka, filled baked potatoes, Caribbean prawn salad, avocado & seafood salad

• Ale – Wadworth's, Bass P – own car park

Worcester, Hereford & Worcs **map 6**

NATURAL BREAK, 4 The Market, off Foregate Street – ☎ Worcester (0905) 26654.

R

In the city centre.

The market really was a hopmarket years ago, and has been many other things including a derelict area. It has now been developed into a pleasant shopping area in the centre of the city.

This is a modern, self-service restaurant which concentrates on savoury flans and salads. It has an agreeable decor in cream and brown, and quarry tiled tables. The Ladies has a chair and a table, and there is room to change a baby there.

£1–5: bacon & mushroom pasties, flans, salads, jacket potatoes

Open 9.30am–4pm (5pm Saturday) Mon-Sat
No credit cards accepted One high chair only
Unlicensed

Wrenbury, Cheshire **map 6**

COTTON ARMS – ☎ Crewe (0270) 780 377.

P *Off the A49 north of Whitchurch.*

The Cotton Arms was a pub in the late 18th century and sits in the middle of the village. Its white pebble-dashed walls are offset by black woodwork; it is well maintained both inside and out, and families will receive a friendly welcome from the owners, who have children of their own.

The bright and agreeable family room has a low, beamed ceiling, while small prints decorate the cream walls. There are several tables with bucket seats.

The enclosed lawned garden is a good spot to be on a summer day. You can relax at one of the bench tables while the children enjoy the swings and the climbing frame. There is also a Wendy house for younger children, and everyone can admire the birds which frequent the two dovecotes.

(12–2.30pm & 6.45–9.30pm) £1–8: mushroom savoury bake, steaks, plaice & chips, vegetable gratin, lasagne
Children: own menu

• Ale – Greenall's, Wem P – own car park

Wytham, Nr Oxford, Oxon **map 3**

WHITE HART – ☎ Oxford (0865) 244 372.

P *Off the A34 north west of the city centre.*

This pub is very close to the Trout Inn at Wolvercote (q.v.) and is yet another classic Cotswold pub, with steep stone roofs over its mellow stone walls. The front wall is bright with trailing plants and flowers.

Families are welcome to use the conservatory which has a paved floor, long scrubbed wooden tables, and plenty of greenery. An iron stove warms the room during the winter months. The main bar is a delight, with its low ceiling, wooden beams, a large dark wood settle and a large open fireplace. A lovely place to sit and chat over a beer or two.

A pretty garden beckons on warmer days. It is part lawn and part terrace, bounded on one side by a stone wall, with several wooden tables and benches and a nice display of flowers.

(12–2pm & 7–9.45pm) £2–8: cold buffet, pork in cider, chicken Kiev, mixed grill, steaks
Children: half portions

• Ale – Ind Coope Burton, Tetley & guests
P – own car park

Yarmouth, Isle of Wight — map 3

BUGLE HOTEL – ☎ Isle of Wight (0983) 760 272.

P

In the centre of the town.

The charming little town of Yarmouth has this attractive pub and hotel, hard by the pier and the Royal Solent Yacht Club. The building is over 300 years old; one part of the facade is made of stone while the other is half-timbered and it is all enlivened by a display of flowers in hanging baskets.

As you might expect the interior has a nautical theme and the main bar is a delightful room with wood panelled walls and presentable wooden tables. The family room is at the back of the pub, beyond the games room with its pool table. It too has wood panelled walls and ceiling and some nice wooden tables, and opens on to a sizeable patio with plenty of bench tables. Barbecues are held here when the weather permits.

During the summer season the pub is open throughout the day and food is available right through to 10pm.

(12–10pm) £1–4: lasagne, plaice & chips, grilled sardines, spit roasted pork & salad
Children: own menu, half portions

• Ale – Flowers, Marston's P – public car park nearby

Yeovil, Somerset — map 2

CORNER HOUSE RESTAURANT, 5 Union Street – ☎ Yeovil (0935) 737 22.

R

In the town centre.

There has been a change of name (formerly Trugs) but not of emphasis at

this large and cheerful wholefood restaurant, where all the food is cooked freshly from ingredients devoid of chemicals, artificial colourings and so on. The restaurant is on two levels with plain and simple pine tables and chairs and over half the eating area is non-smoking. We also noticed a space to park push-chairs – a sensible idea.
The Ladies is on the small side, so it is not easy to change or feed a baby.

£2–7: vegetarian nut loaf, spaghetti Bolognese, peanut & mushroom purse, tagliatelli, steaks
Children: own menu

Open 9.30am–5pm Mon-Sat   Closed Sun & Bank Holidays
No credit cards accepted   Licensed
No smoking upstairs
P – on street and public car park nearby

York, North Yorks — map 10

BETTYS CAFÉ TEAROOMS, St Helen's Square – ☎ York (0904) 659 142.

R

The famous Bettys chain of North Yorkshire tearooms and restaurants are firm favourites of ours and has set out to cater with style for all their customers, including families.
Mothers with babies or small children can dine here with the knowledge that the Ladies offers changing facilities, a play pen and disposable nappies. There are also bibs, beakers, plates and spoons for young children plus both a toddler's and children's menu. They'll even heat up your own baby food if you ask them. There are no less than eight high chairs on the premises.
The main menu is long and varied and offers anything from a piece of granary toast to gammon and eggs, with cakes and confectionery and a host of different blends of tea and coffee.
On Sundays the various breakfasts are very popular and you can eat at leisure, browse through the Sunday papers, and listen to the piano.

£1–7: scrambled eggs with salmon, haddock & prawns au gratin, rarebits, haddock & chips, rosti with bacon
Children: own menu, half portions

Open 9am–9pm every day   Access/Visa
Licensed   Pianist most evenings
No smoking in half the café   P – public car parks nearby

BLAKE HEAD BOOKSHOP & CAFÉ, 104 Micklegate – ☎ York (0904) 623 767.

R

In one of the city's main streets.

At the back of an excellent bookshop housed in a 17th century listed building, you will find this delightful coffee shop and restaurant, which has been designed with some flair to make the maximum use of the available space. Brick pillars, plain wooden beams and a tiled floor set the style, and all down one side there is a glass canopy which gives a light and airy aspect to the place. Attractively plain wooden chairs and tables and interesting prints on the walls complete the picture.

It's a great place to buy books and you can follow up with some excellent salads and vegetarian dishes. Wherever possible organically grown fruit and vegetables are used, and the cheeses are made with non-animal rennet. The wine and beers are also organic.

There are excellent facilities for mothers with babies, including a chair and a pull-down shelf in the spacious toilet area. Bibs, beakers and plastic plates are also provided.

£1–4: salads, vegetable pie, leek & cheese quiche, Brazilian red bean stew, vegetable lasagne
Children: half portions

Open 9.30am–6pm, every day Access/AmEx/Visa
Licensed P – public car parks nearby

TAYLOR'S TEA ROOMS, 46 Stonegate – ☎ York (0904) 622 865.

R

The wonderful aroma of freshly ground coffee greets you as you enter this homely tea room and coffee shop. You'll find the restaurant on the first floor and the first thing which confronts you is an array of different teas and coffees, and an interesting display of unusual and ancient teapots. If you fancy some Formosa Oolong, or some Cuban Extra Turquino Lavado – this is the place.

The bright airy restaurant serves beverages, snacks and light meals all day; sandwiches rub shoulders with an extensive array of salads through to savouries, cakes and desserts.

Mothers with babies can relax here since there is a separate changing room, with a shelf and changing mat and a chair. Nappies, bibs and beakers are also provided.

The only music to reach your ears is the occasional strains of a busker from the pedestrian precinct below.

£1–5: scrambled eggs on toast, rarebits, omelettes, breakfast grill, cream tea
Children: half portions

Open 9am–5.30pm every day
Closed Xmas, Boxing & New Year's days Access/Visa
No smoking in half the restaurant Unlicensed
P – public car parks nearby No music

Yoxford, Suffolk map 8

ELIZA ACTON'S RESTAURANT – ☎ Yoxford (072 877) 637.

R

On the main street, the A1120.

This pink washed tea shop is a cheerful sight alongside the village church and the traditional interior is just as agreeable and welcoming.

There is a wide ranging and enterprising menu, which includes some vegetarian dishes, and the owner puts on a vegetarian evening every month.

On summer days you can take advantage of the patio which faces a delightful garden which is usually crowded with flowers: roses, hollyhocks, delphiniums, lupins and many other blooms.

There are good facilities for mothers with babies in the bathroom upstairs, including a changing mat.

£2–7: prawns au gratin, chicken korma & rice, Somerset pork, chestnut roulade, plaice Mornay
Children: own menu, half portions

Open 10am to 9.30pm every day except Wednesday (closed). Weekends only in winter.
Licensed No credit cards
P – own car park

STORES WITH MOTHER-AND-BABY ROOMS

Aberdeen, Grampian
ASDA, Muir End Road, Portlethen
JOHN LEWIS, George Street
MOTHERCARE, 122 Union Street
TESCO, Danestone Park

Accrington, Lancs
ASDA, Hyndburn Road
MOTHERCARE, 12 Cornhill, Accrington Arndale Centre

Airdrie
BOOTS, 17–19 Graham Street

Aldershot, Hants
MOTHERCARE, Unit C, Wellington Centre, Victoria Road

Altrincham, Cheshire
BOOTS, 13–17 George Street

Andover, Hants
BOOTS, 31-37 Chantry Way

Ashford, Kent
MOTHERCARE, 32 Tufton Walk, The Tufton Centre

Ashton-under-Lyne, Lancs
ASDA, Cavendish Street

Aylesbury, Bucks
MOTHERCARE, 14 Hale Leys High Street
TESCO, Broadfields, Bicester Road

Ayr, Strathclyde
BOOTS, 168-170 High Street
MOTHERCARE, 149–153 High Street

Baldock, Herts
TESCO, 58 High Street

Banbury, Oxon
BOOTS, Castle Shopping Centre
MOTHERCARE, 7 High Street

Barnsley, South Yorks
ASDA, Old Mill Lane
BOOTS, 34–40 Cheapside
LITTLEWOODS, The Metropolitan Centre
TESCO, Wombwell Lane

Barnstaple, Devon
BOOTS, 76 High Street
TESCO, St. Johns Centre, Howard Avenue

Barry, South Glamorgan
TESCO, Highlight Park, Port Road

Basildon, Essex
BOOTS, 25 Town Square
MOTHERCARE, 21 Eastgate

Basingstoke, Hants
BOOTS, 15 Old Basing Mall, Town Centre

Bath, Avon
MOTHERCARE, 44 Southgate
BOOTS, 1 Marchants Passage, Southgate
SAINSBURY'S Green Park Road

Bedford, Beds
BOOTS, 33/35/37 The Harpur Centre, Harpur Street
MOTHERCARE, 16–18 Harpur Street
TESCO, Goldington Road

Bexhill, East Sussex
TESCO, Glyn Gap, Hastings Road

Bexleyheath, Kent
ASDA, The Broadway

Birkenhead, Merseyside
MOTHERCARE, 19 Milton Pavement

Birmingham, West Midlands
ASDA, Coventry Road, Small Heath
BOOTS, City Centre House, 16–17 New Street
MOTHERCARE, 81 High Street

Bishop Auckland, Durham
MOTHERCARE, 11 Newgate Street

Blackburn, Lancs
MOTHERCARE, 38 King William Street

Blackpool, Lancs
BOOTS, 28–38 Bank Hey Street
MOTHERCARE, Victoria Street

Bognor Regis
BOOTS, 47 London Road
TESCO, Shripney Road

Boldon, Tyne & Wear
ASDA, North Road, Boldon Colliery

Bolton, Lancs
BOOTS, 32-36 Deansgate
MOTHERCARE, 1 Market Street
SAINSBURY'S, Moor Lanek

Boroughbridge, North Yorks
GATEWAY, Wetherby Road, Stump Cross

Boston, Lincs
BOOTS, 26 Market Place

Bournemouth, Dorset, Hants
ASDA, Hampshire Centre, Castle Lane
BOOTS, 18–20 Commercial Way
SAINSBURY'S, 1 Lyndhursy Road, Christchurch

Bracknell, Berks
BOOTS, 13 Princess Square
MOTHERCARE, 1 Charles Square
SAINSBURY'S Princes Square
TESCO, Martin's Heron

Bradford, West Yorks
BOOTS, 11 Darley Street
LITTLEWOODS, Kirkgate Centre, Darley Street
MOTHERCARE, 41 Broadway

Bridgend, Mid Glamorgan
GATEWAY, Brackla Shopping Centre
MOTHERCARE, 9 Caroline Street

Bridgwater, Somerset
MOTHERCARE, 2–4 High Street

Brighton, East Sussex
ASDA, Unit 1, Crowhurst Road, Hollingbury
BOOTS, 129 North Street
ASDA, Brighton Marina
MOTHERCARE, 59–60 Churchill Square

Bristol, Avon
BOOTS, 59 Broadmead
CHILDRENS WORLD, Eastgate Centre
DEBENHAMS, 1–5 St James Barton
ASDA, Highwood Lane, Patchway
JOHN LEWIS, The Horsefair
MOTHERCARE, 1 Odeon Buildings
TESCO, Eastgate Road

Bromley, Kent
BOOTS, 148–154 High Street
MOTHERCARE, 156–160 High Street
SAINSBURY'S 17 The Mall

Burgh Heath, Tadworth, Surrey
ASDA, Reigate Road

Burnley, Lancs
MOTHERCARE, 50 The Mall, Burnley Shopping Centre

Burton on Trent, Staffs
MOTHERCARE, 5 Underhill Walk
SAINSBURY'S 19–25 Underhill Walk

Bury, Lancs
ASDA, Pilsworth Road

Bury St Edmunds, Suffolk
BOOTS, 11-13 Cornhill
MOTHERCARE, 4 Brentgovel Street

Caernarfon, Gwyned
BOOTS, 1-3 Pool Lane
BOOTS, 37 Pool Street

Caerphilly, Mid Glamorgan
ASDA, Pontgwindy Road

Camberley, Surrey
LITTLEWOODS, 34/39 Park Street
MOTHERCARE, 6 Princess Way

Cambridge, Cambs
BOOTS, Petty Cury and 65–67 Sidney Street
MOTHERCARE, 12 Lion Yard
TESCO, Cambridge Road, Milton

Canterbury, Kent
DEBENHAMS, Guildhall Street
MOTHERCARE, 12 St Margarets Street

Cardiff, South Glamorgan
ASDA, Longwood Drive
BOOTS, 36 Queen Street and 101–105 Frederick Street
DEBENHAMS, 46–50 St Davids Way
LITTLEWOODS, 82/86 Queen Street
MOTHERCARE, 20 Working Street, St David Centre
TESCO, Culverhouse Cross

Carlisle, Cumbria
ASDA, Chandler Way, Parkhouse
MOTHERCARE, 35 Scotch Street
BOOTS, 43–49 English Street

Carmarthen, Dyfed
BOOTS, 12 Red Street
TESCO, Blue Street, Friars Park

Castleford, West Yorks
ASDA, Leeds Road, Glasshoughton

Chatham, Kent
MOTHERCARE, 159–163 High Street

Chelmsford, Essex
BOOTS, 43 High Chelmer

Cheltenham, Glos
BOOTS, 199 High Street, 12–15 North Street
MOTHERCARE, 36 Regent Arcade, Regent Street
SAINSBURY'S Tewkesbury Road

Chester, Cheshire
BOOTS, 47–55 Foregate Street
MOTHERCARE, 18 St. Michaels Square, Grosvenor Precinct

Chesterfield, Derby
LITTLEWOODS, 9/13 Market Place
SAINSBURY'S, Rother Way
TESCO, Lockoford Lane, Stonegravels

Chichester, West Sussex
MOTHERCARE, 30 East Street

Chippenham, Wilts
SAINSBURY'S, Bath Road

Clacton, Essex
MOTHERCARE, 48 Pier Avenue

Clyde, Strathclyde
MOTHERCARE, 65 Sylvania Way, Clyde Shopping Centre

Cobham, Surrey
SAINSBURY'S, Bridge Way

Colchester, Essex
BOOTS, 6–10 Lion Walk
MOTHERCARE, 16 Culver Walk
SAINSBURY'S Tollgate West, Tollgate
TESCO, Highwoods Shopping Centre

Corby, Yorks
ASDA, Phoenix Park, Phoenix Way

Coventry, Warwicks
BOOTS, 38–42 Corporation Street
SAINSBURY'S, 24/26 Trinity Street

Crawley, W. Sussex
BOOTS, 32–34 Queens Road
MOTHERCARE, 20 Haslett Avenue
TESCO, Hazelwick Avenue, RH10 1GY

Crewe, Cheshire
BOOTS, 56–58 Market Street
MOTHERCARE, 15 Victoria Centre

Croydon, Surrey
ASDA, Marlow Way
BOOTS, The Mall, 12–18 Whitgift Centre
MOTHERCARE, 76 Whitgift Square
SAINSBURY'S 2 Trafalgar Way, Purley Way

Cumbernauld, Strathclyde
GATEWAY, Town Centre

Cwmbran, Gwent
BOOTS, 10-14 The Mall
GATEWAY, Cwmbran Shopping Centre, Tudor Road

Darlington, Durham
MOTHERCARE, 66 Northgate

Dartford, Kent
BOOTS, 48-52 High Street
MOTHERCARE, 36 North Mall, Arndale Centre

Derby
ASDA, Derby Road, Spondon
BOOTS, 1 Devonshire Walk, Eagle Centre
SAINSBURY'S Kingsway

Doncaster, South Yorks
MOTHERCARE, 28–29 High Street
TESCO, Church View

Dorchester, Dorset
BOOTS, 12–13 Cornhill
MOTHERCARE, 9/9A Tudor Arcade, South Street

Dover, Kent
MOTHERCARE, 62 Biggin Street
TESCO, Whitefield Road, Whitefield

Droitwich, Worcs
BOOTS, 50 St. Andrews Square

Dudley, W. Midlands
CHILDRENS WORLD, The Merry Hill Centre, Brierley Hill
DEBENHAMS, Merryhill Centre
GATEWAY, The Merry Hill Centre, Brierley Hill

Dumfries, Dumfries & Galloway
BOOTS, 74 High Street
MOTHERCARE, 70 High Street

Dundee, Tayside
BOOTS, 49–53 High Street
MOTHERCARE, 1 Wellgate Shopping Centre, Cowgate

Dunfermline, Fife
MOTHERCARE, Kingsgate Shopping Centre

Dunstable, Beds
TESCO, Adj Ickfield Way, Skimpot Road

Durham, Durham
BOOTS, 2-5 Market Place
MOTHERCARE, 3 Millburngate
SAINSBURY'S, Arnison Retail Centre, Pity Me

East Grinstead, Surrey
BOOTS, 40-46 London Road

East Kilbride, Strathclyde
BOOTS, 33-37 The Plaza
MOTHERCARE, 9 The Plaza, Town Centre

Eastbourne, East Sussex
BOOTS, 15 Eastbourne, Arndale Centre
MOTHERCARE, 71 Eastbourne, Arndale Centre

Eastleigh, Hants
GATEWAY, Bournemouth Road, Chandler's Ford

Edgware, Mddx
SAINSBURY'S, Unit 25, The Broadwalk Shopping Centre, Station Rd

Edinburgh, Lothian
BOOTS, 101–103 Princes Street
JOHN LEWIS, St. James Centre
LITTLEWOODS, 90/91 Princes Street
MOTHERCARE, 84A Princes Street

Enfield, Mddx
TESCO, Southbury Rd, Ponders End

Exeter, Devon
BOOTS, Boots Corner, 251 High Street
LITTLEWOODS, Guildhall Development

Exmouth, Devon
BOOTS, 21 Chapel Street, The Magnolia Centre

Falkirk, Central
BOOTS, 79–91 High Street
MOTHERCARE, 16 High Street

Fareham, Hants
ASDA, Speedfields Park
MOTHERCARE, Fareham Shopping Centre
BOOTS, Fareham Shopping Centre, 21 Westbury Mall
SAINSBURY'S 21 Thackery Mall, Farnham

Folkestone, Kent
BOOTS, 24-26 Sandgate Road

Gateshead, Tyne & Wear
BOOTS, 46-52 Cameron Walk, The Metro Centre
CHILDRENS WORLD, Retail World, Team Valley
GATEWAY, The Metro Centre
LITTLEWOODS, The Metro Centre
MOTHERCARE, The Metro Centre

Glasgow, Strathclyde
ASDA, Ayr Road, Newton Mearns
ASDA, 20 Rothes Drive, Summerston
BOOTS, 200 Sauchiehall Street
BOOTS, 33–37 The Plaza, East Kilbride
LITTLEWOODS, 56/68 Argyle Street
LITTLEWOODS, 228/239 Sauchiehall Street
MOTHERCARE, 58 Union Street

Glenrothes, Strathclyde
BOOTS, 14 Lyon Square, Kingdom Centre

Gloucester,Glos
BOOTS, 38-46 Eastgate Street

Grantham, Lincs
BOOTS, 42–43 High Street

Gravesend, Kent
ASDA, Thames Way
MOTHERCARE, 5 Kempthorne Street, St. Georges Centre
SAINSBURY'S 12 St Georges Square

Grays, Essex
MOTHERCARE, 3 High Street

Great Yarmouth, Norfolk
ASDA, Acle New Road
BOOTS, 3 Market Gates Shopping Centre
MOTHERCARE, 18 Market Gates Shopping Centre
SAINSBURY'S, St Nicholas Road

Greenock, Strathclyde
BOOTS,43 Hamilton Way
MOTHERCARE, 51 Hamilton Way

Grimsby, Humberside
ASDA, Holles Street
BOOTS, Freshney Mall, Freshney Place Shopping Centre
MOTHERCARE, 15 Friargate

Guildford, Surrey
MOTHERCARE, 23 The Friary

Halesowen, Worcs
SAINSBURY'S 18 The Precinct

Hamilton, Strathclyde
BOOTS, 44 Regent Way

Hampton, Mddx
SAINSBURY'S, 303 Uxbridge Road, St Clares TW12 1AW

Hanley, Staffs
BOOTS, 3-5 Market Square
MOTHERCARE, 13 East Precinct, Charles Street

Harlow, Essex
BOOTS, 37 Broad Walk
MOTHERCARE, 17 Harvey Centre

Harrogate, North Yorks
ASDA, Bower Road
MOTHERCARE, 45–47 Station Parade

Harrow, Middlesex
BRITISH HOMES STORES, 14 St Anne's Shopping Centre
MOTHERCARE, 80/82 St Anne's Road

Hatfield, Herts
TESCO, Mount Pleasant, Oldings Corner

Haverhill, Suffolk
SAINSBURY'S, Hanchett End

Hemel Hempstead, Herts
MOTHERCARE, 64 Marlowes

Hereford, Worcs
SAINSBURY'S Barton Yard
TESCO, Belmont Road

Hertford, Herts
TESCO, Ware Road

High Wycombe, Bucks
ASDA, Holmers Farm Way
BOOTS, 19 The Arcade, The Octagon
MOTHERCARE, 2 Paul Row
JOHN LEWIS, Cressex Centre
SAINSBURY'S Dovecot Road

Hornchurch, Essex
TESCO, 300 Hornchurch Road

Horsham, West Sussex
BOOTS, 1 Swan Walk
MOTHERCARE, 31–32 West Street
TESCO, Wickhurst Lane, Broadbridge Heath

Hounslow, Middlesex
BOOTS, 193–199 High Street
MOTHERCARE, 133 High Street

Huddersfield, West Yorks
BOOTS, 22 King Street
MOTHERCARE, 36 Princess Alexandra Walk

Hull, Humberside
BOOTS, 48–58 Prospect Centre
MOTHERCARE, 57 Whitefriargate

Ilford, Essex
TESCO, High Road, Goodmayes

Inverness, Highland
BOOTS, 11/1 Eastgate Shopping Centre
MOTHERCARE, 15 Eastgate Shopping Centre

Ipswich, Suffolk
ASDA, Goddard Lane, Whitehouse Industrial Estate
BOOTS, 5 Tavern Street
LITTLEWOODS, Tower Ramparts Centre
SAINSBURY'S Felixstowe Road, Warren Heath
TESCO, Copdock Mill Interchg

Keighley, W Yorks
BOOTS, 22-28 Queens Way

Kettering, Northants
BOOTS, 35 Gold Street
MOTHERCARE, 19 The Mall, Newborough Centre

Kidderminster, Worcs
MOTHERCARE, 15 Vicar Street

Kings Lynn, Norfolk
MOTHERCARE, 91–93 High Street
TESCO, Hardwick Road

Kingston, Surrey
BOOTS, 42 Union Street
MOTHERCARE, 20 Church Street

Kirkcaldy, Fife
ASDA, Carberry Road, Mitchelston Ind Est
MOTHERCARE, 22–24 The Mercat

Lancaster, Lancs
BOOTS, 2-12 Rendburg Way

Leamington Spa, Warwickshire
BOOTS, 31 The Parade
MOTHERCARE, 23 The Parade
SAINSBURY'S, The Shires Retail Park, Tachbrook Park Drive

Leeds, West Yorks
ASDA, Howley Park Road, Morley
BOOTS, 19 Albion Arcade, Bond Street Centre
MOTHERCARE, 1 Albion Arcade, Bond Street Centre
TESCO, Roundhay Road

Leicester, Leics
ASDA, Narborough Road South
BOOTS, 30–36 Gallowtree Gate
CHILDRENS WORLD, Belgrave Road
MOTHERCARE, 1 Belgrave Gate

Lewisham
SAINSBURY'S, 14 Burnt Ash Road, Lee Green

Leyland, Lancs
GATEWAY, Towngate

Lincoln, Lincs
BOOTS, 311-312 High Street
BRITISH HOME STORES, 196–199 High Street
MOTHERCARE, 6 Cornhill Pavement, Cornhill

Liverpool, Merseyside
ASDA, Ormskirk Road, Aintree
ASDA, Hunts Cross, Speke Hall Road
BOOTS, Clayton Square Shopping Complex
GEORGE HENRY LEE, Basnett Road
LITTLEWOODS, Church Street
MOTHERCARE, 99 Lord Street

Llanelli, Dyfed
BOOTS, 1-3 Vaughan Street
TESCO, Parc Trostre

London
ASDA, Lavender Hill, Clapham Junction, Clapham
ASDA, Woolwich Road, Charlton E7
ASDA, 130 Chase Side, Southgate N14
BRITISH HOME STORES, 252–258 Oxford Street
BRITISH HOME STORES, 38–42 Selborne Walk, Walthamstow
CHILDRENS WORLD, 317 Cricklewood Broadway, Cricklewood
DEBENHAMS, 334–348 Oxford Street
JOHN LEWIS, Oxford Street, London W1
JOHN LEWIS, Brent Cross, London NW4
JOHN LEWIS KINGSTON, Wood Street, Kingston upon Thames
LITTLEWOODS, 203-211 Oxford Circus
LITTLEWOODS, 49/63 King Street, Hammersmith W6
MOTHERCARE, 416 Brixton Road, Brixton
MOTHERCARE, Unit 7, The Waterglade Centre, 1–8 The Broadway Ealing W5
MOTHERCARE, 64 The Broadway, Ealing W13
MOTHERCARE, 316 North End Road, Fulham SW6
MOTHERCARE, Kings Mall Shopping Centre, Hammersmith W6
MOTHERCARE, 145–147 Brompton Road, Knightsbridge SW3
MOTHERCARE, 41 Riverdale High Street, Lewisham SE13
MOTHERCARE, 461 Oxford Street, Marble Arch W1
MOTHERCARE, 174–176 Oxford Street
MOTHERCARE, Unit 2, Aylesham Centre, Rye Lane, Peckham SE15
MOTHERCARE, 33–34 The Mall, Stratford E15
MOTHERCARE, 14–16 High Street, Tooting SW17
MOTHERCARE, 33 Selbourne Walk, Walthamstow, E17 7JR
MOTHERCARE, 53 The Arndale Centre, Garratt Lane, Wandsworth SW18

MOTHERCARE, 38–40 High Road, Wood Green N22
PETER JONES, Sloane Square, London SW1
SAINSBURY'S, Green Lane, Harrigay
SAINSBURY'S 14 Burnt Ash Road, Lee Green, Lewisham SE12
SAINSBURY'S Kensal Gas Works Site, Ladbroke Grove W10 5AA
SAINSBURY'S, 480 Streatham High Road, Streatham Common, SW16
TESCO, 209 Lewisham Road, Lewisham SE13
TESCO, Coppets Centre, N Circular Road, London N10

Long Eaton, Nottinghamshire
ASDA, Midland Street

Lowestoft, Suffolk
BOOTS, 76A London Road North
MOTHERCARE, 12 The Britten Centre

Luton, Beds
BOOTS, 82-86 The Arndale Centre
MOTHERCARE, 31–33 Arndale Centre

Macclesfield, Cheshire
MOTHERCARE, 30 Mill Street

Maidenhead, Berks
MOTHERCARE, 106–108 High Street

Maidstone, Kent
BOOTS, 56–62 King Street
MOTHERCARE, 34 Week Street
SAINSBURY'S 342 Dukes Walk, Stoneborough Centre
TESCO, Grove Wood Drive, Weavering

Manchester
BOOTS, 32 Market Street
LITTLEWOODS, Unit 2, The Arndale Centre, Market St
MOTHERCARE, Store 6B, Arndale Centre
SAINSBURY'S, Oldham Street, Denton

Mansfield, Notts
BOOTS, 39 Four Seasons Shopping Centre
MOTHERCARE, 22 Four Seasons Shopping Centre

Margate, Kent
MOTHERCARE, 79 High Street

Melton Mowbray, Leics
TESCO, Thorpe Road

Middlesbrough, Cleveland
BOOTS, The Cleveland Centre, 88–90 Linthorpe Road
MOTHERCARE, 6 Oberhausen Mall, Hill Street Shopping Centre
SAINSBURY'S, Wilson Street

Milton Keynes, Bucks
BOOTS, 18 Crown Walk
JOHN LEWIS, Central Milton Keynes
MOTHERCARE, Secklow Gate East
SAINSBURY'S 703 Avebury Boulevard, Secklow Gate East

Mold, Clwyd
TESCO, Chester Road, Old Station Yard

Neath, Glamorgan
BOOTS, 4-6 Water Street

New Malden, Surrey
TESCO, 300 Beverley Way

Newark, Notts
MOTHERCARE, 32 Middlegate

Newbury, Berks
BOOTS, 4–5 Northbrook Street
MOTHERCARE, 44–48 The Mall
SAINSBURY'S 4–10 The Mall

Newcastle-under-Lyme, Staffs
ASDA, Wolstanton Retail Park

Newcastle-upon-Tyne, Tyne & Wear
BOOTS, Eldon Square
BAINBRIDGE, Eldon Square
BRITISH HOME STORES, Kingston Park Centre, Kenton Park
MOTHERCARE, 2 Blacket Bridge, Eldon Square

Newmarket, Suffolk
TESCO, Fordham Road

Newport, Gwent
ASDA, 10 Pencarn Way, Coedkernew
MOTHERCARE, London House, 168 Commercial Street

Newport, Isle of Wight
BOOTS, 122-126 High Street

Newton Abbot, Devon
MOTHERCARE, 5–9 Courtenay Street

Northampton, Northants
BOOTS, 9 The Parade
MOTHERCARE, 15 Abingdon Street

Northwich, Cheshire
BOOTS, 39-45 Witton Street
SAINSBURY'S, Venables Road CW9 5RX
TESCO, Former Station Yard, Manchester Road

Norwich, Norfolk
BONDS, All Saints Green
MOTHERCARE, 47–49 St. Stephens Street
SAINSBURY'S, Pound Lane, Thorpe St Andrew
SAINSBURY'S, 1 Brazen Gate, Queens Road

Nottingham, Notts
ASDA, 184 Loughborough Road, West Bridgeford
BOOTS, 11–19 Victoria Centre
JESSOPS, Victoria Centre
MOTHERCARE, 28 Maid Marian Way
SAINSBURY'S Castle Bridge Road
TESCO, Carlton Hill, Carlton

Nuneaton, Warwickshire
ASDA, Newtown Road
MOTHERCARE, 15 Bridge Street

Oadby, Leics
ASDA, Leicester Road

Oldham, Lancs
BOOTS, 1 Town Square, Shopping Centre
LITTLEWOODS, 37/41 Market Place
MOTHERCARE, 26 Town Square Shopping Centre

Oxford
LITTLEWOODS, 52/53 Cornmarket Street

Paisley, Strathclyde
MOTHERCARE, 24 Causeyside Street

Perth, Tayside
BOOTS, 145–159 High Street

Peterborough, Cambs
BOOTS, Queensgate
JOHN LEWIS, Queensgate Centre
SAINSBURY'S, 110 Oxney Road PE1 5NG

Plymouth, Devon
BOOTS, Boots Corner, 2–6 New George Street
MOTHERCARE, 20 Old Town Street
SAINSBURY'S 23 Armada Way

Pontypridd, Mid Glamorgan
TESCO, Gellihirion Estate, Treforest

Poole, Dorset
BOOTS, 190–196 High Street
MOTHERCARE, High Street
SAINSBURY'S 11 Pitwines Close
TESCO, Ringwood Road, Manning Heath

Portsmouth, Hants
BOOTS, 194–204 Commercial Road
LITTLEWOODS, 129/135 Commercial Road

Preston, Lancs
ASDA, Fishergate
ASDA, East Way, Fulwood
BOOTS, 26–27 Fishergate

Reading, Berks
BOOTS, 47–48 Broad Street
HEELAS, Broad Street
MOTHERCARE, 14–16 King Street

Redditch, Worcs
MOTHERCARE, Kingfisher Shopping Centre

Redhill, Surrey
MOTHERCARE, 26 London Road

Renfrewshire, Strathclyde
BOOTS, 43 Hamilton Way, Greenock

Richmond, Surrey
MOTHERCARE, 1 Lower George Street

Rochdale, Lancs
BOOTS, 50 Market Way
LITTLEWOODS, 31 Market Place

Romford, Essex
BOOTS, 12 The Liberty
DEBENHAMS, Market Place
SAINSBURY'S, Mercury Gardens, Liberty 2 Centre
TESCO, Bryant Avenue

Rotherham, South Yorks
BOOTS, Howard Street
CHILDRENS WORLD, Retail World, Parkgate
MOTHERCARE, 12 Howard Street

Rotherhithe, Surrey
TESCO, Surrey Quays, Redriff Road

Rugby, Warwicks
MOTHERCARE, 5 Manning Walk, The Rugby Centre
SAINSBURY'S 3 Manning Walk, The Rugby Centre
TESCO, Leicester Road

Runcorn, Cheshire
LITTLEWOODS, 54 Runcorn Shopping City

St. Albans, Herts
BOOTS, 9 St. Peters Street

St. Helens, Merseyside
BOOTS, 8 Church Street and 24 La Grange Arcade
MOTHERCARE, 6–8 St. Marys Arcade

Salisbury, Wilts
BOOTS, 41-51 Silver Street
MOTHERCARE, 41 New Canal
TESCO, Southampton Road

Scarborough, N Yorks
BOOTS, 100-101 Westborough

Scunthorpe, Humberside
BOOTS, 43-47 High Street

Sheffield, South Yorks
BOOTS, 26 Market Street, Meadowhall Centre
COLE BROTHERS, Barkers Pool
DEBENHAMS, The Moor
MOTHERCARE, 65 The Moor

Sidcup, Kent
TESCO, Ruxley Corner

Slough, Berks
ASDA, Telford Drive
BOOTS, 178-184 High Street
LITTLEWOODS, 46/55 Queensmere

Solihull, W Midlands
TESCO, Stratford Road, Monkspath

South Ruislip, Middlesex
SAINSBURY'S 11 Long Drive

South Shields, Tyne and Wear
MOTHERCARE, 93 King Street

Southampton, Hants
ASDA, Maynard Road, Totton
BOOTS, 19–29 Above Bar Street
MOTHERCARE, 52 Above Bar
TYRRELL AND GREEN, Above Bar

Southend, Essex
BOOTS, Unit 2, The Royals
MOTHERCARE, 107–109 High Street

Southport, Merseyside
LITTLEWOODS, Chapel Street
MOTHERCARE, 8 Eastbank Street
TESCO, Town Lane

Southsea, Hants
KNIGHT AND LEE, Palmerston Road

Staines, Middlesex
MOTHERCARE, 35 Elmsleigh Centre

Stevenage, Herts
TESCO, The Forum

Stirling, Central
BOOTS, Orchard Croft, 23 Thistle Street
GATEWAY, St Ninians
MOTHERCARE, 39 Stirling Thistle Centre

Stockport, Cheshire
MOTHERCARE, 5 Adlington Walk
SAINSBURY'S Warren Street

Stockton, Cleveland
MOTHERCARE, 47 High Street

Stoke-on-Trent, Staffs
BOOTS, 3–5 Market Square, Hanley
LITTLEWOODS, 2-10 Lamb Street, Hanley

Stratford-upon-Avon, Warwickshire
TESCO, Birmingham Road

Sunderland, Tyne and Wear
ASDA, Leechmere Road Ind Est, Grangetown
LITTLEWOODS, 240 High Street West
MOTHERCARE, 70 High Street West
SAINSBURY'S, Silksworth Lane SR3 1PD

Sutton Coldfield, West Midlands
BOOTS, 44–46 Gracechurch Centre
ASDA, Walmley Ash Road, Minworth
MOTHERCARE, 154 The Parade, Gracechurch Centre

Swansea, West Glamorgan
ASDA, Trallwn Road
BOOTS, 17 St. Marys Arcade, The Quadrant Shopping Centre
MOTHERCARE, 58 Kingway

Swindon, Wilts
ASDA, Tewkesbury Way, Westlea Down
DEBENHAMS, The Parade
MOTHERCARE, 49 The Parade
SAINSBURY'S Oxford Road, Stratton St Margaret

Taunton, Somerset
BOOTS, 64–65 High Street
MOTHERCARE, 56 North Street

Telford, Salop
ASDA, Malinslee
MOTHERCARE, 39 Mall, 4 Telford Shopping Centre
SAINSBURY'S, Colliers Way TF3 4AG

Thornaby, Cleveland
GATEWAY, New Town Centre

Thurrock
BOOTS, 74-75 Lakeside Shopping Centre

Torquay, Devon
MOTHERCARE, Union House, Union Street

Truro, Cornwall
BOOTS, 94 Pydar Street
MOTHERCARE, Pydar Street
TESCO, Garras Wharf

Tunbridge Wells, Kent
BOOTS, 7-11 Calverley Road
SAINSBURY'S, Linden Park Road TN2 5QL

Walsall, West Midlands
BOOTS, 1 Townsend Square
MOTHERCARE, 43 Park Mall Saddlers Centre

Waltham Cross, Herts
BOOTS, Shopping Centre Pavilion, High Street

Warrington, Cheshire
ASDA, Cockhedge Centre, Cockhedge Way
BOOTS, 39–45 Bridge Street
ASDA, Burton Westbrook Shopping Centre
MOTHERCARE, The Mall, Golden Square

Washington, Tyne and Wear
GATEWAY, The Galleries
MOTHERCARE, Town Centre, District 1

Watford, Herts
ASDA, Odhams Trading Estate, St. Albans Road
BOOTS, 147 The Harlequin Centre, High Street
MOTHERCARE, Town Centre, 77 High Street
TESCO, 239–241 High Street
TREWINS, The Harlequin Centre

Wellingborough, Northants
BOOTS, 73 Corn Lane, Arndale Centre
SAINSBURY'S, 260 Northampton Road NN8 3GZ
TESCO, Town Centre

Welwyn Garden City, Herts
JOHN LEWIS, Bridge Street

Weston-super-Mare, Avon
LITTLEWOODS, 66/68 High Street

Weymouth, Dorset
MOTHERCARE, 104F St. Marys Street

Whitley Bay, Tyne & Wear
SAINSBURY'S, Newsteads Drive

Whitstable, Kent
TESCO, Millstrood Road

Wigan, Greater Manchester
BOOTS, The Galleries, 37 Market Street
MOTHERCARE, 7 Standishgate

Windsor, Berks
MOTHERCARE, 12 King Edward Court

Woking, Surrey
BOOTS, 1–9 Commercial Way

Wolverhampton, West Midlands
BOOTS, 4 Queen Street
BOOTS, 29 King Street
LITTLEWOODS, 4 Wulfrun Street
MOTHERCARE, 11 Mander Square, Mander Centre
SAINSBURY'S 20 St Georges Parade

Worcester
BOOTS, 72–74 High Street
MOTHERCARE, 4 Broad Street
TESCO, St Peter the Great St

Worthing, W. Sussex
BOOTS, 48–52 Montague Street
MOTHERCARE, 32/36 South Street

Wrexham, Clwyd
BOOTS, 3-7 Regent Street
BOOTS, 4 Priory Street
MOTHERCARE, 23 Hope Street

Yeovil, Somerset
MOTHERCARE, 3 Vicarage Walk, The Quedam

York, North Yorks
BOOTS, 48 Coney Street and 8–10 Market Street
BRITISH HOME STORES, 44 Coney Street
MOTHERCARE, 25 Coney Street

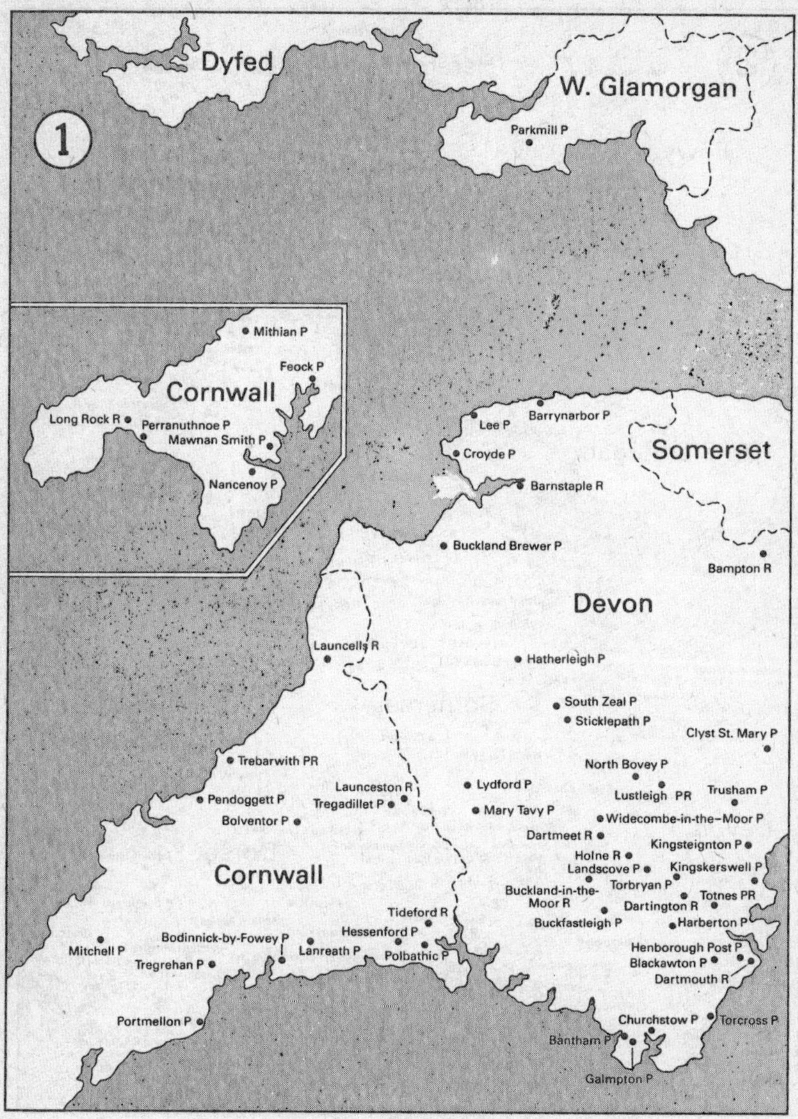
1
Dyfed
W. Glamorgan
Parkmill P
Cornwall
Mithian P
Feock P
Long Rock R
Perranuthnoe P
Mawnan Smith P
Nancenoy P
Lee P
Barrynarbor P
Croyde P
Somerset
Barnstaple R
Buckland Brewer P
Bampton R
Devon
Launcells R
Hatherleigh P
South Zeal P
Sticklepath P
Clyst St. Mary P
Trebarwith PR
North Bovey P
Launceston R
Lydford P
Lustleigh PR
Trusham P
Pendoggett P
Tregadillet P
Mary Tavy P
Widecombe-in-the-Moor P
Bolventor P
Dartmeet R
Kingsteignton P
Holne R
Landscove P
Kingskerswell P
Cornwall
Torbryan P
Buckland-in-the-Moor R
Totnes PR
Dartington R
Tideford R
Buckfastleigh P
Harberton P
Hessenford P
Bodinnick-by-Fowey P
Mitchell P
Lanreath P
Polbathic P
Henborough Post P
Tregrehan P
Blackawton P
Dartmouth R
Portmellon P
Churchstow P
Torcross P
Bantham P
Galmpton P

2
Powys
Hereford and Worcs
Gloucestershire
Gwent
Mid Glamorgan
S. Glamorgan
Avon
Wiltshire
Somerset
Devon
Dorset
Bishop's Frome P
Hay-on-Wye R
Fownhope P
Bretforton P
Twyning Green P
Little Washbourne P
Ross-on-Wye R
Aston Crews P
Withington P
Abergavenny P
Llantilio Crossenny P
Cheltenham P
Elkstone P
Cowley P
Stroud P
Sapperton P
Bibury P
Amberley P
Nailsworth P
Kingscote P
Aust P
Easton Grey R
Tormarton P
Castle Combe P
Ford P
Pewsham P
Bristol R
Hewish P
Congresbury P
Bathford P
Bath PR
Compton Martin P
Litton P
Norton St Philip P
Woolverton P
Brent Knoll R
West Huntspill P
Wells R
Croscombe P
Bradley Green P
West Pennard P
Wheddon Cross P
Williton R
Keenthorne R
Monksilver P
Fonthill Bishop P
Alvediston P
Bishop's Lydeard PR
Somerton P
North Curry P
Semley P
Staple Fitzpaine P
Yeovil R
Trent P
Tintinhull P
Stoke-sub-Hamdon P
Bishop's Caundle P
Dowlish Wake P
Hardington Mandeville P
Misterton P
Tarrant Monkton P
Tiverton R
Ansty P
Chedington P
Plush P
Spetisbury R
Milton Abbas R
Shave Cross P
Axminster R
Rampisham P
Colehill P
Wilmington P
Lytchett Minster R
Bridport P
Shipton Gorge P
Dorchester R
Sidford P
Branscombe P
Poole R
Hurn P
Sandford R
Woodbury Salterton P
Seatown P
West Bay R
Sidmouth P
Osmington Mills P
East Lulworth P
Exmouth R
Corfe Castle P
Weymouth PR
Combeinteignhead P

Warwicks
Welford-on-Avon P
Alderminster P
Shenington P
Northants
Chacombe P
Tempsford PR
Bedfordshire
Ashwell P
Bucks
Bledington P
Stow-on-the-Wold P
Marsh Gibbon P
Knebworth P
Weston-on-the-Green P
Mentmore R
Glos
Whitchurch P
Oxford PR
Little Gaddesden P
Hertfordshire
Stanton St John P
Woodstock R
Burford P
Wolvercote P
Wytham P
Wendover P
Newgate Street P
Lechlade P
Clanfield P
Fyfield P
Bledlow P
Amersham R
Faringdon P
Clifton Hampden P
West Wycombe P
Oxfordshire
Skirmett P
London
Nettlebed P
East Ilsley P
Richmond R
Aldworth P
Lower Basildon P
Shepperton P
Lacock P
Avebury R
Marlborough PR
Berkshire
Staines P
Kingston upon Thames R
Beckhampton P
Cobham R
Wilts
Sherborne St John P
Surrey
Elstead P
Shere P
Coldharbour P
Oakwood Hill P
Hampshire
Frensham R
Lower Woodford P
East Grinstead R
Testcombe P
Salisbury PR
Stockbridge P
Lurgashall P
Nuthurst P
Kingsworthy P
Billingshurst P
North Gorley P
South Harting P
Byworth P
Beauworth P
Elsted P
Stopham Bridge P
Damerham P
Owslebury P
Romsey PR
Edburton P
W. Sussex
Linwood P
Steyning P
Arundel PR
Bramber R
Ditchling P
Hamble R
Chidham P
Chichester R
Burley R
Oving P
Brighton R
East Preston R
Lymington R
Newport R
Highcliffe P
Yarmouth P
Arreton R
Luccombe Chine R
Isle of Wight
Chale P
3

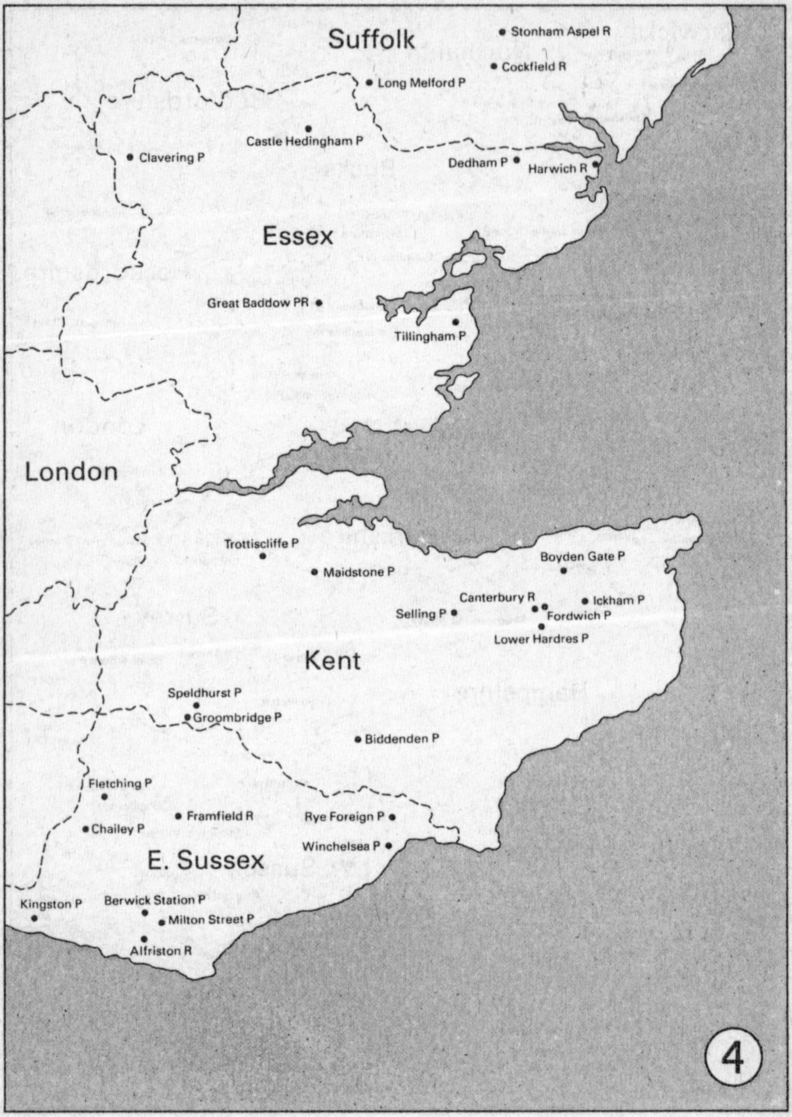
Suffolk
Stonham Aspel R
Cockfield R
Long Melford P
Castle Hedingham P
Clavering P
Dedham P
Harwich R
Essex
Great Baddow PR
Tillingham P
London
Trottiscliffe P
Maidstone P
Boyden Gate P
Canterbury R
Ickham P
Selling P
Fordwich P
Lower Hardres P
Kent
Speldhurst P
Groombridge P
Biddenden P
Fletching P
Framfield R
Rye Foreign P
Chailey P
Winchelsea P
E. Sussex
Kingston P
Berwick Station P
Milton Street P
Alfriston R
4

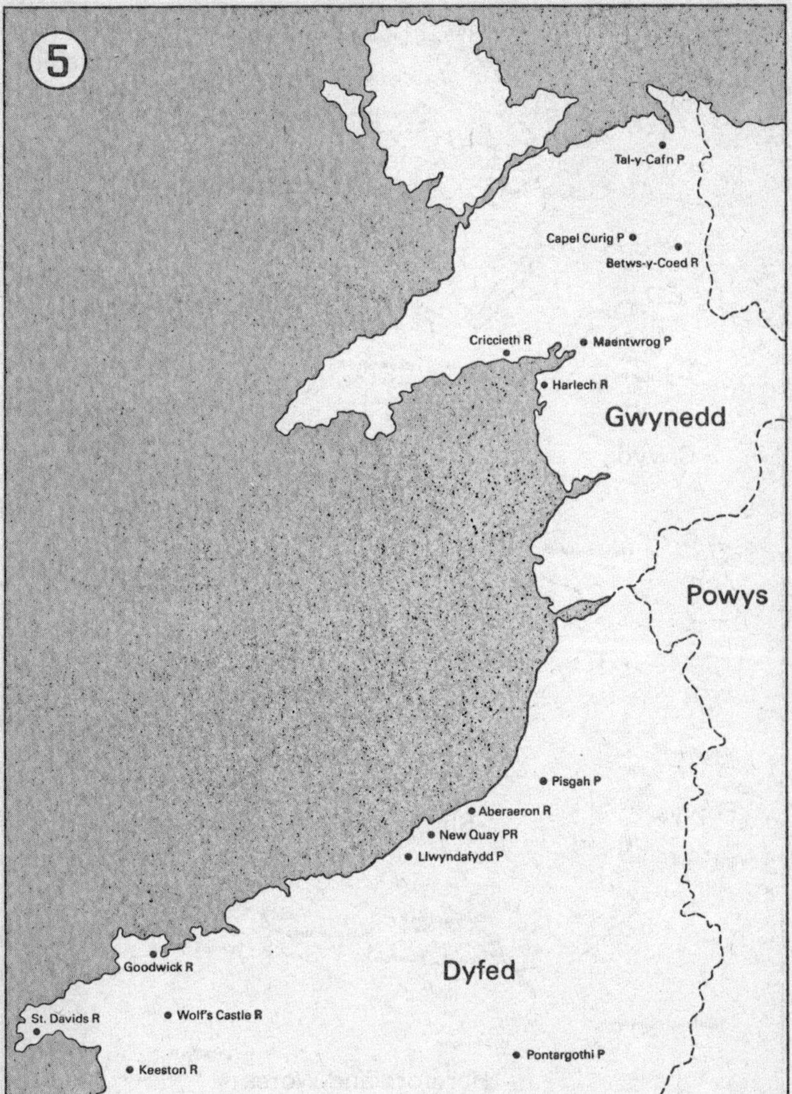
5
Tal-y-Cafn P
Capel Curig P
Betws-y-Coed R
Criccieth R
Maentwrog P
Harlech R
Gwynedd
Powys
Pisgah P
Aberaeron R
New Quay PR
Llwyndafydd P
Goodwick R
Dyfed
St. Davids R
Wolf's Castle R
Pontargothi P
Keeston R

6
Lytham St. Anne's R
Preston R
Lancs
W. Yorkshire
Parbold P
Haskayne P
Holmfirth R
Gtr. Manchester
Stockport R
Derbys
Great Budworth P
Knutsford R
Rowarth P
Chisworth R
Plumley P
Buxton R
Langley P
Northwich R
Mouldsworth P
Over Peover P
Hurdlow P
Bodfari P
Cotebrook P
Wincle P
Chester R
Butterton P
Alstonfield P
Huxley P
Cheshire
Onecote P
Wetton P
Clwyd
Bickerton P
Higher Burwardsley P
Nantwich R
Cholmondeley P
Wrenbury P
Cauldon Low R
Llangollen R
Staffs
Great Bridgford PR
Shrewsbury R
Norton P
Ford P
Clifton Campville P
Llangadfan P
Ironbridge R
Church Stretton R
Powys
Shropshire
Trefeglwys P
W. Midlands
Kinver P
Craven Arms P
Hopton Wafers P
Bewdley P
Ludlow R
Newbridge-on-Wye P
Pembridge P
Studley P
Hallow P
Hereford and Worcs
Worcester R

7
W. Yorkshire
Ledsham P
Airmyn P
Humberside
Cadeby P
S. Yorkshire
Scaftworth P
Bamford P
Castleton P
Calver R
Beeley P
Rowsley R
Eastmoor P
Matlock R
Matlock Bath R
Nottinghamshire
Lincolnshire
Wirksworth R
Derbyshire
Newton P
Langham P
Stretton R
Cottesmore P
Empingham P
Leicestershire
Uppingham R
Lyddington P
Cambs
Warwickshire
Needingworth PR
Northamptonshire
Ryton-on-Dunsmore R
Preston Bagot P
Hail Weston P
Lowsonford P
Ashby St. Ledgers P
Elsworth P
Hatton R
Riseley P
Stratford-on-Avon R

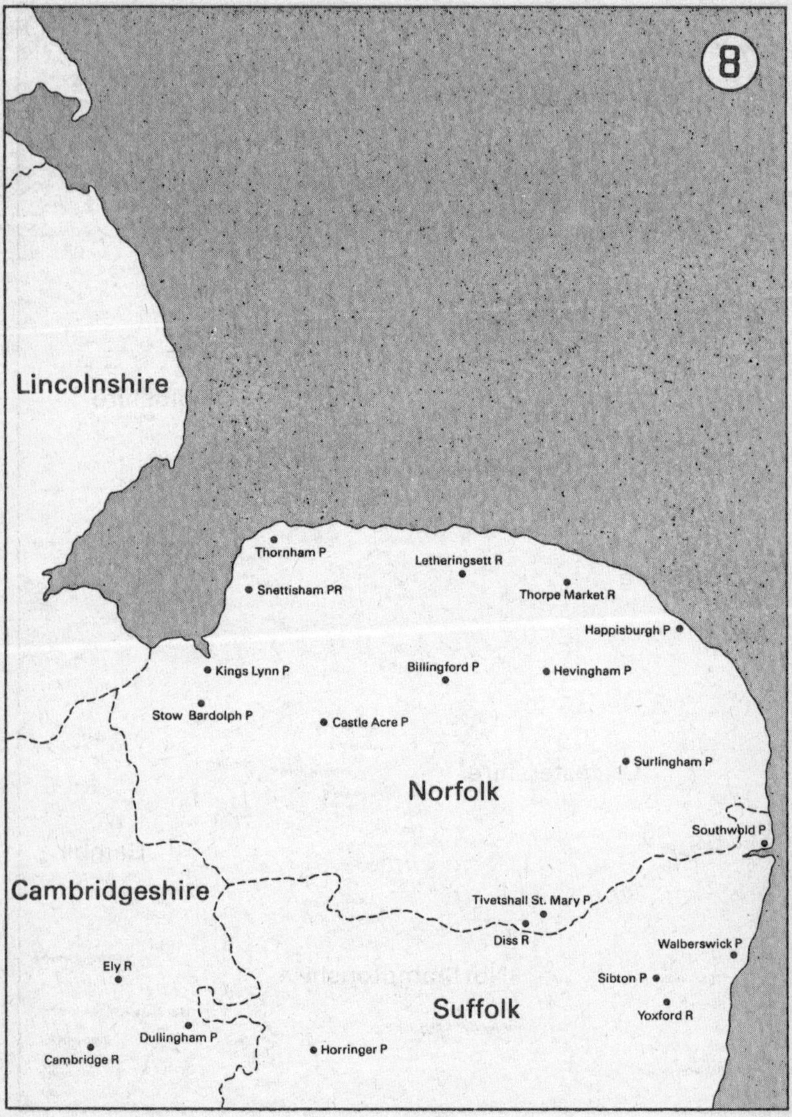
8
Lincolnshire
Thornham P
Letheringsett R
Snettisham PR
Thorpe Market R
Happisburgh P
Kings Lynn P
Billingford P
Hevingham P
Stow Bardolph P
Castle Acre P
Surlingham P
Norfolk
Southwold P
Cambridgeshire
Tivetshall St. Mary P
Diss R
Walberswick P
Ely R
Sibton P
Suffolk
Yoxford R
Dullingham P
Horringer P
Cambridge R

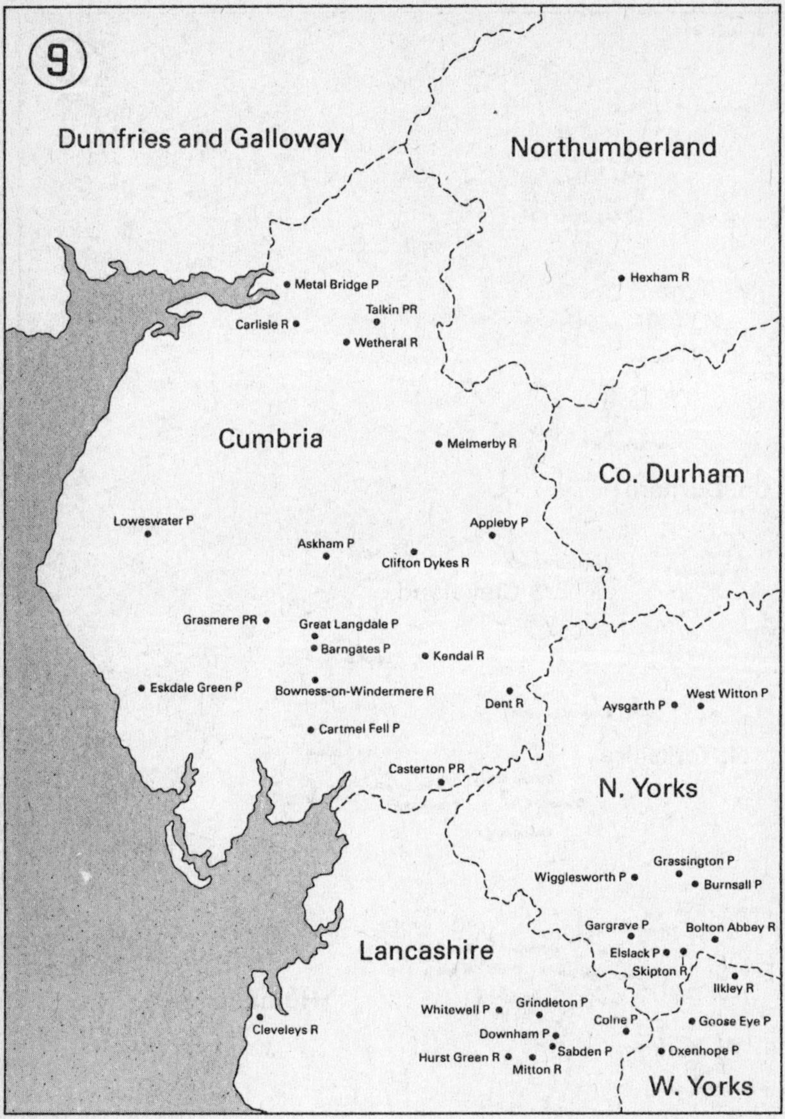
9
Dumfries and Galloway
Northumberland
Metal Bridge P
Hexham R
Talkin PR
Carlisle R
Wetheral R
Cumbria
Melmerby R
Co. Durham
Loweswater P
Appleby P
Askham P
Clifton Dykes R
Grasmere PR
Great Langdale P
Barngates P
Kendal R
Eskdale Green P
Bowness-on-Windermere R
Dent R
Aysgarth P
West Witton P
Cartmel Fell P
Casterton PR
N. Yorks
Grassington P
Wigglesworth P
Burnsall P
Gargrave P
Bolton Abbey R
Lancashire
Elslack P
Skipton R
Ilkley R
Whitewell P
Grindleton P
Colne P
Goose Eye P
Cleveleys R
Downham P
Sabden P
Oxenhope P
Hurst Green R
Mitton R
W. Yorks

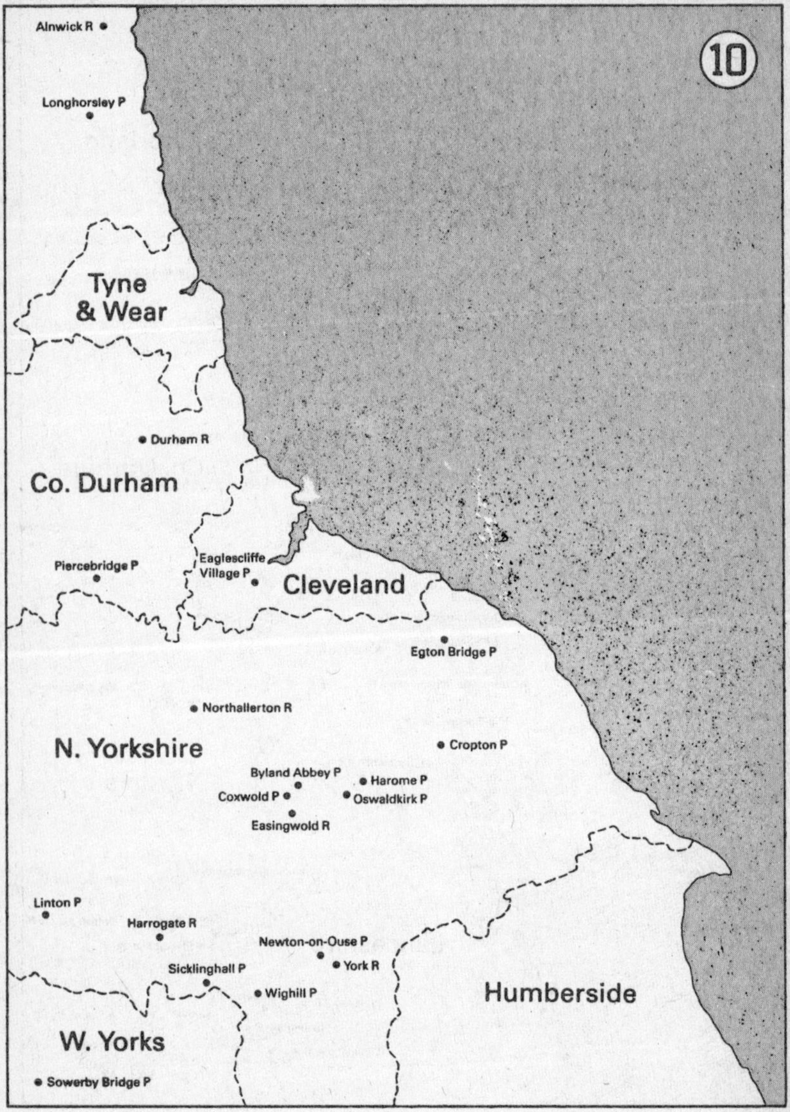
10
Alnwick R
Longhorsley P
Tyne & Wear
Durham R
Co. Durham
Piercebridge P
Eaglescliffe Village P
Cleveland
Egton Bridge P
Northallerton R
N. Yorkshire
Cropton P
Byland Abbey P
Harome P
Coxwold P
Oswaldkirk P
Easingwold R
Linton P
Harrogate R
Newton-on-Ouse P
York R
Sicklinghall P
Wighill P
Humberside
W. Yorks
Sowerby Bridge P

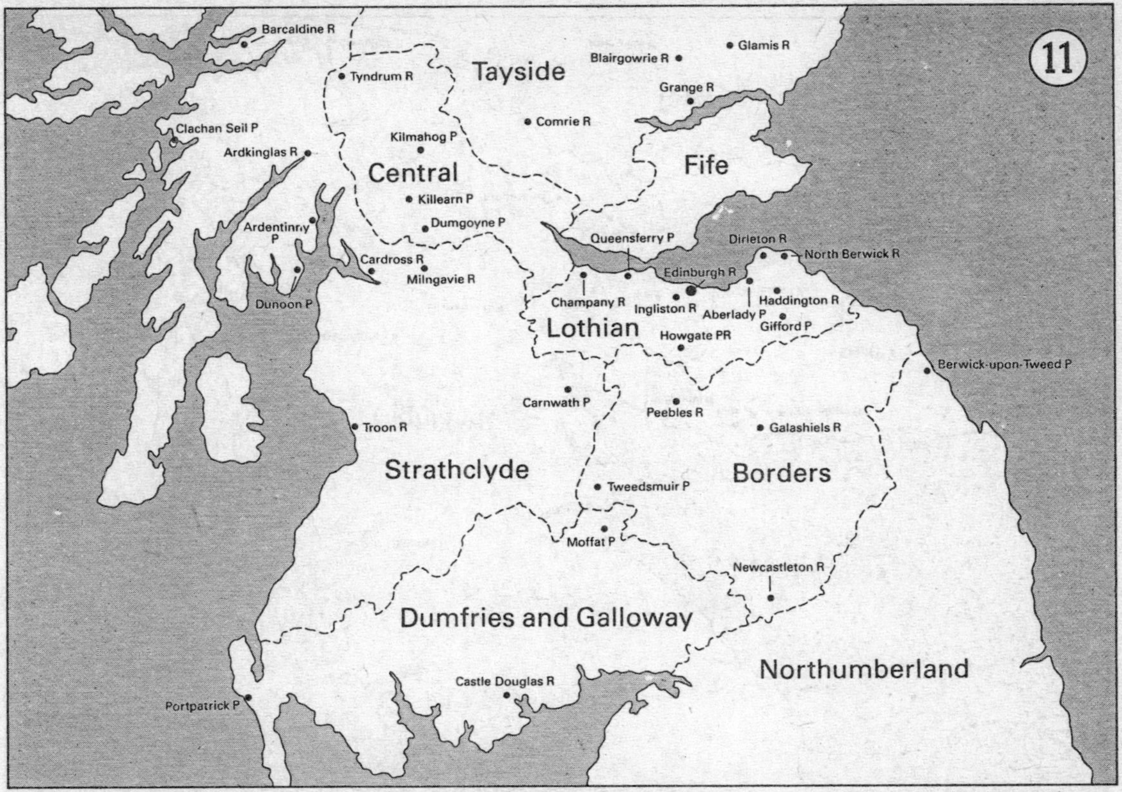
11
Tayside
Central
Fife
Lothian
Strathclyde
Borders
Dumfries and Galloway
Northumberland
Barcaldine R
Tyndrum R
Glamis R
Blairgowrie R
Grange R
Comrie R
Clachan Seil P
Kilmahog P
Ardkinglas R
Killearn P
Dumgoyne P
Ardentinny P
Cardross R
Milngavie R
Dunoon P
Queensferry P
Dirleton R
North Berwick R
Edinburgh R
Champany R
Ingliston R
Haddington R
Aberlady P
Gifford P
Howgate PR
Berwick-upon-Tweed P
Carnwath P
Peebles R
Galashiels R
Troon R
Tweedsmuir P
Moffat P
Newcastleton R
Castle Douglas R
Portpatrick P

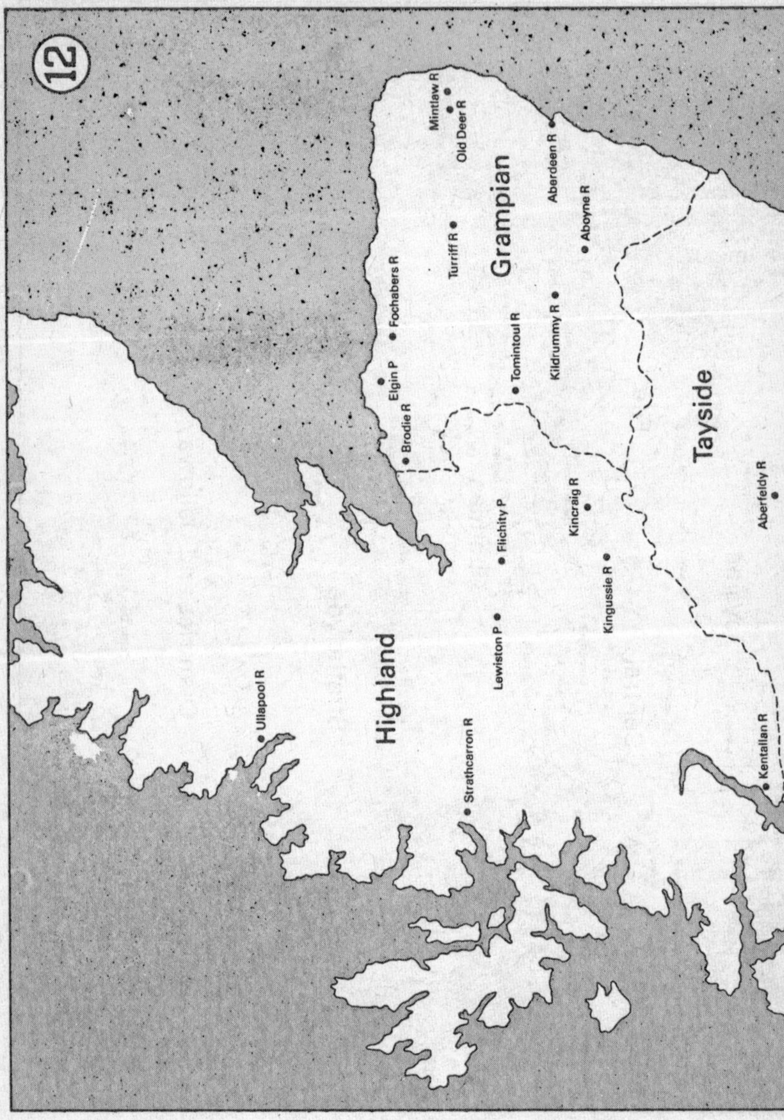
12
Highland
Grampian
Tayside
Ullapool R
Strathcarron R
Lewiston P
Flichity P
Kingussie R
Kincraig R
Kentallan R
Aberfeldy R
Brodie R
Elgin P
Fochabers R
Tomintoul R
Kildrummy R
Turriff R
Aboyne R
Aberdeen R
Old Deer R
Mintlaw R

READERS' COMMENTS

Please use this sheet to recommend establishments which you think should be considered for the next edition of the Guide. The basic facilities we look for are:

Pubs – separate children's or family room

Restaurants – high chairs and children's menus and/or reduced portions

Comments, adverse or otherwise, are welcome about any of the current Guide's entries.

To: The Editors, The Family Welcome Pub & Restaurant Guide 1991, c/o Hamer Books Ltd. Freepost, London SW13 9BR

Full name and address of establishment:

____

____

____

____

____

Phone number:

____

Comments

____

____

____

____

____

____

____

Name and address of sender:

____

____

____

____

____

We regret that we cannot acknowledge these forms, but they will be properly considered.

READERS' COMMENTS

Please use this sheet to recommend establishments which you think should be considered for the next edition of the Guide. The basic facilities we look for are:

Pubs – separate children's or family room

Restaurants – high chairs and children's menus and/or reduced portions

Comments, adverse or otherwise, are welcome about any of the current Guide's entries.

To: The Editors, The Family Welcome Pub & Restaurant Guide 1991, c/o Hamer Books Ltd. Freepost, London SW13 9BR

Full name and address of establishment:

____

____

____

____

____

Phone number:

____

Comments

____

____

____

____

____

____

____

Name and address of sender:

____

____

____

____

____

We regret that we cannot acknowledge these forms, but they will be properly considered.